Autonomy, Informed Consent and Medical Law

Alasdair Maclean analyses the ethical basis for consent to medical treatment, providing both an extensive reconsideration of the ethical issues and a detailed examination of English law. Importantly, the analysis is given a context by situating consent at the centre of the healthcare professional–patient relationship. This allows the development of a relational model that balances the agency of the two parties with their obligations that arise from that relationship. That relational model is then used to critique the current legal regulation of consent. To conclude, Alasdair Maclean considers the future development of the law and contrasts the model of relational consent with Neil Manson and Onora O'Neill's recent proposal for a model of genuine consent.

Having qualified in medicine and worked clinically in both England and New Zealand, Alasdair Maclean studied law and became a lecturer in medical law at the University of Glasgow. He is now a senior lecturer at the University of Dundee.

Cambridge Law, Medicine and Ethics

This series of books was founded by Cambridge University Press with Alexander McCall Smith as its first editor in 2003. It focuses on the law's complex and troubled relationship with medicine across both the developed and the developing world. In the past twenty years, we have seen in many countries increasing resort to the courts by dissatisfied patients and a growing use of the courts to attempt to resolve intractable ethical dilemmas. At the same time, legislatures across the world have struggled to address the questions posed by both the successes and the failures of modern medicine, while international organisations such as the WHO and UNESCO now regularly address issues of medical law.

It follows that we would expect ethical and policy questions to be integral to the analysis of the legal issues discussed in this series. The series responds to the high profile of medical law in universities, in legal and medical practice, as well as in public and political affairs. We seek to reflect the evidence that many major health-related policy debates in the UK, Europe and the international community over the past two decades have involved a strong medical law dimension. Organ retention, embryonic stem-cell research, physician-assisted suicide and the allocation of resources to fund healthcare are but a few examples among many. The emphasis of this series is thus on matters of public concern and/or practical significance. We look for books that could make a difference to the development of medical law and enhance the role of medico-legal debate in policy circles. That is not to say that we lack interest in the important theoretical dimensions of the subject, but we aim to ensure that theoretical debate is grounded in the realities of how the law does and should interact with medicine and healthcare.

General Editors

Professor Margaret Brazier, *University of Manchester*
Professor Graeme Laurie, *University of Edinburgh*

Editorial Advisory Board

Professor Richard Ashcroft, *Queen Mary, University of London*
Professor Martin Bobrow, *University of Cambridge*
Dr Alexander Morgan Capron, *Director, Ethics and Health, World Health Organization, Geneva*
Professor Jim Childress, *University of Virginia*
Professor Ruth Chadwick, *Cardiff Law School*
Dame Ruth Deech, *University of Oxford*

Professor John Keown, *Georgetown University, Washington, DC*
Dr Kathy Liddell, *University of Cambridge*
Professor Alexander McCall Smith, *University of Edinburgh*
Professor Dr Mónica Navarro-Michel, *University of Barcelona*

Marcus Radetzki, Marian Radetzki, Niklas Juth
Genes and Insurance: Ethical, Legal and Economic Issues
978 0 521 83090 4

Ruth Macklin
Double Standards in Medical Research in Developing Countries
978 0 521 83388 2 hardback 978 0 521 54170 1 paperback

Donna Dickenson
Property in the Body: Feminist Perspectives
978 0 521 86792 4

Matti Häyry, Ruth Chadwick, Vilhjálmur Árnason, Gardar Árnason
The Ethics and Governance of Human Genetic Databases: European Perspectives
978 0 521 85662 1

Ken Mason
The Troubled Pregnancy: Legal Wrongs and Rights in Reproduction
978 0 521 85075 9

Daniel Sperling
Posthumous Interests: Legal and Ethical Perspectives
978 0 521 87784 8

Keith Syrett
Law, Legitimacy and the Rationing of Health Care
978 0 521 85773 4

Alasdair Maclean
Autonomy, Informed Consent and Medical Law: A Relational Challenge
978 0 521 89693 1

Autonomy, Informed Consent and Medical Law

A Relational Challenge

Alasdair Maclean

CAMBRIDGE
UNIVERSITY PRESS

CAMBRIDGE UNIVERSITY PRESS
Cambridge, New York, Melbourne, Madrid, Cape Town, Singapore,
São Paulo, Delhi

Cambridge University Press
The Edinburgh Building, Cambridge CB2 8RU, UK

Published in the United States of America by
Cambridge University Press, New York

www.cambridge.org
Information on this title: www.cambridge.org/9780521896931

First published 2009

Printed in the United Kingdom at the University Press, Cambridge

A catalogue record for this publication is available from the British Library

Library of Congress Cataloguing in Publication data
Maclean, Alasdair, M Jur.
  Autonomy, informed consent and medical law : a relational challenge /
Alasdair Maclean.
    p.   cm. – (Cambridge law, medicine, and ethics)
  Includes bibliographical references and index.
  ISBN 978-0-521-89693-1 (hardback)
  1. Informed consent (Medical law) – England.   I. Title.   II. Series.
  KD3410.I54M335 2008
  344.4204′12–dc22   2008049118

ISBN 978-0-521-89693-1 hardback

This book is dedicated to my mother
and the memory of my father.

Contents

Table of cases   *page* x
List of figures   xvi
Acknowledgements   xvii

Introduction   1

Part I   An ethical model   7

1   Autonomy   9

2   The relevance of beneficence, justice and virtue   48

3   The healthcare professional–patient relationship:
    Setting the context for consent   72

4   The concept of consent: What it is and what it isn't   110

Part II   Consent and the law   147

5   The legal regulation of consent   149

6   Rationalising the law and ethics of consent   191

7   Constructing consent: Future regulation and
    the practice of healthcare   220

Summary and conclusion   260

Bibliography   270
Index   290

Table of cases

Abbas *v.* Kenney [1996] 7 Med LR 47, HC.   p. 171

Airedale NHS Trust *v.* Bland [1993] 1 All ER 821, HL.   pp. 149, 153, 194

Al Hamwi *v.* Johnston, The North West London Hospitals NHS Trust [2005] EWHC 206; [2005] Lloyd's LR Med 309, HC.   pp. 83, 179, 180, 221, 223, 224, 249

Allied Maples Group Ltd *v.* Simmons & Simmons [1995] 4 All ER 907; [1995] 1 WLR 1602, CA.   p. 197

Anns *v.* Merton London Borough [1978] AC 728, HL.   p. 215

Appleton *v.* Garrett [1997] 8 Med LR 75.   pp. 161, 192, 237

Attorney General's Reference (No. 6 of 1980) [1981] 1 QB 715. p. 153

Attwell *v.* McPartlin [2004] EWHC 829, HC.   pp. 180, 181, 224

Bancroft *v.* Harrogate Health Authority [1997] 8 Med LR 398, HC.   p. 171

Blyth *v.* Bloomsbury Health Authority [1993] 4 Med LR 151, CA (decided 1987).   pp. 169, 170, 221

Bolam *v.* Friern Hospital Management Committee [1957] 1 WLR 582, HC.   pp. 163–173, 176, 183, 184, 198, 199, 203, 208, 221

Bolitho *v.* City and Hackney Health Authority [1998] AC 232, HL.   pp. 172, 198

Bolton Hospitals NHS Trust v. *O* [2002] EWHC 2871.   p. 160

Breen *v.* Baker (1956) The Times, 27 January.   p. 160

Cambridgeshire County Council *v.* R [1995] 1 FLR 50.   pp. 155, 193

Canterbury *v.* Spence 464 F 2d 772 (DC Cir 1972).   pp. 41, 125, 164, 176, 185, 200, 209

Caparo Industries plc *v.* Dickman [1990] 2 AC 605.   p. 215

Chappel *v.* Hart [1998] HCA 55; [1999] Lloyd's LR Med 223; (1998) 72 ALJR 1344, HCA.   p. 187

Chatterton *v.* Gerson [1981] 1 All ER 257, HC.   pp. 154, 160, 184, 187

Chester *v.* Afshar [2002] EWCA Civ 724, CA.   p. 187

Chester *v.* Afshar [2005] 1 AC 134; [2004] UKHL 41, HL.   pp. 163,
    188, 189, 197, 202, 203, 216, 221
Cobbs *v.* Grant 502 P 2d 1, 12 (1972).   p. 201
Collins *v.* Wilcock [1984] 1 WLR 1172, HL.   p. 150
Cooper *v.* Royal United Hospital Bath NHS Trust [2005] EWHC
    3381, HC.   p. 178
Cornelius *v.* De Taranto [2001] EMLR 12, HC.   p. 189
Cornelius *v.* De Taranto (2002) 68 BMLR 62, CA.   p. 189
Crawford *v.* Board of Governors of Charing Cross Hospital (1953) The
    Times, 8 December, CA.   p. 169
Crouchman *v.* Burke (1997) 40 BMLR 163.   p. 178
Cull *v.* Royal Surrey County Hospital (1932) 1 BMJ 1195.   p. 159
Davis *v.* Barking, Havering and Brentwood Health Authority [1993] 4
    Med LR 85.   p. 192
De Freitas *v.* O'Brien [1995] 6 Med LR 108, CA.   p. 171
Department of Health & Community Services (NT) *v.* JWB and SMB
    (1992) 66 ALJR 300.   p. 153
Deriche *v.* Ealing Hospital NHS Trust [2003] EWHC 3104,
    HC.   p. 178
Devi *v.* West Midlands Regional Health Authority (1981) CA,
    Transcript 491.   p. 159
Doughty *v.* North Staffordshire Health Authority [1992] 3 Med LR
    81.   p. 170
Early *v.* Newham Health Authority [1994] 5 Med LR 214.   p. 171
Enright *v.* Kwun [2003] EWHC 1000, HC.   pp. 180, 181
Eyre *v.* Measeday [1986] 1 All ER 488, CA.   p. 170
Fairchild *v.* Glenhaven [2002] 1 AC 32, HL.   p. 215
Fowler *v.* Lanning [1959] 1 QB 426.   p. 150
Freeman *v.* Home Office [1983] 3 All ER 589; [1984] 2 WLR 130,
    HC.   p. 159
Freeman *v.* Home Office [1984] 1 All ER 1036, CA.   pp. 153, 158
Freeman *v.* Home Office (No. 2) [1984] 1 QB 524, HC.   p. 153
Freeman *v.* Home Office (No. 2) [1984] 1 QB 524, CA.   p. 153
Gascoine *v.* Sheridan [1994] 5 Med LR 437, HC.   p. 170
Gillick *v.* West Norfolk and Wisbech Area Health Authority [1986] AC
    112, HL.   p. 75
Glass *v.* UK [2004] 1 FLR 1019, ECtHR.   pp. 128, 182
Gold *v.* Haringey Health Authority [1988] 1 QB 481, CA.   pp. 169,
    170, 221
Goorkani *v.* Tayside Health Board 1991 SLT 94.   p. 188
Gowton *v.* Wolverhampton Health Authority [1994]
    5 Med LR 432.   p. 185

Gregg *v.* Scott [2005] UKHL 2, HL.   p. 171

Haystead *v.* Chief Constable of Derbyshire [2000] 3 All ER 890; [2000] 2 Cr App R 339.   p. 152

Heath *v.* West Berkshire Health Authority [1992] 3 Med LR 57, HC.   p. 171

Hicks *v.* Ghaphery 571 SE 2d 317, 335 (2002).   pp. 203, 204

Hills *v.* Potter [1984] 1 WLR 641, HC.   p. 184

Hotson *v.* East Berkshire HA [1987] AC 750, HL.   p. 197

Judge *v.* Huntingdon Health Authority [1995] 6 Med LR 223.   p. 171

Junior Books *v.* Veitchi [1983] 1 AC 520.   p. 215

Kelly *v.* Hazlett (1976) 75 DLR (3d) 536.   p. 161

Latter *v.* Braddell (1881) 50 LJQB 166, Common Pleas Division.   p. 157

Latter *v.* Braddell (1881) 50 LJQB 448, CA.   p. 157

LCB *v.* UK (1998) 27 EHRR 212.   p. 194

Letang *v.* Cooper [1965] 1 QB 232, CA.   p. 150

Loveday *v.* Renton [1990] 1 Med LR 117, CA.   pp. 170, 171

Lybert *v.* Warrington Health Authority (1995) 25 BMLR 91.   pp. 177, 178

Malette *v.* Shulman [1991] 2 Med LR 162; 67 DLR (4th) 3.   p. 189

Marriott *v.* West Midlands Health Authority [1999] Lloyd's LR Med 23, CA.   pp. 173, 174

Matthies *v.* Mastromonaco 733 A 2d 456 (1999).   pp. 203, 204

McAllister *v.* Lewisham and North Southwark Health Authority [1994] 5 Med LR 343.   pp. 170, 183, 185, 187

McFarlane *v.* Tayside Health Board [2000] 2 AC 59, HL.   pp. 63, 188, 189, 202, 216

McKay *v.* Essex Area Health Authority [1982] 1 QB 1166, CA.   p. 188

Mink *v.* University of Chicago 460 F Supp 713 (1978).   pp. 151–152

Mohr *v.* Williams 104 NW 2 (1905).   p. 159

Morgan *v.* MacPhail 704 A 2d 617 (1997).   pp. 152, 195

Moyes *v.* Lothian Health Board [1990] 1 Med LR 463, OH.   p. 223

Nancy B *v.* Hotel-Dieu de Quebec (1992) 86 DLR (4th) 385 (Quebec Superior Court).   p. 149

Newell and Newell *v.* Goldenberg [1995] 6 Med LR 371.   pp. 170, 188, 197

The NHS Trust *v.* Ms T [2004] EWHC 1279; [2005] 1 All ER 387, HC.   p. 210

Nishi *v.* Hartwell 473 P 2d 116 (1970).   p. 183

Norfolk and Norwich Healthcare (NHS) Trust *v.* W [1996] 2 FLR 613, HC.   p. 210

North West Lancashire Health Authority *v.* A, D & G [1999] Lloyd's
LR Med 399, CA.   p. 182
Osman *v.* UK (2000) 29 EHRR 245, ECtHR.   p. 80
Palmer *v.* Eadie Lexis Transcript 18 May 1987, CA.   p. 171
Parkinson *v.* St James and Seacroft University Hospital [2001] EWCA
Civ 530; [2001] 3 All ER 97, CA.   p. 216
Pearce *v.* United Bristol Healthcare NHS Trust (1998) 48 BMLR
118, CA.   pp. 173–177, 184, 199, 200, 201, 212, 213, 221, 252,
258, 265
Pretty *v.* UK (2002) 35 EHRR 1, ECtHR.   pp. 183, 189
Putensen *v.* Clay Adams Inc. 12 Cal App 3d 1062 (1970).   pp. 201,
202
R *v.* Bolduc and Bird [1976] 3 CCC 294, SCC.   p. 85
R *v.* Brown [1993] 2 WLR 556, HL.   p. 153
R *v.* Collins, ex parte Brady (2000) 58 BMLR 173.   p. 211
R *v.* Day (1841) 173 ER 1026, Circuit Court.   p. 113
R (Burke) *v.* GMC [2005] EWCA 1003; [2006] QB 273; [2005] 3
WLR 1132, CA.   pp. 123, 125, 181, 182, 213
R *v.* McCoy [1953] 2 SA 4.   p. 158
R *v.* Olugboja [1982] QB 320.   p. 156
R *v.* Richardson (1998) 43 BMLR 21, CA.   pp. 161, 162, 237
R *v.* Tabassum [2000] Lloyd's LR Med 404 CA; (2000) The Times,
26 May.   pp. 162, 239
Ratty *v.* Haringey Health Authority [1994] 5 Med LR 413,
CA.   p. 171
Re AK (Medical Treatment: Consent) [2001] 1 FLR 129.   p. 211
Re B (Consent to Treatment: Capacity) [2002] EWHC 49; [2002] 2 All
ER 449, HC.   pp. 149, 211
Re C (Adult: Refusal of treatment) [1994] 1 WLR 290; [1994] 1 All ER
819, HC.   pp. 155, 193, 194, 211
Re E (A Minor) (Wardship: Medical Treatment) [1993]
1 FLR 386.   p. 210
Re F (Mental Patient: Sterilisation) [1990] 2 AC 1; F *v.* West Berkshire
Health Authority [1989] 2 All ER 545, HL.   pp. 153, 208
Re L (An Adult: Non-consensual Treatment) [1997] 1 FCR 609,
HC.   p. 210
Re MB (An Adult: Medical Treatment) [1997] 2 FCR 541,
CA.   pp. 149, 156, 187
Re R (A Minor) (Wardship: Consent to Treatment) [1992] Fam 11;
[1991] 4 All ER 177; [1991] 3 WLR 592, CA.   pp. 131, 208
Re S [1992] 4 All ER. 671, HC.   p. 210

Re T (Adult: Refusal of Treatment) [1992] 3 WLR 782,
    CA.   pp. 149, 154, 156, 159, 189, 198, 210
Re W (A Minor) (Consent to Medical Treatment) [1993] 1 FLR 1,
    CA.   p. 131
Rees v. Darlington Memorial Hospital NHS Trust [2002] EWCA Civ
    88; [2003] QB 20, CA.   p. 216
Rees v. Darlington Memorial Hospital NHS Trust [2003] UKHL
    52, HL.   pp. 189, 197, 216
Reibl v. Hughes (1978) 21 OR (2d) 14, Ontario CA.   p. 160
Reibl v. Hughes (1981) 114 DLR (3d) 1, SCC.   pp. 160, 161, 165,
    166, 185, 193
Rochdale Healthcare (NHS) Trust v. C [1997] 1 FCR 274,
    HC.   pp. 83, 210
S v. McC; W v. W [1972] AC 24, 43, HL.   p. 149
Schloendorff v. Society of New York Hospital 211 NY 125; 105 NE 92
    (1914).   pp. 149–154
Scott v. Shepherd (1773) 2 W Blackstone 892.   pp. 150, 152
Shine v. Vega 709 NE 2d 58 (1999).   p. 209
Sidaway v. Board of Governors of the Bethlem Royal Hospital [1985]
    AC 871, HL.   pp. 74, 150, 160, 162–169, 171, 183, 192, 198, 199,
    221, 222, 223, 230, 268
Smith v. Barking, Havering and Brentwood Health Authority [1994] 5
    Med LR 285, HC.   p. 184
Smith v. Salford Health Authority [1994] 5 Med LR 321; (1994) 23
    BMLR 137.   pp. 178, 182, 241
Smith v. Tunbridge Wells Health Authority [1994] 5 Med LR 334.
    pp. 170, 173, 177, 185, 241
Spring v. Guardian Assurance [1995] 2 AC 296, HL.   p. 197
St George's Healthcare NHS Trust v. S 3 WLR 936.   pp. 113, 149,
    156, 210, 212
Stobie v. Central Birmingham Health Authority (1994) 22 BMLR
    135, HC.   p. 171
Tameside and Glossop Acute Services Trust v. CH [1996] 1 FLR
    762, HC.   p. 210
Thompson v. Bradford [2004] EWHC 2424, HC.   p. 181
Thompson v. Bradford [2005] EWCA Civ 1439; [2006] Lloyd's LR
    Med 95, CA.   pp. 181, 224
Tysiac v. Poland (2007) 45 EHRR 42, ECtHR.   pp. 128, 182
Vandi v. Permanente Medical Group 9 Cal Rptr 2d 463, 467
    (1992).   p. 203
W v. UK (1988) 10 EHRR 29, ECtHR.   pp. 128, 182

Waters *v.* West Sussex Health Authority [1995] 6 Med LR 362.
  p. 171
Wyatt *v.* Curtis [2003] EWCA Civ 1779, CA.   pp. 176, 177,
  199, 221

Figures

Fig 1 The process leading to consent   *page* 123
Fig 2 Model of consent   144

Acknowledgements

I would like to begin by thanking Professor Sheila McLean who supervised my Ph.D. in the latter half of its development. My approach underwent a metamorphosis, which was crucial to its ultimate coherence, and my discussions with Professor McLean were instrumental in achieving that fundamental change. I would also like to thank Professor Jonathan Montgomery who supervised the Ph.D. from its inception until I moved to Glasgow for my first post as a lecturer in medical law. He helped me to gain important insights and his encouragement was invaluable. I also benefited from discussing the issues with various colleagues at the Universities of Southampton, Glasgow and Dundee. I should specifically thank Dr Colin Gavaghan who often acted as intellectual foil and was willing to put his own work aside to discuss issues with me. I remain responsible for the arguments presented in this book, and, of course, for any errors.

As this book goes to press the GMC has published new guidance on consent entitled 'Consent: Patients and doctors making decisions together' (2008). In it the GMC takes a partnership approach that bears some similarities to my model as described in this book.

Introduction

> The patient who is armed with information, who wants to ask questions, sometimes difficult and awkward questions, should be seen as an asset in the process of care and not an impediment to it.
>
> Sir Liam Donaldson, the Chief Medical Officer (CMO).[1]

In recent years the healthcare professions have been rocked by a number of high-profile scandals including the murderous activities of Harold Shipman and Beverly Allitt, the issue of organ retention and the problems of paediatric cardiac surgery at the Bristol Royal Infirmary (BRI).[2] In addition to these, the cost of clinical negligence litigation and adverse events in general have further focused the government's attention on healthcare practice.[3] The BRI Inquiry's remit included making recommendations to improve the quality of care in the NHS, with patient-centred care forming a bedrock principle underlying the recommendations.[4]

A crucial part of developing a patient-centred service was the need to '[encompass] the notions of respect for and honesty towards patients'.[5] Thus, not only was it important to focus on the mechanics of healthcare but also on the attitudes of the healthcare professionals. For the Inquiry the way forward was to encourage a partnership between the professionals and the patients.[6] It noted that, while healthcare professionals were in general dedicated to the good of the patient, there was a persistent and entrenched culture of paternalism that tended to exclude

---

[1] Speaking at the 2nd National Service Delivery and Organisation Conference (2003).

[2] I. Kennedy, *Learning from Bristol: The report of the public inquiry into children's heart surgery at the Bristol Royal Infirmary 1984–1995*, Cm 5207 (2001).

[3] See Chief Medical Officer, *An Organisation with a Memory* (London: Department of Health, 2000). In 2001, the National Audit Office (NAO) reported a seven-fold increase in costs since 1995–6: NAO, *Handling Clinical Negligence Claims in England*, HC 403 Session 2000–1 (2001), p. 1.

[4] Kennedy, *Learning from Bristol*, Chapter 21, paras. 1, 9.

[5] *Ibid.*, para. 14.   [6] *Ibid.*, para. 23.

patients by limiting information and discouraging them from asking questions.[7]

A whole chapter of the final report was devoted to developing a culture of respect and honesty.[8] It began with a summary of the problems encountered at the BRI, which included a closed culture of paternalism, with patient communication delegated to junior members of staff. The Inquiry emphasised the importance of providing patients and their families with information and support. It suggested that the solution to the endemic paternalism was to redefine the professional–patient relationship as one of partnership 'involving patients, wherever possible, in decisions about their treatment and care'.[9] This approach to respect, information and partnership was something that the Government had already committed to.[10] Furthermore, in submissions to the Inquiry, professional bodies, such as the Royal College of Surgeons and the Royal College of Nursing, also acknowledged the importance of partnership.[11]

The Inquiry's concern for involving patients in treatment decisions gave rise to four key principles regarding information disclosure:[12]

- trust requires an attitude of openness;
- this in turn requires the honest and frequent provision of information;
- this is particularly relevant to information concerning risk and uncertainty; and
- information disclosure should be seen as 'a process and not a one-off event'.

In addition to the problems with a paternalistic approach to information, the Inquiry was also critical of the predominantly functional approach to consent. It emphasised that patients had a right to information and to choose whether or not to consent. For the Inquiry, patient choice was the guiding principle.[13]

The Department of Health (DH) responded by acknowledging a commitment to 'develop an NHS where there is a culture of openness and honesty . . . and where patients and staff work in genuine partnership'.[14] Thus, the DH included in their reform programme 'a consent

---

[7] *Ibid.*, Chapter 22, para. 17.   [8] *Ibid.*, Chapter 23.   [9] *Ibid.*, para. 2.
[10] Department of Health, *Patient and Public Involvement in the New NHS*, Health Service Circular: HSC (99) 210 (1999).
[11] Kennedy, *Learning from Bristol*, Chapter 23, para. 14.   [12] *Ibid.*, para. 18.
[13] *Ibid.*, para. 45.
[14] Department of Health, *Learning from Bristol: The Department of Health's response to the report of the public inquiry into children's heart surgery at the Bristol Royal Infirmary 1984–1995*, Cm 5363 (2002), Executive Summary, para. 2; see also para. 1.4.

process which engages patients fully in decisions about their care'.[15] In fact, as the DH noted, it had already set up the Good Practice in Consent Initiative, as part of the implementation of the 2000 NHS Plan.[16] This involved establishing an advisory group and publishing guidance documents and a model consent form.[17] Apart from the symbolic importance of providing such guidance, the document provides helpful guidance on what is currently required by the law. For certain specific areas, such as consent to anaesthesia, the guidance is particularly helpful in clarifying who has responsibility. Unfortunately, however, it fails to venture far beyond that already required by the law. Nevertheless, it does serve to emphasise the importance of consent and it reinforces the commitment in the NHS Plan.

The commitment to patient-centred care is reinforced by the recent publication *Creating a Patient-led NHS*, which again indicates an intention to provide greater choice and information.[18] Other policies and initiatives, such as the Expert Patient Programme, the Patient Advice and Liaison Service,[19] the National Knowledge Service[20] and the development of information technologies such as HealthSpace (which will allow each patient internet space to record their care preferences), cement the Government's intention to empower patients.[21] In June 2004, the Secretary of State for Health stated:

Patients' desire for high-quality personalised care will drive the new system. Giving people greater personal choice will give them control over these issues, allowing patients to call the shots about the time and place of their care, and empowering them to personalise their care to ensure the quality and convenience that they want.[22]

---

[15] *Ibid.*, Executive Summary, para. 13.

[16] www.dh.gov.uk/PolicyAndGuidance/HealthAndSocialCareTopics/Consent/fs/en.

[17] Department of Health, *Good Practice in Consent Implementation Guide: Consent to examination or treatment* (2001).

[18] Department of Health, *Creating a Patient-led NHS: Delivering the NHS Improvement Plan* (2005), Chapter 1.

[19] Department of Health, *Learning from Bristol*, para. 2.12. See also the PALS website: www.pals.nhs.uk/.

[20] Department of Health, *Learning from Bristol*, para. 2.11. See also the dedicated website: www.nks.nhs.uk.

[21] Department of Health, *NHS Improvement Plan 2004: Putting people at the heart of public services*, Cm 6268 (2004), Executive Summary, para. 12. This commitment is reinforced by the 2008/9 *Operating Framework for the NHS in England*, available at www.dh.gov.uk/en/Publicationsandstatistics/Publications/PublicationsPolicyAndGuidance/DH_081094.

[22] The Rt Hon. John Reid MP, 'Building on the best – An NHS for the future' (2004), available at www.dh.gov.uk/en/News/Speeches/Speechlist/DH_4087161.

However, without suitable legal protection, these political intentions may provide less than they promise.[23] Furthermore, if patients are to be given choices to enable them to 'ensure the quality' of their decisions, then it is important that they are supported in their decision-making so as to prevent the provision of choice simply being used as a way of transferring responsibility to the patient. If patient choice is genuinely intended to enhance the patient's care then it must be supported by an intention to promote the patient's ability to make good decisions.

All healthcare interventions take place in the context of professional–patient contact making the professional–patient relationship – however fleeting – a core feature of healthcare provision. If patient-centred healthcare is to mean anything beyond shallow consumerism and political spin the focus must be on the interactions between the professionals and the patients they are caring for. If consent is necessary for the justification of healthcare interventions then, provided it is given a sufficiently textured interpretation, consent – and the communicative processes that envelop it – should be seen as integral to the creation of a patient-centred system of healthcare. In the recent report examining the professional regulation of doctors, the CMO noted the importance of good communication skills and the need to treat patients with respect by supporting their involvement in making decisions about their care and medical treatment.[24] It therefore seems an appropriate juncture to go back to square one and re-examine the law and ethics of consent to healthcare and the competent adult.

The book grew out of my Ph.D. thesis and is largely written in a way that reflects the journey I travelled in constructing the model of relational consent used as a yardstick to measure the acceptability of the current legal regulation. Central to my argument is the insight that the way in which healthcare professionals approach consent reflects their approach to the patient more generally. As such, consent is central to the professional–patient relationship. I also rely on the assumption that competent patients are responsible agents who want to make good decisions. My final assumption in undertaking this exploration of consent is that responsible agents are equally deserving of respect.

While parts of the journey will inevitably be familiar to some, it should be helpful to those readers with less expert knowledge. Furthermore, it

---

[23] See A. Coulter, 'Whatever happened to shared decision-making?' (2002) 5 *Health Expectations* 185; B. Sang, 'Choice, participation and accountability: Assessing the potential impact of legislation promoting patient and public involvement in health in the UK' (2004) 7 *Health Expectations* 187, 190.

[24] Chief Medical Officer, *Good Doctors, Safer Patients* (London: Department of Health, 2006), p. xi, available at www.dh.gov.uk/en/Publicationsandstatistics/Publications.

should provide useful insights into how and why my model of consent evolved. To that end, I necessarily explore the writings of a selection of other commentators who have commented on consent and the moral concepts that influence the way consent works in practice. The aim, however, is to construct a coherent and useful model of consent that both remains true to its core theory and reflects the value of autonomy. This model may then be used to expose the deficiencies in the legal regulation of consent and provide some suggestions as to how those flaws might be remedied.

In the first part of the book I examine the moral basis of consent. I begin by exploring the meaning and importance of autonomy. Despite some recent challenges to the association between autonomy and consent,[25] if autonomy is seen as the right of moral agents to make self-regarding decisions the connection seems clear. The requirement for consent protects patients from paternalistic or other unjust actions that infringe their rights. While the rules implementing the requirement for consent may be criticised for failing to be sufficiently sensitive to a thick conception of autonomy,[26] this does not undermine the essential relationship between autonomy and consent. However, the healthcare professional's obligation to respect the patient's autonomy should not be examined in isolation from the professional's other duties. In Chapter 2 I therefore consider the relevance of beneficence, justice and virtue and I discuss how they may help to shape the extent of the healthcare professional's duty to respect the patient's autonomy. Then, in Chapter 3, I situate the debate within the context of the professional–patient relationship, which is important because consent always involves at least two parties and the rules necessarily depend on the context of the interaction between them.

In the last chapter of Part I of the book I explore the concept of consent. The approach I take in my analysis is necessarily based in the way others have used the concept. This deconstruction is an essential part of developing a meaningful and useful conception of consent. While analysing the concept I tease out the relevant attributes that reflect the pragmatic and moral aspects of consent to healthcare interventions. Bearing in mind the context of the professional–patient relationship, this allows me to develop a relational model of consent to healthcare interventions.

---

[25] See e.g. J. S. Taylor, 'Autonomy and informed consent: A much misunderstood relationship' (2004) 38 *The Journal of Value Inquiry* 383.

[26] O. O'Neill, *Autonomy and Trust in Bioethics* (Cambridge: Cambridge University Press, 2002), pp. 37–48.

In Part II, I examine the law's approach to consent. I analyse the law chronologically, which is important because it provides insights into the processes of the common law and the interaction between ethical theory and the legal regulation of medical practice. This highlights the problems faced in trying to develop an ethically nuanced standard through the courts.

In Chapter 5, I consider the legal regulation of consent in battery and negligence. As far as possible, I explicate the rules that the courts have developed, particularly those in relation to risk disclosure and the communicative aspects of consent. This necessarily requires a formal and detailed exposition of the leading cases, which then allows, in Chapter 6, a comparison of the legal model of consent with the relational model developed in Part I of the book. The chapter ends with a brief consideration of whether the common law could develop sufficiently to meet the criticisms of the current legal regulation, whether professional regulation could paper over the deficiencies or whether legislation is the most appropriate response.

In the final chapter I consider where the law could go in future. I begin revisiting the developments to date in the legal regulation of consent. This analysis focuses on the cycle of criticism and change allowed by the scope of the concepts of autonomy, rationality and consent. I then examine Manson and O'Neill's recent proposal for a shift from informed consent to their conception of a 'genuine consent'.[27] Given the influential status of Baroness Professor O'Neill it is plausible that Manson and O'Neill's model of 'genuine consent' could influence professional practice. As such, it seems the most likely theory of consent to affect how the common law may develop in future. It is, therefore, important to compare their model with the relational model constructed in Part I of the book. I argue that, while their model may be a valuable stage in the evolution of consent, it fails to provide sufficient support for good decision-making. Furthermore, if it were to be adopted under the current common-law system, the strengths of Manson and O'Neill's model may be undermined by reactive regulation and risk-management approaches that focus on the outcome rather than the process of disclosure. As an alternative I return to my argument that a relational model of consent should be implemented through legislation and I expand the model to illustrate how it may be successfully realised.

---

[27] N. C. Manson and O. O'Neill, *Rethinking Informed Consent in Bioethics* (Cambridge: Cambridge University Press, 2007); O. O'Neill, 'Some limits of informed consent' (2003) 29 *Journal of Medical Ethics* 4.

Part I

An ethical model

1 Autonomy

In the introduction I suggested that consent is predicated on autonomy. If one considers the role consent plays, which I will discuss in more detail in Chapter 4, the connection with autonomy seems apparent. It has not, however, gone unchallenged and I will address this later in the chapter.[1] Starting with the etymological derivation of autonomy, which comes from the Greek and means self-rule, both senses of consent – as a waiver of a right and as a negotiated agreement – depend on the patient's autonomy, at least in the sense of autonomy as self-determination. Consent raises issues of liberty, power, control and responsibility; all of which are also relevant to the importance of autonomy.[2] Because of this connection, it is essential to explore autonomy in some detail. This will allow the attributes of consent to be given more substance, which is a necessary part of determining the moral and legal duties that consent imposes on the healthcare professional. To explicate autonomy and its influence on consent I will explore the nature, value and limits of autonomy. I will then examine the nature of the connection between consent and autonomy.

The nature of autonomy

Various senses and conceptions of autonomy have been expounded.[3] If there are real differences between these approaches to autonomy then the conception adopted may affect the obligations arising from the patient's right of consent. Rather than simply assert my own version of autonomy, recognising these competing conceptions makes it necessary to consider the different views. It seems appropriate to begin with the list

---

[1] Manson and O'Neill, *Rethinking Informed Consent*, pp. 16–22; Taylor, 'Autonomy and informed consent'.
[2] See e.g. K. Lehrer, 'Reason and autonomy' (2003) 20 *Social Philosophy and Policy* 177.
[3] J. Bergsma and T. Thomasma, *Autonomy and Clinical Medicine: Renewing the health professional relation with the patient* (Dordrecht: Kluwer Academic Publishers, 2000), pp. xiii–xiv.

that Gerald Dworkin constructed in his classic exposition of autonomy, which includes autonomy as liberty or freedom to act; as dignity; as 'freedom of the will'; as 'independence'; and as 'critical reflection'.[4] The list may be expanded to include: 'self-mastery; choosing freely; choosing one's own moral position and accepting responsibility for one's choice';[5] 'self-control' and 'self-determination'.[6]

It is apparent from this list that one of the problems with autonomy is that there are almost as many different conceptions as there are commentators writing on the subject. However, this does not mean that there is no single concept and, rather than simply being alternative concepts of autonomy, the various uses of autonomy reflect an amalgam of the different aspects and senses of autonomy. Approached in this way, it may be possible, in the context of healthcare, to determine a core concept with a choice of conceptions. The most meaningful conception may then be determined from the value reflected in the core concept and the context of its application.

The core concept is revealed by the etymology of the word itself. As noted above, autonomy literally means self-rule and this is the central feature of all the various different conceptions. This central notion depends on the claim that we are free-willed agents capable, at least, of making decisions. I will discuss the problem of determinism later, but for now I will assume that adult human beings ordinarily are capable of self-determination. Where rationality is required then this capacity may vary greatly between individuals. Furthermore, the psychological predisposition to exercise the ability may also vary (see p. 91). However, the capacity for self-determination is a necessary feature of agency, which is crucial to the justification provided by consent.

This capacity for self-determination means that, at its core, autonomy is a natural kind concept. However, the different conceptions that have been argued for are, to a greater or lesser extent, social constructs that rely on a mixture of biological and normative claims. The normative claims essentially depend on the type of society, or more specifically to the present discussion, the type of healthcare service that the author is arguing for. A libertarian will construct a different conception of autonomy to the liberal and the liberal view will differ from the communitarian.[7] These fundamentally different perspectives on autonomy

---

[4] G. Dworkin, *The Theory and Practice of Autonomy* (Cambridge: Cambridge University Press, 1988), p. 6.
[5] R. Faden and T. L. Beauchamp, *The History and Theory of Informed Consent* (New York: Oxford University Press, 1986), p. 7.
[6] O'Neill, *Autonomy and Trust*, p. 22.
[7] A. Maclean, 'Consent and sensibility' (2005) 4 *International Journal of Ethics* 31.

mean that it is unlikely that the debate will ever be fully resolved in favour of one conception over another. This is not, however, a problem. In fact, the opposite is true since these different approaches provide the basis for the criticism necessary to a vibrant democratic politic.[8] The caveat is, of course, that unless we are content with incoherent and inconsistent rules, the law, and indeed professional ethical guidelines, must choose one version over another. This choice will not be fixed for all time, but will be subject to the continuing critique of others with differing views. Nevertheless, a conception of autonomy should be selected with the preferred choice determined by the type of healthcare system we want.

Although there are many different conceptions of autonomy they can be broadly grouped into three categories. The libertarian approach is to see autonomy simply as self-determination. The liberal view requires the inclusion of rationality. The communitarian approach would be to require autonomy to also have substantive moral content. While it is possible to discern these three broad characterisations of autonomy this is not to suggest that they are discrete. In particular the inclusion of a requirement for rationality adds another dimension that it is susceptible to one's political persuasion and allows for a complex and nuanced approach to autonomy. The different nuances at play allow the conception of autonomy to be seen as existing on a continuum that spans from the extreme libertarian view of autonomy as atomistic, independent self-determination to the communitarian extreme in which the importance of individual autonomy is subjugated to the needs and interests of the community. Between these caricatured approaches lie many more plausible conceptions. In the subsequent discussion I will begin to construct an argument setting out the conception of autonomy that should ground the legal regulation of consent.

Autonomy as self-determination

In addition to the different conceptions of autonomy, the concept is further complicated by the different senses in which autonomy may be used. For example, the term may be employed to refer to an individual's capacity to 'think, decide and act'.[9] Alternatively, it may be used to

---

[8] A. Maclean, 'Magic, myths and fairytales: Consent and the relationship between law and ethics', in M. Freeman (ed.) Law and Bioethics, Current Legal Issues, vol. 11 (Oxford: Oxford University Press, 2008), Forthcoming.
[9] R. Gillon, Philosophical Medical Ethics (Chichester: John Wiley & Sons, 1985), p. 60.

describe a particular kind of decision or action.[10] It may further refer to a way of living one's life,[11] with autonomy being seen as a virtue rather than a simple ability.[12] Thus, for individual autonomy, one may make a distinction between the *autonomous person*, the *autonomous act* and the *autonomous life*.

For present purposes, because the autonomous life is a derivative of the other two concepts, the most important of these distinctions is between the *autonomous person* and the *autonomous act*.[13] Autonomous persons will not always act autonomously and, where they do not, the act may be contrary to their long-term autonomy or other interests. This raises the thorny, but crucial, question of whether it is more harmful to interfere with a present non-autonomous act or to allow that person to harm his or her autonomous life or future autonomy. Furthermore, the choice between protecting any decision of an autonomous person and only those decisions that are themselves autonomous has implications for the law since the latter position would justify a significantly greater degree of interference. Finally, the distinction between the autonomous person and the autonomous act is also relevant to the nature of the connection between consent and autonomy.

If autonomy is equated with freedom of action then the relevance of any distinction between an autonomous person and an autonomous act disappears since every act of the autonomous person will, by definition, be autonomous. This particularly thin view of autonomy makes no demand for rationality nor does it require the actor to act morally, or even be capable of acting morally. At its most extreme, all that is necessary is the absence of external constraint and the capacity to make (and act on) a decision. Unless individuals are capable of making a rational decision they will be unable to determine the rightness or wrongness of their decisions and will not be responsible members of the moral community. As such, at least one of the reasons to value autonomy vanishes (see p. 23) and, since respect for individuals includes both respecting their autonomy and caring about their welfare,[14] it would be justifiable to interfere with the individual's self-determination to protect him or her from random and dangerous decisions. Because autonomy as self-determination is of less value than conceptions of autonomy that

---

[10] See, T. A. Mappes and J. S. Zembaty, 'Biomedical Ethics', in Mappes and Zembaty (eds.), *Biomedical Ethics*, 3rd edn (New York: McGraw-Hill Inc., 1991), pp. 1, 25–6.

[11] R. Young, 'Autonomy and the "inner self"', in J. Christman, (ed.), *The Inner Citadel* (New York: Oxford University Press, 1989), pp. 77–8.

[12] J. Benson, 'Who is the autonomous man?' (1983) 58 *Philosophy* 5, 9.

[13] Faden and Beauchamp, *The History and Theory of Informed Consent*, p. 235.

[14] See e.g. Dworkin, *The Theory and Practice of Autonomy*, p. 32.

require the capacity to engage with the rationality and consistency necessary for a moral life, and because it is readily overridden, it is better to rely on a thicker view of autonomy.

Autonomy as rational self-determination

Beyond simple self-determination, autonomy requires at least some capacity for rationality. This has the consequence of creating a real distinction between an autonomous act and the acts of an autonomous person, not all of which will be rational. The importance of this distinction will be considered later. However, the inclusion of a requirement for rationality raises two further issues. First, which conception of rationality should be adopted? Second, how much rationality is required?

Rationality may be defined as 'The quality of possessing reason; the power of being able to exercise one's reason',[15] which begs the question of what counts as reason. This may be briefly addressed by considering the point of rationality or reasoning. The purpose of rationality is to provide sufficient consistency to justify reliance on the outcome of the reasoning process. As such, even where it is only relied on by the reasoner, there must be a certain objectivity or 'generality' to the reasoning.[16] This is essentially a practical requirement of rationality. Consider the mundane act of buying milk to put on your cereal. If I choose to buy milk only when the sun shines it is likely, particularly in Britain, that I will sometimes run out of milk. I may also, of course, end up with too much milk and find that some of it is wasted. While it may sometimes work out that I do need to buy milk on a sunny day, this is not because the sun is shining. The sun is an unreliable indicator of when I should buy milk and therefore does not count as a reason. A more rational approach would be to take account of how much milk is in the fridge, the amount of milk used per day and the number of days that the milk will remain fresh. These are reliable indicators that provide a good reason to buy milk provided the aim is to never run out of fresh milk.

Two implications follow from this simple example. First, reasons ground the predictability necessary for statements to be treated as reliable information. Second, if a statement is to be treated as authoritative and be justified as a guide for action, then it must be reliable and hence reasoned. Arbitrary claims are inherently unreliable and do not provide a strong basis for justifying an action.[17] The fact that the sun is shining,

---

[15] Oxford English Dictionary, available at www.dictionary.oed.com.
[16] T. Nagel, *The Last Word* (New York: Oxford University Press, 1997), p. 5.
[17] O. O'Neill, *Bounds of Justice* (Cambridge: Cambridge University Press, 2000), p. 12.

while it may be true, is an arbitrary indicator of the need for milk and thus cannot provide the authority to justify the act of buying milk. Rationality relies on reasons that are authoritative precisely because of their reliability.

There are two aspects of decision-making that raise issues of rationality: the choice of ends and the means of achieving those ends. The law might reasonably be concerned with both of these decisional elements and, as with autonomy, the preference for one form of rationality over another is dependent on one's political view of the role of the agent within society. There are broadly two possible approaches. First, the law could adopt the 'recognitional model'. In this model, the general authority for rational action is that the agent 'represents the action as good', where the 'good' is determined independently of the agent's actions. The second possibility is the 'constructivist' approach in which 'the good simply is constituted as the object of rational choice'.[18]

If the law is to adopt the recognitional model then there must be some objective and non-arbitrary justification of the good that provides the necessary authority and gives the rational actor a motivational reason to adopt that good as an end. However, given the problem of recursion, it seems unlikely that the good life is something that can be wholly based on reason.[19] Ultimately there must be reliance on a belief that cannot itself be fully justified by rational argument.

A standard approach is to base what counts as 'a good end' on the idea of human flourishing. Gaut, for example, draws a connection between the good life and our biology and argues that it is plausible to objectively determine the goodness of an end based on its biological function. The 'good life' can thus be discovered by examining lives that have gone well and those that have gone badly, then using those experiences to arrive at a consensus.[20] This is fine, as far as it goes, but it only provides a very limited view of the good life, which is that part 'determined by her [the agent's] nature: by her capacities, tendencies and needs'.[21] Unless the good life is to be defined solely in terms of biological function, and even that may be open to a degree of interpretation, then we still need some way of choosing between competing philosophies, which problematically may not be fully amenable to objective reasoning.

An alternative is the constructivist model, which may take one of two forms. In the neo-Humean form the agent's motivation comes from

---

[18] B. Gaut, 'The structure of practical reason', in G. Cullity and B. Gaut (eds.), *Ethics and Practical Reason* (Oxford: Clarendon Press, 1997), pp. 161–162.
[19] O'Neill, *Bounds of Justice*, p. 14.   [20] Gaut, 'The structure of practical reason', p. 187.
[21] *Ibid.*, p. 185.

internal states of wants and desires that are neither rational nor irrational.[22] The question of rationality is then purely instrumental: whether the act will satisfy the desire. Unlike Hume, the neo-Humeans add the normative requirement that the desire itself must be reflected on in a knowledgeable way to determine one's ultimate desire. Acting to promote this ultimate desire is rational even though the ultimate desire itself may not be fully rational.[23] This effectively allows individuals to determine their own 'good', provided they have reflected on that end. An example of this approach is the division of desires into first and second order. The first order desire is then considered in light of the agent's second order desires and rationality judged on the basis of consistency between the first and second order desires.[24] This model of rationality, which would accord with a liberal ethic, is not without its detractors.

Perhaps the major criticism is that, while this view of rationality allows for value judgements, it remains self-referential: whether the means is rational is determined entirely against the subjective end chosen by the actors themselves. Under this instrumental approach, morality is irrelevant to the question of rationality.[25] It would, for example, be perfectly rational for someone to steal if they make a reliable judgement that the risk of getting caught and punished is outweighed by the personal gains to be made by stealing. The criticism, that this form of rationality is devoid of moral content, applies to both Humean instrumental rationality and the neo-Humean reflective rationality. As part of a liberal conception of autonomy, it forms the basis for Manson and O'Neill's argument that autonomy cannot be the moral basis for informed consent which I will consider later when discussing the nature of the connection between autonomy and consent.[26]

A second constructivist approach is the Kantian model, in which morality is rational and to fail to act morally is to act irrationally.[27] For Kant, the autonomous will is rational and, as a consequence of rational deliberation, any self-willed autonomous law must obey the categorical

---

[22] G. Cullity and B. Gaut, 'Introduction', in Cullity and Gaut (eds.), *Ethics and Practical Reason* (Oxford: Clarendon Press, 1997), pp. 1, 4.
[23] *Ibid.*, pp. 7–8.
[24] Dworkin, *The Theory and Practice of Autonomy*, p. 20; H. Frankfurt, 'Freedom of the will and the concept of a person', in R. Kane (ed.), *Free Will* (Malden, Mass.: Blackwell Publishers, 2002), p. 127.
[25] J. Kennett, *Agency and Responsibility: A common-sense moral psychology* (Oxford: Clarendon Press, 2001), pp. 99–100.
[26] Manson and O'Neill. *Rethinking Informed Consent*, pp. 20–21.
[27] Cullity and Gaut, 'Introduction', pp. 3–5.

imperative and be willed as universal.[28] Working from Kant's approach, Korsgaard has argued, *contra* Hume, that there is a distinction between actual desires and rational desires and that we ought to pursue our rational desires rather than just our actual desires.[29] This distinction requires that we have some way of distinguishing what is rational, i.e. what we ought to do, from simply what we desire to do and, if this is the case, there must be 'normative principles directing the adoption of ends'.[30] According to Kant, the normative principle is that any self-legislation must also be capable of being willed as universal. Although Kant provided two helpful reformulations of this imperative – treat people as an end in themselves and not merely as a means,[31] and 'every rational being should be regarded as an autonomous legislator in a kingdom of ends'[32] – this approach to grounding the authority of morality in rationality may be accused of being 'a contingent psychological matter' and empty of any substance.[33]

Each of the three approaches to rationality has its defenders and its detractors. The choice between the first two perhaps comes down to whether one sees the good as prior to the right or vice versa.[34] The difficulty with giving primacy to the good arises from the question of why a particular view of the good should be authoritative,[35] and it may lead to an intolerant community with autonomy valued as a means to achieve a societally imposed view of 'self-perfection' rather than for its autobiographical role in determining character and identity.[36] However, the problem with protecting the individual's right to determine his or her own good is that it allows a moral vacuum and underplays the importance of a person's social relationships within the context of a community.

We are all dependent on others, to a greater or lesser extent, throughout our life. Without the nurturing and support from others we would be free

---

[28] I. Kant (tr. M. Gregor), *Groundwork of the Metaphysics of Morals* (Cambridge: Cambridge University Press, 1998), p. 39 (4:431).

[29] G. M. Korsgaard, 'The normativity of instrumental reason', in Cullity and Gaut (eds.), *Ethics and Practical Reason*, p. 230.

[30] *Ibid.*, p. 231.   [31] Kant, *Groundwork*, p. 39 (4:429).   [32] *Ibid.*, p. 39 (4:431–3).

[33] D. O. Brink, 'Kantian rationalism: Inescapability, authority and supremacy', in Cullity and Gaut (eds.), *Ethics and Practical Reason*, p. 272.

[34] See, M. J. Sandel, *Liberalism and the Limits of Justice*, 2nd edn (Cambridge: Cambridge University Press, 1998), p. xi.

[35] It may be argued that the objective ends view of rationality completely undermines the whole idea of autonomy. This is not necessarily the case, but space does not permit a discussion of this issue. For a defence of the view that the two are compatible see J. Varelius, 'Autonomy, subject-relativity, and subjective and objective theories of well-being in bioethics' (2003) 24 *Theoretical Medicine* 363.

[36] M. Oshana, 'How much should we value autonomy?' (2003) 20 *Social Philosophy and Policy* 99, 119; R. Dworkin, *Life's Dominion* (London: HarperCollins, 1993), p. 224.

but that freedom would be relatively impotent. As Gauthier noted: 'No one can attain even . . . [the] minimal human goods alone. They require families and communities that protect, nurture, and support individual well-being and provide for these needs, when necessary.'[37] Given that we could achieve nothing without the support of others we must rely on those others for their help. However, if another person is to provide assistance then he or she must have some reason for doing so and this means that the claim must at least be accepted as reasonable.

The third view of rationality, that links morality and rationality through the constraint of universalisability, has the necessary sensitivity to others to recognise the socially embedded nature of rationality and autonomy (see p. 21). As such, it is the preferable view provided it can be given more substance than exists in Kant's formal imperative. Kant's imperative forms the basis for O'Neill's argument that the individual's ability to reason must be judged against ends, norms or commitments that it is '*possible* for others to follow'.[38] Thus, 'Reasoning is defective when reasoners misjudge or misrepresent what others can follow.'[39] This model perhaps lies somewhere in between the objective-ends and the subjective-ends models of rationality. While it allows individuals to determine the good for themselves, this is open to scrutiny and is only deserving of respect if the ends are accessible to others. This means that the end does not need to be one that the judge *would* accept, but it does need to be one that he or she *could* accept. The judge's identity will depend on context, but could be anyone asked for assistance to enable others to achieve their goals. Whether a particular end is accessible may be influenced by the idea of 'sensus communis', which is 'the sense that founds community'.[40] In this way, the model is sensitive to the objective ends view of rationality. However, because it focuses on what *could* be acceptable, it is also tolerant of more subjective ends. This argument that rationality should have some connection to morality leads neatly on to the third general approach to autonomy as moral rational self-determination.

Autonomy as moral rational self-determination

Although autonomy as rational self-determination allows for the important distinction between the acts of an autonomous person and

---

[37] C. C. Gauthier, 'The virtue of moral responsibility in healthcare decisionmaking' (2002) 11 *Cambridge Quarterly of Healthcare Ethics* 273, 277.

[38] O'Neill, *Bounds of Justice*, p. 24.

[39] O. O'Neill, *Towards Justice and Virtues* (Cambridge: Cambridge University Press, 1996), p. 58.

[40] H.-G. Gadamer, *Truth and Method*, 2nd edn (London: Sheed & Ward, 1975), p. 21.

autonomous acts, it is open to the criticism that it fails to take account of the reality of human existence. This liberal version of autonomy, like the libertarian conception of autonomy as simple self-determination, emphasises the importance of independent decision-making that, when taken to an extreme, isolates individuals and paradoxically mandates self-determination.[41] This approach is criticised for ignoring both the individual's dependence on and their obligations to others who exist in the interdependent network of relationships that surround all but the hermit. While such criticism has a valuable point to make, the liberal version of autonomy is perhaps set up as a straw man since many liberal writers acknowledge this constraint.[42]

While the liberal approach has been unfairly caricatured the criticisms remain valid. It is important to recognise that any valuable or useful conception of autonomy grounded in moral personhood and respect for that personhood – both for the actor and for others – must allow and coexist with influences, constraints and obligations arising from the relationships that envelop us.[43] Reducing individuals to isolated atomistic existences undermines the concept of autonomy, which provides another reason to reject the particularly thin view of autonomy as self-determination. In the absence of relationships autonomy becomes meaningless and unnecessary. Additionally, it is only through and by relationships that individuals can fully develop and express their autonomy.[44] No one would ever get to be an autonomous moral agent without at least maternal support and nurturing. As Nedelsky recognised: 'The collective is not simply a potential threat to individuals, but is constitutive of them, and thus is a source of their autonomy as well as a danger to it.'[45]

Growing up in this world of relationships means that our identities and characters are strongly influenced by other people and the things that happen to us. An extreme determinist view of these influences denies us the possibility of shaping our own lives or claiming authorship of our identity. Without the possibility of critical self-reflection this determinism collapses into a fatalist position that everything is

---

[41] A. Maclean, 'Autonomy, consent and persuasion' (2006) 13 *European Journal of Health Law* 321, 333. And see later discussion.

[42] See T. L. Beauchamp and J. F. Childress, *Principles of Biomedical Ethics*, 5th edn (New York: Oxford University Press, 2001), p. 59; Dworkin, *The Theory and Practice of Autonomy*, p. 21.

[43] J. W. Berg, P. S. Appelbaum, C. W. Lidz and L. S. Parker, *Informed Consent: Legal theory and clinical practice*, 2nd edn (New York: Oxford University Press, 2001), p. 33.

[44] See D. A. J. Richards, 'Rights and autonomy' (1981) 92 *Ethics* 3, 12.

[45] J. Nedelsky, 'Reconceiving autonomy: Sources thoughts and possibilities' (1989) 1 *Yale Journal of Law and Feminism* 7, 21.

beyond our control and we are responsible for nothing. If we are to deny both fatalism and meaningless atomism we must conceive of a third possibility. This third way is to acknowledge that through critical self-reflection agents are able to decide whether to accept or reject the influences to which they are subject.[46] It is only by thinking about the influences and accepting them as one's own that one can be more than just determined entirely by factors outside one's control. It follows from this that, if autonomy is to mean anything more than simple freedom (from external constraints) of action then it must include some notion of critical self-reflection.[47]

Critical self-reflection, while a form of rationality, differs from the more particular skill of being able to determine that one's choices will in fact further one's goals.[48] At least a minimal capacity for both forms of rationality is necessary for the person to be considered autonomous. I have deliberately restricted the requirement to capacity since it is the capacity rather than the use of the ability that grounds responsibility and authorship. Furthermore, critical self-reflection, and perhaps self-regarding rational decision-making should be seen as virtues – character ideals that form the basis for moral aspiration rather than moral duty.[49]

I have already argued that, in order to distinguish the autonomous act from the non-autonomous act of an autonomous person, autonomy must include some requirement for rational reflection. The capacity for rationality is also necessary for autonomy to achieve its full value (see p. 23) and to avoid the more extreme consequences of determinism: that we have no control over who we are and what we believe. All of these reasons suggest that bare self-determination is a less useful conception of autonomy than those views that incorporate rationality. However, even though rationality is necessary it may not be sufficient to justify valuing autonomy because of the absence of internal moral content. For example, it may be just as autonomous to act cruelly as to act the Good Samaritan.[50]

Autonomy as rational self-determination, which may be sufficient for a consumerist free-market competitive ethic, fails to provide moral

[46] P. Huntington, 'Toward a dialectical concept of autonomy' (1995) 21 *Philosophy and Social Criticism* 37.

[47] B. Berofsky, 'Identification, the self and autonomy' (2003) 20 *Social Philosophy and Policy* 199, 203.

[48] R. Noggle, 'The public conception of autonomy and critical self-reflection' (1997) 35 *The Southern Journal of Philosophy* 495, 506.

[49] See the argument in Noggle, 'The public conception of autonomy'.

[50] J. Feinberg, 'Autonomy', in J. Christman (ed.), *The Inner Citadel* (New York: Oxford University Press, 1989), pp. 27, 43.

justification for action in those areas of life that require cooperation rather than competition. This is particularly so where the Humean or neo-Humean approach to rationality is followed. Although the liberal approach to autonomy as rational self-determination may concede that autonomy should be limited by the impact of individual self-determination on the community,[51] some approaches conceptualise autonomy as possessing internal moral content.

In his *Groundwork of the Metaphysics of Morals*, Kant developed and justified his thesis that the sole categorical imperative is 'act only in accordance with that maxim through which you can at the same time will that it become a universal law'.[52] This imperative applies to all rational beings whose rationality presupposes freedom of the will. Kant argued that humans are rational beings but imperfect ones whose rationality is always subject to inclinations and desires. This rational will belongs to the noumenal world of understanding while our non-rational, sensory and emotional self belongs to the phenomenal world. But, it is the will that has intrinsic goodness because if welfare were our proper end we would be governed by instinct rather than reason. Thus, the rational will is an end in itself and, as such, all rational beings should be treated as ends in themselves, 'never merely as means'.[53] This practical imperative is, for Kant, 'the supreme limiting condition of the freedom of action of every human being'.[54] Because rational wills are ends in themselves the rational being has an obligation to treat those wills as ends in themselves.

The role of the will is to provide laws that guide our actions. Since conditional laws are undermined when the condition ceases to exist it is important to establish an unconditional law, which is Kant's categorical imperative. Because laws influenced by anything other than pure reason are conditional any law must come from the rational being's own will. This grounds Kant's view of autonomy as the 'sole principle of morals':

Autonomy of the will is the property of the will by which it is a law to itself (independently of any property of the objects of volition). The principle of autonomy is, therefore: to choose only in such a way that the maxims of your choice are also included as universal law in the same volition.[55]

Kant's view of autonomy makes it a necessary characteristic of a rational being that underpins all moral duty by requiring the actor to be guided

---

[51] J. Feinberg, *Harm to Self* (New York: Oxford University Press, 1986), pp. 28–54; Feinberg, 'Autonomy', p. 45.
[52] Kant, *Groundwork*, p. 31 (4:421).   [53] *Ibid.*, p. 38 (4:429).
[54] *Ibid.*, p. 39 (4:431).   [55] *Ibid.*, p. 47 (4:440).

by laws that could be willed as universal, which means that, in practice, all rational beings must be treated as ends in themselves. Thus, Kant envisaged autonomy as essentially relational[56] and as *the* moral characteristic of a free, rational will.

Manson and O'Neill claim that Kant's approach to autonomy 'cannot be operationalised by informed consent procedures'.[57] Rather, they argue that Kant's autonomy of the will provides the basis for more general duties. They then go on to use Kant's categorical imperative to argue that the healthcare profession has a duty not to coerce or deceive the patient. While these are general rules, Manson and O'Neill have argued that these duties should be specifically implemented as rules of consent. This may not be directly reliant on Kant's view of autonomy, but it is derived from autonomy of the will since the categorical imperative constitutes a constraint on the autonomous will that helps to define it.

While Manson and O'Neill may be correct insofar as the current approach to informed consent *does not* operationalise Kant's version of autonomy, this clearly does not mean that it *cannot* do so. Rather than completely abandoning autonomy, what Manson and O'Neill have actually done is to take a duty-based approach to consent in opposition to the more common rights-based approaches that pervade bioethical and legal debate. This creates the appearance that their approach is not autonomy-based, but it still has its origins in a respect for the autonomous will – or the agent – which lies at the heart of Kant's ethic. Furthermore, in focusing on the healthcare professional's duty they have ignored the possibility that the patient also has duties.

As I have suggested, Kant's view of autonomy, for all of its problems of being over-inclusive and under-determined,[58] is essentially relational. Wholly self-regarding decision-making, even if possible, falls foul of both the universalisability formulation and the ends/means formulation of Kant's imperative. To live in the context of a social existence means that, in making decisions, the individual should take into account the impact of the decision on at least those others who exist in a close relationship with the individual. The impact on society of a rule that

---

[56] B. Secker, 'The appearance of Kant's deontology in contemporary Kantianism: Concepts of patient autonomy in bioethics' (1999) 24 *Journal of Medicine and Philosophy* 43, 48.

[57] Manson and O'Neill, *Rethinking Informed Consent*, p. 18.

[58] See e.g. the criticism of O'Neill's approach in J. Wilson, 'Is respect for autonomy defensible?' (2007) 33 *Journal of Medical Ethics* 353 (written before Manson and O'Neill's book was published).

requires only self-regard in making decisions would be as great in severing the social bonds as a rule that permits lying. When applied in the context of healthcare, this universal rule would impose on patients a duty to at least take into account the impact of their decision on those others that exist in close relationships with them. There is no reason why this could not be included as a rule of consent.

Having said that, while Kant's theory supports a relational approach, its flaws of over-inclusiveness and under-determination suggest that other arguments need to be brought in to provide a more robust conception of autonomy. Furthermore, the absoluteness of Kant's approach may also be problematic. There are for example, times when lying may be justified.[59] Thus, what is most important for my purposes is the more general notion that other persons should be treated as ends and that the impact of our choices on those others should be taken into account. This notion may be developed drawing on the feminist conceptions of relational autonomy that take into account the need for social support, but also its constraints as well as the importance of caring about how one's decisions impact on those relational others.[60] This 'principle-directed' relational view of autonomy provides the third conception of autonomy that I have considered in this book.[61]

To summarise, I have suggested that there are three broad categories of conceptions of autonomy. These different approaches are essentially political and include autonomy as freedom of action/choice, autonomy as the capacity for rational/reflective choice and the principle-directed relational view of autonomy. However, I have also argued that, if it is to retain its value, autonomy must include some requirement for rationality and so autonomy as freedom of action was rejected. I have also distinguished the autonomous act from the autonomous person and the autonomous life. These distinctions are important because they justify different degrees of intervention and it is therefore important to determine which type of autonomy the law should protect. Before I can undertake that task I must address the other questions posed at the beginning of this chapter. I turn, then, to why autonomy is valued.

---

[59] The classic example being the situation in the Second World War of lying to Gestapo officers about the presence of a Jew hiding in the attic.

[60] See e.g. the essays in: C. MacKenzie and N. Stoljar (eds.), *Relational Autonomy: Feminist perspectives on autonomy, agency and the social self* (New York: Oxford University Press, 2000).

[61] H. T. Engelhardt Jr, 'The many faces of autonomy' (2001) 9 *Health Care Analysis* 283, 287.

The value of autonomy

Autonomy has both intrinsic and instrumental value. The intrinsic value of autonomy arises from its relationship with rationality and its necessity for agency, moral personhood and the ascription of moral responsibility. As O'Neill recognised, 'ethics can be addressed only to those who can reason, deliberate and act; ... [such] debates must take agency ... seriously'.[62] If I am to be held responsible for both the good and bad things I do, then I must have sufficient agency to be counted as the author of those acts, which demands that I have chosen to do the act for my own reasons, irrespective of the existence of possible alternatives.[63] This in turn requires that I am an autonomous individual. If I shot someone because a more physically powerful person forced the gun in my hand and squeezed my finger on the trigger I would not be held responsible for the death. Similarly, if I had been brainwashed or hypnotised into shooting someone I would not be held responsible.

The importance of autonomy here is that it is an essential constitutive element of agency and the more autonomous one is the better one is able to act as an effective moral agent.[64] However, while autonomy may be necessary to agency it is arguably not sufficient. It is possible for people to be autonomous, in the sense of instrumentally rational self-determination, but not be morally responsible agents because they lack the capacity to recognise, and be motivated by, moral norms.[65] This does not wholly undermine the connection between autonomy and agency since rationality, even in the 'thin' sense of instrumental rationality, remains necessary for agency.[66] This simply shifts the debate to the value of agency, which derives from the control agents have over their lives; while agency does not stop us from being acted upon it does allow us to shape and affect the world and our own lives within it.

Although the value of agency rests in the possibility of control, its importance does not lie in independence from others' influence. The claim that I would rather make a bad decision than cede the decision

---

[62] O'Neill, *Autonomy and Trust*, p. 7.
[63] H. Frankfurt, 'What we are morally responsible for', in J. M. Fischer and M. Ravizza (eds.), *Perspectives on Moral Responsibility* (Ithaca, NY: Cornell University Press, 1993), p. 286.
[64] Hurka, 'Why value autonomy?' (1987) 13 *Social Theory and Practice* 361, 366.
[65] See M. A. L. Oshana, 'The misguided marriage of responsibility and autonomy' (2002) 6 *The Journal of Ethics* 261, 267.
[66] See also J. Harris and K. Keywood, 'Ignorance, information and autonomy' (2001) 22 *Theoretical Medicine* 415, 420.

to an expert does not undermine my agency.[67] Rather, it is a necessary part of responsible agency that I decide whether or not to accept the expert's advice, or indeed allow the expert to decide for me. The value of agency is predicated on the equality of moral agents such that, without some justification other than the claim that he or she knows better than me, no moral agent has the authority to impose his or her opinion or decision on any other moral agent. It is perfectly rational and autonomous to acknowledge and rely on the expertise of others where there is good reason to do so. However, if autonomous persons are to be moral agents, they must be allowed to make those decisions and it smacks of the arrogance of infallibility to claim that simply because healthcare professionals are recognised as experts they should be allowed to override the patient's agency.

The alternative to agency is that we are only capable of reaction rather than action: that the environment and our instinctive responses to that environment wholly shape our lives. In such a world praise and blame would be tools of 'manipulation or training' and we would have no reason to retain 'reactive attitudes' such as gratitude and admiration.[68] This would undermine ideas of responsibility, personhood and a sense of self.[69] As Wolf commented:

A world in which human relationships are restricted to those that can be formed and supported in the absence of the reactive attitude is a world of human isolation so cold and dreary that any but the most cynical must shudder at the idea of it.[70]

Thus, if we are to see ourselves as responsible agents, and we must if we wish to hold on to reactive attitudes to each other, autonomy is essential.[71] Furthermore, far from being isolationist, autonomy is crucial to developing social relations that have any meaning beyond purely instinctive behaviour.

Additional support may be gained, for this argument that autonomy is intrinsically valuable, from the similarities between the characteristics of personhood that give the individual intrinsic moral value and the nature of autonomy. The features that constitute personhood include conscious

---

[67] See the discussion in J. Varelius, 'The value of autonomy in medical ethics' (2006) 9 *Medicine, Health Care and Philosophy* 377.

[68] S. Wolf, 'The importance of free will', in J. M. Fischer and M. Ravizza (eds.), *Perspectives on Moral Responsibility* (Ithaca, NY: Cornell University Press, 1993), pp. 101, 104–6.

[69] *Ibid.*, pp. 113–14.   [70] *Ibid.*, p. 106.

[71] C. C. Gautier, 'Moral responsibility and respect for antonomy: Meeting the communitarian challenge' (2000) 10 *Kennedy Institute of Ethics Journal* 337, 344.

awareness of self and others; the ability to reason; the ability to act independently of external control; and an awareness of the self as a being with a future.[72] The more persuasive accounts of autonomy tend to require a rational being that is consciously self-aware and hence would count as a person.[73] If personhood is seen as intrinsically valuable then so must autonomy. As Richards suggested, 'The development of . . . [autonomy] is, from the earliest life of the infant, the central developmental task of the becoming of a person.'[74] What this means is that morality is contingent on the existence of autonomy, which is the central characteristic of personhood that allows us to be treated as equal members of the moral community, be held responsible for our actions and be capable of relationships based on reactive attitudes.

The primary argument against the intrinsic value of autonomy is based on a determinist position that attacks the very possibility of autonomy. However, if autonomy is not wholly undermined and some degree of self-determination is possible then the argument that autonomy is intrinsically valuable holds fast.

Determinism holds that all of our decisions and actions result from the interaction between our genetically controlled characteristics and the environment (including other beings). Every thought I have is a consequence of the interaction between the environment and the physical architecture of the cognitive part of my brain. I am acted upon by external factors and I react to them in a way that would be entirely predictable if only we knew enough about the laws of nature. I am not capable of self-reflection or rationality and the appearance of, and belief in, such behaviour is an illusion caused by chemical reactions that result from the interactions mentioned earlier.

There is insufficient evidence to know whether this extreme form of determinism is true. However, even assuming it is, we behave as if it is not and for some people the belief that one has some control over one's own life is psychologically valuable. Irrespective of whether autonomy is an illusion, those people with a strong internal locus of control are adversely affected if their autonomy is obstructed by, for example, the withholding of information.[75] It is also arguable that treating people as if they have autonomy is valuable because it may mean that that those

[72] Adapted from, M. A. Warren, 'On the moral and legal status of abortion', in L. Gruen and G. E. Panichas (eds.), *Sex, Morality and the Law* (London: Routledge, 1997), p. 302.
[73] See e.g. B. H. Levi, *Respecting Patient Autonomy* (Chicago: University of Illinois Press, 1999), p. 37; B. Rössler, 'Problems with autonomy' (2002) 17 *Hypatia* 143, 146–7.
[74] Richards, 'Rights and autonomy', 7.
[75] B. M. Waller, 'The psychological structure of patient autonomy' (2002) 11 *Cambridge Quarterly of Healthcare Ethics* 257.

'determined' to respond to moral obligations will do so if such moral obligations exist. Thus, treating people as if they are autonomous may result in behaviour that is beneficial both to themselves and to others within the community. Similarly, behaving as if people have autonomy allows us to retain reactive attitudes towards them making the world more 'human' and less mechanistic than it might be in their absence. Finally, it is also arguable that the very idea of scholarship and argument about autonomy suggests that we implicitly believe that we have some degree of autonomy.

Rössler has suggested that:

The failure to lead, or at least the difficulty of leading, an autonomous life is something we are able to comprehend as such, in its very recalcitrance, only because and insofar as we both do and want to understand ourselves always already as being autonomous . . . Otherwise the possibility of that failure would not always be our irritating and disquieting companion.[76]

This point, that our very concern with autonomy betrays our desire to be autonomous, may be taken one step further. If extreme determinism is true, and it is important to 'live in accordance with the facts', then it is important to accept that we have no free will. This acceptance requires us to adopt a particular reactive attitude towards ourselves: that we are blameless for our lives and our conduct. However, extreme determinism precludes reactive attitudes. Even the attitude that we do not have free will presupposes and asserts that we at least have sufficient free will to take the stance that we lack free will.[77] This means that living in accordance with extreme determinism would prevent us from adopting any attitude towards ourselves, including that, as beings lacking autonomy, we are blameless. Thus, it is paradoxically illogical to argue that we should behave as if extreme determinism were true.

Finally, autonomy may also be intrinsically valuable because of its role in our identity. By making particular choices such as our choice of career and our friends, we foster the development of our character. Thus, autonomy, in the sense of rational self-determination, is essential to our 'integrity' as a person.[78] The capacity for rational self-reflection allows us to question the values and beliefs to which we are exposed. This in turn allows us to decide for ourselves whether or not to identify with the value or belief in question. Autonomy allows us to choose our goals and the way in which we go about achieving them. It allows us to decide how

---

[76] Rössler, 'Problems with autonomy', p. 157.
[77] Wolf, 'The importance of free will', p. 113.
[78] Dworkin, *Life's Dominion*, p. 224.

to behave towards others. Autonomy is, in other words, crucial to our self-definition.

Apart from its intrinsic value, autonomy is also important for its instrumental value. Two instrumental values have already been mentioned. First, for people with an internal locus of control, respecting autonomy is beneficial to their well-being.[79] Even when the researchers do not take account of the differing needs of patients with an external locus of control, there are many studies that suggest that the provision of information, which is one aspect of respecting autonomy, is clinically efficacious.[80] It may further be the case that helping those with an external locus of control to become more autonomous may be a valuable long-term strategy providing it is done sympathetically and supportively.[81] Second, treating people as autonomous may encourage some to take responsibility, accept their obligations and so act in a morally good way, which may be beneficial both to themselves and to the community in general.

Another instrumental value is that through reason a person will be better, and more consistently, able to attain desired outcomes (known in this context as 'goods').[82] Since the capacity for autonomy is a matter of degree and people can be more or less autonomous, this means that the more autonomous a person is the better.[83] This has, as a consequence, the possibility that respecting a person and treating him or her as an end, and not just a means to an end, requires us to recognise not only a duty of non-interference but also a positive obligation to support and enhance that person's autonomy. It is, however, important to recognise that this value is contingent.

J. S. Mill argued that since each person's self-knowledge is usually better than other-regarding knowledge, and since the person who cares most for someone is usually him or herself – and this is especially so when considering society's interests in its members – competent persons should be allowed the liberty to decide for themselves on matters that affect their own lives.[84] This argument supports the principle of

---

[79] Waller, 'The psychological structure of patient autonomy'.

[80] See e.g. M. Valimaki et al., 'Self-determination in surgical patients in five European countries' (2004) 34 Journal of Nursing Scholarship 305, 309; G. C. Williams, G. C. Rodin, R. M. Ryan, W. S. Grolnick and E. L. Deci, 'Autonomous regulation and long-term medication adherence in adult outpatients' (1998) 17 Health Psychology 269.

[81] Waller, 'The psychological structure of patient autonomy', 263.

[82] R. F. Ladenson, 'A theory of personal autonomy' (1975) 86 Ethics 30, 43.

[83] Ibid., 46.

[84] J. S. Mill, 'On Liberty', in J. Gray (ed.), On Liberty and Other Essays (Oxford: Oxford University Press, 1991), pp. 5, 75–85. It should be noted that Mill does not use the term 'autonomy' but the concept is implicit in a lot of what he argues (see especially

autonomy in general, but leaves individual irrationally self-harming decisions open to interference. This is because there will certainly be occasions when others can see more clearly than I and are better able to make a good decision for me. Mill's argument did, however, predict a major criticism of medical paternalism that doctors are only competent to know the best clinical choice but, because patients are the experts concerning all other aspects of their lives, the final decision regarding treatment should rest with them.[85] This is particularly so given that, while it may be an end in itself, health's greatest value is instrumental; being healthy allows us to follow our life plans and achieve our goals. Conceived in this way it is self-fulfilment rather than health or welfare per se that is, in a secular world, of fundamental importance. The primacy of self-fulfilment over health or welfare requires that each of us is ultimately allowed to be autonomous.

It may be argued that, while we may know ourselves better than others do, we still make mistakes and that others should be allowed to prevent us from making or acting on such bad decisions. Excluding decisions based on wrong or inadequate information, the problem from a developmental perspective is that the capacity for rational decision-making may be stunted unless the individual is required to exercise his self-determination and making mistakes is an important part of learning. Thus, self-determination should be encouraged and practised so as to improve on one's autonomous capacity, which is important if rationality is seen as a good thing. It may, of course, be countered that allowing someone to make mistakes is all very well but is self-defeating if the mistake is such that the person's future autonomy or his life will be lost. It should, therefore, at least be justifiable to coercively prevent someone making such an extremely harmful mistake. I will consider this in more detail later but for now it is enough to note that even if that argument is accepted it only requires that we not treat autonomy as an absolute right.

Finally, but nonetheless importantly, autonomy acts as a protection against the 'tyranny' of the state and its institutions,[86] and, as Levi argued, 'one's autonomous status is important for demarcating certain political boundaries between persons'.[87] It is, therefore, essential for a democratic state.[88] Furthermore, allowing people the important liberties of freedom of thought and speech is essential for the advancement of

---

p. 17). Even if it is not, freedom of action and decision-making is an important aspect of autonomy.

[85] For example see Berg *et al.*, *Informed Consent*, pp. 18–19, 22–4.

[86] Mill, 'On Liberty', pp. 8–9.   [87] Levi, *Respecting Patient Autonomy*, p. 24.

[88] Oshana, 'How much should we value autonomy?', 107.

knowledge and understanding. Without that liberty, established views would go unchallenged and knowledge would remain static.[89]

I have argued that autonomy has both intrinsic and instrumental value. The instrumental value of autonomy justifies respecting those decisions that are either autonomous or at least not significantly harmful to the individual. The difficult decisions are those irrational decisions that may significantly impair the person's future autonomy. I will discuss this issue in more depth in Chapter 2. However, it is the intrinsic value of autonomy and not its instrumental value that provides the strongest justification for respecting an agent's decisions.

As an intrinsic value, autonomy is a necessary capacity for an agent to be a morally responsible member of the community. The value of having a community of moral agents justifies respect for the autonomous person. Furthermore, if I see myself as a moral agent and would like that agency respected I must, if I am to be consistent, respect the agency of others with a similar capacity. Unless I believe that I am the only person with the capacity to be an agent then it would be unjust to privilege my decisions over the decisions of others.[90] This means that if any person is to be treated as an agent then all persons of a similar capacity should be treated likewise. Thus, to have any form of government, or indeed any politics at all, requires the recognition of agency. However, while autonomy is intrinsically valuable this does not mean that the capacity for autonomy grounds an absolute right to self-determination.

The limits of autonomy

If autonomy were to be seen as an absolute right to decide for oneself the consequence would be the risk of chaos with the vulnerable left to the mercy of the strong. Furthermore, if conceived as a right then it is logically impossible for it to be absolute. If A decided to exercise his or her autonomy by locking B inside a room this would interfere with B's autonomy and B could not be said to have a right to autonomy unless A is restrained from exercising his or her right in this way. Thus, ignoring the problem of ability, any right to autonomy cannot be the freedom to do what one wants.

That trite example suggests that any right to autonomy must be limited by having regard to the autonomy of others. It might be suggested that A has the right to do what he or she wants providing it does

---

[89] Mill, 'On Liberty', esp. pp. 22–41.
[90] See T. Takala, 'Concepts of "person" and "liberty", and their implications to our fading notions of autonomy' (2007) 33 *Journal of Medical Ethics* 225, 227–8.

not prevent B from doing what he or she wants. This formulation, however, would be overly restrictive and would paralyse much of our life. It may be reasonable if resources were plentiful and we lived completely independent lives. But, in a world in which we must compete for scarce goods and interact with others, autonomy would lose much of its value if A cannot do something simply because it would prevent B from doing it. Imagine if A wants to build a house on a particular spot next to the sea with good access to fresh water and a supply of food. If no one else wants to build there then he or she is free to do so. But, if B also wants to build there then there is a problem. Neither A nor B may exercise his or her autonomy if it prevents the other from doing so, which means that A can only build there if B does not want to and vice versa. However, if both want to build there then neither can and the plot must remain unused. This means that they must each select other plots but the same problem may recur ad infinitum meaning that neither can build anywhere. This would be a ridiculous state of affairs and so a middle ground 'capable of public justification' must be found,[91] which suggests that any limitation must conform with the 'morality of duty' rather than the more individualistic ideal 'morality of aspiration'.[92]

The harm principle

Perhaps the least contentious ground for limiting autonomy is to prevent harm to others. Mill explicated the most famous version of this principle in his essay 'On Liberty'. He argued that:

the only purpose for which power can be rightfully exercised over any members of a civilised community, against his will, is to prevent harm to others. His own good, either physical or moral, is not a sufficient warrant. He cannot rightfully be compelled to do or forbear because it will be better for him to do so, because it will make him happier, because, in the opinion of others, to do so would be wise, or even right. These are good reasons for remonstrating with him, or reasoning with him, or persuading him, or entreating him, but not for compelling him, or visiting him with any evil in case he do otherwise.[93]

This limitation of course depends on what is meant by 'harm'. Since limiting autonomy may itself be seen as harmful, the outcomes that might justify limiting autonomy should be more than temporary or

---

[91] Noggle, 'The public conception of autonomy', 500.
[92] L. L. Fuller, *The Morality of Law*, 2nd edn (New Haven: Yale University Press, 1969), p. 5.
[93] Mill, 'On Liberty', p. 14.

trivial upsets.[94] The limitation must also require that the harm be wrongfully inflicted. One possible way of defining harm is to characterise it as a setback to someone's interests.[95] The problem with this is that, as a justification for limiting autonomy, such a definition would be overly restrictive. Returning to my earlier example of choosing a plot of land to build one's house on, allowing A to build on the most desirable plot would certainly be a setback to B's interests if building on that plot was one of B's autonomous goals. Thus, it would constitute a harm and we could justify limiting A's autonomy to prevent harm to B. However, as I have shown, this would result in neither being able to build and both would be harmed. This explains why 'harm' as a justification for limiting autonomy must incorporate both damage (setback to interests) and the notion of a wrong.[96] The notion of a wrong is something that must be defined independently of autonomy and a full exploration is beyond the scope of this book. Suffice it to suggest that someone is wronged if they have a justifiable claim obstructed and that our justifiable claims are defined by the rules determined by the society in which we live.

One difficulty in determining the limits of autonomy is that most, if not all, decisions made by any individual will have an impact on other people. This is true even if the decision seems to be essentially self-regarding. For example, imagine that A is a vegan with strongly held views that humans should not use other animals solely for their own benefit. A has developed a condition that will leave him severely disabled unless he accepts a transplant of tissue taken from a pig. Such a decision would contravene A's deeply held autonomous views about the relationship between humans and animals but his decision to refuse treatment, which will leave him severely disabled, will harm his wife. It will also affect others who have a relationship with A and will place an additional burden on the community's resources. It is arguable that A ought to consider the effect of his decisions on others and he should take them into account when making a decision. If possible A ought to make decisions that will be good for all concerned. It would be especially good of A to make decisions that put others' interests ahead of his own. However, if morality and the meaningfulness of individual existence is to survive state coercion then A should not be prevented from exercising his autonomy unless the affected other has a justified claim that would be obstructed by his choice.

---

[94] J. Feinberg, *Harm to Others* (New York: Oxford University Press, 1984), p. 12.
[95] Feinberg, *Harm to Self*, p. 10.
[96] *Ibid.*, pp. 10–11. A stronger version of the setback to interests definition of harm, limits the interests to 'vital ones': H. Hayry, *The Limits of Medical Paternalism* (London: Routledge, 1991), p. 21.

It might be argued that A's wife does have quite a strong claim – arising out of their relationship – requiring that A accepts the necessary treatment to prevent the disability. However, for state coercion to be justified it would need to be clearly established that such a claim would be created when entering into such a relationship. In other words, A would need to consent in advance and this would mean that unless he could predict the need to compromise his principles his consent would not be normatively effective in relation to the pig organ transplant. If his views are deeply held it is unlikely that he would enter such an agreement voluntarily. Being able to define our own relationships, and that includes the obligations that arise from them, is an important part of what it means to be a person. State interference is only warranted where it is not possible for one of the parties to autonomously negotiate the nature of the relationship.

As indicated earlier, choices that are essentially self-regarding may burden the community. If the cost to the community is too high then it may be justifiable to limit individual autonomy. This may be explained by Feinberg's garrison model: in a situation when the community's very existence is under threat then the selfish decision of a single person may tip the balance. Under those circumstances the community may be justified in seeking to preserve itself by overriding an autonomous choice.[97] This justification, however, is simply the harm principle applied to the community rather than to individual others. It depends on seeing the destruction of the community as harm and on the existence of a minimal obligation towards the community that would be breached by failing to assist it in such times of need. While it is theoretically possible that this model may be relevant in the context of individual medical treatment it does not pertain in present-day Britain nor is it foreseeable in the near future. However, it may also be justifiable under the harm principle to limit an individual's autonomy to prevent lesser levels of community harm.

Certain interests may be considered as public interests if they are sufficiently widely held. These interests may be raised as justifiable limits on autonomy either when the specific interests of a sufficiently large number of individuals are harmed or when a 'common' interest is harmed.[98] Public-health threats, such as the risk of transmitting an infectious disease, may justify coercion. Similarly, threats to the environment may be coercively prevented even though it may not be possible to identify an individual directly harmed. The protection of these community interests is simply an extension of the harm principle to cover

[97] Feinberg, *Harm to Self*, p. 22.   [98] Feinberg, *Harm to Others*, pp. 222–3.

those harms where the victims are the indeterminate members of the community.

Other limiting principles

Apart from the harm principle, there are four principles that might justify limiting an individual's autonomy:

- prudence
- offence to others
- self-harm and
- morality.[99]

Although allowing that actions offending good manners or decency may be prohibited if done in public,[100] all of these possible constraints may be rejected as interfering with the general development of people's ability to decide their own lives and to actually decide for themselves how their life should go, which is what gives life its personal value.[101] These judgements justify argument, persuasion and remonstration but not coercion. Certainly if, when it matters, our autonomy is restricted to making decisions that others see as wise it would be fatally undermined as a concept. Apart from the impact such a strategy would have on our ability to identify with any of our choices when we know we could not have chosen otherwise, it also threatens the principle that all moral persons are equal. Dominant views of rationality would hold sway and subjugate the 'incomprehensible' minority.

It might be argued that if autonomy requires rationality then an irrational action is not autonomous and does not, therefore, need to be protected.[102] For example, the US President's Commission suggested that 'A second limitation on self-determination arises where a person's decisionmaking is so defective or mistaken that the decision fails to promote the person's own values or goals.'[103] This constraint protects the overtly autonomous act but not the other acts of an autonomous person. One problem with this approach is that acts may be autonomous but not obviously so, for example, where people autonomously choose to

---

[99] Hayry, *The Limits of Medical Paternalism*, p. 25.
[100] Mill, 'On Liberty', pp. 108, 109.   [101] Mill, 'On Liberty', p. 14.
[102] Hayry, *The Limits of Medical Paternalism*, p. 36.
[103] The President's Commission for the Study of Ethical Problems in Medicine and Biomedical and Behavioral Research, *Making Health Care Decisions: The ethical and legal implications of informed consent in the patient–practitioner relationship, vol. 1: Report* (1982), p. 49.

act in a way that does not appear to coincide with their goals or interests. A related problem is the incomprehensibility that arises because observers are unable to understand the person's goals. This results from a difference in the conception of the 'good life' and what goals a person ought to aim for. It is also likely, as Mill claimed, that – subconscious influences notwithstanding – we know ourselves better than others do. While I may not always be able to explain my actions, my own knowledge of my interests and goals and my own understanding of what life means for me will almost certainly be better than some other person's appreciation of those crucial decision-making factors. Thus, an external judge of rationality may easily be mistaken about the logic of my decision.

It may further be argued that we learn best by being allowed to make mistakes. If I am only allowed to make rational decisions I will not be allowed to make mistakes and my ability to reason will improve less quickly. This argument can only apply to those mistakes that will not cause permanent and significant harm to my ability to be autonomous. It would be self-defeating to argue that I should be allowed to make mistakes so that I can learn better how to make decisions if, as a result, I am unable to exercise that rationality. Related to this argument is perhaps the stronger point that, since no one is infallible and I am the person who will have to live with the consequences, I should be the one who makes the decision. If, because you profess an expertise, I choose to rely on your judgement I am responsible for the decision and should accept the consequences with equanimity. Certainly, I have no justifiable reason to blame you for my misfortune. However, if you force a choice on me against my will and I am harmed as a consequence that harm will be amplified precisely because you chose to act against my will. Just as stifling free speech suggests infallibility,[104] so too does preventing free choice. Such an unwarranted profession of infallibility makes a bad outcome seem all the worse especially as it is I rather than you who will have to live with the consequences.

Apart from when the harm principle is invoked, limiting autonomy on the basis of morality is problematic. The reality of moral relativity and the existence of a pluralistic society make it difficult to base rules on particular moral principles. Again the problem of a dominant view is raised and allowing such moral judgements to justify coercive law hints at an arrogant intolerance. As Hayry noted, 'there are an infinite variety of interpretations of what is moral, and to a person defending any one of them, its opponents will always appear more or less irrational'.[105] If a

---

[104] Mill, 'On Liberty', p. 22.   [105] Hayry, *The Limits of Medical Paternalism*, p. 126.

particular view of morality is enforced this implies that the followers of a different morality are somehow less equal. If living by a particular code is not harmful to others then the value of such a code can only be coercively denied by a society that sees those individuals as less worthy of respect. Since moral equality is one of the assumptions behind my argument, harmless moral (or 'immoral') beliefs/actions cannot justify limiting autonomy.

It is arguable that offensive actions fall within the purview of the law. It may be legitimate, as Mill argued (see p. 33), to restrict offensive activities by banning them from public display. In general, however, it would be a greater invasion of liberty and autonomy to coercively prevent an action seen by some as offensive. What counts as offensive is, to a large extent, simply a matter of opinion. Categorising something as offensive is an appeal to individual sensibilities and is not subject to reason but to feelings and, as such, it is less objective than the more legitimate harm principle. To infringe one person's autonomy because another finds the idea of it offensive is to treat the actor as less equal because it subjugates his or her autonomy to the irrational emotions of the other; it becomes a conflict between two different wants.

Even though it may be rational to have an interest in not being offended, the content of that interest is populated by feelings. If the offensive actions solely further the actor's interest in being offensive, then there is a conflict of equal interests. Other autonomous interests, however, will usually be weightier than the interest in not being offended and setbacks to those other interests may be more permanent than the relatively temporary impact of offensiveness. The interest in not being offended may be infringed by offensive behaviour but the offence will not persist beyond the incident. The setback caused to others by banning the 'offensive' activity may, however, have a much more permanent and total impact. In the context of medical care this argument is particularly apt. The types of treatment that may be seen as offensive include operations like abortion and sex change.[106] The impact of preventing an abortion because such operations offend a section of society would be huge, both for the individual woman and for society. History demonstrates the misery and harm caused to women through having to deal with unwanted pregnancy when abortion is unlawful.

---

[106] Of course, if the fetus is seen as a person then the harm principle may be raised as an argument against allowing abortion. Also, abortion may be criticised on moral grounds.

The protection of future autonomy

I will consider the issue of paternalism and the restriction of autonomy to prevent self-harm in more detail in Chapter 2 following a discussion of the principle of beneficence. For now I will confine the debate to an examination of whether it is legitimate to restrict present autonomy in order to protect the autonomy of the future self. One argument that would support restricting present autonomy in order to protect future autonomy relies on a utilitarian position that if autonomy is a good thing then it should be maximised and what really matters is not how much autonomy I can exercise now but how much I am able to exercise over my whole life. This may mean that present autonomy should not be respected if it would undermine my future autonomy.[107] Parfit's reductionist argument, based on the relative unimportance of personal identity, that 'we ought not to do to our future selves what it would be wrong to do to other people', forms the basis for a second argument.[108] If the harm principle justifies restricting autonomy to protect others from harm then, if my psychological connectedness to my future self is no greater than it is to current third parties, just as my autonomy may be justifiably restricted to prevent harm to others so it may be constrained to protect my future self.

As I noted earlier, for autonomy to be constrained the harm principle requires the act to be wrongful. What this implies is that for harm to future autonomy to count as a justifiable limit I must owe myself a duty not to cause such a setback to my autonomy. This is problematic not least because if I owe myself the duty there is no good reason why I cannot waive it and that undermines any such duty. This consequence may be avoided if I am held to be the subject of the duty but the duty is owed to the community (or state). However, for such a duty to be justifiable, the harm caused by infringing my present autonomy must be less than the harm that would otherwise be caused to my future autonomy. Furthermore, any claim that I owe a duty to protect my future autonomy must survive the following arguments.

The starting point is that many choices restrict my future options. To use Parfit's railway analogy, if I choose the right – rather than the middle or left – track I lose all of the opportunities associated with the middle and left track. In this way, every time I exercise my autonomy I restrict my future autonomy. Avoiding making choices cannot solve this problem because it defeats the point of being autonomous and, since many

---

[107] See the similar argument in Levi, *Respecting Patient Autonomy*, p. 84.
[108] D. Parfit, *Reasons and Persons* (Oxford: Clarendon Press, 1984), p. 320.

choices are lost by inaction, it would not guarantee protection of future autonomy. Thus, if present autonomy is to be restricted it must be to protect future *capacity* for autonomy.

The question of whether an individual's self-determining decision should be overridden is most likely to arise when the stakes are at their highest. This is precisely when it is most important for the autonomous agent to be allowed to be self-determining. By overriding a person's decisions whenever the decision really matters undermines the whole point of recognising the individual as moral agent and it essentially makes the right to self-determination an empty right. There is little point in being an autonomous agent if, just when it matters most, some authority intervenes to prevent you from exercising that autonomy.[109] This is exacerbated by the realisation that the person's future autonomy is equally vulnerable to being overridden.

Levi argues that the 'sacrifice' of present autonomy for the sake of future autonomy 'involves uncoupling ends and means in such a way that one's present activities no longer reflect the principles that ground one's values, upon which one's priorities, and in that sense "meaning", are based'.[110] A classic example of this would be ignoring the Jehovah's Witness' refusal of blood in order to prevent him or her suffering permanent harm or death from major blood loss.

One important implication of Levi's argument is that it appears to address only those instances in which the exercise of autonomy concerns one's values, goals or life plans. This justifies non-interference only where the decision itself was autonomous rather than respecting all the primarily self-regarding decisions of an autonomous person. Because the argument protects only autonomous decisions it fails to justify non-interference where the actor decides irrationally or simply makes a mistake. It may be argued that there is no good reason to protect such decisions if they will damage the actor's future autonomy. However, being self-determining is, as I discussed earlier, an intrinsically important aspect of authorship, responsibility and moral personhood. It is our actions as autonomous persons rather than our autonomous actions that ground these crucial parts of who we are, which means that not only should others respect our autonomous choices but also our non-autonomous choices.

---

[109] Levi, *Respecting Patient Autonomy*, p. 84. The argument depends on accepting that valuing the capacity for autonomy requires us also to value being able to exercise that autonomy. Just as having money but no opportunity to spend it seems pointless, so too is having an unusable capacity for autonomy.

[110] *Ibid.*, p. 85.

It may be argued that, since the capacity for autonomy is so import-ant, only autonomous choices should be respected, as these will – if truly autonomous and hence rational – take account of the effect on future capacity. However, it is an empty respect for someone to say that his decisions will be respected but only if they are objectively right. If taken to an extreme these objective judgements would be applied not just to our decisions but also to our goals and life plans and would be the moral equivalent of Henry Ford's famous restriction that the customer could choose whatever colour he liked as long as it was black. In fact, it may be psychologically worse as alternatives may be apparently available only to be whisked from under our noses if we make the mistake of opting for the 'wrong' one.

The argument that non-autonomous decisions should be respected is given further support by recourse to one of Mill's justifications for liberty (see p. 27 above). This is that we know ourselves better than others know us, which makes each of us the expert regarding our own lives. While others may inform us of the likely effect of a chosen action, it is for us to determine the relative importance of that consequence. It is worth repeating that Mill's argument that we should be allowed to make mistakes because it is the best way to learn would not apply where the consequence was catastrophic. There seems little point in learning a lesson if the consequence of that lesson is to so undermine autonomy that the actor is unable to utilise any new knowledge. Notwithstanding the limits of Mill's argument I would suggest that, based on its intrinsic value, a respect for autonomy requires respect for both autonomous choices and the non-autonomous decisions of autonomous persons. This position, however, is still vulnerable to Parfit's arguments regarding the protection of future selves, which I will now briefly address.

Future selves

Parfit argued that identity is important only in so far as it is constituted by psychological continuity and connectedness. The importance of these latter two factors he persuasively established by considering scenarios involving split brains.[111] Thus, he argued that when his brain is split into two parts (left and right) and each half is placed in a new body the question of his existence is irrelevant. More important is whether he shares a psychological connectedness with Lefty and Righty. Since, in a normal life, connectedness decreases over time (I share a greater

---

[111] See, Parfit, *Reasons and Persons*, pp. 199–345.

psychological connection with my 30-year-old self than with my 10-year-old self) it is not irrational to act for instant pleasure even if that would cause harm to my future self. However, as the connectedness decreases so my future self becomes less like me and increasingly like someone else. As such it makes little sense to deny my future self the same protection afforded to others who may be wrongly harmed by my actions. This would suggest, amongst other things, that my present autonomy might be constrained to protect my future self's autonomy.

There are a number of reasons why Parfit's argument should not be applied to restrict present autonomy.[112] The first is the familiar point that the present self is the person best placed to be considered expert about the best interests of the future self. As I noted earlier, this will not always be the case and at best it only provides a conditional argument in favour of respecting present autonomy. A second argument is that for the vast majority of our decisions the person most directly affected is sufficiently psychologically connected to the decision-maker to be considered the same self. This is perhaps the most telling counter-argument in the context of contemporaneous decision-making. Acknowledging that human life is a narrative provides the necessary connection.[113] Dworkin, for example, argued that the best justification for autonomy is that it is through the exercise of personal choice that we construct our own identity. On this 'integrity' view, autonomy is causally necessary for authorship and the development of a unique character.[114] The narrative thread that connects the individual stages of the human being's life creates the necessary unity of identity, which means that any duty owed to the future self is a duty owed to myself and may thus be waived.

Parfit's argument may also be countered by appealing to an agency-based account of an individual's life. For Korsgaard the 'agent' unifies the person's life,[115] which means that the agent's choices are constitutive of the person's identity.[116] Thus, any choice authored by the agent has a special significance. Furthermore, an agent-based view of the person means that the present self is an empty concept. All decisions made by the agent are based on the persistence of the agent over time and the

---

[112] Levi, *Respecting Patient Autonomy*, pp. 88–91.

[113] M. Quante, 'Precedent autonomy and personal identity' (1999) 9 *Kennedy Institute of Ethics Journal* 365, 372; B. A. Rich, 'Personhood, patienthood, and clinical practice: Reassessing advance directives' (1998) 4 *Psychology, Public Policy, and Law* 610, 614.

[114] Dworkin, *Life's Dominion*, pp. 223–4.

[115] C. M. Korsgaard, 'Self-constitution in the ethics of Plato and Kant' (1998) 3 *The Journal of Ethics* 1, 22.

[116] C. M. Korsgaard, 'Personal identity and the unity of agency: A Kantian response to Parfit' (1989) 18 *Philosophy and Public Affairs* 101, 103.

psychological identification of the present self with the self in the future. Thus:

the extent that you regulate your choices by identifying yourself as the one who is implementing something like a particular plan of life, you need to identify with your future in order to be *what you are even now*. When the person is viewed as an agent, no clear content can be given to the idea of a merely present self.[117]

It is, therefore, arguable that the qualitative changes in our person resulting from our agent-authored choices do not affect the identity of that person, which is only fragmented by external influences. Thus, barring some radical discontinuity, I remain the same person throughout my autonomous life and I can waive any duty I owe to myself. This argument has the further consequence of limiting external interference, since major interference with the agent will fracture the person's unity.

A third objection to Parfit's view is that, any protection of future selves should apply across the board and not just to medical decision-making.[118] Thus, decisions about career, relationship, financial and leisure activities should be constrained where the decision risks significant harm to the future self. This raises the issues of who would be qualified to make such decisions and whether anyone could ever make such decisions. This point has particular force in light of Korsgaard's argument about agency as it would seriously undermine an individual's integrity if every major decision in life was subject to the constraint of 'objective' rationality.

A fourth argument is that, any future self is likely to share values, interests and goals with the present self as these will have evolved from those possessed by the present self. This argument may apply to the future selves that develop gradually, especially those unified by the 'agent', but will be far less relevant where the future self is created by a devastating event (i.e. where psychological continuity is disrupted by, for example, head trauma).

Finally, the fact that autonomy, in whatever guise, is generally valued may lead to a profound resistance to formal attempts by state authorities to interfere with essentially self-regarding decisions.[119] Proposals to restrict what people see as civil liberties are usually met with strongly voiced objections and the more self-regarding the decisions involved the greater the resistance is likely to be. While this is not a principled objection to Parfit's approach it does at least suggest a counsel of caution.

---

[117] *Ibid.*, 113–14.   [118] Levi, *Respecting Patient Autonomy*, p. 88.
[119] Hayry, *The Limits of Medical Paternalism*, p. 137.

Although the agency-based arguments provide the strongest case, all of these objections suggest we should be allowed to make our own choices even if they are irrational. Others may be allowed – or even have a duty – to advise, persuade and remonstrate, but if autonomy is the guiding principle then the final decision should remain with the individual. However, autonomy is not the sole principle and others need to be included in the final balance. Before I consider the relevance of other moral principles and approaches in Chapter 2 there is one further issue that needs to be addressed.

Autonomy as the moral basis for consent

I stated earlier that there is a clear connection between autonomy and consent. This has been a working assumption in bioethics and medical law for many years but has recently been challenged. It is, therefore, important to revisit the connection and address the challenges. I will begin with Taylor's attack on the relationship between autonomy and consent.

Taylor argued that 'concern for human well-being' rather than autonomy is really the basis for informed consent.[120] Before considering the justification for this claim, it should be noted that he refers specifically to 'informed consent'. The term 'informed consent' has acquired a certain amount of baggage over the years and it is reasonable to suggest that it has lost sight of its origins. Indeed, the term itself implies that the focus of the interaction should be information disclosure.[121] In *Canterbury* v. *Spence*, for example, Robinson CJ stated: 'The scope of the physician's communications to the patient . . . must be measured by the patient's need and that need is information material to the decision.'[122] Because I am concerned specifically with consent, rather than the more loaded concept of 'informed consent', and because I am reducing that concept to first principles I avoid some of the criticism that follows from the way 'informed consent' has developed in practice.

This brings me to the first problem with Taylor's approach. In his paper he initially begins by noting that commentators have traditionally drawn a connection between informed consent 'as an ethical doctrine' and autonomy. He then goes on to focus largely on the legal approach to implementing the doctrine. His discussion, however, fails to acknowledge

---

[120] Taylor, 'Autonomy and informed consent', 384.
[121] D. H. Smith and L. S. Pettegrew, 'Mutual persuasion as a model for doctor–patient communication' (1986) 7 *Theoretical Medicine* 127, 133.
[122] *Canterbury* v. *Spence* 464 F 2d 772, 786 (DC Cir 1972).

that his criticism of the association between autonomy and informed consent might simply reflect an imperfect implementation of ethical theory by the law. Simply because the legal rules do not seem to respect the patient's autonomy does not undermine the connection between autonomy and informed consent as an ethical doctrine. The criticism should be aimed at the law's implementation and not at the underlying theory.

This point, that the law may implement theory imperfectly, is an important one. The effect of an imperfect implementation may be exacerbated by the response of those affected by the regulation. For example, the defensive response by healthcare practitioners and the impact of the machinery of risk management has, at least in some contexts, distorted the theoretical ideal of informed consent into the gargantuan monster of 'full disclosure'. The law assesses the healthcare practitioner's performance on the basis of whether particular risks have or have not been disclosed. Since common law is necessarily reactive to cases brought before the court, it is not possible to know in advance which risks must be disclosed to avoid liability in negligence (see p. 214). Thus, the easiest way to avoid liability is to disclose all the risks, regardless of whether this is in fact helpful to patient decision-making. The result of this is that a theoretical model requiring 'adequate' or 'reasonable' disclosure is rapidly transformed into a practice of 'full disclosure'. This, however, does not make the theory itself flawed. Rather, it is the execution of the theory that has caused the problems and, rather than being a concern for welfare, this excessive disclosure is more reflective of a concern to avoid being sued.

This attack on the connection between autonomy and consent also fails to take account of context. While consent in abstract liberal theory is predicated on the idea of autonomy, in practice consent always engages at least two parties. This means that, when devising the rules of consent, both parties' interests must be considered. In the context of healthcare this engages the professional's duty of beneficence and concern for the patient's welfare, which may act as constraints on the duty to respect autonomy. However, simply because patient autonomy is not the *sole* concern in the regulation of consent this does not undermine its role as the *primary* justification for consent.

My main criticism of Taylor's approach is that his argument is based on a flawed premise. The relevant assertion is: 'A necessary condition for one person to exert control over the decisions of someone else is that the person must intend to do this.'[123] It is this claim that allows Taylor to

---

[123] Taylor, 'Autonomy and informed consent', 386.

argue that an unintentional but negligent failure to disclose relevant information prevents an informed consent but does not undermine the patient's autonomy because his or her control over the decision is unaffected by the failure to disclose. However, the crucial question is not whether A has exerted control over B's decisions but whether A has interfered with, or undermined, B's ability to control his or her decisions. If children are playing near a railway track and carelessly run into the track-switching lever so that the approaching train runs on to a different track, the children have altered the train's route but have not intended to do so. It may be argued that, because they lack the requisite intention, the children have not exerted control over the train's route. Nevertheless, regardless of their intention, they have undermined the train company's control of the train's route.

Taylor supports his claim by using the example of Iago and Othello. Where Iago intends to manipulate Othello by 'controlling the information Othello receives' Iago compromises Othello's autonomy.[124] However, where 'pseudo-Iago' makes no attempt to manipulate 'pseudo-Othello' and 'simply reports . . . the facts as he understands them', Othello remains fully autonomous although he still possesses only the same information in the original case, in which his autonomy had been undermined. This example, while superficially attractive, fails to acknowledge a crucial issue. That is: whose responsibility was it to ensure that Othello was sufficiently informed to make the decision? If the duty is Othello's then his capacity for autonomy has not been compromised because it is his responsibility, and not Iago's, to ensure he is sufficiently well informed; Iago has done nothing that would constrain Othello's ability to satisfy himself that the information is sufficient and reliable. However, if the duty is Iago's, and it is reasonable for Othello to rely on the information, then Othello's autonomy has been compromised because he has been caused to believe that he is sufficiently informed.

In modern society it is impossible to live without relying on information provided by experts. Where the expert has a duty to provide sufficient information, as the physician does, then any failure to do so, whether intended or not, will lead to a false reliance that undermines the individual's autonomy. By inducing a false belief in the patient, that he or she knows enough to make a rational decision, the patient's motivation for seeking additional information is removed. Thus, although the patient is free to seek additional information, he or she falsely believes there is no reason to do so and, because the physician has caused this reasonable but false belief, that physician is responsible for the patient

---

[124] *Ibid.*, 385.

making an insufficiently well-informed decision. This means that where a physician, or other healthcare professional, misinforms the patient this reduces the patient's ability to make a rational – and hence autonomous – decision. Thus, Taylor's argument fails to sever the connection between consent and autonomy.

The second challenge comes from Manson and O'Neill's argument that the dominant conception of autonomy is devoid of moral content and thus it provides no ethical reason to respect a competent person's consent or refusal of consent.[125] The basis for this attack lies in conceiving autonomy as self-determination or rational self-determination. Manson and O'Neill criticise this reliance because those conceptions of autonomy do not require decisions that necessarily have moral value. They contrast these libertarian and liberal approaches with Kant's autonomy of the will, which does carry moral value, but suggest that Kant's autonomy cannot ground specific rules of consent. Because the liberal and libertarian conceptions of autonomy are essentially reducible to choice some other ethical basis must be found for consent.

Manson and O'Neill's tactic of emphasising the importance of an agency model of information is implicitly reliant on the argument that Kant's categorical imperative requires a general rule that prohibits coercion and deception. Without these prohibitions trust would be undermined, effective communication would be precluded and society would be unable to function. It is these two normative proscriptions that provide consent with its ethical importance. Thus, rather than the ethical basis for consent lying in the patient's right to (respect for) autonomy, it resides in the healthcare professional's duty to be trustworthy and not to coerce or deceive the patient.

While I agree that the professional has a duty to be trustworthy (see Chapter 3), this shift of focus simply creates the illusion that consent is not ethically grounded in a respect for autonomy. There are two problems with Manson and O'Neill's account of autonomy. First, they have completely ignored the wealth of scholarship that has grown up around the conception of relational autonomy. As I noted earlier, this view of autonomy, like Kant's, has ethical content. While the liberal version of autonomy may be the dominant conception in bioethics and law, there has been a groundswell in favour of the relational approach and this version of autonomy could be used to construct rules of consent that make ethically valuable decisions more likely. Furthermore, as I argued earlier, Manson and O'Neill are too ready to assert that Kant's autonomy of the will cannot form the basis of rules of consent.

[125] Manson and O'Neill, *Rethinking Informed Consent*, pp. 16–22.

The second problem with Manson and O'Neill's argument is that they fail to distinguish the autonomous person from the decisions of an autonomous person. Their argument essentially states that since not all decisions are themselves autonomous they are not necessarily valuable or automatically worthy of respect. However, the connection between consent and autonomy lies in the fact that effective consent is granted by an autonomous person or agent. As I argued earlier, the capacity for rationality, and hence autonomy, is necessary for moral agency and it is this that provides the value rather than the actual decision the agent makes.

The ethical value of consent lies in its connection with the intrinsically valuable moral agency of each autonomous person.[126] It both protects that person's liberty to be self-determining and it requires that person to take responsibility for his or her decisions. If Manson and O'Neill meant to argue that the ethical basis for consent does not lie with the patient's actual decision then they are correct. However, this does not mean that the individual's autonomy has no moral connection to the importance of consent. That importance lies in a respect for the person as an autonomous moral agency; it requires the person to be treated as an end and not just a means to an end.

Conclusion

In this chapter I have explored the nature, the value and the limits of autonomy. I noted that there are broadly three conceptions of personal autonomy: self-determination, rational self-determination and moral rational self-determination. I suggested that it was also important to distinguish between the autonomous person, the autonomous act and the autonomous life. Because simple self-determination obscures these distinctions, and because it fails to engage the justification that autonomy enables moral responsibility, I rejected it. Furthermore, since autonomy must take into account its relational nature any useful conception must acknowledge the need for rational self-reflection. This leaves autonomy as rational self-determination or as moral rational self-determination. I declined to make a final choice between these two conceptions at this point, although I recognised that autonomy as moral rational self-determination is more valuable than autonomy as rational self-determination. I will address this choice in Chapter 3, when I explore the relevance of the healthcare professional–patient relationship.

---

[126] See, J. Wilson, 'Is respect for autonomy defensible?' (2007) 33 *Journal of Medical Ethics* 353.

I suggested that autonomy has both intrinsic and instrumental value. The intrinsic value arises primarily because of the necessity of autonomy for the ascription of moral personhood and responsible agency. It follows from this that autonomy is intrinsically valuable because it is necessary for personal integrity and it allows us to adopt the reactive attitudes that instil life with the warmth of humanity. Instrumentally, autonomy is valuable because it is beneficial to the well-being of those with an internal locus of control. It is also important because respecting autonomy allows people to get better at attaining goods and to learn from their mistakes. Finally, it serves as a layer of protection against the tyranny of the state.

Although autonomy is both intrinsically and instrumentally valuable, it is not protected absolutely. The main limit on personal autonomy is to prevent harm to others. Other potentially limiting factors, such as offence to others and moralism, are insufficient – at least in the context of healthcare provision – to justify restricting individual autonomy. Imprudence and the possibility of self-harm only justify the use of remonstration, pleading and rational persuasion. The most difficult situation is where the choice risks harm that is catastrophic for the individual's future autonomy, but even here I suggested that any interference should fall short of force or coercion. Furthermore, this protection for autonomy extends to both autonomous and non-autonomous acts provided the person has the capacity for autonomy.

Finally, I briefly considered two challenges to the connection between autonomy and consent. Both of these challenges have perhaps arisen because of the inadequate implementation of consent in professional ethics and in the law and both fail to take into account the effects of the implementation of theory in practice. I argued that both of these challenges fail. Taylor's criticism of the connection was flawed because it assumed that control could not be undermined unintentionally. Manson and O'Neill's challenge only establishes that it is not the value of the individual's decision that provides the ethical justification for consent. However, the connection between the value of the autonomous moral agent and consent is left intact by their approach.

In this first chapter, I have examined the concept of autonomy and discussed its nature, value and limits to come to some limited conclusions, which I will develop further in subsequent chapters. I have not yet considered the internal and external constraints on autonomy that arise in the particular context of healthcare. These include the patient's illness, psychological differences that affect an individual's capacity for autonomy,[127] the power imbalance in the doctor–patient relationship and perhaps the institutional discourse of healthcare. These important constraints have implications for the way doctors and patients interact, which I will address in Chapter 3. In the next chapter I will explore some of the other relevant moral principles and approaches that may interact with autonomy. This will include consideration of beneficence and paternalism, which will allow further discussion of the problematic issue of autonomy and self-harm. I will then go on to explore the relevance of justice. This will particularly focus on the relevance of autonomy to the individual's responsibility for outcome. Finally, I will also consider the importance of character and virtue ethics and the relevance of consequences.

---

[127] Waller, 'The psychological structure of patient autonomy'; J. Bergsma, 'Cancer and autonomy' (2002) 47 *Patient Education and Counseling* 205, 206.

2   The relevance of beneficence, justice and virtue

In Chapter 1 I considered the concept of autonomy, which through its relationship to agency may be seen as the driving force of consent. However, autonomy is not the sole guiding principle. In this chapter, I will examine other moral principles and approaches that may be relevant to determining how the law should regulate consent to medical treatment. Rather than attempt to provide a complete model of how the different concerns interact I will in this chapter focus on the relevance of beneficence, justice and virtue in order to provide sufficient background to enable the subsequent development of a more textured model.

I have little to say about the principle of non-maleficence, the essence of which is to do no harm. As Szasz noted, this is – if taken too literally – 'an absurd' prescription.[1] Much of what the professional does necessarily risks or causes harm and the obligation is, if interpreted literally, an impossible one. It makes better sense to consider the obligation in tandem with the duty of beneficence. An alternative approach is to use a normative concept of harm that requires the act to be both harmful and wrong.[2] Most of the specific duties that arise from this, such as the obligations not to kill, cause injury or pain are relevant only in so far as consent provides the necessary justification to prevent the act being wrongful. Thus, other than reinforcing the general duty to respect the other's autonomy, it adds little to the consent debate and will not be considered further.

It will be noted that I am saying nothing explicitly about the role of consequences. This is because, as far as consent is concerned, the discussion in Chapter 1 on the limits of autonomy and the concepts of beneficence and paternalism largely exhaust the issue. Consequences do have an additional relevance, which is the resource implication of any particular approach to consent. The more demanding the approach, the

---

[1] T. Szasz, 'The moral physician', in *The Theology of Medicine* (Syracuse, NY: Syracuse University Press, 1977), p. 1.
[2] Feinberg, *Harm to Self*, pp. 10–11.

greater the resources required to meet those demands and the fewer resources there will be available for other purposes. Since respect for patient autonomy is only one of many competing goods it is important to bear in mind the effects on those goods of any diversion of resources necessary to enhance patient autonomy. This is a difficult political question that I will return to later. For now, I will begin by discussing the role of beneficence, the issue of paternalism and the relationship between beneficence, paternalism and autonomy.

Beneficence

The principle of beneficence has a long and close association with medical practice. The duty forms part of the Hippocratic Oath and, as the British Medical Association (BMA) noted: 'Doctors are trained to recognise that they have a duty to benefit others and to avoid the risk of harm unless this is outweighed by potential benefit to the patient.'[3] This duty, of acting to benefit the patient, is an important and reasonable duty that makes the healthcare professional–patient relationship a caring one and demands that the professional's role is more than just salesman or technician. Although the obligation to benefit the patient seems an intuitively good thing, it is important to determine the limits of the duty and consider how it interacts with the obligation to respect autonomy. Importantly, does the healthcare professional's duty of beneficence affect the patient's right to autonomy, or does the patient's right to autonomy define the extent of the professional's duty of beneficence?

It would be a mistake to see the duty of beneficence as solely concerned with tangible goods such as health. The duty has a wider application that includes both tangible goods as well as intangible interests. Since the duty of beneficence subsumes the duty to prevent avoidable harm, and individual rights serve to protect the interests that all persons have, then the duty of beneficence requires the healthcare professional to protect and defend those rights.[4] This certainly includes an imperative not to infringe any of the patient's rights. Thus, the healthcare professional's duty of beneficence incorporates an obligation to avoid or to prevent an infringement of the patient's autonomy.

As well as proscribing harmful interventions, the duty of beneficence also creates an obligation to provide a positive benefit to the patient. This duty includes those interests that are protected by the patient's

---

[3] British Medical Association, *Medical Ethics Today: Its practice and philosophy* (London: BMJ Publishing, 1998, 1993), p. 154.
[4] Beauchamp and Childress, *Principles of Biomedical Ethics*, p. 167.

rights and this requires healthcare professionals to act in a way that furthers those interests. This applies just as much to the patient's autonomy as it does to the patient's health or other welfare interests. Thus, professionals have an obligation to further the patient's agency. In the present context this requires the professional to act in a way that not just respects the patient's formal right to consent but also reflects the spirit behind that requirement. However, this has not always been the way in which the duty of beneficence has been conceived.

The traditional goals of medicine are to preserve, protect and/or restore the patient's health.[5] This perhaps makes it understandable that the emphasis of the duty may be focused on benefits to the patient's health as objectively determined by the healthcare profession. Sometimes this clinical view will coincide with the patient's, or else the patient will defer to the professional's expertise. At other times, however, it may conflict with the patient's belief of what constitutes a benefit. This apparent conflict, between healthcare professionals' approach to their duty of beneficence and patient autonomy arises because of the focus on health and life as the primary object of the professional's duty. The problem with this approach is that it fails to respect the patient as a holistic person since it concentrates on just one aspect of that person's life.[6] It fails to distinguish between the individual as a biological being and the individual as a person.[7] Thus, the conflict is 'apparent' because it arises not from beneficence per se but from the clinical perspective of beneficence seen through gauze-covered spectacles.[8] Within an institutional discourse that defines beneficence by reference solely to the medical effects on health the patient is disempowered and becomes a body to be acted upon rather than a person to be interacted with.[9]

Health is just one aspect of well-being; it is of instrumental rather than intrinsic value; it is not wholly objective and may often be adequately achieved by more than one route.[10] As well as health, well-being involves the person's sense of self. By creating a feeling of powerlessness,

---

[5] See the Declaration of Geneva 1948 (as amended 1983).

[6] P. Byrne, 'Divergence on consent: A philosophical assay', in G. R. Dunstan and M. J. Seller (eds.), *Consent in Medicine: Convergence and divergence in tradition* (London: King Edward's Hospital Fund, 1983), pp. 45, 51.

[7] K. A. Richman, *Ethics and the Metaphysics of Medicine: Reflections on health and beneficence* (Cambridge, Mass.: The MIT Press, 2004), p. 28.

[8] M. Foucault, *The Birth of the Clinic* (New York: Vintage Books, 1973), p. 145.

[9] P. McGrath, 'Autonomy, discourse, and power: A Postmodern reflection on principalism and bioethics' (1998) 23(5) *Journal of Medicine and Philosophy* 516, 521.

[10] D. W. Brock, *Life and Death* (New York: Cambridge University Press, 1993), pp. 25–6; See also K. Draper, 'The personal and impersonal dimensions of benevolence' (2001) 36 *Nous* 201, 219.

constraining or infringing a person's autonomy may adversely affect his or her well-being. This may be exacerbated by the effect of treatment choices and the consequential effects of disempowerment on the patient's goals and life plan. Thus, a duty of beneficence ought to require respect for the individual's autonomy. Furthermore, the physician's duty of beneficence should not be allowed to override his duty of ordinary humanity and part of this duty is to respect the other person as a moral equal. As Kant wrote: 'I cannot do good to anyone according to my conception of happiness (except to young children and the insane), but only according to that of the one I intend to benefit.'[11] Thus, the duty of beneficence is one that should take account of and perhaps be defined by the patient's autonomy.

Paternalism

Brock argued that 'The physician's ultimate responsibility is to use his or her medical skills to serve patients' overall well-being in this broad sense, to facilitate patients' pursuit of their plans of life.'[12] If this is the case, it raises the question of whether the healthcare professional is justified in overriding a competent patient's decision when that decision appears to conflict with the patient's values, long-term goals or life plan. This is where the distinction between an autonomous decision and a self-determining decision of an autonomous person becomes particularly important. If a decision is autonomous, it will, by definition, accord with the patient's values and life plan. If it is merely self-determining then it may not.

Although it has been suggested that beneficence was redefined as paternalism during the rise of rights-based movements in the 1960s and 1970s,[13] this is to misrepresent the relationship between the two concepts. Beneficence and paternalism overlap, in that both involve acting for another's benefit, but beneficence is constrained by the beneficiary's will, while paternalism is not. An act of morally problematic paternalism may be defined as one that incorporates the following two elements:[14]

---

[11] I. Kant, *The Doctrine of Virtue: Part two of the metaphysics of morals* (New York: Harper & Row, 1964), p. 122.

[12] Brock, *Life and Death*, p. 27.

[13] D. J. Rothman, 'The origins and consequences of patient autonomy: A 25-year retrospective' (2001) 9 *Health Care Analysis* 255, 257.

[14] These elements are gleaned or adapted from R. J. Arneson, 'Mill versus paternalism' (1980) 90 *Ethics* 470; Dworkin, *The Theory and Practice of Autonomy*, pp. 121–9; Levi, *Respecting Patient Autonomy*, p. 16; Feinberg, *Harm to Self*, pp. 3–26; A. Buchanan, 'Medical paternalism' (1978) 7 *Philosophy and Public Affairs* 370.

1 It is for the benefit of the other person.
2 It is done contrary to the other's will in such a way as to undermine that other person's self-determination either by:
  a overriding or
  b circumventing that person's self-determination by withholding information or deliberately providing misinformation.

The act may – but does not have to – interfere with the other person's liberty and it does not necessarily have to involve an infringement of a right. In this context, however, I am concerned with those acts that do infringe the other person's right to self-determination. I am not here concerned with those acts of 'soft' paternalism, which do not violate autonomy because the other person lacks capacity and is therefore not competent to make the decision.[15] Nor am I concerned with strong, hard paternalism, which results from a 'moral prudentialism' rather than a concern for the best interests of the person per se.[16] The arguments presented in the previous chapter about the value of autonomy are sufficient to show that such extreme paternalism is unjustified. The question I seek to answer here is whether 'weak hard' paternalism can be justified when the competent patient makes an irrational and harmful decision.

One objection to paternalism is that professionals are not infallible and may be mistaken in their judgement that a patient's decision is irrational. It is important here to emphasise the distinction between a decision that is difficult to comprehend and one that is truly irrational and, although the risk may be reduced through training, guidelines and oversight, it is unlikely that the problem will be completely eliminated. One of the dangers that lie behind the problem of incomprehensibility is the risk that minority beliefs and values are subjugated to the dominant majority. Judgements regarding another person's best interests have a tendency to collapse into moralism; decisions based on values and beliefs alien to our own may be difficult to understand and will seem irrational if, from our own perspective, the outcome of the choice appears to be needlessly harmful.[17] Regarding others as irrational because they do not share the same view of the morally good life predisposes to paternalism and raises difficult questions of moral equality.

The second problem arising from the professional's fallibility is that it will be the patient who is left to live with the consequences of a bad decision. Although compensation can alleviate the financial burdens and

---

[15] Hayry, *The Limits of Medical Paternalism*, p. 64.   [16] *Ibid.*, p. 76.
[17] *Ibid.*, pp. 13–15, 126.

may soften the blow, in most cases it is a poor substitute for a good outcome. Bad outcomes are difficult enough where they result from the person's own choices but where another person's paternalistic decision goes wrong this may be more likely to lead to disappointment, disillusionment and resentment.[18] If there is a risk of a decision being harmfully wrong then it should be the person who has to live with the consequences who makes the decision. Again, the risk of mistake can be reduced through procedural requirements but it is unlikely to be completely eliminated and thus, the healthcare professional should avoid paternalistically overriding the patient's agency.

Even if patients' irrational decisions are correctly identified their impulsiveness may be a central part of their characters and, if patients are to be held responsible then they should be allowed to make their own decisions.[19] Patients can always choose to place the decision in someone else's hands if they are worried that their impulsiveness or irrationality will be harmful. Even if someone regrets their impulsiveness it remains rational to prefer to live with the consequences of one's irrational choices rather than have other people impose their opinion of what might be good for them.[20] For the sake of further argument, however, assume that the healthcare professional is correct with regard to both the judgement that the patient's decision is irrational and the clinical decision regarding the best treatment choice.

A decision is irrational where it fails to reflect the person's values, goals or long-term plans. It may be argued that intervening in such a case, where although the person is autonomous the decision is not, may be justified by an argument that paternalism respects the autonomous person's genuine desires. In other words, the act of paternalism simply replaces a non-autonomous decision with the choice that the person would have made had he or she acted autonomously. This argument for instrumental intervention is the most difficult issue to resolve because it is uncertain whether we respect the individual more through interference or non-interference.

I argued in Chapter 1 that respect for the patient's autonomy did not permit overriding that person's autonomy in order to protect his or her future autonomy. It might be argued that this is fine as far as defining a general position but that paternalism may still be justifiable in the short term to prevent irrational harm if such decisions are made on a

[18] A. Coulter, *The Autonomous Patient: Ending paternalism in medical care* (London: The Stationery Office, 2002), p. 107.
[19] D. Lavin, 'Practical reason and the possibility of error' (2004) 114 *Ethics* 424, 425.
[20] D. Scoccia, 'Paternalism and autonomy' (1990) 100 *Ethics* 318, 323.

case-by-case basis. The problem with this argument is that it is impossible to isolate cases in this way. As soon as such cases occur they begin to create a more general position and it becomes natural to use each case as a precedent for a new situation with slightly different circumstances so that such a casuistic approach soon starts to resemble a general principle.

This may not completely defeat the casuistic, consequentialist approach if sufficient safeguards can be established to prevent the slippery slide into a general principle. However, overriding a person's decision may undermine their confidence in the security of their autonomy. Once one's decision-making has been overridden it implies that the same could happen again, which is problematic – especially when it is a decision that actually matters and the stakes are high – since it threatens to undermine the whole value of autonomy. As Arneson noted, '[t]he consequences of coming to rely on the dispensation of paternalistic aid are mischievous, as are the consequences of dispensing paternalistic aid and the consequences of observing paternalistic aid dispensed to others'.[21]

A further point supporting a non-paternalist position arises from the risk of bad luck. Even with the best will in the world things sometimes go badly. Most, if not all, medical interventions carry some risk, often of quite serious consequences. Since the patient will have to live with those consequences it should be the patient who controls whether or not the treatment is undergone. Requiring that control of the decision rests with the patient does not affect the position that it is possible, and perfectly reasonable, for the patient to abdicate from making the decision and leave it almost entirely up to the physician.

It may be argued, by a non-paternalist, that overriding a competent person's decision shows a lack of respect for that person because personhood is grounded in the capacity to be autonomous. However, it is equally possible to argue that caring about the other person's welfare demonstrates a respect for that person and, since welfare includes both autonomy and health, balancing one value against the other does show respect for that person. If one value is balanced against the other then both are given respect. This is perhaps especially the case where the preservation of health protects the individual's capacity for autonomy.

It is only if one believes that it is moral personhood – rather than the individual as a whole – that deserves respect that the health of the individual becomes a matter for that person alone to control. Whether paternalism is justified when a person makes an irrational choice depends on the value one places on autonomy. There is no doubt

21 Arneson, 'Mill versus paternalism', 481.

that all of us sometimes make bad decisions and the harmful consequences could be avoided by paternalistic intervention. Thus, if 'weak hard' paternalism is to be condemned it ultimately must be on deontological rather than teleological grounds. In other words, paternalistically overriding an irrational decision, even if it would avoid a serious consequence, is wrong because it undermines the person's agency and fails to treat him or her as an equally authoritative decision-maker.[22]

The higher the value given to autonomy the less the individual's health can be taken into account and the less justifiable paternalism becomes. While health is only of instrumental value, autonomy has intrinsic value and is of fundamental importance for ascribing moral personhood and responsibility. As such, it is certainly a defensible position that autonomy should take precedence when in conflict with welfare. At this point, the paternalist may argue that an irrational decision is not autonomous and therefore does not need to be respected. However, as I have already noted, since it is the patient who must live with the physical consequences of the choice he or she ought to be allowed control over the decision. Furthermore, if one is to respect the autonomous individual, rather than autonomy as an abstract concept, then even the non-autonomous decisions of an autonomous person should be respected.

Although one should respect the choices of an autonomous person this does not mean that the precedence for autonomy requires others to abandon individuals to their decision. Rather, they should seek to foster and support the other's autonomy, especially where there is a special obligation to the other party. I will discuss this in more detail in Chapter 3. However, for now it is sufficient to suggest that a respect for autonomy, far from preventing value judgements (even if it is possible to do so), arguably requires the healthcare professional to attempt to persuade the patient that their choice is mistaken.

Provided that professionals treat their patients as moral equals, stick to using rational argument and avoid autonomy-undermining techniques, such as withholding relevant information, then they will be respecting their patients' autonomy far more than if they simply accept the patient's initial decision regardless of how good or bad it is. If the patient's decision is truly autonomous then he or she will resist the professional's reasonable efforts to persuade him. Healthcare professionals must obviously be sympathetic to the condition of their patients as their ability to resist persuasion may be undermined by illness.

[22] D. N. Husak, 'Paternalism and autonomy' (1981) 10 *Philosophy and Public Affairs* 27, 28–9.

But, if healthcare professionals are sensitive to this, they can, by 'non-interventional paternalism', enhance the way their patients exercise autonomy and do all that is justified towards protecting their patients' health.[23]

While a respect for the other person's autonomy may ultimately mean that he or she must be allowed the authority to make essentially self-regarding decisions, this does not mean that the autonomous person must be abandoned to the consequences of that decision if it seems likely that the outcome will be bad. Such an approach would be to treat a respect for the autonomous person as solely a duty of non-interference. Rather, the duty of beneficence and, as I will argue in Chapter 3, a positive duty to respect autonomy requires healthcare professionals to intervene where they foresee a bad outcome. However, that intervention must stop short of coercion, deception or manipulation – at least in a pejorative sense – and should be restricted to a sensitive enquiry into the reasons behind the decision, the offering of advice and an attempt to rationally persuade the patient to change his or her mind.

Another situation in which paternalism may be justified is in the timing of any disclosure of information. It might be argued that autonomy requires the healthcare professional to disclose personal information, such as test results, at the earliest practical opportunity. However, where such disclosure may overburden or unduly distress a patient, it is equally arguable, from the duty of beneficence, that professionals should use their discretion to decide on the best time and kindest way to inform their patients. This limited form of paternalism may be justified provided the professional intends to and does disclose the information before it becomes relevant to any decision the patient might need to make.

There is an obvious danger here, which is exemplified by Beauchamp and Childress' argument that the paternalism is justified provided the information is disclosed prior to surgery.[24] However, medical decisions are not the only ones that the information may be relevant to. Information about the patient's illness, or the possible consequences of the proposed intervention may also affect social, family and work decisions. For this reason, if this type of paternalism is to be justified, it needs to be tightly constrained so that the professional discloses the information at the earliest practical opportunity when any distress may be minimised.

---

[23] J. Savulescu, 'Rational non-interventional paternalism: Why doctors ought to make judgements of what is best for their patients' (1995) 21 *Journal of Medical Ethics* 327.
[24] Beauchamp and Childress, *Principles of Biomedical Ethics*, p. 186.

Beauchamp and Childress' actual example involved inconclusive test results that hint at a dangerous pathology.[25] However, this may not be a case of paternalism at all. In the situation they describe, the professional should honestly disclose his uncertainty, which is arguably necessary as part of seeking the patient's consent for the repeat test. Since the first test has not provided sufficient certainty regarding the possible pathology it would be perfectly truthful, and respecting of the patient's autonomy, to simply inform the patient that the results were inconclusive and another test needs to be performed. There is no need to disclose the possible pathology unless it is sufficiently likely that a repeat test is unnecessary. If there is still sufficient doubt in the professional's mind that the pathology exists then it is both unkind and unnecessary to mention the possibility. It may, of course, become necessary if the patient refuses consent to the second test, but if the patient is willing to undergo the second test on the basis of an inconclusive first test then the failure to disclose the suspicion has not infringed the patient's autonomy since it was unnecessary for the decision. Such an approach would not be paternalistic.

The role of justice

Justice is relevant in any situation where conflict may not be resolved through the cooperative relationship of care or love. In something as impersonal as the state, justice is essential to legitimise power and the exercise of authority.[26] Although justice may be said to be concerned with fairness, there are both different senses of justice and different conceptions of what it means to be fair. As a starting point, however, the concept of justice may be reduced to the Aristotelian ideal of justice as equality where those who are equal are treated equally but those who are unequal are treated unequally.[27]

One of the assumptions that ground my model of consent is that all members of the relevant community should be treated as prima facie equals, which means that any different treatment of individuals must be justifiable on the basis of morally relevant differences between them. This also means that individuals should not be treated differently on the basis of morally irrelevant factors. This view of justice, however, still leaves the work of determining what counts as morally relevant. As

---

[25] *Ibid.*, pp. 185–6.
[26] A. Ryan, 'Introduction', in A. Ryan (ed.), *Justice* (Oxford: Oxford University Press, 1993), p. 1.
[27] Aristotle, *Politics III* (Oxford: Oxford University Press, 1998), p. 103 (1280a7).

Stone noted: 'Recognition of . . . human equality . . . is . . . a necessary step toward raising the questions of justice, toward asking when persons shall be treated unequally or equally according to their badges of entitlement.'[28]

These 'badges of entitlement' include many different outcome measures that might justify different treatment: for example, need, effort, merit, desert, contribution and free market competitiveness. However, since treatment may be different both in kind and in degree, it is not enough to simply point to a morally relevant difference. There also needs to be some way of evaluating the value of the difference between individuals so that the effect of treating that person differently is proportionate to that value.[29] I am not here concerned with constructing a particular theory of justice, which would take a book in itself. Nevertheless, it is necessary to have at least a working definition in order to determine how the principle of justice interacts with autonomy and consent. The approach briefly outlined above forms the starting point for my discussion of how justice is relevant to consent to medical treatment.

Justice is relevant only when conflict exists and it is most pressing when the conflict is between claims of comparable value. There are three points at which justice must interact with autonomy and consent to resolve any discord. First, justice is relevant to the question of whose autonomy should be respected as well as the degree and limits of that respect. Second, justice is relevant to the availability of resources that might be necessary to support the individual's autonomy. Third, justice is important when considering the question of responsibility for outcome.

Before I can outline these three interactions it is necessary to determine to whom this duty of justice applies. As I noted above, it certainly applies to the state and to the institutions and agents that comprise the state and allow it to function as a machine to support and promote social cooperation. However, it also applies to individuals as much as it does to the state,[30] which is reflected in the idea of justice as a virtue (see p. 68). Although one of the functions of the state is to achieve the collective justice that would otherwise be impracticable, this does not reduce the duty of individuals simply to pay their taxes and abide by the state's laws. If it is the individual's obligation to act justly that permits at least some state intervention then why should the state intervention wholly

---

[28] J. Stone, 'Justice not equality', in E. Kamenka and A. Erh-Soon Tay (eds.), *Justice* (London: Edward Arnold, 1979), pp. 97, 102.

[29] N. M. L. Nathan, *The Concept of Justice* (London: Macmillan Press, 1971), pp. 14–15.

[30] See L. B. Murphy, 'Institutions and the demands of justice' (1998) 27 *Philosophy and Public Affairs* 251.

relieve the individual of any further duty of justice? As Murphy suggested: 'once we accept that the principles that govern the ideal design of ideal institutions essentially describes a means to an end, the oddness of thinking that justice is concerned with some means to that end but not others becomes rather evident'.[31]

The demands that the principle of justice makes of particular individuals or institutions depend on the context in which those individuals and institutions are interacting. This is not to suggest that context necessarily alters what counts as just, merely that in order to determine whether two cases are, in a morally relevant way, the same or different those cases must be seen in context. While developing principles of justice requires generalisations, applying those principles in practice demands attention to the particular circumstances of the case that defines the issue and the more specific the context the more the focus must be on the particular.

In the discussion that follows I will set out what justice might generally require in regulating autonomy and consent. I will then consider the more particular demands of justice and autonomy in the context of the healthcare professional–patient relationship in Chapter 3.

Justice and respect for autonomy

I argued in Chapter 1 that autonomy is necessary for moral responsibility and, through this and its association with moral personhood, it is intrinsically valuable. Because of this it would be unjust to deny any one autonomous individual the same respect for his or her decisions as we allow other autonomous persons.[32] If autonomy is judged worthy of legal protection, which it currently is, then the principle that the different treatment of certain individuals or groups must be justifiable means that, prima facie, each person deserves an equal respect for his or her autonomy. This raises the question of what counts as a sufficient reason to respect a person's autonomy less.

Since the right to (respect for) autonomy is predicated on the ability of the individual to be at least rationally self-determining, then where that ability is impaired it is just to treat the individual differently. In fact, it may be unjust not to treat them differently because it would require them to be responsible when they lack the necessary capacity. However, where individuals have the necessary ability to be rational and are

---

[31] *Ibid.*, 282.
[32] R. A. Tsanoff, 'Social morality and the principle of justice' (1956) 67 *Ethics* 12.

capable of making autonomous choices then it would be unjust not to allow them to do so. It is, of course, for society to determine the level of capacity required and how that capacity should be tested, but those important concerns are beyond the scope of this book, which is limited to an examination of the rules that apply to those persons deemed legally competent.

One of the arguments sometimes raised against the current emphasis on patient autonomy is that, because of their illness, patients are incapable of exercising their autonomy.[33] If the patient's ability to be autonomous has genuinely been diminished to the point at which he or she lacks the capacity to make a rational decision then it is just to treat him or her differently from the patient who has retained sufficient capacity. However, not all patients will suffer from such a reduction in autonomy that they cannot be supported and empowered to make a reasoned decision. Where patients still retain sufficient capacity to make rational decisions then it would be unjust to treat them differently, unless there is some further reason that would justify different treatment. This brings the argument back to the question of whether paternalism is ever just.

As I have already argued, it may be just to act paternalistically where the individual's capacity for autonomy is sufficiently diminished to make it reasonable to protect them against their own inability to make rational decisions. However, where the person has sufficient capacity – even where it may be diminished by illness – it would be to treat them as an inferior, and hence to act unjustly towards them, to override a decision except where it falls within the penumbra of the harm principle.

Outside the constraints of the harm principle then, as I suggested earlier, where the individual is capable of achieving the degree of autonomy necessary for moral responsibility, the ordinary duty of beneficence is generally constrained by the individual's autonomy. I further argued that, while it may be just to temporarily infringe a person's liberty, it is not justifiable to infringe autonomy in order to protect the individual from a potentially catastrophic choice. These arguments support the fact that in ordinary life we are largely allowed the freedom to take risks that could lead to permanent harm or death. This holds even where that choice will impact on others and defeat our obligations to them. Thus, the mother or father of a young family remains free to climb dangerous mountains, parachute out of planes or join the army. The question that remains is whether the context of healthcare provision

---

[33] A. I. Tauber, 'Historical and philosophical reflections on patient autonomy' (2001) 9 *Health Care Analysis* 299, 311.

provides a good reason to make an exception to this freedom to make self-determining decisions. I will return to this question in Chapter 3.

There is one final point to make here, which is that it is also a matter of justice what sanctions the law provides when an individual has been treated unjustly whether by another individual or by an institution. There are two issues that fall to be justly determined: the reparation that should be made to the victim and the penalty that should be imposed on the individual or institution that has transgressed the victim's rights. Both of these are highly context-dependent since justice requires recognition of all the relevant factors that vary both between individuals and the particular circumstances in which the individuals find themselves. Because justice is concerned with treating like alike and unalike differently, a just response demands flexibility and sensitivity to the relevant differences between one situation and another. This explains why it is necessary to situate consent within the context of the healthcare professional–patient relationship rather than simply importing the rules that govern consent in other areas of social life.

Justice, resources and support for autonomy

The capacity for autonomy depends both on the liberty to make decisions and on the resources and support necessary to enable decisions. This reflects the negative and positive aspects of the right to autonomy.[34] The positive right to autonomy may be further split into two aspects: the support necessary to enable a decision and the resources required to make a decision meaningful. Because a rational decision is based on reason it requires access to understandable information. A positive right to autonomy creates an onus to provide the information and the support to enable people to understand it and so make possible a rational decision.

Given that people have different abilities, justice requires them to be treated differently. If there is an equal right to autonomy then those that are less able should be given more support to help them exercise their autonomy as effectively as other, more able persons, or at least as effectively as they can given the limits of their ability. This is so whether the lesser ability is innate or due to other influences, such as illness, stress, disempowerment, a lack of confidence or a lack of education. Since justice requires us to act so as to benefit the disadvantaged then it arguably requires the provision of necessary support to foster and improve the ability of the less able to be autonomous. If autonomy is

[34] I. Berlin, *Four Essays on Liberty* (Oxford: Oxford University Press, 1969).

necessary for moral community and responsibility then autonomy is the trigger for prima facie equality. If equality is to mean anything then it must at least require that the community supports and fosters each individual's ability to be autonomous – to enable him or her to exercise their innate capacity – and hence be an equal member of the moral community.

This need to enable at least reasonable autonomy is further supported by the arguments for behaviour-based systems of distributive justice. If resources are to be distributed on the basis of desert, merit or the competitive free market then it would be unjust to significantly disadvantage a section of the community in order to further disadvantage them by rewarding those who were better placed to succeed because they started with a greater ability to be autonomous.[35] Since we cannot return to a starting point for distribution, the best we can do is to respond to the needs of those whose autonomy is constrained by factors that may be relieved by additional support.[36] This has implications for the ability of patients to be autonomous and for the duty of healthcare professionals to further that end (see Chapter 3).

Apart from the requirement to support the ability to make decisions, justice is also relevant to the issue of resource allocation. Without the choices available to the individual the right and the capacity to make decisions are empty. The relevance of this is that there is a clear distinction between the obligations to protect the freedom to be autonomous and the obligation to provide the individual with meaningful choices. The freedom to be autonomous is instantiated through the protective rights, such as the right to bodily integrity, and the derivative right to control those protections through the device of consent.

Consent is primarily a device of negative not positive autonomy (see Chapter 4). However, as I argued above, there is a positive obligation on the community to empower individuals to exercise that consent. The driving force for this positive obligation is formal justice combined with the right to negative autonomy, which is the minimum liberty necessary for moral responsibility. On the other hand, substantive justice and positive autonomy drives the right to choice through the availability of scarce resources. The relevance of this will become apparent in Chapter 4 when I discuss the concept of consent in detail. For now it is sufficient to note that there are many different outcomes that may be used to determine a just distribution of these resources. These include *welfare*

---

[35] Nathan, *The Concept of Justice*, pp. 32–6.
[36] T. D. Campbell, 'Humanity before justice' (1974) 4 *British Journal of Political Science* 1, 12–13.

need and the *capacity to benefit*, both of which engage the healthcare professional's duty of beneficence.

Justice and responsibility for outcome

This final interaction between justice, autonomy and consent is perhaps the most complex: it engages issues of agency, luck, responsibility, corrective and distributive justice. Whenever an agent acts to cause a change in the world that change may be for the better or worse and may affect only the agent or it may also impact on others. Sometimes the change will be exactly as the agent intended, sometimes things will end badly because the agent has been careless, and sometimes the outcome will depend on good or bad luck. The question is who should carry the responsibility for the outcome and, particularly for the present purposes, what effect does consent have?

As I noted earlier, autonomy is a prerequisite for moral responsibility and if that responsibility is to mean anything then it is that, in the absence of a condition that undermines moral sensitivity,[37] autonomous agents should accept responsibility for the consequences of their actions. This is a reasonable starting point; if we want to be treated as responsible then we should accept responsibility. However, as I suggested above, sometimes things happen that are outside the control of an autonomous agent and these accidents of good or bad luck may alter the outcome. Since the agent is not responsible for the luck should he or she be held responsible for the outcome?

The situation is further complicated when a second agent acts by giving consent to the first agent. Who should be responsible for the outcome of the act when both agents have exercised their autonomy? I have indicated that the two relevant forms of justice are distributive and corrective. Distributive justice is concerned with the proportionate distribution of benefits and burdens, and freedoms and responsibilities. Corrective (rectificatory, commutative) justice is concerned with 'equalising' losses and gains caused by an unfair or wrongful transaction.[38] Although these two forms of justice are traditionally seen as distinct types their boundaries are not so clear in practical application. The connection between the two types of justice was recently commented on by Lord Steyn who claimed, in *McFarlane* v. *Tayside HB*, that

---

[37] See, M. A. L. Oshana, 'The misguided marriage of responsibility and autonomy' (2002) 6 *The Journal of Ethics* 261, 267.
[38] Aristotle, *Ethics*, tr. J. A. K. Thomson (London: Penguin, 1976), pp. 176–80 (V. ii–iii 1130b–1132a).

tort law was 'a mosaic in which the principles of corrective justice and distributive justice are interwoven'.[39]

I have argued elsewhere that distributive justice and corrective justice are more closely linked than other commentators have previously acknowledged.[40] My argument follows Honoré who explained that distributive justice is as concerned with the fair distribution of responsibility for outcome as it is with a fair distribution of resources, rights or freedoms.[41] If society is seen as an animated structure, which acknowledges the possibility of future interactions between members of society, then the losses and gains that result from those interactions may be allocated on the basis of distributive justice principles. When regarded in this way, corrective justice is simply one way of sharing responsibility for outcome. It does this by associating responsibility for outcome with agency and moral accountability. Under a system of corrective justice the agent is allowed to keep the benefits of any action but the loss lies where it falls unless the agent is morally blameworthy.[42] This is a type of distributive justice based on desert, but it is a particular approach to desert that favours the actor over any other person that may be affected by the act. There are other, less one-sided, approaches to desert and other material principles of justice, such as need, that might be relevant to determining a fair allocation of responsibility for outcome.

The relevance of concluding that corrective justice is simply a species of distributive justice is that it questions the current association of consent to medical treatment and responsibility for outcome (see p. 118). Consent and responsibility for outcome are not inherently linked. The association is one of convention dependent on assumptions about agency and responsibility that rely on the more atomistic liberal conception of autonomy. Once the relevance of luck and the interdependent nature of socially situated individuals are acknowledged the issue of outcome responsibility is more complex than a simple direct causal association with agency. This is not to deny the importance of agency and autonomy but merely to suggest that, when luck and the relational nature of autonomy are acknowledged, autonomy is insufficient justification to necessarily transfer all responsibility with consent.

---

[39] *McFarlane* v. *Tayside Health Board* [2000] 2 AC 59, 83.

[40] A. R. Maclean, 'Distributing the burden of a blessing' (2004) 1 *Journal of Obligation and Remedies* 23.

[41] T. Honoré, 'The morality of tort law: Questions and answers', in *Responsibility and Fault* (Oxford: Hart Publishing, 2002), pp. 67, 79.

[42] It may be noted that tort and delict are imperfect systems of corrective justice because the element of fault inherent in those branches of law is based on objective rather than subjective criteria.

Dickenson suggested that the problem of 'moral luck'[43] might be overcome by transferring responsibility for outcome with consent. It is necessary to restrict the healthcare professional's responsibility in this way because, where the procedure has been competently performed, a bad outcome is simply bad luck. Thus, she concluded, 'an absolutist interpretation of consent protects both doctor and patient: the doctor from moral luck, and the patient from invasion of autonomy'.[44] But why is it, simply because the healthcare professionals have not acted in a way that is morally blameworthy, that they should be shielded from all responsibility for outcome? The patients have also acted in a way that is morally blameless, but we are expected to accept that not only should they suffer the physical consequences of the harm, they should also bear the financial responsibility. There is a distinction here between responsibility for outcome and moral responsibility, and consent cannot be made to bear the full weight of determining both issues. Rather, it is a determination that should engage not just consent, but also agency and justice.

Consider the situation if you were to ask to borrow my brand new bicycle and I consent to you using it. While you are riding the bicycle one of the tyres is punctured. This may be seen as largely a matter of bad luck because, while you had control over the bicycle and choice as to when and where to ride it, you lacked the knowledge to enable you to predict where the nail was that would cause the puncture.[45] However, I also had some control over the situation because it was my bicycle and I could have refused you permission to use it. Who then should bear the expense and inconvenience of mending the puncture?

Certainly, if you had taken my bicycle without asking then, barring some humanitarian emergency that might excuse your conduct, many people would, I suspect, agree that you should make right any damage. This is because only your agency is engaged and you have wrongfully caused a loss. You alone are morally responsible for the fact that the bicycle was in a position to get the puncture, and under the principle of corrective justice you deserve to bear the cost of that loss. But, where you have my consent you have not acted wrongly and so the principle of corrective justice is no help. If responsibility for outcome automatically transfers with consent then no other facts will be relevant and it should

---

[43] A term coined by Bernard Williams to reflect the paradox that morality requires us to be responsible for our actions but luck is a pervasive causal influence on all outcomes, which appears to undermine the possibility of moral responsibility: B. Williams, 'Moral Luck', in *Moral Luck* (Cambridge: Cambridge University Press, 1981), p. 20.

[44] D. Dickenson, *Risk and Luck in Medical Ethics* (Cambridge: Polity Press, 2003), p. 85.

[45] This is not to suggest that the possibility of a puncture was unforeseeable.

be left for me to deal with the puncture. However, just because no one has acted wrongly does not necessarily mean that there are no factors that might influence the answer to the question and I suspect that people's responses to the question of responsibility for outcome would be more mixed than for the example where you took the bicycle without consent.

Perhaps the most relevant factor would be your purpose in borrowing the bicycle. Consider the following possibilities. In the first variation you are a courier and you borrowed my bicycle so that you could make a delivery and carry on earning while your own bicycle was being repaired. In the second case I have asked you to deliver some food to my elderly mother. In the third case you have borrowed the bicycle to help you in your work as a volunteer at the local children's home where you were supposed to be taking the children out for the day for a bicycle ride into the country. In the final variation, I am a sixteen-year-old schoolboy with a Saturday job while you are earning £50,000 a year and, instead of a puncture, the wheel was buckled.

In the first case it seems reasonable to suggest that since you stood to benefit then you should be responsible for the puncture. In the second situation, since you are benefiting me by fulfilling one of my obligations to my mother, it likewise seems fair that I should deal with the puncture. The third case is more difficult since you are acting to benefit a third party. In this case, one might argue that because your act is charitable then you should not suffer the added burden of dealing with the puncture. However, because charity is supererogatory it does not seem fair that I should necessarily be left with the cost of the puncture. Since the children's home is gaining considerably from your help and my loan of the bicycle, perhaps the home should take responsibility for the loss. Alternatively, the burden could be shared.[46]

The final variation is of a different type. In this case there is a huge difference in the resources that the two parties have and it seems reasonable to suggest that, since you have a greater capacity to bear the cost, it would be fair for you to pay to have the buckled wheel replaced. It may still be relevant to ask who stood to benefit from the bicycle loan, but the important point is that the fact I gave consent does not appear to be determinative in all of these situations. This is not to suggest that autonomy and consent are irrelevant, merely that consent simply determines whether the act was wrong and it is really principles of justice

---

[46] The idea of sharing the cost of a bicycle puncture may strike one as faintly ridiculous but it is really the principle that I am arguing here. We could equally well be talking about a more expensive loss.

that do the work of determining who should bear the responsibility for outcome. I will consider the particular relevance of this for consent to medical treatment in Chapter 4.

The relevance of virtue

In contrast to deontology and teleology, which are concerned with the right kind of action, virtue ethics are concerned with character – with 'determining what sort of person one should strive to be'[47] – and this is necessarily dependent on an account of the good life that provides a goal or *telos* for individuals interacting within a social community.[48] While these different approaches are often presented as an either/or choice, there is a third option, which is to recognise the importance of both character traits and right action. Since action is to at least some extent controlled by the actor's character and the way we judge character is by observing a person's behaviour, the two seem mutually interdependent and it makes sense to be concerned with both.[49]

This book is primarily concerned with the regulation of consent, which is essentially a set of rules governing behaviour. This is because the law tends to operate through rules that create rights and obligations, the stock in trade of action rather than character. Because the law is concerned with adjudicating between individuals when one is affected by the other's behaviour it must be more concerned with action than with character. However, simply because behaviour is the primary focus of the law this does not mean that character should be ignored. In criminal law, for example, the convicted person's character may influence the punishment. Thus, the focus in this brief discussion will be on how attention to the actor's character may be relevant to consent.

A feature of principles and rules is that they underdetermine action and require that the actor interpret them appropriately. Language is often vague, or even ambiguous, and it is difficult, if not impossible to construct a rule that is so precise as to leave no room for interpretation. In one sense this may be an advantage since there is often more than one acceptable approach. However, the problem is that this indeterminacy, while it gives scope for individuality, also means that it is possible to wrongly interpret the rule. Acknowledging this imprecision emphasises

---

[47] E. F. Paul, F. D. Miller and J. Paul, 'Introduction', in E. F. Paul, F. D. Miller and J. Paul (eds.), *Virtue and Vice* (Cambridge: Cambridge University Press, 1998), p. vii.
[48] A. MacIntyre, *After Virtue*, 2nd edn (London: Duckworth, 1985), pp. 184–6.
[49] G. Sher, 'Ethics, character and action', in Paul, Miller and Paul (eds.), *Virtue and Vice*, pp. 1–7.

the need for, and importance of, judgement. Judgement, however, is not something that can be legislated for as it depends on the presence of virtues such as prudence, wisdom, temperance, justice, courage[50] and – at least in healthcare – compassion, empathy and caring for, and about, others.[51] This makes it crucial to attend to individual character and to find ways to foster virtue. In the absence of virtue, rules – no matter how well defined – will tend to be interpreted and applied formalistically and the spirit behind the rule risks being lost. Even staunch defenders of the principles-approach acknowledge that virtues 'are needed . . . for moral obligations to be instantiated and sustained in the moral life of real people'.[52]

In virtue ethics, the right action is determined by what a virtuous person would do in the circumstances. In the approach adopted here, this would translate as 'the interpretation of the rule is that which would be made in the circumstances by an agent with a virtuous character'. Furthermore, in virtue ethics the good is prior to the right. Deontology, however, prioritises the right. In this combined approach, it is neither necessary nor possible (as is evidenced by the lack of consensus on the issue) to definitively prioritise either. Rather the good and the right might be seen as iteratively and symbiotically related to each other: the good informs the right which in turn informs the good.

Virtues are seen as 'objectively good'.[53] This claim may be problematic in relation to persons in general because it requires somebody with the authority to say that subjective opinion is irrelevant. It is, however, less problematic when applied to someone in their professional role where the professional community is defined, at least in part, by its goal (or set of goals). Where that professional community has been given a social mandate to operate then the society granting the mandate has the authority to determine the professional virtues. Where a person voluntarily enters such a profession then they take on the ethical obligations of that community and their own personal attitudes and values become subject to those professional ethics.[54]

---

[50] P. Foot, *Virtues and Vices* (Oxford: Clarendon Press, 2002), pp. 1–18.

[51] G. Clement, *Care, Autonomy, and Justice: Feminism and the ethic of care* (Boulder, Colo: Westview Press, 1998). See also, E. H. Loewy, *Moral Strangers, Moral Acquaintance, and Moral Friends: Connectedness and its conditions* (Albany, NY: State University of New York Press, 1997), pp. 121–5.

[52] R. Gillon, 'Ethics needs principles – four can encompass the rest – and respect for autonomy should be "first among equals"' (2003) 29 *Journal of Medical Ethics* 307, 309.

[53] J. Oakley, 'A virtue ethics approach', in H. Kuhse and P. Singer (eds.), A *Companion to Bioethics* (Oxford: Blackwell Publishing, 1998), pp. 86, 90.

[54] MacIntyre, *After Virtue*, p. 190.

The importance of the virtuous professional was recognised by the Bristol Royal Infirmary Inquiry, which emphasised 'the values of caring, of comforting, of supporting and of truthfulness and honesty'.[55] However, because people may not be, and cannot be relied on to be, perfectly virtuous, rules of behaviour are needed. But the rules require interpretation and so exist symbiotically with the need for judgement and hence a virtuous disposition. In other words, while neither deontological rules nor virtuous dispositions are sufficient by themselves, iteratively combining the two approaches may resolve the weaknesses of both. As Pellegrino and Thomasma argued: 'Virtue-based ethics link principles and obligations as abstract entities to the circumstances of our personal lives through the virtue of prudence.'[56] By highlighting the relevance of, and need for, virtue, the law can at least add symbolic importance to the development of, and emphasis on, the dispositions as an aspect of the professionalism of medicine.

As I will discuss in subsequent chapters, the essence of consent to medical treatment is that patients give their permission for healthcare professionals to perform the relevant intervention. This function of consent naturally lends itself to regulation through a number of rules that require certain behaviour from the professional. However, as I have argued above, implementation of these rules requires interpretation, which is where the professional's character becomes relevant because character inclines or motivates an individual to act in a particular way.[57] Healthcare professionals could, for example, adopt a formalistic approach to the rules and do the minimum required in order to satisfy the obligation without any thought as to how well such an approach suits the individual patient. Alternatively, they might adopt a paternalist approach and use the indeterminacy of the rules to allow them to manipulate the patient's decision. For example, the obligation to inform patients would be met by disclosing the relevant risks, but the mode and order of presentation of those risks are likely to influence the patient's decision. Risks can be underplayed by using descriptors such as 'only' or 'less than', while they might be overplayed by the use of terms such as 'more than' or 'as many as'. However, if the patient's autonomy is to be truly respected then the healthcare professional should adopt an ethically sensitive, purposive approach to the rule.

---

[55] Kennedy, *Learning from Bristol*, Chapter 23, para. 36.
[56] E. D. Pellegrino and D. C. Thomasma, *The Virtues in Medical Practice* (New York: Oxford University Press, 1993), pp. 23–4.
[57] M. Slote, 'The justice of caring', in Paul, Miller, and Paul (eds.), *Virtue and Vice*, pp. 171, 173.

Getting healthcare professionals to approach the rule in an ethically sensitive way cannot be achieved by refining the rules. Furthermore, a highly regulated approach may lead to an overly restricted relationship where the rules replace rather than support trust and encourage formalism rather than empathy. Allowing a reasonable amount of professional autonomy in applying the rules may be more conducive to a caring relationship than a more restrictive approach. However, if professionals are to be afforded that degree of latitude then it is important to encourage them to develop the relevant virtues that will incline them to interpret the rules appropriately so as to determine the healthcare professional–patient relationship as one that fits both the caring practice of medicine and the respectful practice of the wider community. Engaging with the virtues, therefore, will allow the law to support the professionalism of the healthcare professional, avoid treating the patient as a consumer and may encourage a more nuanced interaction between the two autonomous persons.

Virtues may also be relevant to the patient's role in the clinical encounter. Although patients are not required to interpret rules, it would be helpful if they had the inclination to act in certain ways. It is easy to imagine how the tendency to honesty, openness, empathy, courage and prudence may be valuable in the discursive process leading up to the consent decision. If patients have obligations arising out of the professional–patient relationship, as I will argue in Chapter 3, then there is no theoretical reason why the law should not also be concerned with encouraging them to be virtuous, or at least to act in a way that would be consistent with what might be expected of the virtuous patient.

Conclusion

In this chapter I have explored the ethical issues that interact with autonomy and consent to medical treatment. I have focused on beneficence, paternalism, justice and virtue and suggested that beneficence is best seen as a duty constrained by the patient's autonomy. In this way, paternalism towards the competent patient is unjustified except in the limited sense of intervening to ensure that the patient is acting as autonomously as possible. This would allow, and might perhaps require, the healthcare professional to challenge an apparently irrational decision and to try to persuade the patient to decide otherwise if the likely outcome will be significantly harmful. It may also justify the healthcare professional controlling the timing of any disclosure, provided that the delay does not undermine any significant decisions that the patient must make.

I suggested that justice is relevant in three ways. First, it is engaged when deciding whose autonomy should be respected. Second, it is relevant to the provision of resources to support autonomy, both in a negative and a positive sense. Third, it is germane to the question of responsibility for outcome. In this last regard, I argued that responsibility for outcome, as distinct from moral accountability and responsibility, is determined by principles of justice rather than by autonomy and consent, although consent is necessary as a qualifying requirement that enters the individual into the distributive equation.

Finally, I also discussed the relevance of virtue. I argued that attention to individual virtue is necessary because of the indeterminacy of rules. I suggested that virtues and deontological rules exist in an iterative and symbiotic relationship, where both are important to the morality of individual acts. The relevant virtues are determined by the *telos* or goal of the community, which is less problematic for a professional community that has been given a social mandate to exist and practice predicated on certain societal goals.

In the next chapter I will situate these ethical issues within the context of the healthcare professional–patient relationship. This will provide sufficient texture for a more sensitively nuanced approach to the concept of consent, which will be addressed in Chapter 4.

3 The healthcare professional–patient relationship: Setting the context for consent

> A model must incorporate respect for the personhood and self-determination of the patient and should enhance dialogue between the two parties of the relationship.
>
> P. G. Smith and L. H. Newton, 'Physician and patient' (1984)[1]

Consent is not unique to healthcare and, while it may serve parallel functions in different contexts, the regulation of consent should be sensitive to the setting. For example, the requirements for a valid consent in the context of non-commercial sexual relationships are influenced by the necessary absence of formality, which is not the case for consent to healthcare interventions. Furthermore, because consent must always involve at least two agents it is not a free-floating device that can exist in the absence of a relationship. The way healthcare professionals approach consent indicates their attitude towards their patients, which should reflect a moral sensitivity to the issues discussed in the first two chapters, and is central to the relationship between them and their patients. The patient's role in the relationship is equally important and the way in which the patient approaches consent will impact on the effectiveness of the communicative process and the consent decision that results. Thus, it is important to situate consent within the context of the relationship between the patient and the healthcare professional.

Positing consent as central to the professional–patient relationship emphasises its communal aspect. Community may be seen as a functional process of participation and interaction,[2] and it is notable that consent derives from the Latin *con sentire* (feel together), suggesting an element of communion between the parties. The idea of *com*munity is further emphasised if *com*munication is seen as an important part of consent. Thus consent, or at least the process leading up to consent,

---

[1] D. G. Smith and L. H. Newton, 'Physician and patient' (1984) 5 *Theoretical Medicine* 43, 55.

[2] D. Micah Hester, 'What must we mean by "community"? A processive account' (2004) 25 *Theoretical Medicine* 423, 433.

may be seen as a community interaction. While it has been argued that 'A turn to processive community demands that participation, and not consent, be the primary concern of physicians and patients alike',[3] this is to isolate the final act of permission (see Chapter 4) from the other elements of consent. If consent is seen as requiring both the communication of permission and a preliminary agreement, then it more readily may be seen as a communal act requiring the participation of both parties. Even the final event of seeking permission may be seen as a communal enterprise since it reflects mutuality through a respect for the equal status of the other.

The importance of setting consent within the context of a relationship is that the relationship itself is a source of obligations and responsibilities. Given that autonomy and beneficence are meaningless in the absence of a social context and that the social context centres on the relationship between the relevant parties, it is essential to explore the relationship between the patient and the healthcare professional. It is through this examination that the rights and obligations of the two parties can be resolved. This is important because it allows a more sensitive approach to determining consent and the rules required to regulate consent in this context.

The professional–patient relationship

The most important contact for people as patients is with the professionals providing their care. Although they may only need to enter into a single relationship – for example, where their GP can provide the necessary treatment – on many occasions they will be cared for by a number of professionals. Sometimes their care will progress vertically, by referral from one professional to another, but at other times there may be a more horizontal progression with many professionals being involved cooperatively in caring for the patient. As such it may be a simplification to discuss the professional–patient relationship as if it exists in isolation as a discrete relationship. Nevertheless, since every interaction is conducted within the context of such a relationship, it provides a useful focus for discussion.

Montgomery has suggested that paradigms of regulating consent should move away from 'a relationship between individuals . . . [and] move towards models recognizing the importance of institutions'.[4]

---

[3] *Ibid.*

[4] See J. Montgomery, 'Time for a paradigm shift? Medical law in transition' (2000) 53 *Current Legal Problems* 363, 395.

Sensitivity to the relevance of the institution is essential since the organisation of the institution inevitably influences the professional–patient relationship through the time and resource constraints imposed on the professional.[5] Furthermore, institutional priorities may differ from those of the individual parties and this is likely to have an effect on the implementation of consent. This influence, which may be exacerbated by constraints of external institutions such as the law, will – if not accounted for – cause consent in practice to look very different from the model of consent in theory. However, this does not mean that the process and regulation of consent can ignore the importance of individual professional–patient relationships.

Focusing on the institutional effects to the exclusion of the individual relationships that are responsible for its final delivery would be to ignore the human side of healthcare. Individual relationships, even where short-lived or where responsibility for the patient is shared, are both desirable and unavoidable. Care, compassion and empathy are characteristics of humans, not institutions, and the professional–patient relationship is an 'essential' element of medical communication,[6] and one of the dominant concerns of the patient.[7] Thus, the professional–patient relationship remains the most appropriate context for defining the procedural and regulatory approach to consent, provided that the approach is sensitive to the institutional, legal and political constraints.

Although a number of models have already been used to represent the moral relationship between healthcare professionals and their patients, they reflect the end products of the authors' attempts to balance the various values that are thought to be relevant to the relationship. Furthermore, the doctor–patient relationship is usually presented as analogous to other relationships such as priest–parishioner, or seller–consumer and in some jurisdictions – such as Canada – the courts have treated the relationship as fiduciary.[8] However, there is no reason why it

---

[5] S. J. Potter and J. B. McKinlay, 'From a relationship to encounter: An examination of longitudinal and lateral dimensions in the doctor–patient relationship' (2005) 61 *Social Science and Medicine* 465; C. Provis and S. Stack, 'Caring work, personal obligation and collective responsibility' (2004) 11 *Nursing Ethics* 5.

[6] G. Makoul, 'Essential elements of communication in medical encounters: The Kalamazoo consensus statement' (2001) 76 *Academic Medicine* 390.

[7] E. Burkitt Wright, C. Holcombe and P. Salmon, 'Doctors' communication of trust, care, and respect in breast cancer: Qualitative study' (2004) 328 *British Medical Journal* 864, 866–7.

[8] The English courts have rejected the idea that the doctor–patient relationship is fiduciary in nature: *Sidaway* v. *Board of Governors of the Bethlem Royal Hospital* [1985] AC 871, 884 per Lord Scarman. For a discussion see P. Bartlett, 'Doctors as fiduciaries: Equitable regulation of the doctor–patient relationship' (1997) 5 *Medical Law Review* 193.

should be defined in these terms. It is a unique relationship that may involve aspects – but is unlikely to share all the features – of any one of these models. As such, it may be better simply to identify the interests, values and obligations that form the basis for the relationship.

By definition, a relationship involves at least two parties. It is possible to *be in* a relationship where the other party is not of equivalent moral status: for example, the parent and young child or baby, or the carer and a mentally incapable person. These relationships are one-sided and the imbalance between the two parties justifies the dominant party treating the weaker party paternalistically. The origin of the term derives from the paradigm of the caring father and his child. However, as the child gradually develops the ability to be autonomous so the relationship between the parent and the child changes, eventually reaching one where the two parties are of equal moral status. This developing moral status has been recognised in law. For example, in *Gillick* v. *W. Norfolk and Wisbech AHA* the House of Lords acknowledged that parental rights are extinguished once the child has matured sufficiently to no longer need the protection of his or her parents.[9]

As the child matures and develops an increasing capacity to be autonomous so the nature of the relationship between the parent and the child should change. If the parent and child are to *have* a relationship, rather than simply *be in* a relationship, each must recognise the other as an autonomous agent: the parent as fully autonomous, the child as a person with developing autonomy, eventually becoming fully autonomous. An essential aspect of moral agency is that the person is responsible for his or her actions. To gain a sense of responsibility, that allows him or her to exercise moral agency, a person's capacity for autonomy must be recognised by the other agents that exist in relationships with that person.[10] But, part of being autonomous in a moral or relational sense is the recognition of the other as a moral agent and the acknowledgement and acceptance of the moral obligations that arise out of the relationship. Through this mutual recognition, which is an important influence on the individual's sense of dignity and agency,[11]

---

[9] *Gillick* v. *W. Norfolk and Wisbech AHA* [1986] AC 112, 184 per Lord Scarman.

[10] P. Benson, 'Feeling crazy: Self-worth and the social character of responsibility', in C. Mackenzie and N. Stoljar (eds.), *Relational Autonomy: Feminist perspectives on autonomy, agency and the social self* (New York: Oxford University Press, 2000), pp. 72, 78–88.

[11] This may be particularly important for the less dominant party to the relationship: A. Werner and K. Malterud, 'It is hard work behaving as a credible patient: Encounters between women with chronic pain and their doctors' (2003) 57 *Social Science and Medicine* 1409, 1415.

each party allows the other to fully participate in the relationship, which is necessary for the parties to *have* a relationship.

The point of approaching consent through the professional–patient relationship is to emphasise the importance of social dependency and obligations but equally to recognise that any relationship involves individuals.[12] If too much emphasis is placed on the individual as an independent decision-maker we risk relationships of care being undermined with the patients being abandoned to the cold harshness of their isolated self-determination. On the other hand, too much emphasis on the communal and the importance of relational others risks undermining the moral agency of the individual and may prejudice that individual's interests for the sake of the community. There should, therefore, be a balance between the individual's agency and the relevance of that person's obligations arising from his or her relationships.

The recognition that autonomy involves both individuals and relationships emphasises the distinction between *being in* a relationship and *having* a relationship. When one of the parties to the relationship is not respected as a moral agent then that person may *be in* the relationship but he or she does not *have* a relationship, which requires mutual recognition of the other's agency and hence allows mutual participation. In the context of the patient–professional relationship, this is important because it requires both parties to recognise the moral agency of the other. Thus, it empowers the patient to be autonomous and it maximises the outcome of that autonomy because, through the patient's respect, the professional is empowered to exercise his or her expertise to further the patient's goals. The consequence of this is that, where the patient and professional have a relationship, this mutually dependent interaction is likely to improve the outcome. A second consequence is that, because the two parties will be working together, it should also lead to greater satisfaction for both parties. There is evidence to support both of these claims.[13] Furthermore, as noted earlier, patients place a high value on a good relationship with their healthcare professional and valuable or significant relationships tend to be associated with specific responsibilities.[14]

There are two further reasons for acknowledging and focusing on the professional–patient relationship as the context for consent. First,

[12] A. I. Tauber, 'Sick autonomy' (2003) 46 *Perspectives in Biology and Medicine* 484, 490.

[13] Potter and McKinlay, 'From a relationship to encounter: An examination of longitudinal and lateral dimensions in the doctor–patient relationship', 476–7; E. J. Speeding and D. N. Rose, 'Building an effective doctor–patient relationship: From patient satisfaction to patient participation' (1985) 21 *Social Science and Medicine* 115.

[14] S. Scheffler, 'Relationships and responsibilities' (1997) 26 *Philosophy and Public Affairs* 189, 190.

because it requires both parties to recognise and respect the moral agency and expertise of the other party, having a relationship is morally better than simply being in a relationship. Second, if patients expect professionals to care and to engage with them in anything more than a purely functional manner then it is reasonable to expect the patient, as a moral agent, to accept the reciprocal obligations that flow from *having* such a caring relationship.

Of course, the patient may decide that he or she does not value the relationship. Since it is only those relationships that one has reason to value that generate specific obligations, this relieves the patient of the specific obligations that are examined in more detail below. The professional, however, does not have the same degree of freedom. As I will discuss later, by voluntarily entering the profession, the professional's autonomy is constrained by the values of the profession. As long as the profession values the professional–patient relationship then so must the professional.

Relationships are characterised by two central features: they are based on need and they create bilateral obligations. In the absence of obligation, any relationship between individuals is purely formal and has no substance: there may *be a* relationship but they do not *have a* relationship. The distinction between formally being in a relationship and actively having a relationship was evidenced in a recent survey of cohabiting or married couples. In analysing the responses, Eekelaar and Maclean found that the formality of marriage was seen as neither 'necessarily, or even characteristically . . . a significant source of personal obligations'.[15] Rather, the situation of having a relationship grounded the perceived obligations to the other.

For a relationship to be 'good' – or, in other words, mutual – certain other characteristics are important. First is the need for trust. While this need not be absolute or equal, it would be a poor relationship in which trust was wholly lacking. The point of trust is that, if it is well placed, it allows us to rely on the skills and knowledge of the other person. It is impossible, and arguably undesirable, for any individual to be wholly self-reliant in the context of a social existence. We cannot be expected to be experts in everything and thus reliance on others is unavoidable. Furthermore, placing trust in the other party to a relationship demonstrates a necessary respect for that other person that will help the relationship to flourish and make it more effective. Provided the trust is not

---

[15] J. Eekelaar and M. Maclean, 'Marriage and the moral bases of personal relationships' (2004) 31 *Journal of Law and Society* 510, 536.

abused, both parties will be the richer for it. Trust is the bedrock of any relationship and the professional–patient relationship is no exception.[16]

On a similar note, the second feature of a mutual relationship is that both parties should respect the other. This, in turn, is necessary for maintaining the trust essential to a good relationship: trust and respect interact iteratively within a relationship. Putting these elements together, the third characteristic is the need for each party to feel, and be, (at least) morally responsible to the other. Without that sense of moral responsibility it is unlikely that the individual parties to the relationship will feel obligated to the other. This places any trust between them at risk of being abused or neglected. The fourth characteristic of a mutual relationship is empathy.[17] Since need is a central part of any relationship, it is important that each party is sensitive to the needs and vulnerabilities of the other party to the relationship. This can only be achieved if there is sufficient empathy between the persons involved in the relationship. The final characteristic of a good relationship is care, which may be for the other party, for the relationship itself or for both the relationship and the other party. If neither party cares about the relationship, or the other party to the relationship, this demonstrates a lack of respect for the other. Without that respect the relationship is unlikely to survive in anything but its formal sense.

While, for our purposes, the most central relationship is that of professional and patient, both parties exist in their own network of relationships which comprise a complex system of obligation, responsibility and dependence. When the potential demands and benefits of the professional–patient relationship are added to this system it is clear that situating autonomy is not straightforward and whatever solution is reached it will only be capable of limited justification and is unlikely to receive unanimous approval. Nevertheless, any attempt to construct an institutional regulation of consent should recognise the relevance of the professional–patient relationship and its context within the web of both professional and social relationships that surround it. The aim is to acknowledge, embrace and take advantage of the benefits offered by the various social relationships that support the patient. However, as well as supporting the dependent patient, relationships that are not wholly one-sided also bring obligations and responsibilities.

---

[16] L. B. McCullough, 'Trust, moral responsibility, the self, and well-ordered societies: The importance of basic philosophical concepts for clinical ethics' (2002) 27 *Journal of Medicine and Philosophy* 3, 5.

[17] N. Quist, 'The paradox of questions and answers: Possibilities for a doctor–patient relationship' (2003) 14 *The Journal of Clinical Ethics* 79, 81.

If patients are to rely on the support of others, as they must, then it is fair to expect them to meet at least some reasonable obligations in return, and hence to *have*, not just *be*, in a relationship with the healthcare professional. Any obligations must take account of the patient's ability to meet them and must also be sensitive to the danger that the patient's autonomy might be rendered impotent if the duty is too onerous.[18] Thus, the rules of consent should situate respect for individuals, their autonomy and their self-determined choices within the context of their community-based social relationships. This necessarily requires a relational approach to autonomy; and the context of consent provides a reason to prefer autonomy as moral, rational self-determination rather than the more individualistic liberal view of autonomy as rational self-determination. In this way, the concerns of the individual, those in close relationship and the wider community can be balanced without sacrificing the individual, his or her dependants or the community.

The professional's obligations within the professional–patient relationship

The first thing to note is the trite caution that professionals are only human. Humans are imperfect and have a finite ability to process and retain information, to communicate effectively and to cope with the emotional demands placed on them by others and by themselves. These limitations should be incorporated into any determination of what may be expected from healthcare professionals. Furthermore, some people are more capable of the empathic aspects of providing healthcare while others are more technically gifted. Even where sufficient time is available, these factors may make it difficult, and perhaps impossible for some, to develop excellence in both the technical and the empathic aspects of medical care.

Our limitations as humans (bearing in mind the constraints of time and resources) mean that any system of regulation must take into account the effect that emphasising empathic skills will have on the professionals' technical abilities (and vice versa). The more that is expected of healthcare professionals in the human side of caring the more the technical side is compromised and it is important to achieve a balance that facilitates both aspects of healthcare.[19] While either

---

[18] J. Cohen, 'Patient autonomy and social fairness' (2000) 9 *Cambridge Quarterly of Healthcare Ethics* 391, 396.

[19] M. Gregg Bloche and K. P. Quinn, 'Professionalism and personhood', in D. C. Thomasma, D. N. Weissrub and C. Herve (eds.), *Personhood and Health Care* (Dordrecht: Kluwer Academic Publishers, 2001), pp. 347, 350–2.

empathic or technical skills may be given greater priority it should not be to the extent that the other aspect is jeopardised. Patients need to be treated with adequate levels of both technical skill and empathic humanity. This means that, in constructing the rules of consent, and the consequential obligations, care must be taken not to make the demands on professionals so great that it undermines their ability to satisfy the required technical demands.

Professional obligations arise from two sources. First are those obligations that fall equally on all moral agents, which derive from the recognition that all agents are ends in themselves. Second, professionals have obligations that derive from their role within the healthcare professional–patient relationship.

Perhaps the most important general duty is to respect the other person's autonomy, which provides a reason to trust those persons and give prima facie respect to their decisions.[20] Furthermore, any interference with an autonomous person's decision must be justified. The need for justification is strongest where the decision is clearly autonomous. However, even where the decision appears to be non-autonomous, humility (the acknowledgement of fallibility) requires that any interference is proportionate and justified. This general obligation to respect the autonomous person's decision is a negative duty, but a respect for autonomy may also entail positive duties. Although the libertarian may reject the existence of positive duties they are widely acknowledged both in principle and practice.[21] In any case, even if positive obligations do not arise from the professionals' general moral duty they certainly do from their role as healer in the context of the professional–patient relationship.

Realising one's autonomy requires at least minimal choice and the resources necessary to act on that choice. Within the professional–patient relationship it is professionals who control the resources necessary for patients to exercise their autonomy,[22] including availability of treatment choices, access to other professionals and the information necessary to make a rational decision. While an ever-increasing amount of information is readily available through technologies such as the Internet, without assistance to process it patients may end up overwhelmed and unable to use the information effectively. Paradoxically, although autonomous decisions should be informed, more is not necessarily better and too much

---

[20] W. A. Rogers, 'Is there a moral duty for doctors to trust patients?' (2002) 28 *Journal of Medical Ethics* 77, 77–8.

[21] See e.g. *Osman* v. *UK* (2000) 29 EHRR 245.

[22] The professional's access to some of these resources – the tangible goods – may be restricted by the chain of healthcare management.

information – especially if unfiltered – may serve to confuse and so undermine autonomy.[23] On the other hand, it has been shown that where information is desired it can be empowering.[24]

Within the professional–patient relationship both parties should possess the power required to exercise their roles.[25] Professional power comes from a number of sources, including their knowledge base, their control of the treatment options and their social role as healer.[26] While this power is necessary it may have a profound effect, and it should be used in a way that respects patients and enables them to exercise their autonomy effectively to arrive at a mutually acceptable treatment plan. The implication for consent is that the professional, who possesses the expertise and information necessary to the treatment decision, is the dominant party in the relationship.

Since communicative acts, or processes, necessarily involve at least two parties and require some degree of cooperation, both parties have responsibilities, but – as the dominant party – it behoves the professional to facilitate the patient's involvement. This at least requires the healthcare professional to support and facilitate the patient's ability to make an autonomous decision. Where healthcare professionals are supportive of patient autonomy this has been shown to increase the patient's willingness to be self-determining, which may improve that patient's cooperation with a treatment regime and hence improve the clinical outcome.[27]

In a survey of 410 patients McKinstry found that 'Patients' preferences for shared or directed versions of scenarios were significantly associated with . . . their perception of their own doctor as one who shared or directed [decision-making].'[28] This supportive approach is necessary partly because people naturally vary in their ability to make autonomous decisions, partly because the patient's ability may be compromised by illness or by the context of the decision and partly because, like any skill, the ability to make autonomous decisions should improve with practice and the assistance of others. Thus, patients must

[23] H. P. Grice, 'Logic and conversation', in R. M. Hamish (ed.), *Basic Topics in the Philosophy of Language*, (Harvester Wheatsheaf: New York, 1994), pp. 57, 61.

[24] E. Krupat, M. Fancey and P. D. Cleary, 'Information and its impact on satisfaction among surgical patients' (2000) 51 *Social Science & Medicine* 1817, 1824.

[25] F. Goodyear-Smith and S. Buetow, 'Power issues in the doctor–patient relationship' (2001) 9 *Health Care Analysis* 449, 459.

[26] H. Brody, *The Healer's Power* (New Haven: Yale University Press, 1992), pp. 16–17.

[27] Valimaki *et al.*, 'Self-determination in surgical patients in five European countries', 309.

[28] B. McKinstry, 'Do patients wish to be involved in decision making in the consultation? A cross sectional survey with video vignettes' (2000) 321 *British Medical Journal* 867, 868.

be supported and encouraged if they are to exercise their autonomy effectively. However, autonomy does not require patients to make every decision themselves and, since healthcare professionals are experts, it may be reasonable for patients to defer to their judgement because they reasonably believe healthcare professionals have greater capacity to make the decision.

In such a case, professionals should ensure that patients understand the implications of ceding the decision and should also enquire whether there is any information the patient desires. There are two reasons for this. First, consent is not the sole reason for needing information. For example, knowing how long it will take to recover, or when they will be able to return to work, is necessary to allow patients to organise their life or to know what to expect. Second, patients may defer decisions, not because they see themselves as wholly unable to make them but because it is more efficient and expedient to do so. In this case, they may require authoritative reasons why they should accept the professional's decision. This type of authority differs from persuasion in that reasons are provided to explain the decision rather than to convince the other that one choice is better than another. Professionals do not need to bring the patient round to their way of thinking; they simply need to justify the patient's trust in their judgement.[29]

Even where patients choose to make their own decision, this does not reduce healthcare professionals to technical advisers as their clinical autonomy, their duty to respect patient autonomy and their duty of beneficence all require them to try and persuade patients to accept their preferred treatment choice (see Chapters 1 and 2). This is particularly so where the patient's decision appears irrational and risks irremediable harm to the patient's future autonomy. In these circumstances, it is more respectful to question the decision than abandon the patient to his or her fate.[30]

In Chapter 2 I argued against allowing healthcare professionals the authority to override an irrational decision. Further to that argument, the knowledge that one's self-determination might be overridden may undermine the trust necessary to sustain the professional–patient relationship and risks causing patients to avoid seeking healthcare. In the US, for example, compulsory drug testing or compelling pregnant women to undergo non-consensual treatment caused some to go into

---

[29] J. Cunliffe and A. Reeve, 'Dialogic authority' (1999) 19 *Oxford Journal of Legal Studies* 453, 459–63.

[30] See A. Maclean, 'Autonomy, consent and persuasion' (2006) 13 *European Journal of Health Law* 321.

hiding or give birth at home.[31] However, just because people should ultimately be free to be wrong and make irrational decisions this does not mean that they should be abandoned. As Mill argued:

> It would be a great misunderstanding of this doctrine to suppose that it is one of selfish indifference, which pretends that human beings . . . should not concern themselves about the well-doing or well-being of one another . . . Human beings owe to each other help to distinguish the better from the worse and encouragement to choose the former and avoid the latter.[32]

An alternative approach would be to challenge decisions, ensure that patients are not making decisions on the basis of misinformation or a misunderstanding, and attempt to persuade them that their reasoning is flawed or their goal or belief is unjustified. This may be seen as a compromise that tries to balance a respect for autonomy with a respect for the individual's welfare and his or her potential for future autonomy.[33] However, it is also arguable that it is more respectful to the individual's present autonomy than simply abandoning that person when he or she makes a catastrophic choice.

In *Rochdale Healthcare (NHS) Trust* v. *C*,[34] C refused a caesarean section because she would rather die than go through another one after a previous caesarean left her with a painful scar and a bad back. Even though it may be reasonable to value the avoidance of pain it seems irrational, unless the pain is unbearable, to give that goal a greater weight than continued life. It is only by challenging such decisions that healthcare professionals can be sure that their patients have reflected on, or at least had the opportunity and resources to reflect on, the values and goals that guided their decisions. This is particularly true in circumstances, such as genetic counselling, where either accepting or rejecting the offered intervention may be seen as equally rational.[35] It is only by questioning the patient's decision and requesting an explanation of the reasons behind the choice that the professional can determine whether the decision is consistent with the patient's values and goals.

---

[31] W. Chavkin, M. H. Allen and M. Oberman, 'Drug abuse and pregnancy: Some questions on public policy, clinical management, and maternal and fetal rights' (1991) 18 *Birth* 107, 111; N. K. Rhoden, 'The judge in the delivery room: The emergence of court-ordered cesareans' (1986) 74 *California Law Review* 1951, 2028.

[32] Mill, 'On Liberty', p. 84.

[33] Respect for the person is arguably a wider duty than simply respecting that person's autonomy. See M. T. Lysaught, 'Respect: Or, how respect for persons became respect for autonomy' (2004) 29(6) *Journal of Medicine and Philosophy* 665.

[34] *Rochdale Healthcare (NHS) Trust* v. *C* [1997] 1 FCR 274.

[35] See *Al Hamwi* v. *Johnston, The North West London Hospitals NHS Trust* [2005] EWHC 206; [2005] Lloyd's LR Med 309.

Furthermore, requiring patients to explain their goals may cause them to reconsider their beliefs and perhaps change their decisions. Alternatively, the patient's explanation may satisfy the healthcare professional that the decision was autonomous.

It may be objected that the professional lacks the authority to interfere with a competent patient's decision.[36] However, to fully respect another individual's autonomy arguably requires positive obligations – especially when in a caring relationship – as well as the simple negative duty not to obstruct the decision. In this context there may be a balance between the two duties as there is a certain amount of conflict between non-interference, which protects the liberty aspect of autonomy, and the interference necessary to ensure that individuals possess the resources, and have the opportunity, to exercise their autonomy effectively.[37] Care must be taken to ensure that the interference does not become obstructive, but – while professionals should be sensitive to the circumstances (the potential consequence of the decision, the power imbalance, patient vulnerability and the fragile nature of a sick person's autonomy) – it seems reasonable to suggest that they should question an apparently irrational decision.

This argument is premised on the presumptions that most patients want to make reasonable decisions, that they do not see the professional–patient relationship as antagonistic and that they are willing to engage in a discussion of the decision and attempt to reach an agreement that is acceptable to both of them. All of these presumptions may be normatively justified as features of a trusting relationship between autonomous – and hence responsible – moral agents.

Persuasion, which is the use of reason to convince the other to accept the correctness of one's position, is a form of influence that may be justified by either of two arguments.[38] The 'negative strategy' argues that the professional's influence is allowed because it is important to combat the negative effect of the patient's sickness on his or her autonomy. The 'positive strategy', which is the primary approach I have adopted, is based on the argument that a true respect for autonomy requires more than simply abandoning patients to whatever choice they

---

[36] See S. A. M. McLean, *A Patient's Right to Know: Information disclosure, the doctor and the law* (Aldershot: Dartmouth, 1989), p. 22.

[37] T. E. Quill and H. Brody, 'Physician recommendations and patient autonomy: Finding a balance between physician power and patient choice' (1996) 125 *Annals of Internal Medicine* 763.

[38] T. Tomlinson, 'The physician's influence on patients' choices' (1986) 7 *Theoretical Medicine* 105, 109.

make.[39] As Barilan and Weintraub argued: 'Abiding by unexplored expressed wishes does not necessarily amount to respect for persons, since respect for persons is much more than submission to social boundaries.'[40] Through the use of dialogue and persuasion the tension between the individual and the community may be resolved without undermining the individual's autonomy.

In some cases patients may be mistaken as to the choice that best serves their goals and values. This is not a reason for professionals to simply usurp the patients' role in making the decision and substitute their own views for those of their patients. Without the patients' involvement and cooperation, the professionals cannot discover the patients' goals, and hence their best interests. But, where patients have not formalised their thoughts concerning their higher-order desires or long-term goals, they may need both support and facilitation to determine the most appropriate decision. Similarly, intervention, such as pointing out logical inconsistencies or irrational reasoning, may also be necessary where patients have formalised their goals but are mistaken in how best to achieve them. Thus, not only is persuasion morally permissible, it is also the healthcare professional's duty. However, the limits of persuasion may blur with those of manipulation, at which point patient autonomy is undermined rather than enhanced.

The ultimate aim of the manipulator is to 'motivate' the other person to do something that will serve the manipulator's goal rather than respecting the other person's right to determine his or her own ends.[41] This may also be the aim of rational persuasion, which might be directed at either the means of achieving a particular goal or at the reasonableness of the goal itself. However, perhaps what distinguishes manipulation from persuasion is that the manipulator seeks to avoid the open use of honest reasons to convince the other. Instead, manipulation relies on devices such as deception to undermine the other person's control of the decision. In addition to deception, which includes both lying and withholding relevant information, the manipulator's tools include playing on the other person's fears, inducing a feeling of guilt, taking advantage of the other's good nature and the offer of exploitative

---

[39] S. Wear, 'Patient autonomy, paternalism, and the conscientious physician' (1983) 4 *Theoretical Medicine* 253, 262–4.

[40] Y. M. Barilan and M. Weintraub, 'Persuasion as respect for autonomy: An alternative view of autonomy and the limits of discourse' (2001) 26 *Journal of Medicine and Philosophy* 13, 20.

[41] J. Rudinow, 'Manipulation' (1978) 88 *Ethics* 338, 346; M. Kligman and C. M. Culver, 'An analysis of interpersonal manipulation' (1992) 17 *The Journal of Medicine and Philosophy* 173, 183.

inducements. All of these avoid the use of reason and, by utilising the patient's weaknesses, undermine autonomy.[42] Furthermore, especially when done for 'beneficent' reasons, withholding or manipulating information demonstrates a lack of trust in the patient's ability to use that information effectively. If exposed, this lack of trust may fatally undermine a therapeutic relationship.

On the other hand, rational decision-making may reasonably take fear, guilt, goodwill and inducements into account and it is not always easy to distinguish between, for an example, an appropriate appeal to patients' obligations to others and the manipulative use of the guilt they will feel should they fail those others. One example of where the use of an inappropriate sense of guilt may occur is where patients decline to ask questions or engage in further dialogue for the expressed reason that they do not want to bother the busy physician. If patient autonomy is valued then it is part of the professional's duty to spend a reasonable length of time in dialogue, and allowing patients to cut short any discussion because they feel guilty about taking up the professional's time is exploitative and may be used as a tool of manipulation.

Another difficulty arises because what may be offered as honest information may still mislead. Misunderstanding arises because the patient must necessarily interpret information and that interpretation – or misinterpretation – will inevitably be affected by their existing knowledge, beliefs and experiences. It is impossible to convey information without the meaning of that information being affected by the patient as he or she processes the information and tries to incorporate it within his or her existing and complex state of knowledge and belief. Knowing this, professionals could adopt one of two strategies.

One approach would be for professionals to disclose what they honestly believe to be the truth even where they suspect that the patient will misinterpret it. Alternatively, they could present the information in a way that will cause the patient to achieve a more reasonable picture. Both strategies could be justified as respecting the patient's autonomy and the situation is complicated because, unless one discloses all information in a neutral fashion, which is arguably impossible, it will always be necessary to make judgements about what to disclose and how to disclose it. Thus, the boundary between the two approaches is blurred, which makes it difficult to draft a rule explicitly permitting one while preventing the other.

Although both strategies arguably respect autonomy, there are problems with the second approach. First, it shows a lack of trust in the

---

[42] Tomlinson, 'The physician's influence on patients' choices', 114.

patient's openness to rational persuasion and hence reflects a diminished respect for that person's autonomy. Second, it relies on the assumption that the healthcare professional can reliably predict that the patient will misinterpret the information. Third, if the patient does interpret the information differently, it assumes that the healthcare professional's interpretation is the correct one. Where there is reasonable doubt it may be more respectful to trust the patient and provide a more open disclosure. However, provided the information is merely non-specific rather than a lie, the rationally autonomous patient should be astute enough to notice the lack of specificity and ask for more detail. Giving non-specific information may be a more sensitive approach because it allows patients, provided they are sufficiently empowered, to determine the level of detail required. This approach may be acceptable provided it satisfies certain constraints.

First, any exceptions would need to be well publicised so as to ensure that all patients are aware that seeking certain types of information is their responsibility. Second, because of the power dynamics of the professional–patient relationship and, in many cases, the patient's vulnerability, healthcare providers and professionals would need to be sensitive to their patients' disadvantage and facilitate the exercise of their responsibility. Acknowledging such a duty further supports the claim that this is a more sensitive means of communication rather than deception or a lack of candour. Third, if the manoeuvre is to respect patient autonomy, and arguably their welfare, then any lack of candour should be intended to advance patients' ends and not those of the professionals. Fourth, creating rules to delimit those circumstances when a lack of candour would be acceptable raises all the usual problems of how those rules might be open to interpretation.

While rules may be drafted to prohibit lying, deception and other forms of manipulation, they will inevitably be open to interpretation and will rely on the physician's character, in the form of virtues with concomitant imperfect duties, to implement those rules within the spirit of the justification that underlies them. This acknowledges that there may be, for example, occasions where the professionals' duty of beneficence and their personal knowledge are enough to justify the 'manipulation' of their patients' prejudices in order to instil a true belief about the decisional relevance of the proposition. The law can formulate precise duties regarding the more overt forms of pejorative manipulation and can guide healthcare professionals towards the appropriate dispositions and interpretation but, because manipulation may be well disguised and hidden from anyone lacking the necessary insight into the history and context of the situation, there will always be difficult cases that depend on the professional's character. Ultimately then, rules can only provide so much security and the good or virtuous character is essential to enhance or complete that protection.[43]

In addition to the ordinary duty to respect the patient as a person, healthcare professionals have role-specific obligations arising from their privileged position and the professional–patient relationship. Perhaps the most widely accepted specific duties are those of beneficence and non-maleficence. In Chapter 2 I argued that the duty of non-maleficence only made sense when incorporated into the duty of beneficence, which is constrained by the duty to respect autonomy. The duty of beneficence requires professionals to act for the benefit of the patient, which is a vague and general obligation requiring further explication. In Chapter 2 I suggested that beneficence should be directed holistically at the patient as a person rather than solely at the patient's health. An additional constraint is that the benefit of the intervention should be balanced against its costs, both to the individual patient and to the wider community. Thus, even if a particular treatment would benefit the patient, healthcare professionals are under no duty to provide it if the costs outweigh the benefit. This caveat of 'utility' has obvious implications for the post-modern consumer clamour for choice and justifies the role played by bodies like the National Institute for Health and Clinical Excellence (NICE) which determine the use of treatments on just such a basis.

The interaction between the professional's duties of beneficence and respect for the patient's autonomy requires professionals to act in a way that not just respects the patient's formal right to consent but also reflects the spirit behind that requirement. If harm is seen as a wrongful setback to the other person's interests, the duty again requires that professionals are concerned to justify any intervention by gaining the competent patient's consent. In addition to this, they should pay heed to the patient's other interests. The most basic interests of health and life should be protected, but not necessarily at the expense of the patient's other interests. Going beyond the sphere of medical goods takes professionals outside their area of expertise and their lack of knowledge regarding the patient's values, goals and interests means that they must engage the patient cooperatively in the decision-making process or provide the patient with the necessary information and cede the decision.[44]

---

[43] F. J. Ingelfinger, 'Informed (but uneducated) consent' (1972) 287 *New England Journal of Medicine* 465, 466.

[44] R. M. Veatch, 'Doctor does not know best: Why in the new century physicians must stop trying to benefit patients' (2000) 25 *Journal of Medicine and Philosophy* 701, 703–5.

Although both respect for autonomy and the duty of beneficence require healthcare professionals to involve patients in decisions that affect them this does not mean that patients should be abandoned to their decision. Both obligations also require healthcare professionals to try and persuade them to change their decision if it appears unwise;[45] in particular, the duty of beneficence requires that healthcare professionals act so as to avoid their patients suffering harm. As discussed earlier, the duty of beneficence does not justify the professional in absolutely overriding the patient's autonomy, nor does it justify coercion or dishonest manipulation of the patient's will. It does, however, support the same kinds of interference required by a respect for their patients' autonomy to ensure that patients are competent, have an adequate understanding of the facts and potential consequences (both to themselves and relevant others) and have given the matter appropriate consideration.

The obligation to challenge an apparently unwise decision is further supported by the virtue of care. Abandoning a patient to an unwise decision that is likely to result in significant harm is the antithesis of caring for and about that person. To care for someone means wanting them to achieve their goals but at the same time respecting their values. One cannot do this by simply accepting whatever decision the patient makes. Equally, caring for another does not justify smothering that person's agency. Rather, someone committed to a caring relationship must engage with the other and support that person in exercising his or her autonomy. Only by engaging with the patient's decision-making process and the reasons behind the decision can the professional fulfil his or her role as carer. Thus the virtue of care, like beneficence and respect for autonomy, requires the healthcare professional to challenge, and if necessary argue with the patient.[46]

As I argued in Chapter 2, the rules of beneficence, particularly when combined with a sense of justice, require additional support to be provided where the individual is less able to be autonomous. For many patients their desire and ability to be autonomous will be affected by their illness. One study even found that when doctors become patients they also prefer the treating physician to take the primary role in decision-making, and this tendency increased with the severity of the sickness.[47]

---

[45] The caveat is that the doctor should, in determining the best course of action, take the patient's goals and values into account.

[46] D. H. Smith and L. S. Pettegrew, 'Mutual persuasion as a model for doctor–patient communication' (1986) 7 *Theoretical Medicine* 127, 137–8.

[47] J. Ende, L. Kazis and M. A. Moskowitz, 'Preference for autonomy when patients are physicians' (1990) 5 *Journal of General Internal Medicine* 23.

This is compounded by the power imbalance between professional and patient, the alien environment of the hospital and the individual's social conditioning. These may all diminish the competent patient's ability to exercise his or her autonomy by encouraging heuristic decision-making that often relies on intuition and 'folk-wisdom' and precluding the rational reflection ideally required by autonomy.[48]

While the effects of illness may completely undermine the autonomy of some patients, other patients will be less severely compromised and even where patients' autonomy is diminished it may be possible to encourage, support or facilitate their autonomy. Furthermore, one of the most important functions of medicine is to restore the patient's autonomy.[49] This does not mean that patients should be forced to exercise autonomy, especially where it is undermined by illness. However, where at least some of these effects may be countered, the professionals' duty of beneficence and their role within the professional–patient relationship require them to enhance their patients' autonomy by creating a sympathetic environment, encouraging their patients to participate and providing the support and time necessary to enable that participation.[50] This is important because it is the patients who will necessarily bear the physical and psychological consequences that follow any healthcare decisions.

An essential element of the healthcare professional's role is to care for the sick. Because the unifying consequence of sickness is the loss of control that patients experience, this translates into an obligation to help the patient regain that control.[51] Where a quick and effective cure is available then perhaps the best way to do this is simply to treat the patient. In other cases, however, the doctor must educate patients and teach them how to regain as much control as possible in the face of their sickness. Since autonomy and control are intrinsically connected, this beneficence-based argument adds further weight to the autonomy-based arguments that professionals should be honest with patients. Deception and manipulation are arguably wrong because they undermine autonomy and trust. However, if discovered, they also undermine the patient's sense of control. Thus, if professionals are to help their patients exercise maximal control over their sick bodies, honesty is crucial.

[48] C. Schneider and M. Farrell, 'The limits of informed consent', in M. Freeman and A. Lewis (eds.), Law and Medicine, Current Legal Issues, vol. 3 (Oxford: Oxford University Press, 2000), pp. 107, 120–2.

[49] E. Cassell, 'The function of medicine' (1977) 7 Hasting Center Report 16.

[50] L. Doyal, 'The moral foundation of the clinical duties of care: Needs, duties and human rights' (2001) 15 Bioethics 520, 530–1.

[51] E. J. Cassell, The Healer's Art (Cambridge, Mass.: MIT Press, 1985), p. 163.

Interacting with the patient is complicated by the fact that not all patients want to exercise their autonomy. The desire to act autonomously is affected by a number of demographic variables such as age, sex and culture.[52] These differences may be explicable on the basis of two psychological variables: the locus of control and self-efficacy.[53] The locus of control is a sense of how much influence individuals have over their lives: those with an external locus of control see their lives much more as the subject of fate and largely outside their own control, while those with an internal locus of control see their lives as primarily shaped by themselves. This has a number of consequences.

First, persons with an external locus of control may be reluctant to engage in autonomous decision-making, especially in the fragile state of sickness, with its attendant loss of control, and the intimidating environment of the hospital. Second, they may find it hard, even in ideal circumstances, to make autonomous decisions. Third, persons with an internal locus of control may find it more difficult and stressful to deal with the loss of control caused by their sickness. Consequently, it may be psychologically beneficial to support their autonomy as far as possible. Also following from this, it may be both more distressing and more harmful to those with an internal locus of control if insensitively paternalistic professionals undermine what autonomous capacity they do have. On the other hand, it may be equally harmful or distressing to unduly pressure or compel patients with an external locus of control to exercise their autonomy.

The issue is more complicated because people do not fall neatly into one of these two types. While individuals may in general tend towards one or other of these types, this tendency may be affected by surrounding circumstances. In addition to having an internal locus of control, autonomy requires that individuals see themselves as capable of successfully completing a task, or, in this context, capable of making an autonomous decision.[54] A loss of this confidence may undermine the positive effect on autonomy of an internal locus of control and may cause stress and a feeling of helplessness. However, patients' confidence may be influenced by the surrounding circumstances and by the attitude and behaviour of healthcare professionals. For example, the patient's desire for information or to engage in the decision-making process may be underestimated.[55]

---

[52] H. Leino-Kilpi et al., *Patient's Autonomy, Privacy and Informed Consent* (Amsterdam: IOS Press, 2000), p. 64.
[53] Waller, 'The psychological structure of patient autonomy'.   [54] *Ibid.*, 258.
[55] In a recent Department of Health survey of NHS patients it was found that 46% of patients who responded wanted greater involvement in treatment decisions: *NHS*

This lack or loss of confidence may be expressed as an unwillingness to make a decision. However, rather than simply accept this reluctance at face value, the healthcare professional should attempt to restore the person's confidence by supporting his or her autonomy. This may be more difficult where the patient tends towards an external locus of control, in which case professionals would need to be sensitive to the patient's psychological disposition and vary their support and involvement accordingly as some may be overwhelmed if given control and deserted.[56] Nonetheless, since psychological traits are not static, and are tendencies rather than absolutes, it may be worthwhile supporting and enabling patients to be as autonomous as possible. As such, any rules or guidelines regulating consent should be sensitive to these two psychological characteristics.

The professional–patient relationship, as a caring relationship, can also benefit the patient's health.[57] To be successful in this, the relationship at least needs to be cooperative, and requires mutual trust if it is to be most effective. The need for patients to trust professionals, which encourages shared decision-making[58] and is essential to the whole process of care, obliges the professional to act in a trustworthy way. In many circumstances, particularly in acute care situations where the professional–patient relationship may be very short-lived, patients must trust professionals simply by virtue of the professional's role and their own vulnerability. Because of this need to place trust in the role as well as in the person, the obligation to be trustworthy is owed not just to their patients, but also to present and future colleagues. This reinforces the professionals' duty to be open, honest, non-manipulative, proficient and concerned for their patients.

A caveat to the professionals' duty to be trustworthy is that, while they should avoid deception, their duty of beneficence may justify controlling the timing of disclosure, particularly of distressing information.[59] This does not mean that professionals can withhold the information but it would allow them to decide when and how to disclose. Arguably, any such decision should, if it is to respect the patient's autonomy, involve

---

Patients Survey Programme 2001/02: Key findings (2003). A similar result was obtained in the Healthcare Commission's 2005 inpatient survey.

[56] C. E. Schneider, *The Practice of Autonomy: Patients, doctors, and medical decisions* (New York: Oxford University Press, 1998), p. 115.

[57] H. M. Adler, 'The sociophysiology of caring in the doctor–patient relationship' (2002) 17 *Journal of General Internal Medicine* 883, 885–6.

[58] N. Kraetschmer, N. Sharpe, S. Urowitz and R. B. Deber, 'How does trust affect patient preferences for participation in decision-making?' (2004) 7 *Health Expectations* 317.

[59] E. J. Gordon and C. K. Daugherty, '"Hitting you over the head": Oncologists' disclosure of prognosis to advanced cancer patients' (2003) 17 *Bioethics* 142, 162–3.

negotiation, placing a degree of responsibility on the patient to request further information when the professional makes a tentative offer.

As a final point, a recent study has suggested that patients' most important concern appears to be the need to trust their doctor. In a qualitative study of thirty-nine breast cancer patients, Burkitt Wright *et al.* found that the patient's desire for information primarily related to maintaining trust and hope, rather than as a tool to enable them to be the decision-maker. Trust was undermined where the patients felt they had been misled and, conversely, trust was enhanced where the doctor was perceived as being open. For this subset of patients, 'what patients sought diverged from the current emphasis on providing information. It was a function not of amount of information but of the nature of information and manner of presentation.'[60] Although this study provides helpful insights into the needs and desires of patients it may be that some of the patients' concerns are influenced by their underlying pathology. Thus, the results may not be applicable to non-cancer sufferers. Nevertheless, the study does emphasise the central importance of trust and respect.

The patient's obligations within the professional–patient relationship

While patient autonomy generates obligations for healthcare professionals, accepting the role of moral agent also imposes obligations on the patient. These arise because of the socially situated nature of autonomy and from the more specific context of the professional–patient relationship. As suggested earlier, relationships create bilateral obligations and the professional–patient relationship is no different. Furthermore, a non-reciprocal relationship is more likely to fail the parties and thus lose the benefits that justify the relationship's existence. It might be argued that the patient's vulnerability relieves him or her of at least some of the obligations that would normally arise in a relationship and – because of the imbalance of knowledge and power – justifies an asymmetry of responsibility in the healthcare professional–patient relationship.[61] It is, however, insufficient to always justify a denial of the consequential duties.

---

[60] Burkitt Wright, Holcombe and Salmon, 'Doctors' communication of trust, care, and respect in breast cancer: Qualitative study', 866–7.

[61] M. Kelley, 'Limits on patient responsibility' (2005) 30 *The Journal of Medicine and Philosophy* 189.

Vulnerability makes people susceptible to exploitation and it would be reasonable for the law to protect them from that eventuality, but vulnerability per se does not prevent someone from being an agent with the authority to make decisions and the responsibility for the consequences of the decisions.[62] Although the balance of power may lie with the professional, patients are not completely impotent and may, for example, manipulate the professional or abuse the provision of state-funded healthcare. Furthermore, the patient's power may be bolstered by the rise in self-help groups, the increased involvement of lawyers and the scrutiny of medicine by the media. Just as the healthcare professional's power within the relationship demands responsibility, so does the patient's.

Perhaps the primary obligation arising from autonomy is the duty to respect others as persons or ends in themselves, which is necessary to allow those other persons a fair opportunity to exercise their own autonomy. It requires patients to give due concern to the impact of their behaviour on other people. More specifically, because they have entered into a personal relationship, they should treat the professional with respect; just as competent patients come to the professional–patient relationship as autonomous persons, so do the professionals.

Three types of autonomy are relevant.[63] First, the professionals' personal autonomy means that they come to the relationship with their own values, interests and goals. Second, the values and goals of the autonomous professional influence and constrain their personal autonomy, which results in, third, the restricted 'clinical autonomy', which provides the professional with both the power and the responsibility 'to act according to the shared standards of that profession'.[64] The relevance of the professionals' personal autonomy is that, within the constraints of the general duty to respect others, their profession, the contractual obligations of their employment and the duties arising by virtue of their roles as healer, they should be allowed to bring those personal values and goals to the decisional process. It would, perhaps, be impossible for professionals to prevent their deeply held values from affecting their interpretative judgement. However, the importance of these constraints requires them to be alive to that possibility. It is also

[62] H. Draper and T. Sorrell, T. 'Patients' responsibilities in medical ethics' (2002) 16 *Bioethics* 335, 339.

[63] E. D. Pellegrino, 'Patient and physician autonomy: Conflicting rights and obligations in the physician–patient relationship' (1994) 10 *Journal of Contemporary Health Law and Policy* 47, 52.

[64] C. MacDonald, 'Relational professional autonomy' (2002) 11 *Cambridge Quarterly of Healthcare Ethics* 282, 284.

one reason why their behaviour should be supported and guided by reasonably specific principles and rules. Ideally, perhaps, they should also be encouraged to become virtuous professionals.

The professionals' personal autonomy may cause them to see the patient's decision as unwise or even morally wrong and, excluding the emergency situation, it may justify them refusing to provide the requested treatment. As May suggested: 'In protecting a patient's rights to treatment options, we must be careful not to hold the health care professional hostage to the patient's values by forcing the provision of services that would not otherwise be offered, simply because the patient holds certain beliefs or values.'[65] This mirrors the patient's right to refuse treatment and, just as professionals should respect that decision, so patients should respect the professionals' stance. However, while it may justify a refusal to treat this does not absolve them of their professional duty to care for their patients, which at least requires the professional to support their patient and help him or her find another professional who may be willing to provide the treatment.

Given the imbalance in power, it may not be fair to allow the professional, who has voluntarily entered the profession, absolute rights of conscience. There are some types of treatment, such as abortion, that raise particularly contentious moral issues. It seems reasonable to allow professionals to conscientiously object to these types of treatment. However, this does not mean that a professional can refuse to treat simply because the intervention or the patient's motives clash with his or her personal values. A balance must be sought that respects the professional's values without unjustly compromising the patient's autonomy. Thus, there will be situations where a professional's personal values and beliefs must surrender to the profession's ethics.

It is also arguable that their autonomy does not allow healthcare professionals to refuse treatment simply because they believe it to be a riskier or less beneficial alternative. Risk and benefit have strong subjective elements that make it unjustifiable for professionals to impose their view of risk on the patient. However, the balance between patient and professional autonomy does not require healthcare professionals to provide treatment that is not 'medically indicated', and it remains the professionals' prerogative to prioritise treatments on medical grounds and to advise patients accordingly. But, where treatments are 'medically indicated' then the healthcare professional should not refuse to provide them simply because they are not 'medically optimal'. An alternative

---

[65] T. May, 'Rights of conscience in health care' (2001) 27 *Social Theory and Practice* 111.

approach that may avoid conflict is to negotiate with the patient to see if a compromise can be reached. This may need persuasion, but also requires the professional, in turn, to be open to persuasion.[66] The mutual obligation to be open to persuasion means that if patients choose not to accept the professional's recommended treatment then it is reasonable to expect them at least to explain why.

This openness to mutual persuasion, which is essential to truly shared decision-making, is reflected in the type of duties that may be seen as basic to an effective professional–patient relationship. These include a duty to communicate openly with the professional; to genuinely try to make a responsible decision; to respect the healthcare professional as a moral agent with a duty to perform a particular role, which means giving due consideration to the professional's advice;[67] and to actively participate in the professional–patient relationship and their own care.[68] In particular, patients arguably have a duty to engage in the process of open and honest dialogue that will enable the most autonomous decision possible. As moral agents, patients also have the more general duties of being responsible for their own health and behaving as reasonable citizens; these general obligations also require the patient to respect the healthcare professional and to follow their advice unless they have good reason not to.

Beyond this, the very point of seeking medical assistance perhaps justifies an obligation on patients to allow the professional to confront apparently irrational decisions. If someone is asked for assistance it seems reasonable for that person to require the other to explain why an apparently irrational course of action deserves assistance. Even though acceding to the patient's request that turns out badly may not directly harm them, professionals may still have feelings of guilt and regret as a consequence because, unless healthcare professionals are to act purely as technicians (without independent agency), then they share responsibility for a bad outcome. The duty to allow apparently irrational decisions to be challenged may also follow from the argument that each of us owes other members of the community a duty to behave in a morally responsible way, which includes considering the impact of one's decisions on others.[69]

---

[66] Barilan and Weintraub, 'Persuasion as respect for autonomy', 21–2.

[67] Draper and Sorrell, 'Patients' responsibilities in medical ethics', 346.

[68] M. J. Meyer, 'Patients' duties' (1992) 17 *The Journal of Medicine and Philosophy* 541, 550–3.

[69] C. C. Gauthier, 'The virtue of moral responsibility' (2005) 30 *The Journal of Medicine and Philosophy* 153, 161.

A respect for professionals as beneficent and caring experts may require patients to explain their decisions and provide the motivating reasons allowing the healthcare professional to understand the decision or to spot any factual or logical errors. Although consent is primarily predicated on respect for the patient, it would be an unjustly one-sided relationship if professionals could not also claim some respect for their role from patients who have requested their assistance. However, if professionals are to justify such respect, they should be sensitive to the different narratives that professionals and patients bring to the encounter. This is particularly important where the decision is intimately connected to the patient's conception of self, life-plan or future goals. As such, where patients' decisions seem unintelligible, while it is appropriate for professionals to question them, they should try to understand the decision from within the patients' narrative.[70]

From the patient's perspective, the professional's trust is an important feature of the professional–patient relationship. This is important because professionals cannot be certain that patients have been open and honest, that they will behave responsibly in using the disclosed information nor that the apparently cooperative patient will follow their advice. Since healthcare professionals lack complete control over their patients they have little choice but to trust their patients to some extent. However, they do have scope to act in a way that minimises the need to trust their patients. For example, they could deliberately withhold relevant information or emphasise certain risks to manipulate their patients because they do not trust them to make the 'right' decision. These consequences of distrust undermine patient autonomy and threaten the mutuality of the relationship and thus, professionals *ought* to trust their patients beyond the minimum level of unavoidable trust.

Although the law could regulate professional conduct to limit these undesirable consequences it seems reasonable to suggest that, because patients potentially benefit from the professional's trust, they should also support that trust by acting in a trustworthy manner, which at least requires open and honest communication.

The patient's obligations and mandatory autonomy

It is sometimes argued that not only do people have a right to respect for their autonomy but they also have an obligation to be autonomous and this applies just as much to patients as anyone else. As Schneider noted,

---

[70] J. L. Hallenbeck, 'What's the story: How patients make medical decisions' (2002) 113 *The American Journal of Medicine* 73, 74.

these arguments in favour of mandatory autonomy rely on one or more of four possible justifications:[71]

- the prophylaxis argument
- the therapeutic argument
- the 'false consciousness' argument
- the moral argument.

The prophylaxis argument is based on the view that patients must be self-determining in order to protect themselves from professionals who abuse their authority. While professionals do indeed possess power they will not all seek to abuse their position and patients are not completely powerless and unsupported.[72] The very idea that patients are autonomous suggests they ought to be capable of dealing effectively with professionals. However, this implies an all-or-nothing approach to autonomy while, as a capacity, it is a variable ability that may be modulated by the more powerful partner in a relationship. Although the professional is in a position to exploit the patient, this risk may be managed without needing to mandate autonomy. The organisation of the institution of healthcare, or – more locally – the hospital or surgery, may include checks and balances to minimise the risk of abuse. These arrangements can be supported by legal rules and by regulation that is sensitive to the possibility. The idea of requiring the patient to be self-determining as a way of constraining professional power implies such a lack of trust that the professional–patient relationship would be jeopardised by this approach. Rather than requiring autonomy the rules of consent should seek to facilitate and encourage it.

The therapeutic argument is based on the idea that it is clinically beneficial for the patient to be self-determining. Schneider criticised the view that greater control maximises health outcomes because of the problems patients have in assimilating information and using it rationally.[73] Contrary to this view, there is evidence to suggest that, if given appropriate information and decisional support, reasonably rational decision-making is possible.[74] Furthermore, there is also empirical

---

[71] Schneider, *The Practice of Autonomy*, pp. 137–79.

[72] *Ibid.*, pp. 139–42; J. Nessa, 'Autonomy and Dialogue: About the patient–doctor relationship', in D. C. Thomasma, D. N. Weisstub and C. Herve (eds.), *Personhood and Health Care* (Dordrecht: Kluwer Academic Publishers, 2001), pp. 355, 360.

[73] Schneider, *The Practice of Autonomy*, pp. 143–51.

[74] L. A. Hembroff, M. Holmes-Rovner and C. E. Wills, 'Treatment decision-making and the form of risk communication: Results of a factorial survey' (2004) 4 *BMC Medical Informatics and Decision Making* 20; Valimaki *et al.*, 'Self-determination in surgical patients in five European countries', 309.

evidence demonstrating the beneficial effect of informing the patient and involving them in their care.[75] On the other hand, it is also true that too much information – especially in an unsupportive environment or in situations where the patient does not have the time to process it – may be as detrimental as too little information. However, given the different psychology of patients, even if information and control may be beneficial for some it will not be for all. Again, it may be better to encourage the patient to be autonomous rather than require it.

The 'false consciousness' arguments hold that patients who are reluctant to make their own treatment decisions would lose their reticence if they could be 'freed from some enslaving delusion':[76] if they had not been conditioned into this way of thinking they would want to be autonomous. However, as Schneider noted, some of the reasons patients have for ceding the decision are 'deep-seated', and may be difficult to shift without adopting coercive strategies that may cause more distress and harm than good. Some patients may be so profoundly conditioned that, in the limited time available in the healthcare setting, it may be impossible to ensure that a decision is autonomous. And, what can be done with the obstinate patient who steadfastly refuses to autonomously engage with the decision? Furthermore, it is paradoxical to suggest that someone should be coerced or forced to be autonomous. This problem is best tackled in the wider community by encouraging autonomy through education. In the healthcare context, patients might be encouraged to be autonomous and supported in their efforts but mandating autonomy is likely to be neither effective nor just.

The moral argument is that the essential connection between autonomy and identity creates a non-delegable duty to be self-determining. Thus, all significant decisions, including medical ones, should be made autonomously. However, as I argue below, it is possible to act autonomously but still cede certain decisions to those who, by virtue of their authority or expertise, are better placed to make a wise decision. This autonomously chosen dependence may be a necessary response to debilitating sickness and it may allow individuals to avoid decisions that would permanently damage their future autonomy. Furthermore, provided the decision to delegate is procedurally autonomous, moral responsibility is not transferred with the decision and individuals remain instrumental in constructing their identity. Finally, given the nature of

[75] See e.g. Valimaki, *et al.*, 'Self-determination in surgical patients in five European countries'; Williams, Rodin, Ryan, Grolnick and Deci, 'Autonomous regulation and long-term medication adherence in adult outpatients'.
[76] Schneider, *The Practice of Autonomy*, p. 151.

our social existence and our relational interdependence, it is unlikely that we can completely avoid some form of dependency. The question then becomes on *whom* should we depend and not *whether* we should depend on anyone at all. Besides which, avoiding dependence on the healthcare professional may unduly burden friends and relatives.

A final argument that can be added to Schneider's list might be termed the 'logical' argument: mandatory autonomy requires patients to make their own decisions, which means they must listen to the rationally necessary information. Under the most extreme view, this must be communicated without recommendation or attempt to direct the patient, such as the non-directive counselling practised by some clinical geneticists.

I suggested, in Chapter 1, that there is a distinction between the right to waive information and the right to waive consent and that it might be rational, and hence reasonable, for patients to trust their healthcare professional – as an expert – to make medical decisions for them. This means that there is no need for those patients to be provided with the background information required to make that decision. However, they cannot, in effect, waive their right to consent; because consent itself is a waiver, in order to waive their right to consent they must consent to not consenting. Because this is a recursive argument, the nature of consent means that it is inalienable, but only in the sense that the patient must make a decision – even if that decision is simply to allow someone else to make the actual treatment decision. Thus, an attempt to avoid any decision at all is impossible and that very limited aspect of autonomy is an obligation. However, it is a minimal obligation and does not require any medical information. It is enough that patients are aware that while they are not obliged to make the treatment decision they must make the decision not to decide, which carries the same legal and ethical responsibility as if they had made the treatment decision.

The distinction between the two decisions reflects that between procedural and substantive dependence. For individuals to be autonomous, it is only necessary that they are procedurally independent. On this view, if the reasons for being substantively dependent are one's own then an individual may autonomously choose to be dependent.[77] A classic example of this is when Odysseus asks his sailors to tie him to the ship's mast in order to avoid succumbing to the sirens' song and making the (non-autonomous) decision to sail towards them.[78] In the same way,

---

[77] L. Haworth, *Autonomy: An essay in philosophical psychology and ethics* (New Haven: Yale University Press, 1986), p. 20.
[78] Dworkin, *The Theory and Practice of Autonomy*, pp. 14–15.

patients may recognise their decision-making limitations and allow the professional to make the treatment decision for them. By ensuring that patients understand the ethico-legal implications of their decision, the professional ensures that they have sufficient knowledge to make an autonomous waiver and thus the idea of mandatory autonomy is severely constrained: patients are allowed to cede the treatment decision and professionals are permitted to recommend a treatment choice, directively advise patients or try to persuade them to adopt the professional's preferred choice.

Although the focus is usually on the professional's duties, I have argued that patients also have obligations to the professional. These obligations are justified on the basis of the patient's autonomy, the mutuality of the professional–patient relationship and the need to support the professional's trust. In the present context, perhaps the most relevant of these duties are the duty to communicate openly, the duty to actively participate in the relationship, the duty to take seriously the professional's advice and the duty to make responsible decisions. These serve to facilitate autonomous decision-making and, if patients expect healthcare professionals to respect and foster their autonomy, then it follows that they *ought* to act in a way that allows healthcare professionals to fulfil their obligation. In moral terms these duties seem reasonable to expect of patients, especially as they themselves will usually benefit by fulfilling them. However, there is no obligation on the patient to actually make all self-regarding decisions themselves and it is reasonable to rely on the professional's advice. All that autonomy requires of patients is that they decide whether to cede the treatment decision-making, share it or retain it.

The virtuous patient

In the subsequent section I will argue that the professionals should be encouraged to be virtuous. There is no reason why the same should not also apply to patients. Again this comes down to what the patient is hoping to gain by consulting a healthcare professional and the recognition that the patient is seeking the help of another autonomous agent. Since virtues such as wisdom, judgement and autonomy increase the likelihood of acting autonomously then these virtues would improve the patient's ability to make rational decisions. Other-regarding virtues such as charity, justice, beneficence and moral responsibility favour a more relational or socially sensitive autonomy. This last virtue includes such traits as honesty, a willingness to actively engage in self-regarding decisions and a disposition to consider the impact of one's decisions on others.[79]

While the law is not well placed to affect these character traits it may facilitate the expression of virtuous dispositions and hinder the expression of vices. One approach would be to construct an ideal 'virtuous patient' and then design the regulation of consent in a way that would encourage or require real patients to act similarly. By attending to the patient's character in this way, the principles and rules of law (and morality) could be supplemented. Such a law would need to be drafted carefully as it would be easy to forget that the model is an ideal and requiring too much of real patients may significantly constrain their liberty. If, however, it is autonomy rather than bare liberty that is intrinsically valuable, this concern need not be prohibitive. Because of the unbridgeable gap between the real and ideal patient the law should focus on facilitating – rather than requiring – expression of the relevant virtues. Similarly, it may be better to discourage rather than wholly prohibit expression of the vices. Nevertheless, the law may justifiably prohibit particular instances that express a vice.

The virtue of professionalism and the professional virtues

The ability of healthcare professionals to deliver care crucially depends on the social institutions that support them and protect their monopoly. In other words, professional autonomy is mandated by the society that supports it.[80] This means that professional autonomy is a privilege carrying with it certain obligations that require professionals to behave in concordance with the privilege. Thus, it is just for society to expect the profession to encourage its members to develop what might be called the virtue of professionalism. Furthermore, there is something more distinctly human, and hence more appealing, about someone who is disposed to act well as a matter of character rather than someone who simply follows rules.[81]

The virtue of professionalism requires the professional to be inclined to develop the ideal characteristics of the virtuous professional. These dispositions may be derived from the professional's duties of care as

---

[79] Gauthier, 'The virtue of moral responsibility in healthcare decisionmaking', 278.

[80] C. MacDonald, 'Clinical standards and the structure of professional obligation', (1999) 8 *Professional Ethics* 7.

[81] J. Griffin, 'Virtue ethics and environs', in Paul, Miller and Paul (eds.), *Virtue and Vice*, pp. 56, 58.

determined by healthcare's goal of supporting, caring for and curing the sick,[82] and from the recognition that the patient is a vulnerable moral agent. This latter concern means that medicine must be about more than just the technical mastery of pathology but must also be concerned with the patient as both a person and a moral agent. Furthermore, the inevitable necessity for the patient to trust the professional adds weight to the need for the professional to be disposed to act in a way that fulfils the spirit of the professional's obligations. The virtuous professional is more likely to act in a way that preserves rather than destroys the patient's trust, both in the individual professional and the institution of healthcare as a whole.

These two fundamental concerns, for patients' health and their moral agency, justify three broad duties. These are that healthcare professionals should act so as to benefit their patients' health; that they should respect their patients' agency, which means respecting their autonomy; and that they should do so justly, without unfairly favouring one patient over another.[83]

The first duty points to the virtues of caring, compassion, conscientiousness and benevolence. As a virtue, caring for someone is to be concerned with that person's physical and mental well-being but also with that person's goals, values and aspirations. To care for someone requires the carer to want the person to achieve his or her goals. This concern can only be fully realised by supporting or restoring that person's autonomy. Thus, the virtue of caring disposes the professional to pay due heed to the patient's autonomy as well as the patient's health. There is, of course, the danger that care may become oppressive and controlling where the person is dominated by his or her carer.[84] However, while this risk should be taken seriously and guarded against, it should be noted that a similar danger threatens many other virtues unless moderated by prudence.

Compassion requires professionals to identify with the patient's suffering and through that empathy to assist the patient in making the right decisions.[85] In this way the patient is able to get the most out of what medicine has to offer. However, compassion and empathy require the healthcare professional to approach the decision from the patient's perspective with the right decision being one that is good for the patient on the patient's own terms. In other words, compassion, like caring, is

---

[82] Pellegrino and Thomasma, *The Virtues in Medical Practice*, pp. 52–3.

[83] Doyal, 'The moral foundation of the clinical duties of care', 530.

[84] J. Kultgen, *Autonomy and Intervention: Parentalism in the caring life* (New York: Oxford University Press, 1995), p. 8.

[85] Pellegrino and Thomasma, *The Virtues in Medical Practice*, p. 81.

also ultimately concerned with the patient's autonomous goals and values. These two virtues are further supported in their concerns by the virtue of benevolence, which should predispose professionals to place importance on and strive to address the patient's needs and goals.

The second duty requires virtuous professionals to be open, honest, empathetic and to have integrity. Integrity as a virtue refers to the idea of 'moral wholeness' or the willingness and sensitivity necessary to respect others as moral agents.[86] It disposes virtuous persons to act in a morally sensitive and consistent way. Temperance and humility may also have a role to play in countering any tendency in professionals to over-confidence in their competence and knowledge and their ability to know what is best for their patients.[87] Tolerance may also be a relevant virtue since the tolerant person will be predisposed to negotiate rather than ride roughshod over people whose values appear to conflict with their own. This is clearly relevant if the professional–patient relationship is to be cooperative and caring. However, there is a danger with tolerance in that it implies the other's views must be put up with and this further implies that those views are less worthy than the views of the person tolerating them. While tolerance is preferable to intolerance, it may be better to aim for the less judgemental virtue of acceptance, which would be a disposition to treat another person's beliefs and goals as prima facie equally worthy of respect as one's own.

The third duty can only be fulfilled if healthcare professionals have the virtues of justice and prudence (or practical wisdom).[88] Justice is concerned with ensuring all persons are given their due, including due respect, and is engaged in knowing how to act fairly when patient autonomy threatens harm to other parties. The virtue of justice also concerns the disposition to treat each patient equitably and, given that healthcare is essentially beneficent, this should be determined by reference to need and capacity to benefit. Furthermore, given the beneficent goals of medicine, and the altruism inherent in any profession, the virtue of justice, along with the virtue of benevolence, would also dispose professionals to act in their patient's interest rather than in self-interest.[89] Prudence is essential because it disposes virtuous professionals to grasp the goal of any interaction and to make appropriate use of reason to guide their actions towards that end. In doing this, prudence moderates the expression of the person's other virtues. Thus, prudence would dispose

[86] *Ibid.*, p. 132.   [87] *Ibid.*, pp. 118–24.
[88] D. Putman, 'Virtue and the practice of modern medicine' (1988) 13 *Journal of Medicine and Philosophy* 433, 440.
[89] Pellegrino and Thomasma, *The Virtues in Medical Practice*, pp. 105, 144.

caring professionals to avoid the danger of oppression and would pre-dispose tolerant or accepting professionals to restrict their tolerance or acceptance to non-harmful goals and values. For example, the tolerant but prudent professional still acts virtuously by being intolerant of the practice of female circumcision.

In addition to these three duties, because trust is crucial to the professional–patient relationship and to the effective delivery of health-care, professionals have an obligation to be trustworthy. The corres-ponding virtue of trustworthiness requires healthcare professionals to try to understand the patient as a person, to avoid manipulation and deception, and to be sensitive to the patient's vulnerabilities. It both supports and provides a backdrop for the professional's substantive obligations and other virtues. In this it is supported by the virtue of fortitude,[90] which counters any temptation to take the path of least resistance in the face of a moral challenge and so encourages consistency and reliability, both of which are important to trust.

External factors

Although the professional–patient relationship provides the contextual setting for the regulation of consent, the relationship cannot be con-sidered in isolation from the external factors that affect it. These include the interaction between the patient and important others, the relevance of a team approach to healthcare, the organisation and behaviour of the institution, the politics of healthcare and the regulation of consent. Other important constraints are the impact of social conditioning and education, the effects of which may explain why older patients and those from a lower social class are more likely to prefer their interactions to be directed by the healthcare professional.[91] Since the book as a whole deals with regulating consent my focus here is on the other factors.

It is important for the law to take into account the relevance of third parties to the relationship. Patients may be empowered by the support of relevant others who can help them understand the information, facilitate decision-making and provide emotional support. However, just as third parties can be supportive they can also undermine the patient's auton-omy by placing unfair emotional pressure on the patient or trying to manipulate the patient's decision to suit their own ends.

[90] *Ibid.*, p. 114.
[91] McKinstry, 'Do patients wish to be involved in decision making in the consulta-tion?', 868.

The healthcare institution may influence patient autonomy in two ways. The first is its attitude towards patient autonomy and consent. If little value is given to consent then that approach will filter down and it may become a low priority for the healthcare professionals working directly with the patient. While this may have been the usual attitude twenty or thirty years ago, the increasing burden of litigation and the recent high-profile incidents, such as the Shipman case, and the Bristol heart surgery and organ retention scandals, have perhaps made healthcare providers place more value on consent. However, this value has become defensive as evidenced by the rise of risk management, which makes the avoidance of litigation a prominent – if not the primary – value of consent.[92] Recent guidance from, amongst others, the Association of Anaesthetists and the Department of Health reflects this defensive approach to consent by focusing primarily on the minimal requirements of the law and the legal and professional consequences of failing to gain an adequate consent.[93] While this bias is understandable it encourages an undesirable adversarial tone and, unless it is taken into account, will cause the implemented model of consent to become misshapen.

The second way in which the healthcare provider may influence patient autonomy is in the actual delivery of care. This includes a restriction of choices available to the patient and the practical organisation of healthcare delivery. Consider, for example, the provision of day surgery. Unless anaesthetists are given sufficient opportunity to see patients before the operation they may be unable to adequately counsel them, make them aware of the available choices and obtain an adequate consent. While this could be amalgamated with the consent for the surgical procedure, the surgeon is unlikely to be able to properly discuss the options available, which may be restricted either because of the patient's health or the experience of the anaesthetist. In the absence of a pre-admission clinic, the anaesthetist's only contact with the patient may be on the day of the operation. This may only allow a hurried chat in the anaesthetic room while the operating department practitioner is applying the monitoring equipment, which is hardly conducive to an autonomous decision. While it would be both impractical and presumptuous for the law to dictate such practical arrangements, it might,

---

[92] S. M. White, 'Consent for anaesthesia' (2003) 30 *Journal of Medical Ethics* 286, 289; E. Peters and M. Challis, 'Most doctors see consent from functionalist perspective' (1999) 318 *British Medical Journal* 735.

[93] The Association of Anaesthetists, *Consent for Anaesthesia* (2006), available at: www.aagbi.org/publications/guidelines/docs/consent06.pdf. Department of Health, *Reference Guide to Consent for Examination or Treatment* (2001), available at: www.dh.gov.uk.

through the use of a code of practice and a regulatory/advisory body, encourage the development of systems that are more sensitive to and facilitative of patient autonomy and consent.

This example also highlights the relevance of a team approach to healthcare, which adds a level of complexity to the preceding discussion for two reasons. First, it may mean that many of the relationships are short-lived, which perhaps makes a relationship of trust more difficult to establish unless the trust predates the relationship. Second, if different professionals, each of whom is independently responsible, carry out different elements of the patient's care then this raises questions about their responsibilities for seeking the patient's consent.

Individual healthcare professionals may not be sufficiently conversant with the different interventions to inform and advise the patient. For example, should surgeons with little formal training in anaesthetics counsel the patient about the pros and cons of different options, assuming that they are even aware that those options exist? But, if anaesthetists are to take that responsibility then there needs to be appropriate practical arrangements that allow patients sufficient time to reflect on the available choices. Furthermore, consideration needs to be given to whether these elements of care require separate consents or are subsumed by a more general consent to the care plan as a whole.[94]

Patients may see their care holistically and raise questions about an aspect of care that the professional currently counselling them will not be providing. By answering the question healthcare professionals may step on a colleague's toes and may not give the same answer that their colleague would have given. This could cause misunderstanding and confusion. Furthermore, it is important for patients to know who is responsible for each aspect of their care so that they know who to approach for advice and who to contact if there is a problem. Essentially, all of these issues create problems of coordination and communication, which means that it is not enough for the individual professional to behave well. It is equally important to ensure that an appropriate system is in place and that someone is responsible for that system.[95]

Finally, it is important to recognise the necessary relationship between politics and consent.[96] For example, if healthcare is provided within a true market system, patients may be treated as consumers and their legal

---

[94] See A. R. Maclean 'Consent, sectionalisation and the concept of a medical procedure' (2002) 28 *Journal of Medical Ethics* 249.

[95] C. Black and A. Craft, 'The competent doctor: A paper for discussion' (2004) 4 *Clinical Medicine* 527, 530.

[96] A. R. Maclean, 'Consent and sensibility' (2005) 4 *International Journal of Ethics* 31.

protection based on the libertarian or liberal conception of autonomy with greater demands for independent patient choice and decision-making. In such a system, responsibility for outcome might be more tightly linked to consent but the principle of *caveat emptor* may be more relevant, tilting the balance from the professional's duty to disclose to the patient's responsibility to ask questions. Furthermore, the emphasis would more likely focus on rights rather than obligations and this may increase the possibility of litigation and introduce an adversarial element into what perhaps ought to be a cooperative encounter. Exacerbating this, a market approach will encourage a commodification of healthcare with practice driven by financial concerns rather than the community's health needs. In the market environment there is a risk that a 'factory model of care' will pay more attention to a high throughput of patients than to the psychosocial or ethical interests.

On the other hand, if the healthcare system is provided by the state and based on a social ethic then autonomy may be seen in a more relational sense, with the focus on obligations rather than rights. Responsibility for outcome may be more readily divorced from the patient's consent. Taking this to a more communitarian extreme, utility becomes more important, the issue of individual consent becomes less relevant and responsibility for outcome is borne by the community as a whole rather than any single patient. It is, of course, possible for the state to pragmatically adopt a mixed approach rather than commit to a purer political vision. However, this can still only be achieved if it is clear what is wanted from the healthcare system. For example, is it more important to maximise patient throughput or should the emphasis be on how those patients are treated as persons? Is choice more important than quality or equity? How much money are we willing to spend on health and do external financial constraints justify withholding treatment that the patient wants? What the community wants from its healthcare system – and what it is prepared to pay for – inevitably affects the approach to consent as much as it affects the provision of any of the more tangible resources.

Conclusion

In this chapter I examined the professional–patient relationship as a context for regulating consent. I argued that a good relationship requires mutual trust and mutual respect. Both parties come to the relationship as autonomous persons. However, the professionals' autonomy is constrained by the ethics of their profession. Perhaps the most important consequence of the relationship is that it generates obligations for both parties. While healthcare professionals should respect and support their patients' autonomy, they should not abandon them to unwise and harmful decisions. Although they do not have the authority to override a competent patient's decision, healthcare professionals have a duty to use rational persuasion to guide the patient towards a mutually acceptable outcome. In order to facilitate this process, patients should also be open and honest with their healthcare professionals, be prepared to explain their decisions and be willing to listen to their healthcare professionals' advice. The mutual trust and respect needed for this process means that both healthcare professionals and their patients should behave in a trustworthy way. However, because of the difficulties of encapsulating these obligations in rules, attention must be directed to the healthcare professional's character. In order to apply the rules of consent in practice, healthcare professionals should be encouraged to develop the virtue of professionalism. The institution of healthcare must be organised to facilitate the practice of these obligations. However, as a final caveat, it is acknowledged that the conception of consent and its implementation are ultimately political and depend on what the community wants from its healthcare system and how much it is prepared to pay.

4 The concept of consent: what it is and what it isn't

In the first three chapters I discussed the ethical basis and practical context of consent to medical treatment. I argued that the primary justification for consent is the patient's agency expressed through his or her autonomy but that the context of the professional–patient relationship constrains the implications of that autonomy. On entering the relationship both the professional and the patient acquire certain obligations towards the other party that shape how the patient's autonomy is given effect. In this chapter I will explore the concept of consent itself bearing in mind the arguments and conclusions of the earlier chapters.

For my purposes there are four reasons why it is essential to explore the concept in some depth. First, without an insight into consent any attempt to determine the regulation of consent will be flawed. Second, arguments advanced about consent may in fact be about a primary underlying claim right rather than about consent per se. This type of argument will remain hidden and inadequately dealt with unless it is exposed and to do this requires recognition of both the meaning and extent of consent. Third, an understanding of consent and its requirements is necessary to predict the interaction between consent and the provision of healthcare. Fourth, elucidation of consent will then allow a critique of the current law.

In the discussion that follows I approach consent from first principles to construct a model that reflects the roles of both parties to the healthcare professional–patient relationship. In developing this model of relational consent I will examine the various claims that have been made about consent in order to determine both its core meaning and its context-specific attributes. While this may seem overly formal it is necessary because of the way the concept has been used and abused in both theory and practice.

A preliminary definition

It seems reasonable to start this analysis with a standard definition of consent. The Oxford English Dictionary lists consent as both a verb and a noun. As a verb, it has two senses. The first sense is 'to agree together . . . to come to agreement upon a matter or as to a course of action'. The second sense is 'to agree to a proposal, request etc . . . voluntarily to accede to or acquiesce in what another proposes or desires'. Etymologically the word derives from the Latin conjunction of *con*, meaning 'together' with *sentire*, meaning 'to feel, think or judge'. Thus, it is the first sense of the word that is closest to the original meaning of the term. As a noun, the only current use is 'voluntary agreement to or acquiescence in what another proposes or desires; compliance, concurrence, permission', which is closest in meaning to the second sense of the verb consent.

It is interesting that the earliest use of the word refers to shared decision-making while the later use refers to a proposal and voluntary acceptance of that proposal. In its role as a check on physician autonomy this etymological development is reversed. Thus, the traditional use of the word is to refer to the patient voluntarily agreeing to undergo the treatment proposed by the doctor. With the early attacks on paternalism this meaning of consent was championed as a shield for patient rights. When this shield was swapped for a sword and the requirements of individual autonomy taken to an extreme, some commentators felt that both doctors and patients suffered, which led to a move away from perceiving consent as two parties negotiating a 'contract' at arm's length. Instead, these writers championed the cause of shared decision-making and called for a partnership or 'therapeutic alliance'.[1]

In the previous chapters I argued that the patient's autonomy grounds the right to give or withhold consent but that this right must be framed by the mutual obligations arising from the professional–patient relationship. A reasonable conception of consent ought to take both of these factors into account. Thus, both senses of consent are relevant; while the patient must give or withhold consent this decision is not free-floating but is made as part of an ongoing relationship.

In both senses of the word it initially appears that an agreement lies at the very heart of the concept of consent. However, while it can be used to refer to an agreement it has been argued that this sense of consent is irrelevant in the healthcare context. Gillon, for example, states that:

consent means a voluntary, uncoerced decision, made by a sufficiently competent or autonomous person on the basis of adequate information and

---

[1] H. Teff, 'Consent to medical procedures: Paternalism, self-determination or therapeutic alliance' (1985) 101 *The Law Quarterly Review* 432.

deliberation, to accept rather than reject some proposed course of action that will affect him or her.[2]

Other writers, however, preferred to see consent as a '*shared process* of decision making'.[3] This partnership approach was seen as important because it recognises both the patient's autonomy and the healthcare professional's role as healer. Even in the context of consent to research, writers have cautioned against the danger of consent being seen as an adversarial procedure.[4] This provides me with a starting point for analysis and, at this stage, I will define consent as either a 'mutually arrived at agreement to an intervention' *or* as 'an agreement, by the patient, to undergo an intervention offered by the healthcare professional'.

There is a problem with both of these primitive definitions since agreements are necessarily joint decisions that engender a joint commitment to the agreed proposals. This joint commitment generates a mutual obligation that requires both parties to honour the agreement, which means that neither party may withdraw unilaterally.[5] This creates a difficulty for consent to healthcare interventions since it is widely accepted that persons giving consent to a breach of bodily integrity may withdraw their consent and with it the permission that justifies action. If consent is to be characterised as an agreement then this makes it unacceptable for patients to unilaterally withdraw their consent.

In one sense, consent operates to create mutual obligations and properly constitutes an agreement. This is the situation when contracts are created, and is also the sense of consent when the healthcare professional agrees to provide treatment. In the current context, however, because our bodies are so fundamentally important to our self-identity and autonomy, it seems inequitable to hold patients to their consent. This means that consent to medical treatment is either not an agreement or it is a particular kind of agreement that does not impose a binding obligation on the consenter. The difficulty with this latter position is that it threatens to undermine fatally the social and normative meaning of agreement, which suggests that perhaps it is better to conceptualise consent in this context as something other than, or in addition to, an agreement.

As noted earlier, consent has two senses and both seem relevant to an exercise of the patient's autonomy within the context of the

---

[2] Gillon, *Philosophical Medical Ethics*, p. 113.
[3] A. Meisel and M. Kuczewiski, 'Legal and ethical myths about informed consent' (1996) 156 *Archives of Internal Medicine* 2521, 2522.
[4] R. Horton, 'The context of consent' (1994) 344 *Lancet* 211, 212.
[5] M. Gilbert, 'Agreements, coercion, and obligation' (1993) 103 *Ethics* 679, 691–3.

professional–patient relationship. The mutuality of the relationship suggests the relevance of both parties' involvement and agreement, while respect for the patient's autonomy is reflected through the control allowed by consent as permission. Thus, it may be appropriate to acknowledge that patient decision-making involves both consent as an agreement (consent$_A$) and consent as permission (consent$_P$). The agreements between professionals and their patients arise at an earlier stage of the encounters and are precursors to consent$_P$. While consent$_A$ creates obligations, consent$_P$ acts by waiving the obligation of non-interference with the patient's body.

One potential problem with 'permission' is its connection with 'permit'. Where someone permits an act this may imply an active grant of a power to act that, like consent$_P$, removes the moral and legal prohibition on acting, assuming the person giving permission has the right to do so. Alternatively, permit may mean a passive submission or failure to resist. Although submission may follow – and, in certain circumstances, imply – consent$_P$ there are other reasons for failing to resist including violence, force and coercion. Such a submission would not affect the moral or legal status of the act and would not, therefore, amount to consent$_P$.[6] As Coleridge J stated: 'Every consent to an act involves a submission; but it by no means follows that a mere submission involves consent.'[7] Thus, a distinction must be made between passively 'permitting something' and actively 'giving permission'.

The centrality of permission to consent means that the two primitive definitions that I used as a starting point must be revised. Rather than focusing on agreement, consent to a healthcare intervention may be defined as either 'a simple permission granted by the patient' *or* as 'a permission granted by the patient consequent on a mutually arrived at agreement'. Because of the moral and legal effect of the permission, an attribute may now also be included to reflect that consent 'removes the healthcare professional's obligation of non-interference'.

The nature and function of consent to medical treatment

There are three broad views of the nature of consent. First, it may be seen solely as a mental state. This view of consent focuses exclusively on the agency and autonomy of the person granting consent. It consists solely of the person intentionally adopting the appropriate attitude towards the proposal. Once this 'propositional attitude' has been adopted

---

[6] See e.g. *St George's Healthcare NHS Trust* v. *S* [1998] 3 WLR 936, 949.
[7] *R* v. *Day* (1841) 173 ER 1026.

the proposed intervention is permitted and the actor will be justified in performing it.[8] A second approach to consent characterises it as an intentional act.[9] On this view the focus shifts from the person giving consent (agent) to the person performing the intervention (actor). The issue is not whether the agent granted permission but whether the actor had sufficient reason to believe that the agent consented to the act. In its pure form the mental state of the person granting consent is unimportant and the justification that flows from consent arises from the existence of certain social conventions of communication that allow consent to be deemed. Others, often for pragmatic reasons, have suggested that consent is both a state of mind and a signifying act.[10]

The characterisation of consent as a mental state or as an intentional act represents different ends of a spectrum of political approaches to the nature of society. Consent as a state of mind depends on the libertarian caricature of the agent as a wholly independent, self-reliant decision-maker. The communication of consent is unimportant to the question of justification because relationships are irrelevant to the person's agency. At the other end of the spectrum lies the equally extreme communitarian view, which subjugates the importance of independent agency. In this view the person's state of mind is irrelevant. All that matters is whether the two parties interacted in such a way that the intervention can be seen as justified or excused. Consent is not morally important but is simply a device for resolving conflict within a relationship.

My approach to autonomy and the balance between the individual's independence and his or her relational dependence supports a view that lies in between these two extremes. In other words consent should be seen as a combination where both communication and the agent's mental state are important. This combined approach is supported by an examination of the work expected of consent.

Consent works in two ways. It either legitimates an otherwise forbidden act or it creates new obligations. As a creator of obligations, consent is crucial to an agreement (or contract). Consent's other role is to provide a rights-bearer with control of that right, which it does by allowing the transformation of an illegitimate act into a permitted one.[11]

---

[8] H. M. Hurd, 'The moral magic of consent' (1996) 2 *Legal Theory* 121; L. Alexander, 'The moral magic of consent (II)' (1996) 2 *Legal Theory* 165; O'Neill, *Autonomy and Trust*, p. 43.

[9] A. Wertheimer, 'Consent and sexual relations' (1996) 2 *Legal Theory* 89, 94.

[10] H. H. Malm, 'The ontological status of consent and its implications for the law on rape' (1996) 2 *Legal Theory* 147; E. Sherwin, 'Infelicitous sex' (1996) 2 *Legal Theory* 209, 209, 217.

[11] Alexander, 'The moral magic of consent (II)'.

THEORETICAL, ADD TO INTRODUCTIO
IF TIME

Hurd's view of consent, however, goes beyond its role of legitimisation and this is reflected in her claim that 'when we give consent, we create rights for others'.[12] While this may be true for consent$_A$, it is over-inclusive. For consent$_P$, it is perhaps more accurate to view consent as generating permissions rather than rights per se.[13] Although some of those permissions may also grant rights this will not be universally so. For example, consider the consent$_P$ given to a surgeon to perform an operation. This does not give the surgeon a right to operate since the patient still retains sufficient control of his or her right to bodily integrity to withdraw permission. In this context consent$_P$ operates as a form of waiver rather than as a transfer of a right.

In her discussion of consent$_P$ in the context of rape law, Hurd suggested that it alters the morality of another's actions in two ways. First, she posited that 'consent can function to transform the morality of another's conduct – to make an action right when it would otherwise be wrong'. Second, she claimed that 'consent can generate a permission that allows another to do a wrong act . . . [This] does not morally transform a wrong act into a right act, but it grants another a right to do a wrong.'[14] Both claims are problematic.

Hurd's first suggestion is flawed because she assumes that since doing a non-permitted act would be wrong it must be right to perform a permitted act. This is wrong because it places the whole normative judgement at consent's door and ascribes consent too much power. Consent simply prevents an act being a wrong against the consenter. This does not affect the rightness or wrongness of the act more generally. Thus, if it is wrong to kill for reasons other than simply infringing bodily integrity, the 'victim's' consent does not alter the wrongness of the act. For a couple not wanting children, consent to unprotected sex does not make it 'right'. It arguably remains morally wrong for being an irresponsible act.

If the act is not inherently wrong but is only forbidden because it affects something over which I have the right of control, then consent makes the act morally permissible. Even here, however, consent is unable to alter the inherent value of an act. Giving consent does not make an inherently bad act – nor even a morally neutral act – good. It simply provides permission for the act. This means that for consent to have any effect the act must be one that society already sees as essentially

---

[12] Hurd, 'The moral magic of consent'.
[13] T. McConnell, *Inalienable Rights: The limits of consent in medicine and the law* (New York: Oxford University Press, 2000), p. 8.
[14] Hurd, 'The moral magic of consent', 123.

a good thing, or at least something that is acceptable. Medical treatment, for example, is seen as a societal good. However, because it also involves intentionally infringing individual bodily integrity, consent is a necessary justification. Female circumcision, on the other hand, is seen as essentially wrong and the woman's consent is insufficient to justify the act. The same is true in relation to the legal function of consent.

Hurd's second mechanism is similarly flawed. As an example, Hurd utilised the 'wrong' of abortion as a form of contraception.[15] While the woman's consent permits the doctor to perform an abortion it is only by virtue of the fact the woman herself is permitted to act 'wrongly' that she may give another permission to assist her in that act. However, where the consenter has no right to do something then his or her consent is ineffective in granting the actor permission. For example, if my car has no road tax my consent cannot give you permission to drive it on a public road. Furthermore, even when persons are permitted to do a particular act, it is not always the case that they can transfer that permission to another. I may be permitted to cut off my own leg. However, without external justification (such as the leg is gangrenous and you are a surgeon) I cannot give you a legally effective permission to perform the amputation.

Hurd's explanation of how consent works is too broad because it ignores the fact that consent is insufficient as a normative tool to justify all acts. Some acts are justified irrespective of the person's consent, such as quarantining people with infectious diseases that are a public health hazard, 'sectioning' and treating the dangerously mentally ill, and incarcerating convicted criminals. Other acts – such as routine therapeutic medical procedures on competent adults – will be justified only if consensual. Finally, there are acts that consent cannot justify. From a legal perspective, these include consent to be killed or maimed.

While this third group may be larger from a legal rather than a moral perspective, it is also arguable that there are morally wrong acts that cannot be justified or excused by the 'victim's' consent. Consider someone who consents to be killed. If that person is healthy, with obligations towards a partner and young children, then it is wrong for that person to kill him or herself. Even if that person consents to being killed by another, it would be wrong of that other to kill him or her. While consent may give actors permission it cannot relieve them of their duty to make – and take responsibility for – an independent moral judgement. A valid consent does mean that the consenters have no right to complain if they are harmed by the act: consent affects the wrongness

---

[15] Hurd, 'The moral magic of consent', 123–4.

of an act within the context of the relationship between actor and consenter. It does not, however, affect the wrongness of an act if that wrongness is external to the relationship.

It is apparent then, that consent acts to transform the status of an act between the actor and the consenter. It removes the consenter's right to complain about the act. For some acts consent provides the necessary justification and where those acts are beneficial in nature consent transforms the act into a morally good one. Consent, however, is neither necessary nor sufficient to make an act good. Where a person is unable to consent the act is still justified if it is in the person's 'best interests'. Where an act is wrong then consent is unable to make it right or even justify the act. Where the act is seen as a serious wrong, such as killing a person for whom life is not seen as harmful, then consent is wholly ineffective and both the act and the actor are condemned. Where an act is seen as a less serious harm the act remains wrong but the person's consent may excuse the actor from moral blame. Thus, while consent may be sufficient to alter the rights and obligations between the actor and the consenter, it is insufficient to make a wrong act right.

Too much may be demanded of consent if it is treated as a primary right, equivalent in nature to the right to life or the right to bodily integrity. To discuss consent in this way is mistaken.[16] Consent is not a right in the same sense as these other rights. It is not something possessed equally by all persons within the rights-holding community. Persons who are incapable of giving or withholding consent still possess the right to bodily integrity but it is not necessary to gain their consent before, for example, subjecting them to an operation. Allowing others to provide proxy consent goes some way to creating the impression that the right may be more similar to the primary right than it actually is. Consent, however, is a derivative or secondary right. In the absence of a right to bodily integrity, consent would not be required to give someone permission to interfere with our bodies. Thus, unlike these other rights, consent is contingent. Furthermore, unlike the other rights it is dependent on the person's ability or their status. In this way, consent is perhaps best seen as an aspect of all other rights that arises because it is inherent to the concept of a right that someone, usually the right-holder, has control over it. This is important because it means that no one can consent to something unless they have a right that may be waived or alienated. In this context, consent reflects the negative aspect of liberty.

---

[16] R. Brownsword, 'The cult of consent: Fixation and fallacy' (2004) 15 *King's College Law Journal* 223, 225.

Apart from operating either to legitimise an action or to create an obligation, consent may also affect responsibility for the outcome of the action. It might be thought that responsibility necessarily travels with consent,[17] but there is no reason why this should be the case. If I give you consent to use my bicycle, there is no prima facie reason why I should be responsible for any damage you might cause to my bicycle. However, it is certainly arguable that, in the absence of an explicit agreement, I should be responsible for the 'wear and tear' that is the natural and foreseeable consequence of use. For consequences that do not necessarily follow from the act consented to it is arguable that the actor should bear responsibility where he is morally or legally culpable. If you damage my bike because you ride at night without lights then you should be responsible for the damage that results. This is because whether or not you act negligently is – at least partly – a consequence of your agency and not a necessary consequence of my own agency in the shape of my consent. The 'wear and tear' damage is different since it is entailed by your exercise of the permission I have granted.

A third type of consequence results from luck.[18] Certain things that happen do so outside of anyone's control or influence and may be put down to good or bad luck. If it happens that you ride over a nail, puncturing one of the tyres on my bicycle, who should be responsible for repairing the damage? Certainly, if you have taken my bike without consent, it would be your responsibility. However, does my consent cause that responsibility to shift to me? The answer to this is that it perhaps depends more on convention and political stance than on any underlying moral argument. Both parties have exercised agency and the damage is nobody's fault. It might seem unfair that either party should be held responsible but, by default, if responsibility is allowed to lie where it falls it will be me, the bicycle owner, who will shoulder the cost of the repair. One option is to argue that it might depend on who benefits most from the act, or alternatively, who would gain from good luck.[19]

Consider a person who consents to a non-therapeutic research intervention. In this case, the person giving consent does not stand to gain from the act in any direct sense.[20] It is both society and the

---

[17] M. Epstein, 'Why effective consent presupposes autonomous authorisation: A counter-orthodox argument' (2006) 32 *Journal of Medical Ethics* 342, 344.

[18] T. Honoré, 'Responsibility and luck' (1988) 104 *Law Quarterly Review* 530.

[19] T. Nagel, 'Moral luck', in *Mortal Questions* (Cambridge: Cambridge University Press, 1979), p. 24; P. Cane, *Responsibility in Law and Morality* (Oxford: Hart Publishing, 2002), p. 76.

[20] Ignoring the speculative psychological benefits accruing from an altruistic act.

researcher who gain. Society gains by the advancement in medical science while the researcher gains prestige and an improvement in his or her potential for career advancement. Under these circumstances, it might be thought unfair to allow research subjects to bear the responsibility for injury caused by bad luck. Instead, they should be compensated either by society or the researchers, since it is those parties that stand to gain most from the research. It is perhaps for this reason that the Declaration of Helsinki states that 'the responsibility for the human subject must always rest with a medically qualified person and never rest on the subject of the research, even though the subject has given consent'.[21] However, where consent is to conventional medical treatment, it is the patient who stands to benefit and thus it is the patient who accepts responsibility for the outcome caused by bad luck.

Although consent is neither necessary nor sufficient to shift responsibility for outcome from the actors, where they require the other party's consent to legitimise their action then consent is necessary to allow that party to be included in the apportionment of responsibility. Once a valid consent is given, responsibility for outcome is determined by principles of justice. This, of course, is not to say that pragmatic arguments could not affect legal responsibility for the outcome. For example, it might be argued that, in order to reduce the economic inefficiencies of the legal system, a no-fault compensation system should be established. Whatever approach is taken to outcome responsibility, it is important to recognise that any harm consequential to the intervention is distinct from the harm to the patient's autonomy caused by an infringement of the right to consent. This separation will become relevant when I consider the way the law has developed to regulate risk disclosure through the tort of negligence.

I now return to the fundamental nature of consent. As noted earlier, there are three competing views of consent: that it is a state of mind, a signifying act or a state of mind evidenced by an appropriate act. It may be thought that since consent is predicated on autonomy, which in turn requires free will, it must at least be a state of mind. Where the actor is not to be held responsible, and the post-act beliefs and evidence of the person accurately reflect his or her state of mind at the time of the act, then that person's state of mind would be sufficient to constitute a valid consent (or refusal). However, where the actor is held responsible for the act unless legitimised by consent, given the problems of hindsight, then some tangible evidence of consent is required. At the very least, this would require some communication from the person to the actor that

---

[21] Principle 15, Declaration of Helsinki 1964 (as amended, Edinburgh 2000).

the person is consenting. It might even be argued that until communication of consent has occurred the act remains illegitimate. An uncommunicated consent, while still consent, may be ineffective as far as
granting the actor permission to act.

It is arguable, particularly from a libertarian view of agency, that
providing the person has formed the relevant state of mind, communication to the actor is irrelevant and the act is morally legitimate.
Whatever the actor believes, the act has been permitted and the act is
therefore not wrong for lack of consent. On the other hand, while the
authority of moral agency is important, if a *respect* for the agency of
others is central to the justification provided by consent then the actor's
state of mind is also important.[22] Without any form of communication
of the person's state of mind, the actor will be unable to form any
rational belief about the existence of consent. The act would then be
performed without believing it was permitted and this would fail to
respect the person irrespective of whether he or she had the requisite
state of mind. As such, the act would be morally wrong.

In Chapter 3 I suggested that consent must be placed in the context of
the professional–patient relationship and that the approach to consent
helps to define that relationship. A good relationship requires mutual
trust and respect, which includes an obligation to respect the other's
autonomy. This mutual respect requires open and honest communication allowing both parties to play their role within the relationship. If
healthcare professionals are to respect their patients' autonomy, they
must believe that the patient is consenting before they act. This belief
can only be reliably achieved by communication of the consent.

Pragmatically, communication of consent is necessary to allow the law
to apportion responsibility for outcome or to hold the actor legally
culpable in the absence of consent. In a very real sense, it is impossible to
avoid the issue since the two parties will draw inferences from both
verbal and non-verbal signals. Irrespective of whether the person has
formed the relevant state of mind, if he or she behaves in such a way as
to cause the actor reasonably to believe that he or she is consenting, it
would be unjust to hold that the act was unlawful.

Given the arguments above, and the fact that it would be impossible
for two persons to interact without some degree of communication, it
seems reasonable to suggest that consent exists but is ineffective in the
absence of communication. This means that communication of consent
is not part of the core theory but is an attribute of consent, albeit one

---

[22] J. McGregor, 'Why when she says no she doesn't mean maybe and doesn't mean yes: A
critical reconstruction of consent, sex, and the law' (1996) 2 *Legal Theory* 175, 191.

that is necessary in the context of this enquiry. Consent as a state of mind, however, seems to be essential to the core theory.

To summarise, the two possible definitions of consent are:

> Consent 1   A state of mind of the patient formed with the intention of permitting an intervention offered by the healthcare professional.

> Consent 2   A state of mind of the patient with the intention of permitting an intervention formed as the result of a mutually arrived at agreement.

These alternative central theories are currently fleshed out by two attributes:

> Attribute A   The communication of the patient's state of mind to the healthcare professional.

> Attribute B   Effect
> Values:
>
> 1. Alters obligations for:
>   a. the healthcare professional by removing the obligation of non-interference;
>   b. both the patient and healthcare professional by negotiation to establish new obligations of cooperation and treatment.
> 2. Justifies intervention through moral/legal transformation.
> 3. Permits apportionment of outcome responsibility.

As discussed earlier, as a derivative right, consent would be meaningless in the absence of the relevant substantive right. If there were no right to bodily integrity then we would be unable to use consent to waive that right. It might be argued, however, that a pre-existing right is unnecessary to the individual's agreement to an intervention, which may be given irrespective of whether he or she has control over the variable affected by the act. But, without the necessary control the agreement would be unable to legitimise the act. The law would have to look elsewhere to determine if the act was permissible. Furthermore, should the actor intervene without the individual's agreement, the law would not treat this any differently from the case where the individual has agreed.

It might then be argued that acting without the individual's consent is in itself a breach of a right and so the existence of an underlying right is unnecessary. This, however, raises the question: consent to what? The answer cannot be to everything since the world would grind to a complete halt if that were the case. It would be a practical impossibility to seek, let alone obtain, everyone's agreement before acting. In order to allow society to function the limits of consent must be defined and as soon as this happens the things over which we have the power of consent become our 'right'. If society allows that you may only legitimately disclose my medical information with my consent then it becomes a 'wrong' for you to disclose it in the absence of consent. *Ipso facto*, I have a 'right' to confidentiality. If consent is to have any moral or legal force, it must be derived from an underlying right. This underlying right is one of the necessary attributes of consent and, in the present context, it is a broadly construed right to bodily integrity that is relevant.[23] Thus, consent must have a third attribute, *Attribute C*: the primary right. For consent$_P$ this primary right is bodily integrity and for consent$_A$, it is self-determination.

Consent as a process

Some commentators have suggested that consent should be seen as a process. Meisel and Kuczewski, for example, argued that a rights-based approach to consent is too restrictive and often inapplicable to the clinical realities. Instead of a model characterising physicians as technical experts advising their patients who then make decisions based on their own beliefs and values, they see consent as a 'shared process of decision-making'.[24] The problem with this is that it conflates consent with the process of enabling patients to give a valid consent to the intervention on offer. If consent is a state of mind then it only serves to confuse matters to argue that it is also a process. Rather, consent should be preceded by a process of information disclosure, expert advice from the physician and negotiation, which means that the idea of a process does not form part of the central theory of consent. However, because negotiation/shared decision-making (see below) recognises the professional–patient relationship and allows patients greater involvement and control without wholly abandoning them to their own devices, it is important to include the process of consent as an attribute with two values: *negotiation* and *patient's decision*. This is modelled in Figure 1.

---

[23] More expansively, it might be argued that the relevant right is privacy.
[24] Meisel and Kuczewiski, 'Legal and ethical myths about informed consent', 2522.

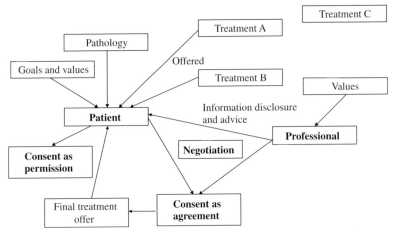

Fig 1 The process leading to consent

The professional, who controls the treatments available, has offered the patient a choice of two treatments (A and B). In other cases, the professional may only offer one treatment to the patient. Whether or not this is legitimate is independent of the patient's right to bodily integrity and hence is independent of consent as permission. Consent$_P$ is a device for controlling negative liberty rights. The exercise of positive liberty rights comes in the form of a demand or request rather than a waiver and may be served to some extent by the requirement of consent$_A$. This re-connects with the first sense of consent to engage both parties in negotiation to determine the final management decision.

At this point of the process patient autonomy meets clinical autonomy. Patients may choose to waive their right to be involved in the decisional process, leaving the treatment choice at the professionals' discretion. However, insofar as professionals are legally obliged to offer a choice of effective treatments, patients' positive claim rights may impinge on the professionals' clinical autonomy.[25] Patients' claim right to treatment, while it may engage their autonomy, is determined prior to their consent and is a matter of distributive justice,[26] which is beyond the scope of this book and will not be further considered.

---

[25] Unlike a liberty right, which simply allows the rights-holder the freedom to do something, a claim right imposes a duty on another person. This may be a negative duty of non-interference or, as here, it may be a positive duty requiring the other person to provide the rights-holder with the requisite goods or services.

[26] *R (Burke)* v. *GMC* [2005] EWCA 1003 at [31].

This model of consent is rights-based, but does not reduce the professional's role to one of technician. All it does is recognise that professionals may not legitimately treat competent adult patients without their consent. They must still act as advisors and the treatment options open to the patient remain under their control. Finally, it should be remembered that consent is a state of mind, which may change over time. As such, even when patients have communicated their consent, professionals have a duty to ensure that their patient is still consenting at the time of the intervention.

Time course of consent

The time course (duration) of consent constitutes an additional attribute and depends on whether consent is purely a state of mind or whether communication is an integral component. As a state of mind, consent persists for as long as the individual maintains that particular state of mind. This is problematic where the patient is to be anaesthetised since the requisite state of mind will be lost while unconscious, which again emphasises the importance of communication. When communication is taken into account, consent may be seen as having a continuing effect until a withdrawal is communicated. Given the professional's role within the professional–patient relationship, this need for consent to be terminated by withdrawal underscores the professional's duty to determine whether the patient is still consenting at the relevant time.

Consent as a choice

In a limited sense consent is always associated with the choice of whether to give or withhold consent. In the present context, this equates to accepting or rejecting the proffered treatment. It is sometimes argued further that consent requires, where available, a range of treatment options.[27] Consent, however, is primarily a device that protects autonomy in the negative sense. By giving or withholding consent rights-bearers control when and who may infringe one of their primary underlying rights. A claim for control over the choice of proffered interventions goes beyond the traditionally negative role of consent and extends its role beyond that of permitting or justifying interventions.

---

[27] See e.g. Schneider, *The Practice of Autonomy*, pp. 7–9; J. Austoker, 'Gaining informed consent for screening' (1999) 319 *British Medical Journal* 722; R. Worthington, 'Clinical issues on consent: Some philosophical concerns' (2002) 28 *Journal of Medical Ethics* 377, 378.

The push to extend the role of consent to protect positive autonomy is reflected in the development of 'informed consent' and arguments for 'shared decision-making'. For example, in the leading US case of *Canterbury* v. *Spence*, Robinson CJ stated: 'True consent to what happens to one's self is the informed exercise of a choice, and that entails an opportunity to evaluate knowledgeably the options available.'[28] This pressure to engage with positive autonomy is reflected in Stirrat and Gill's suggestion that '[t]he term "informed choice" is often to be preferred over "informed consent"'.[29] Although the move to enhancing patient choice recognises that the patient must still consent to the intervention agreed upon, by viewing consent as a process and arguing for shared decision-making, this 'consumer rights' approach seeks to make consent a weapon for positive autonomy.[30] The emphasis on patient choice has become a mantra for, amongst others, the British government.[31] The consequence of this emphasis is that the value placed on informed consent derives from its role in promoting choice rather than from its role in allowing the agent control over an existing right. The danger of this is that it sidesteps, or perhaps even usurps, the roles of clinical judgement and distributive justice in determining the choice of resources available.

It might be argued that consent merely requires information about alternative options rather than that those options are made available. However, if an option is unavailable then knowledge about it is irrelevant to consent. In order to give valid consent patients must appreciate the implications of their decision. This includes understanding that by consenting to treatment A they will be excluding non-treatment and alternative treatment options. However, if treatment C is unavailable they will not be excluding the implications of C by consenting to A. Thus, it would be nonsensical to require they be informed about treatment C. It is not consent, at least as a waiver, but distributive justice and the professional's duty of care that drives the treatment options on offer.[32] The power to determine the treatments that should be offered,

---

[28] *Canterbury* v. *Spence* 464 F 2d 772, 780 (1972).
[29] G. M. Stirrat and R. Gill, 'Autonomy in medical ethics after O'Neill' (2005) 31 *Journal of Medical Ethics* 127, 129.
[30] C. Charles, A. Gafni and T. Whelan, 'Shared decision-making in the medical encounter: What does it mean? (Or it takes at least two to tango)' (1997) 44 *Social Science and Medicine* 681, 681–2. The more recent push for shared decision-making aims to make the patient a 'responsible partner', and so blunt the earlier consumerist approach.
[31] See the Department of Health's web pages on patient choice: www.dh.gov.uk/en/ Policyandguidance/PatientChoice/index.htm.
[32] *R (Burke)* v. *GMC* [2005] EWCA 1003 at [32].

while constrained by the patient's consent, lies with healthcare budget holders, bodies such as NICE and healthcare professionals.

It appears that consent is unable, without a significant reconceptualisation, to require options other than the right to say 'yes' or 'no' to an intervention on offer. Consent in this context is permissive and the patient's consent carries no power to oblige professionals in any way. However, there are two arguments that suggest this view of consent is too narrow. First, if patients' right to withhold consent acts as a veto then treatments refused cease to be options. Professionals still owe a duty to act in their patients' best interests and if a treatment exists that would be better than none at all then they must either offer that alternative or refer the patient to a colleague. In this way, even if healthcare professionals are unwilling to offer a treatment option, their patients' right to withhold consent may oblige them to offer it.[33] As such, it is perhaps preferable, at least from an autonomy perspective, to make patients aware of the options even before any refusal. While professionals arguably should advise their patients as to their preferred choice the patients would then be in a position to weigh up the pros and cons of all beneficial treatment options.

The second argument arises from the sense of consent as an agreement. While an agreement per se cannot force either party to do something they are unwilling to offer up for agreement, it is also arguable that any reasonable conception of a negotiation requires more than simply a 'take it or leave it choice'. If consent is to operate in this way then professionals' obligations and their own right of consent (in the sense of creating obligations rather than in the sense of a waiver) must be considered.[34] However, the concept of negotiation still requires that there are options to negotiate. Thus, consent requires more choice than a simple acceptance or refusal of a single treatment option.

Although consent as a waiver can, if the offered treatment is refused, require alternative treatments to be offered, the case for disclosure of alternatives is strengthened if consent is also approached in the sense of an agreement. The argument for consent as choice is suggestive of the type of negotiated consent seen in contractual negations where the consent is mutual and establishes bilateral obligations. Since consent as a waiver is necessary to justify medical treatment, consent as a choice appears to be a hybrid of its two senses: agreement and permission.

---

[33] It should be noted that this is driven by the patient's right to sue in negligence rather than any claim right to a particular treatment (see below).

[34] This is exactly what negligence law does in requiring disclosure of alternatives (see Chapter 5).

These arguments only address the issue of those treatments that are available to the patient but where the choice has been constrained by the professional's clinical autonomy. There is also the limit on choice imposed by the distribution of available resources. Consider the situation where three treatments are available. Treatments A and B are offered by the NHS but treatment C is available only privately. Does the patient's right to give or withhold consent require the healthcare professional to disclose treatment C as an option? The same argument applies as justified disclosure where the constraint came from clinical judgement. Although the public healthcare professional is not under a duty to provide treatment C, where the patient rejects both A and B, the professional's continuing duty of care requires that the patient be informed of the option and referred to a professional who can provide it. Thus, treatment options that are only available privately should be disclosed where the patient is being treated in a state-funded healthcare system.

The only possible exception to this is where the healthcare professional can be certain that the patient will be unable to pay for the treatment. In such circumstances the treatment is effectively unavailable and a failure to disclose the treatment has no implications for the patient's decision whether to accept one of the other treatment options. However, this then raises the question of how certain must be the professional. On the one hand, to disclose possible treatments that are unaffordable may be cruel and may affect the patient's ability to decide on the available options. On the other hand, it is always possible, even if unlikely, that the patient will win the lottery or find a philanthropist willing to fund the treatment. There are no clear-cut answers to this dilemma, which is exacerbated by a market approach to healthcare, and it is perhaps best dealt with on a case-to-case basis depending on the patient involved and the precise circumstances. This again highlights the relevance of the virtuous professional and indicates the importance of focusing the regulatory gaze on the process that precedes the consent decision as much as on the decision itself.

Consent and non-treatment

Following on from this is the suggestion that consent should also be necessary for non-treatment decisions. Biegler, for example, argued that, if consent is predicated on respect for autonomy and autonomy has positive as well as negative aspects then patients would 'be justified in requesting treatments that are in their best interests'.[35] He discussed this

---

[35] P. Biegler, 'Should patient consent be required to write a do not resuscitate order?' (2003) 29 *Journal of Medical Ethics* 359, 360.

in the context of 'do not resuscitate' orders and concluded that 'consent ought to be required to withhold treatment that is in a patient's best interests to receive'.[36] It appears that he was arguing for a claim right to those treatments that are in the patient's best interests and that the patient's consent is necessary to waive that right and permit the professional to withhold it. The difficulty with this is that it has implications for resource allocation and for professional autonomy. Furthermore, it should be noted that consent does not do the initial work here: to make consent relevant an initial right must exist that may then be waived. Thus, before consent even becomes relevant the claim right to particular treatments must be justified on grounds of distributive justice.

A second way in which consent may be relevant here engages the other sense of consent. Where there is no pre-existing right to treatment then, because non-treatment does not breach the patient's bodily integrity, consent$_P$ is irrelevant. The duty to treat is regulated by the law of negligence and, providing healthcare professionals act reasonably, they will fulfil their obligation and avoid liability. The professional's duty in negligence does not create a consequential right to treatment; the associated right is the right to sue for damages. However, Article 8 of the ECHR, incorporated into domestic law by the Human Rights Act 1998, allows the right to a private and family life. This subsumes autonomy and, as far as the family is concerned, has allowed that parents have a right to be involved in decisions about their children[37] even where they have been taken into care.[38] Subsequently, in *Tysiac v. Poland*, the European Court of Human Rights noted that Article 8 required that the 'individual has been involved in the decision-making process, seen as a whole, to a degree sufficient to provide her or him with the requisite protection of their interests'.[39] These cases suggest that patients should be involved in decisions concerning non-treatment, and consent$_A$, rather than consent$_P$, might be an appropriate mechanism for regulating this involvement. At the very least, patients may be able to claim a right to know that such a decision has been made even if they have no claim right to require the actual treatment. In this context, consent can only be relevant in the sense of an agreement because the primary right of bodily integrity is not engaged by a decision not to treat.

Using consent in the context of non-treatment raises certain issues regarding the consequences of patients refusing to give their consent to the withholding of treatment but this is not the place to discuss those

---

[36] *Ibid.*, 363.   [37] *Glass* v. *UK* [2004] 1 FLR 1019.
[38] *W* v. *UK* (1988) 10 EHRR 29 at 50.
[39] *Tysiac* v. *Poland* (2007) 45 EHRR 42 at [115], ECtHR.

issues. Strictly speaking the model I am constructing in this book is concerned with consent to medical treatment, which – if narrowly interpreted – does not include non-treatment decisions. However, deciding not to provide a particular treatment, or any treatment at all, is an important aspect of medical decision-making and arguably involves consent$_A$ even if it does not engage consent$_P$. Because of this relationship between treatment and non-treatment decisions, both of which engage the patient's autonomy, it may be worthwhile considering the legal regulation of non-treatment decisions at the same time as I consider consent to treatment. This would acknowledge the sibling relationship between the two types of consent, which might then be categorised under a more general heading of consent to a medical management plan.

Consent and shared decision-making

The idea of shared decision-making is sometimes discussed as if it is synonymous with consent.[40] This partnership approach to medical decisions is proselytised as a way of balancing or respecting both the patient's autonomy and the healthcare professional's role as beneficent care-giver. Beauchamp and Childress, however, dismiss shared decision-making as a 'worthy ideal in medicine' but one that 'neither defines nor displaces informed consent'.[41] They may make a valid point but it is perhaps misleading as to the role of shared decision-making.

Rather than being seen as an alternative model to consent, shared decision-making can be seen as a way of achieving a more meaningful consent.[42] In this sense, the patient's consent is still necessary but, instead of disclosing the relevant information and abandoning patients to their decisions, professionals work through them with their patients.[43] Once they arrive at a mutually acceptable treatment option the patient's state of mind will be one of consent and the professional should be

---

[40] Meisel and Kuczewiski, 'Legal and ethical myths about informed consent', 2522; D. Giesen, 'From paternalism to self-determination to shared decision making in the field of medical law and ethics', in L. Westerhall and C. Phillips (eds.), *Patient's Rights – Informed consent, access and equality* (Stockholm: Nerenius & Santerus Publishers, 1994), pp. 19, 37.

[41] Beauchamp and Childress, *Principles of Biomedical Ethics*, p. 78.

[42] H. Teff, *Reasonable Care* (Oxford: Clarendon Press, 1994), particularly Chapter 3; J. Marta, 'Whose consent is it anyway? A poststructuralist framing of the person in medical decision-making' (1998) 19 *Theoretical Medicine and Bioethics* 353, 354; J. Katz, *The Silent World of Doctor and Patient* (Baltimore: Johns Hopkins University Press, 1984, 2002).

[43] See J. Bridson, C. Hammond, A. Leach and M. R. Hester, 'Making consent patient centred' (2003) 27 *British Medical Journal* 1159.

aware of this. Provided that the procedural requirements of consent are satisfied, the intervention would be morally and legally justified. This view of shared decision-making reflects the relevance of the professional–patient relationship explored in Chapter 3.

The US President's Commission saw shared decision-making as an ethical ideal:

[T]he patient and physician will arrive at a joint decision in which the physician agrees to care for the patient and the patient agrees to be treated . . . The resiliency of the relationship will depend importantly on the extent of trust and confidence exchanged between patient and professional.[44]

However, this does not mean that this vision was meant to replace the law's doctrine of informed consent. Rather, it was to supplement the physician's legal obligation. The Commission's approach also included the idea of patient choice, although a choice constrained by accepted medical values and others' claims on scarce resources. This reinforces the suggestion above that consent should be seen as a hybrid involving both consent$_A$ and consent$_P$. It is, however, important to recognise that consent$_P$ is essential while consent$_A$ is desirable but, because it is fundamentally dependent on the political questions of clinical autonomy and distributive justice, it is perhaps better treated as a possible attribute rather than a central part of the theory. This is particularly so since some decisions are so clinically certain and have relatively low importance to the patient such that there may be little need or desire for negotiation.[45]

Consent and refusal: two sides of the same coin?

It is reasonable to suggest that the right to give consent necessarily implies the right to refuse consent. Since 'right' carries with it the idea of 'control' there can be no right where the individual (or lawful proxy) has no control. If one has no option but to exercise the 'right' then that option is not really a right but a duty. This argument explains why consent as a waiver of a primary right even exists. However, the very justification for consent also defines its limitations. Although refusal of consent is the opposite side of the same coin, this does not mean that a refusal of consent is sufficient to prohibit a breach of bodily integrity.

---

[44] President's Commission, *Making Health Care Decisions: The ethical and legal implications of informed consent in the patient – practitioner relationship*, vol. 1 (Washington D.C., 1982), p. 37.

[45] S. Whitney, 'A new model of medical decisions: Exploring the limits of shared decision making' (2003) 23 *Medical Decision Making* 275.

When A gives B consent to perform an intervention, A waives his or her right to bodily integrity. This means that the subsequent intervention is not a breach of bodily integrity. If B intervenes without A's consent then B will be breaching A's right to bodily integrity. However, unless a right is absolute, consent will not be the only justification for performing the intervention. For example, imagine that A has a highly contagious disease that threatens the health of other members of the community. Although it would be respectful of the individual to seek consent to intervene to isolate and treat A, it may still be justified – because of the risk of harm to others – to intervene even if A refuses to give consent. In this case the justification comes from the rights of the other members of the community. If the intervention is non-consensual then A's right to bodily integrity has been breached, but it is a justified breach.

What this means is that there will be occasions when, despite a refusal (or lack) of consent, an intervention will be legitimate even though it breaches the primary right of bodily integrity. This argument perhaps provides some insight into Lord Donaldson MR's judgments in *Re R* and *Re W*.[46] In *Re R*, Lord Donaldson MR adopted the analogy of a key-holder to explain that even where a child is capable of giving consent their refusal may be overridden by someone with parental responsibility. The relevance of my argument here is that, providing the law allows two or more individuals the right of consent, then a refusal of either of those parties will be insufficient to prohibit the intervention. This does not claim that the law is right in allowing two parties the right of consent, merely that unless a right is absolute, the individual's refusal to give consent is insufficient as a veto.[47]

Interestingly, in *Re W*, Lord Donaldson withdrew his key-holder analogy and replaced it with one involving flak jackets.[48] In one way, this is unfortunate since the key-holder analogy fits better with the concept of consent as a waiver of a right. However, it could be argued that the key-holder analogy tallies with the child's right to consent while the parents' right to consent has a different justification and is better represented by the flak jacket analogy. If the right to bodily integrity truly belongs to the child then the parents cannot legitimately waive that right. While the child is incompetent to consent, some other means of justifying necessary interventions is required. This comes from allowing the

---

[46] *Re R (A Minor) (Wardship: Consent to Treatment)* [1992] Fam 11; *Re W (A Minor) (Consent to Medical Treatment)* [1993] 1 FLR 1.

[47] It could be argued that parental consent merely prevents the intervention from being a violation of the child's right to bodily integrity but, without the child's consent, the intervention remains a breach (or infringement) – albeit justified – of that right.

[48] *Re W (A Minor) (Consent to Medical Treatment)* [1993] 1 FLR 1, 9.

parents the power to determine whether or not a particular intervention is a justifiable breach of the child's bodily integrity. Legally, this has two parts. The first is to agree that the intervention is necessary, the second is to waive the right to complain about the intervention and it is only by virtue of this latter part that the permission to intervene is legitimately called 'consent'. The consent, however, is not a waiver of the right to bodily integrity but a waiver of the right to sue. As such, it may still persist even when the child is competent to consent to the intervention itself. In this way, the child's consent is like a key while the parent's consent is more like the flak jacket.[49]

Some commentators have argued that competence to consent should be assessed on the basis of the risk posed by the intervention.[50] This would allow that someone might be competent to consent to a procedure, but not competent to refuse consent. I have argued elsewhere that competency should be based on the complexity rather than the risk of the decision and that the relevance of risk lies in ensuring that the competency assessment reaches the correct conclusion.[51] This is not the place to reiterate the arguments in favour of that conclusion. It is, however, worth noting that if my argument here about the nature of consent is correct then the decision to give or withhold consent is a single decision. Refusal of consent may not be divorced from the giving of consent since the decision not to give consent is equivalent to a refusal of consent.

Some of the difficulties over consent perhaps arise because it is easy to forget that the individual's consent is only one of the possible justifications for performing an intervention. For example, Harris asserted that: 'The idea that a child (or anyone) might competently consent to a treatment but not be competent to refuse it is palpable nonsense.'[52] This statement is only true if he means refusal of consent rather than refusal of treatment. A refusal of consent only means that the individual's right to bodily integrity has not been waived. This does not mean that it may not legitimately be infringed provided a suitable justification can be found. A justifiable breach is not a violation of the individual's right. However, the breach must be justified if it is to be a legitimate act.

[49] This argument is entirely a legal argument and would not preclude criticism of this position on moral grounds.

[50] See e.g. D. W. Brock, 'Decisionmaking, competence and risk' (1991) 5 *Bioethics* 105; I. Wilks, 'Asymmetrical competence' (1999) 13 *Bioethics* 154.

[51] A. Maclean, 'Now you see it, now you don't: Consent and the legal protection of autonomy' (2000) 17 *Journal of Applied Philosophy* 277, 281–7. See also: M. R. Wicclair, 'The continuing debate over risk-related standards of competence' (1999) 13 *Bioethics* 149.

[52] J. Harris, 'Consent and end of life decisions' (2003) 29 *Journal of Medical Ethics* 10.

Consent, power and control

There can be little doubt that consent is concerned with issues of power and control. The language used when discussing consent and the factors that invalidate it reflect the tussle between the parties for control of the relationship. Both a lack of knowledge and undue influence – whether coercive or not – are capable of shifting the balance of power. Similarly, the language of rights, the protection that rights afford against exploitation, and the enforcement of those rights by the law all indicate the relevance of power and control. Thus, consent, predicated as it is on the right to self-determination (or autonomy), demands that the decision to give or withhold consent is voluntary.

The importance of consent lies in allowing individuals to control particular aspects of their life. It is necessary precisely because without the protection of consent and the underlying right individuals will lack control in all relationships in which they are the subordinate party. This is particularly important in the healthcare setting. There are a number of reasons why professionals occupy the dominant position: their social position, their superior knowledge, their control over access to healthcare, the patient's illness and the fact that the patient has come to them for help.[53] Apart from the deontological justification for consent, it has been shown that a sense of control has valuable and sustainable benefits for the individual's health.[54] What consent does in this context is not to neutralise the power imbalance but to legitimise it. Ensuring that patients have the ultimate control over their own body, consent prevents the professional's authority from being exercised in an authoritarian fashion. It is precisely because the power imbalance is unavoidable that consent is necessary.

Despite the power that consent gives to the patient, it is important to realise that this does not emasculate the professional who remains the dominant 'partner'. This is not, however, a bad thing. Power is not simply repressive and the power professionals possess is what enables them to help their patients.[55] This power allows professionals to discover things about their patients that they would not otherwise be allowed to know; it allows them to advise, care for and heal their

---

[53] Brody, *The Healer's Power*, pp. 16–17; M. R. Haug and B. Lavin, 'Practitioner or patient – who's in charge?' (1981) 22 *Journal of Health and Social Behavior* 212.

[54] M. Seeman and T. E. Seeman, 'Health behavior and personal autonomy: A longitudinal study of the sense of control in illness' (1983) 24 *Journal of Health and Social Behavior* 144.

[55] M. Foucault, 'Body/Power', in C. Gordon (ed.), *Power/Knowledge* (Brighton: The Harvester Press, 1980), pp. 55, 59.

patients. Without it a professional would become simply a dispenser of tablets or a technician. This power, however, must be exercised fairly and responsibly if it is to remain legitimate.

Even within the context of information disclosure, while consent may go some way to reducing its authoritarian potential, it is unable to negate completely the potential for repression inherent in power. This is not to argue that power is itself repressive, but simply to recognise that it may be exercised repressively. For example, the way in which professionals present the information and advice to their patients will affect the 'truth' that the patient accepts. While it may be argued that this manipulation would invalidate consent in a moral sense, it may not be susceptible to legal regulation.

In practice, then, professionals may manipulate the timing and presentation of information in such a way as to gain the patient's agreement, which currently the law would deem sufficient for consent. Similarly, exercising power repressively during the consultation may affect the ability of patients truly to engage in the decision-making process and any 'consent' would simply involve an acceptance of the professional's advice. Interrupting patients and ignoring questions, whether or not done consciously, may reduce patients' ability to exercise their autonomous power.[56] This is important because the realisation that formalised rules of consent may be unable to prevent an unethical exercise of power highlights the need for professionals to be sensitive to an appropriate ethical framework.

This discussion suggests another value to be included under *Attribute B* Effect: [consent has the effect of] legitimising a beneficent exercise of the professional's power.

The prerequisites for consent

Consent, information, knowledge and risk

The purpose of providing information is to help individuals gain the knowledge necessary to allow them to consent to the proposed intervention. It is certainly trite that in order to consent individuals must know something. At the very least they must know that their consent is required. If they must know this, then since consent is not an abstract state of mind but always exists in relation to something, they must also know that there is something for which their consent is required. This

---

[56] N. Ainsworth-Vaughan, *Claiming Power in Doctor-Patient Talk* (New York: Oxford University Press, 1998), p. 51.

much is entailed by the knowledge that consent is required. The real issue is whether consent requires more than this.

The crucial point, and one that may not be determined definitively, is what the patient must know in order to consent to procedure X rather than to some inadequate conception X. However, it seems reasonable to start with the suggestion that patients have no need to know about the mechanics of the procedure. If knowledge is seen as an ability to utilise the information possessed then knowing about the mechanics is only necessary if one is required to perform the procedure.[57] For example, it is completely unnecessary for patients to know that a purse-string suture is employed to close the defect left when an appendix is excised. It may even be counter-productive as it might confuse patients or deflect their attention from more important information. A second piece of information that could be safely omitted is details of the scientific evidence in support of the procedure. While patients may need to know that research has shown procedure X to be more effective than procedure Y, they would not need to know how the studies showed this to be the case.

At this point it is tentatively suggested that patients need to have sufficient knowledge to *distinguish X from the alternatives in terms of the risks and effects of the procedure*. At the very least this requires patients to be able to distinguish the implications of procedure X from the implications of no treatment at all. However, as I have already discussed, for consent – both as a waiver and as an agreement – the professional may be obliged to disclose alternative options and patients should therefore be able to appreciate the implications of accepting treatment X rather than treatment Y.

When discussing the information disclosure aspect of consent, attention is often focused on the risks. This is understandable since, from a legal perspective, issues of consent often arise in relation to the harm caused by an undisclosed risk materialising. While risk is crucial to the consent decision, it is important not to ignore the relevance of other types of information. As suggested above, if patients are to consent to a procedure they must know the implications of their decision, which requires knowledge of the alternatives on offer. The reason for this may be explained as follows. If I am to consent to X, I must know the implications of consenting to X. But, if I consent to X this may exclude (or at least affect the implications of) the alternatives to X.[58] Therefore,

---

[57] It would also be required if one was called upon to explain the mechanics of the procedure to someone else, i.e. in an exam.

[58] If I consent to X I am excluding not-X. For other options, at the very least my decision will make those options unavailable at that time and may have implications for the future use of those options. For example, consider patients with an injured spleen.

since consenting to X excludes other alternatives, I cannot know the implications of X unless I know the implications of not consenting to the alternatives, which includes the consequences of not being treated.

What is perhaps surprising about this argument is that, in order to consent to X, I do not need to know the procedure in order to consent to it. This explains the fallacy of arguing that informed consent cannot be achieved by laypersons because they lack medical training and so cannot possibly understand complex procedures. Instead, what is required is knowledge of the implications of the procedure.

Focusing on the implications of the intervention rather than on the nature of the procedure has the consequence of highlighting that what must be disclosed cannot be fully determined in the abstract. Rather, the duty to disclose must be referenced to the particular professional–patient relationship, the needs of the patient and the communicative interaction between the two parties. In this regard, Manson and O'Neill's examination of the two different approaches to information is apposite.[59]

Manson and O'Neill distinguish two different metaphorical models of information: the container/conduit model and the agency/communicative model. The container model treats information as essentially discrete packets of information that can be transferred from one container – or person – to another. While acknowledging that this model captures one sense of information, they argue that focusing exclusively on this model has caused the problem that haunts the current approach to informed consent. The consequence of the container metaphor of information is that the duty to inform is interpreted simply as the duty to convey the requisite packets of information with little or no thought for the needs of the patient, the different purposes of consent or the problems of the process of communication.[60]

As an alternative, Manson and O'Neill argue persuasively for an agency metaphor that focuses on the process of communication and the purposes behind the communicative interaction. They point to a number of features of information and informing that are obscured by the

---

Assuming – for the sake of argument – they are sufficiently competent to consent then their options may be 'wrapping' or 'removal' of the spleen. If they choose 'removal' then 'wrapping' is permanently excluded and the implications include permanent loss of splenic function. If they choose 'wrapping' this may fail to halt the bleeding and they may require further surgery and more blood transfusion. Although they retain the option of 'removal' this will be at a later time and will require a second operation.

[59] Manson and O'Neill, *Rethinking Informed Consent*, pp. 26–67.

[60] The association of consent with autonomy, particularly the liberal conception, which demands the information necessary for a rational decision, exacerbates the problems of the container metaphor. I have already discussed Manson and O'Neill's approach to consent and autonomy in Chapter 1.

container metaphor.[61] These include that informing depends on context; is subject to rules; is propositional and seeks to affect the other person's behaviour; is rational and rationally evaluable. Furthermore, 'informing is referentially opaque', which means that the listener may not appreciate the same implications as the speaker intends. Indeed, because of different beliefs and background knowledge listeners may draw very different inferences from the information. These latter points highlight the agency of the listener. The importance of this is the recognition that the listener will, through processing and interpretation, shape the information: the listener is not simply a passive receptacle for the packets of information conveyed by the speaker.

The agency metaphor is a crucial insight into the communicative aspects of consent and the process that precedes it. It is important to remember that consent is not simply the state of mind of the person giving consent but engages two persons, both of them agents with rights, responsibilities and duties. Acknowledging the relevance of both agents explains why the attributes of consent depend on the context of the relationship that grounds the interaction between the person seeking and the person granting consent. The nature of this relationship will vary depending on the nature and purpose of the interaction. Thus, the obligations that arise from the right to consent may differ where the context is clinical care as opposed to research.

The agency model of information also explains why the regulatory focus should not simply reside in the information that has, or has not, been disclosed. The outcome of the communicative process may be the easiest thing to measure to determine whether a duty has been fulfilled. However, it only concerns one aspect of the two parties' duties and completely ignores the other duties that arise out of the relationship between the healthcare professional and the patient. Importantly, it does not require either party to engage with the other and, without that mutual engagement, communication will inevitably fail. This failure is independent of the packets of information that have been disclosed and is reflected in the patient's ability, or inability, to respond appropriately to the course of action proposed by the healthcare professional. This holds regardless of whether the patient is intent on making the treatment decision or is content to trust the healthcare professional and cede the decision.

I will return to the importance of the process of communication in the final chapter, where I will compare Manson and O'Neill's model of consent with my own and discuss how the models might be

[61] Manson and O'Neill, *Rethinking Informed Consent in Bioethics*, pp. 41–8.

implemented and the possible consequences of that implementation. Moving away from the models of information, the final point I will consider in this section is whether patients are obliged to receive the information in order to give a valid consent.

The waiver of the right to information is distinct from the question of whether patients may waive the right to consent. Unfortunately the distinction is not always maintained. For example, Wear stated:

> The least troublesome exception [to disclosure] would seem to occur when the patient voluntarily gives up his right to an informed consent. Various reasons may lie behind such an action, including that the patient does not want to be upset by hearing the gory details, or he feels incapable of making decisions and would prefer that his doctor decide.[62]

The problem with this is it concatenates the right to information with the right to consent. The two are distinct, although a valid consent requires that the patient's right to information has not been unjustifiably breached. As with other rights, the right to information may be waived, since, without the power to waive the right becomes an obligation and, as I will explain below, there is no reason why that should be the case in this context.

Providing patients are aware that they have a right to the information, and that by waiving the right they are accepting risks determined by the healthcare professional, then it is reasonable for them to relinquish their right to information. It is reasonable to trust experts where they have a duty to act in one's interests and there is no reason to suspect that they will do otherwise. As long as patients are aware of the implications of refusing information and it is reasonable for them to trust the healthcare professional's advice then they are acting autonomously. To argue that autonomy requires that patients actually make the clinical decision itself, on the basis of a 'neutral' disclosure, prioritises that decision and constrains patients' autonomy by preventing them from making the alternative decision to rely on expert advice. Thus, patients may legitimately waive their right to information.

This argument reflects an agency approach to information that recognises the importance of seeing information as something more than just packets of data. Rather, information and knowledge (or the ability to use information) are inseparable from the communicative process that unites the parties in a relationship. This distinction between the two different models of information is a crucial part of Manson and O'Neill's

---

[62] S. Wear, *Informed Consent: Patient autonomy and clinician beneficence within health care*, 2nd edn (Washington D.C.: Georgetown University Press, 1998), p. 23.

critique of informed consent and their argument that informed consent should be discarded in favour of a genuine consent. Their explication and argument in favour of an agency approach over the conduit/container model is insightful and persuasive. It is an approach that is implicit to the relational approach to consent that I am arguing for here. However, although both of our approaches recognise the crucial importance of communication and the relevance of human agency, we draw different conclusions. I will return to consider Manson and O'Neill's model of genuine consent later. For now it will suffice to note that the agency approach highlights the importance of focusing as much, if not more, on the process of communication as on the actual information that is conveyed.

Consent and voluntariness

The primary purpose of consent is normatively to transform the legitimacy of an act. Following from this transformation, consent also protects the actor against complaint and justifies including the consenter in the allocation of outcome responsibility. All of these roles rely on the relationship between autonomy, control and responsibility. Autonomy is concerned with the idea of moral agency: that we should be free to make our own decisions and to take responsibility for the ensuing consequences. Thus, if consent is to act as a permission that alters the legitimacy of an act then it must be wilfully and freely given. Without the freedom to give or withhold it, consent loses its moral (and legal) force and is reduced to being a normatively meaningless assent that lacks the power to legitimise the act.

Two possible strategies exist for coping with the interaction between consent and voluntariness. First, voluntariness could be seen simply as essential to the normative force of consent. This would mean that an involuntary consent would still be consent but it would not have the power to legitimise the intervention. This is perhaps the way in which the courts have traditionally handled consent since judges usually talk of consent being vitiated rather than defeated *ab initio*. The second strategy would be to argue that a lack of voluntariness means that the given permission is not, in fact, consent. This second manoeuvre would further develop consent as a term of art and distance it from its everyday use. Which of these strategies is chosen is, to a large extent, a matter of personal preference. In both cases consent loses its normative and legal force and the consequences may be broadly similar. Because the second strategy has the advantage of simplicity and clarity, that is the approach I will adopt.

It is, of course, important to determine exactly what is meant by voluntariness. All of us are subject to both internal and external constraints that affect our choices and none of us makes choices in a vacuum. We live in a network of relationships all of which enmesh us in mutual obligations and expectations. These obligations and expectations ought to be considered when making our decisions and as such should form the background conditions of freedom, which emphasises the importance of contextualising consent within the professional–patient relationship (see Chapter 3). On top of this, our decisions may be subject to more direct and immediate pressures. It is these influences that may affect the voluntariness of our choices. The difficulty lies in distinguishing between legitimate background constraints and the illegitimate pressures that undermine the normative force of consent.

Consent and competence

Competence is relevant whether consent is conceived of as a mental state or a signatory act of communication. It is relevant because consent always requires an active input. Clearly, persons unable to perform the necessary act – either the formation of a particular mental state or the requisite communicative behaviour (or both) – are also unable to consent. The difficulty comes when individuals have some ability but it is deficient in some way. One problem arises because ability is a continuous variable while competency is biphasic – an individual is either competent or incompetent. One way around this is to adopt the approach taken by the law, which is to make competency task- or decision-specific. Another problem arises where someone is capable of making and communicating a decision but lacks the ability to make a rational autonomous one.

First, and most importantly in this context, overriding the decision of persons lacking the mental capacity for autonomy should be justified. One approach to this would be to argue that if consent is to act as a morally transformative permission then the consenter must be a moral agent. Moral agency requires the appropriate autonomous ability and where individuals lack that ability their consent cannot be permissive. Legal agency is similarly justified on the basis of when society believes that individuals should be held legally responsible for their actions. This is largely derived from the idea of moral agency, as indicated by the law's emphasis on autonomy.[63] Second, there is the problem of deciding the ability necessary to justify respect for that person's decision. I do not

---

[63] It should be noted that in some circumstances the law deems agency even if moral agency is in fact lacking (and vice versa). The idea of legal responsibility, however, is

need to go into this here because it is sufficient for me to simply establish that competence is a prerequisite for consent. This is achieved if it is accepted that for consent to be morally or legally transformative, agency is required.

Summary of the nature, attributes and function of consent

It is now possible to summarise a final definition of consent to medical treatment:[64]

Consent Theory	A state of mind of the patient formed with the intention of permitting treatment suggested by the healthcare professional.
Attribute A	Primary right *Value*: 1. Bodily integrity (broadly construed to include both direct and indirect interference).
Attribute B	Explicit or implicit communication of consent from patient to healthcare professional *Value*: 1. The patient's attitude towards the proposed intervention.
Attribute C	Effect *Values*: 1. Alters obligations for: a. the healthcare professional by removing the obligation of non-interference; and, if Attribute D, value 1 is present, b. both the patient and healthcare professional by negotiation to establish

derivative of the idea of moral agency. It should also be noted that, for adults, agency, and hence competence, are presumed.

[64] I do not here include the sense of consent in the context of non-treatment, where consent is an agreement rather than a permission or waiver.

new obligations of cooperation and treatment.
2. Justifies intervention or non-intervention through moral/legal transformation.
3. Legitimises a virtuous exercise of power.
4. Allows apportionment of outcome responsibility.

Attribute D   Process of communication
Values:

1. Shared decision-making/negotiation culminating in consent as an agreement.
2. Patient's decision.

Attribute E   Time course
Values:

1. Until withdrawn.
2. Until relevant circumstances change.

Prerequisites   1. Competence.
2. Relevant knowledge
  a. disclosure
  b. understanding.
3. Voluntariness.

Conclusion

In this chapter I have explored the concept of consent and determined the underlying theory and important attributes. I argued that consent should be seen as a permissive state of mind that waives the right to bodily integrity. Once communicated to the actor the permission takes effect by justifying the intervention and legitimising the virtuous exercise of the doctor's power. I also suggested that consent as agreement, while not an essential part of the theory of consent, should be incorporated as an attribute. This reflects the context of the professional–patient relationship and allows patients the opportunity to negotiate treatment options prior to giving permission. It also highlights the importance of recognising the mutual engagement of both parties as agents in a communicative process. Once the negotiation is complete the patients and their professionals have entered into morally binding agreements that create obligations and expectations for both.

I further noted the limits of consent in that a refusal of consent, while it may operate as a veto for certain treatment, is not the same as a refusal of treatment and other justifications may exist that normatively transform the act. Furthermore, although consent lacks the power to oblige performance of a particular act, in combination with the professional's duty to the patient it may be valid to utilise the concept of consent, particularly as agreement, when dealing with non-treatment decisions. This may be seen as a secondary function of consent, with the primary purpose – in this context – being the justification of an intervention. Finally, some acts remain forbidden, even in the presence of an otherwise valid consent.

Addendum

To close this first part of the book I will pull together the various strands of my argument to present a model of consent to medical treatment (Figure 2) that will form the basis for critiquing the current legal regulation. I have argued that consent should be contextualised within the professional–patient relationship that grounds it. The context of the relationship establishes the mutual obligations that give practical substance to the theory and moral justifications underlying consent.

Consent is the act of communicating the patient's mental attitude towards the healthcare professional's proposal. It is predicated on the patient's personal autonomy but, since it is set in the context of the professional–patient relationship, it must also account for the professional's autonomy and his or her role responsibilities. This is achieved by incorporating consent$_A$ into the model as an attribute (Figure 2). While, through consent$_P$, patients retain control of what happens to them, consent$_A$ allows the professional to challenge apparently irrational decisions and to attempt to persuade the patient to change his or her mind and accept the professional's advice. The professional's duties to the patient, of beneficence and respect for autonomy, mean that this power to persuade becomes an obligation. Furthermore, the patient's obligations, which arise from the relationship and are expressed through consent$_A$, require patients to respect the professional's role within the relationship. They should explain their decisions, listen to the professional and be open to persuasion. Similarly, the professional should also be open to persuasion that the patient's decision is appropriate. The relationship between the healthcare professional and the patient justifies imposing positive obligations on the healthcare professional to engage the patient in a mutual dialogue where each party is open to persuasion. This mutual participation is a crucial part of consent$_A$.

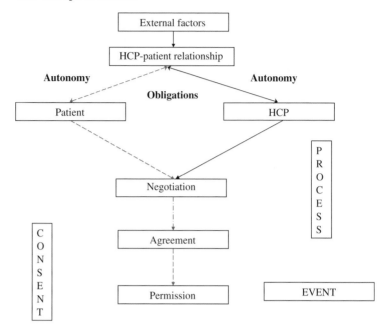

Fig 2 Model of consent

Because consent is justified by autonomy, and is an expression of agency, the patient must be competent to make the decision. The patient should also be sufficiently well informed, which requires an understanding of the implications of the treatment chosen. The healthcare professionals have a duty to facilitate their patients' autonomy by supporting them throughout the decision-making process. The extent of the disclosure should be determined through negotiation with patients having the right to waive information, or even to cede the treatment decision to the professional. However, where patients choose to waive their right to information, or to cede the treatment decision, the healthcare professional should ensure that they appreciate the implications of their choice. Any decision made by the patient should be made not in the absence of any influence (both the healthcare professional and the patient's loved ones may be allowed to influence the patient), but in the absence of undue influence that attempts to control the patient's decision by unfairly exploiting the patient's weaknesses or vulnerability. A consent that satisfies these criteria is valid until withdrawn by the patient, or until circumstances change so as to undermine the rationale for the decision.

Consent$_P$ protects the patients' right to control the underlying primary right of bodily integrity, which may be communicated explicitly or implicitly. However, there is no room for presumed consent, which is a misnomer and not really a type of consent at all. Nor is there any need for consent$_P$ to be obtained to non-intervention decisions. However, consent$_A$ does require that patients be involved in any such decision, and that they be provided with the opportunity to influence the healthcare professional's decision. Even if patients lack the power to require a particular treatment, a respect for their autonomy requires that they are engaged in the process, are informed of the reasons for the decision, are given an opportunity to disagree and are asked for their agreement. Although consent$_P$ cannot independently drive the obligation to disclose alternative treatments to the professional's preferred option, when combined with the healthcare professional's duty of care, disclosure of alternatives is required. This obligation is further justified by the inclusion of consent$_A$ as an attribute.

Since not all medical interventions involve a direct infringement of bodily integrity, any regulatory model needs to account for those indirect interferences. These include treatments where the healthcare professional prescribes and directs the treatment but it is the patient who performs the final act by, for example, taking oral medication, applying topical creams and ointments or self-injecting (in such cases as diabetes). In all of these cases the healthcare professional's agency is mediated through the patient. Although the patient acts intentionally, the healthcare professional's involvement is a relevant causal factor. Given the imbalance of knowledge and power, and the reasonableness of relying on the expert's advice, the healthcare professional may be seen as causally responsible for the patient's act: in performing the final act of treatment, the patients are acting as the healthcare professional's agents. Even if this argument is not accepted, these types of treatment may still be covered by consent$_A$, which I argued was an important attribute of consent to medical treatment. Thus, any regulation of consent should be able to deal with treatment where the patient performs the final act. This ensures that consent protects the negative aspects of individual autonomy for both direct and indirect medical interventions.

Because of the importance of consent$_A$, the dialogical process that precedes consent$_P$ should be accounted for in the regulation of consent to medical treatment (Figure 2). Given the relational nature of any communication, the law should accept that both parties have responsibilities. For example, although the balance of power and knowledge lies with the professional, patients should be responsible for letting the professional know how much information is wanted, what their baseline understanding is and whether they are happy to give consent on the basis of the information disclosed. The professional should do what is reasonable to facilitate autonomous decision-making. This means that the standard of disclosure should not be based solely on what was disclosed but should take account of how the two parties have conducted the process of communication that culminated in the particular disclosure made.

The law must also deal with the consequences of an ineffective or absent consent. Perhaps the most serious failures are where the healthcare professional has shown a complete lack of respect for both the welfare and the autonomy of the patient. This should be a rare occurrence but may nonetheless occur where a healthcare professional coerces or deceives a patient in order to obtain consent to a procedure where the motivation was primarily to benefit the healthcare professional (e.g. unnecessary work for financial gain). The complete failure to obtain consent is also a serious wrong. Perhaps less serious are those cases where the consent has been obtained negligently, for example, by simply forgetting to disclose a relevant risk. Arguably, legal regulations should acknowledge the differing degrees of infringement in the remedies available to the claimant.

Because autonomy is the moral basis for consent, whether the risk materialises or whether the patient would have made a different decision should be irrelevant to the question of liability. These factors, however, may affect the amount of any damages awarded. As I discussed earlier, liability for consent and outcome responsibility should be determined independently, although a valid consent would be needed to include the patient in the apportionment of responsibility. This, however, does not mean that patients can only be held responsible when a risk materialises if that risk has actually been disclosed. Where patients have consented knowing that some risks have not been disclosed then there is no reason why they should not be held as responsible for the undisclosed risks as for those that have been disclosed.

Finally, the law must allow the competent patient's refusal of consent to act as an effective refusal of treatment unless to do so would directly harm others. This protection should be extended to any decision, whether rational or not. However, the law should require that the healthcare professional challenge any decision that does appear to be irrational and attempt to persuade the patient to change his or her mind. While the law should not force the patients to change their decisions, it should require the healthcare professional to seek both reasons and explanations for the decision. If the patient is unwilling to engage with the healthcare professional to provide these reasons and explanations, the law should allow the professional to transfer the patient's care to another healthcare professional.

Part II

Consent and the law

5   The legal regulation of consent

The courts repeatedly proclaim the value that the law gives to the individual's right to self-determination. For example, in *S* v. *McC; W* v. *W*, Lord Reid stated:

There is no doubt that a person of full age and capacity cannot be ordered to undergo a blood test against his will . . . The real reason is that English law goes to great lengths to protect a person of full age and capacity from interference with his personal liberty.[1]

Similarly, in *Nancy B* v. *Hotel-Dieu de Quebec*, Dufour J quoted with approval the words of Professor Beaudoin (a justice of the Quebec Court of Appeal) who stated:

For a competent person of the age of majority, the making of his own decisions with respect to his own body is the legal expression of the principle of personal autonomy and of the right to self-determination.[2]

This right exists regardless of the consequences for the individual. In principle the law protects the individual's right to self-determination even when the likely consequence is the person's death.[3] In *Re T*, Lord Donaldson even went so far as to claim that, at least for competent adults, making decisions about their medical treatment the right is absolute.[4]

---

[1] *S* v. *McC; W* v. *W* [1972] AC 24, 43.
[2] *Nancy B* v. *Hotel-Dieu de Quebec* (1992) 86 DLR (4th) 385, 391 (Quebec Superior Court). See also Cardozo J's statement in *Schloendorff* v. *Society of New York Hospital* 211 NY 125, 129 (1914).
[3] *Airedale NHS Trust* v. *Bland* [1993] 1 All ER 821, 860 per Lord Keith.
[4] *Re T (Adult: Refusal of Treatment)* [1992] 3 WLR 782, 786. Lord Donaldson MR did consider that a woman's choice may be limited by the prospect of that choice resulting in the death of a viable fetus. However, it has since been held that this is not the case: *Re MB (An Adult: Medical Treatment)* [1997] 2 FCR 541; *St George's Healthcare NHS Trust* v. *S* [1998] 3 WLR 936. See also *Re B (Consent to Treatment: Capacity)* [2002] EWHC 49.

For the law to protect personal autonomy, it must prohibit an invasion of that right and provide for sanctions when a breach does occur. This protection is achieved by allowing individuals a personal sphere of control mediated by consent. In this context, the personal sphere is the right to bodily integrity and a breach of consent renders the actor liable in tort law for a battery and in criminal law for at least a battery (and possibly one of the more serious offences under the Offences Against the Person Act 1861).[5]

This right to refuse treatment follows from the legal protection that allows individuals to claim a right to bodily integrity. The most expansive protection of this right is found in tort, and my focus is on this branch of law. Within tort law, it is battery that provides the most obvious protection and grounds the right to refuse treatment. As I suggested in Part I, the idea of control is inherent in the concept of a right and that control is facilitated through consent. This protection of personal autonomy requires both the underlying right to bodily integrity, and the secondary right of consent. As such it is necessary to consider both the extent of the protection of bodily integrity and the nature of the control allowed by consent in the law of battery.

Battery

In the context of medical treatment, a battery may be defined as an intentional and unjustified act that causes direct contact with the claimant's body.[6] The primary justification that makes that act lawful is the claimant's consent. For my purposes there are two elements to examine. First is the restriction to direct contact. The second is the meaning and limits of consent.

Despite the lack of clarity arising from *Collins* v. *Wilcock*,[7] in which Goff LJ stated that 'a battery is the actual infliction of unlawful force on another person',[8] directness is still required for contact to be battery.[9] According to Blackstone J,[10] the meaning of direct is 'immediate' – as opposed to consequential or 'mediate'. This is of little help. Surgical operations would certainly be direct, as would the physical contact

---

[5] *Sidaway* v. *Board of Governors of the Bethlem Royal Hospital* [1985] AC 871, 882 per Lord Scarman.

[6] F.A. Trinidade, 'Intentional torts: Some thoughts on assault and battery' (1982) 2 *Oxford Journal of Legal Studies* 211, 216.

[7] *Collins* v. *Wilcock* [1984] 1 WLR 1172.   [8] *Ibid.*, 1177.

[9] *Fowler* v. *Lanning* [1959] 1 QB 426; *Letang* v. *Cooper* [1965] 1 QB 232.

[10] *Scott* v. *Shepherd* (1773) 2 W Blackstone 892.

required to examine the patient, take blood or give an injection. However, consider the situation in which a doctor writes a prescription for a patient who takes it to the pharmacy where it is filled out and then taken home before, some hours later, the patient ingests a tablet. Could this amount to a battery where an effective consent had not been obtained?[11] This would almost certainly not be actionable as a battery. The connection between the doctor's prescription and the non-consensual contact with the offending tablets is insufficiently direct. However, consider the same scenario except, instead of writing a prescription for the drug, the physician hands the patient a plastic cup containing the tablets, which the patient then ingests (alternatively, the doctor leaves the cup on the side and merely indicates to the patient that she should take the tablets). Is this sufficiently direct to constitute a battery?

In *Mink* v. *University of Chicago*, a number of pregnant women were given diethylstilbestrol (DES) as part of a medical research programme.[12] The women were not told that they were part of an experiment, nor were they told that the pills were DES. The plaintiffs alleged, inter alia, that the defendants committed battery by experimenting on them without their consent. The administration of DES was alleged to be an 'offensive invasion of their persons'. Grady J acknowledged that most cases involving a lack of knowledge concerned the doctrine of 'informed consent', which should be bought in negligence. However, the fact that these patients neither knew that they were part of a research trial nor that the pills were DES meant that the situation was more closely analogous to an unauthorised operation than to a failure of information disclosure.[13] In deciding that the defendants were liable for battery, Grady J stated:

We find the administration of a drug without the patient's knowledge comports with the meaning of offensive contact. Had the drug been administered by means of a hypodermic needle, the element of physical contact would clearly be sufficient. We believe that causing the patient to physically ingest a pill is indistinguishable in principle.[14]

In the US, the American Restatement (Second) of Torts (1965) erased the need to show that, in battery, the force was direct. However, it may be argued that Grady's judgment should be equally applicable in England and other common-law jurisdictions. Grady held that a

---

[11] See G. Seabourne, 'The role of the tort of battery in medical law' (1995) 24 *Anglo-American Law Review* 265, 270.
[12] *Mink* v. *University of Chicago* 460 F. Supp. 713 (1978).   [13] *Ibid.*, 717.
[14] *Ibid.*, 718.

non-consensual injection would be a sufficiently direct application of force to constitute a battery. It follows that if 'causing the patient to physically ingest a pill is indistinguishable in principle' then that action would also be a battery. It may also be feasible to draw an analogy between this situation and *Scott* v. *Shepherd* in which the defendant threw a lighted firework into a crowded marketplace.[15] The firework was thrown onwards by two of the stallholders acting in self-preservation. It finally exploded in the plaintiff's face causing him to lose an eye. The act was held to be sufficiently direct because the intermediaries were not acting under the control of their own independent rational wills. The onward passage of the firework was considered to be a continuous chain of events set in motion by the defendant. In *Mink*, it could equally be argued that the women, by virtue of their lack of knowledge and power within the doctor-patient relationship, were not free to act controlled only by their own rational will. As such, it is arguable that the ingestion of the pill was simply another link in the chain initiated by the doctor.[16]

It is equally arguable that if *Mink* were heard in England it would have a different outcome. It may be significant that the drug was provided as part of a research programme rather than simply as therapy. Given the judicial reluctance to find doctors liable for battery (see p. 192), it is unlikely that, in a therapeutic context, English courts would accept Grady's argument that causing someone to ingest a tablet is equivalent in principle to injecting them with a hypodermic syringe.[17] Although it is arguable that the women may be acting under undue influence and hence that they are akin to a passive instrument in the hands of the doctor, an English court is more likely to hold that the act of ingesting was distinct from the doctor's act of providing them with the tablet and that the connection was an indirect one. Even if the court did adopt Grady's approach it is extremely unlikely that it would be extended to include prescription drugs.[18] Rather, the courts would probably hold that any liability would be in negligence rather than battery.

---

[15] *Scott* v. *Shepherd* (1773) 2 W Blackstone 892.

[16] See the criminal law case of *Haystead* v. *Chief Constable of Derbyshire* [2000] 3 All ER 890, in which it was held that it was sufficiently direct for the force to be applied through a 'medium controlled by the actions of the assailant'.

[17] In one US jurisdiction that treats informed consent as an aspect of the law of battery, rather than negligence, the Supreme Court even held, contrary to Grady J's opinion, that a therapeutic injection was insufficiently invasive to constitute a battery: *Morgan* v. *MacPhail* 704 A 2d 617 (1997).

[18] But see *Happell* v. *Wal-Mart Stores, Inc*, unreported (2006) WL 1840382 (Westlaw) in which the ND Illinois District Court followed *Mink* and held that providing a prescription drug could amount to a battery.

Consent and battery

Consent justifies rather than excuses the permitted contact.[19] Thus, in *Freeman* v. *Home Office*, Sir John Donaldson MR stated that 'consent . . . deprives the act of its tortious character',[20] and in *Airedale NHS Trust* v. *Bland*, Lord Mustill noted: 'The reason why the consent of the patient is so important is not that it furnishes a defence in itself, but because it is usually essential to the propriety of medical treatment.'[21] Consent functions as a justification because a lack of consent forms part of the offence.[22] This means that the burden of proof falls on the claimant, who must show an absence of consent.[23] Although in criminal law consent does not justify contact causing actual bodily harm,[24] it is likely that it would be effective in civil law, which is concerned with a private complaint and the correction of a wrong rather than the more public concerns of criminal law. In any case, in the present context of consent to medical treatment, a valid consent is also completely effective in the criminal law.[25]

Although consent functions as a complete justification to medical treatment, it is not the only justification recognised by the law. Where treatment is required to prevent a risk of harm to others, healthcare interventions may be justified by the public interest in preventing that harm materialising. Most noticeably this arises in the public-health context of communicable diseases and where the patient poses a risk because of mental illness.[26] It should also be noted that mental health law also allows non-consensual treatment of the competent person's mental health condition where there is a risk of self-harm.[27] A general exception to the need for consent is where the defendant's contact 'is acceptable in the ordinary conduct of everyday life'.[28] Finally treatment

---

[19] *Re F (Mental Patient: Sterilisation)* [1990] 2 AC 1, 73.

[20] *Freeman* v. *Home Office* [1984] 1 All ER 1036, 1044, CA.

[21] *Airedale NHS Trust* v. *Bland* [1993] 1 All ER 821, 889.

[22] *Freeman* v. *Home Office (No. 2)* [1984] 1 QB 524, 539. Although the case went to appeal, this point was not disputed: *Freeman* v. *Home Office (No. 2)* [1984] 1 QB 524. That lack of consent forms part of the offence in English law was also noted by McHugh J in the Australian case *Department of Health & Community Services (NT)* v. *JWB and SMB* (1992) 66 ALJR 300, 337.

[23] *Freeman* v. *Home Office (No.2)* [1984] 1 QB 524 at 539.

[24] See *R* v. *Brown* [1993] 2 WLR 556.

[25] *Attorney General's Reference (No. 6 of 1980)* [1981] 1 QB 715, 719. Lord Lane CJ actually specified 'reasonable surgical treatment', but it is likely that anything accepted as legitimate medical practice would be justified by the patient's consent.

[26] Sections 35–8 Public Health (Control of Disease) Act 1984; ss. 3(2)(c), 58, 62, 63 Mental Health Act 1983, as amended by the Mental Health Act 2007.

[27] Sections 3(2)(c), 62 Mental Health Act 1983.

[28] *Re F (Mental Patient: Sterilisation)* [1990] 2 AC 1, 73 per Lord Goff.

may also be justified by the doctrine of necessity, but only where the patient lacks the competence to give a valid consent.[29]

Competence   Although this book is primarily concerned with the competent adult, the relevant population cannot be defined without determining who is competent. Furthermore, if competency is decision-specific and related to the complexity of the decision, it is necessarily related to the informational element of consent: whether someone is competent should be determined by reference to the complexity of the information needed for a legally valid consent. Because of this relationship, a basic understanding of competence is relevant to the context of any discussion of consent. Finally, given the relationship between information and competence, how the law regulates these two issues is relevant to whether the law is coherent. For these reasons, it is important to consider how the law determines competency.

In *Re T*, Lord Donaldson MR noted that, while the law presumes that adults are competent, the right to self-determination requires the capacity to make the decision in question and the presumption of competence can be rebutted.[30] This means that there must be a standard of competence that allows the law to identify which adults lack the requisite capacity and should be deemed incompetent.

An early indication of the legal standard is found in Cardozo J's classic statement, which referred to the requirement of a 'sound mind'.[31] Although vague, this reflects a low-level test of capacity, which suggests that those persons capable of making the other decisions that are part of an ordinary adult life will also be competent to make their own medical treatment decisions. In *Chatterton v. Gerson*, Bristow J held that, for consent to be 'real' the patient must be 'informed in broad terms of the nature of the procedure'.[32] Since there is little point in requiring the transfer of information if it will not be understood, the law must, at least, require that the patient is capable of understanding 'in broad terms the nature of the procedure'.[33] This test remains easy to satisfy.

---

[29] *Ibid.*, 73–4 per Lord Goff. Section 5 of the Mental Capacity Act 2005 puts the 'best interests' justification on a statutory basis and under s. 9 medical treatments may also be justified by proxy consent.

[30] *Re T (Adult: Refusal of Treatment)* [1992] 3 WLR 782, 796.

[31] *Schloendorff* v. *Society of New York Hospital* 211 NY 125, 129 (1914).

[32] *Chatterton* v. *Gerson* [1981] 1 All ER 257, 265.

[33] M. Gunn, 'The meaning of incapacity' (1994) 2 *Medical Law Review* 8; M. Brazier, 'Competence, consent and proxy consents', in M. Brazier and M. Lobjoit (eds.), *Protecting the Vulnerable: Autonomy and consent in health care* (Routledge: London, 1991), pp. 34, 36.

In *Re C*, Thorpe J accepted the test of capacity proposed by one of the expert witnesses,[34] which requires the individual: '(1) to take in and retain treatment information, (2) to believe it and (3) to weigh that information, balancing risks and needs'.[35] Subsequently, in *Cambridgeshire CC* v. *R*, Hale J cited the *Re C* test and stated: 'The test of competence . . . has always been the capacity to understand the nature and effect of the transaction or other action proposed.'[36] Unlike the *Re C* test, this view of competency does not require that the person believes the information. Furthermore, although requiring an understanding of the effect of the intervention, Hale J's test avoids explicit reference to risks. However, the Mental Health Act Code of Practice quotes the tripartite *Re C* test as the appropriate test for competence and states that the knowledge required for consent includes: 'the purpose, nature, likely effects and risks of th[e] treatment including the likelihood of its success and any alternatives to it'.[37]

Following *Re C*, the Law Commission adopted a 'functional' approach to capacity based on the ability to make and communicate the requisite decision.[38] A person is unable to make a decision if:

he or she is unable to understand or retain the information relevant to the decision, including information about the reasonably foreseeable consequences of deciding one way or another or failing to make a decision.[39]

The Law Commission would also require the person to be capable of effectively using the information in making the decision.[40] However, it recommended that the 'belief' requirement of the *Re C* test should be dropped, which the Law Commission saw as superfluous to the requirement that the person must be able to use the information.[41] The proposal to drop the 'belief' element of the *Re C* test was followed by

---

[34] *Re C (Adult: Refusal of treatment)* [1994] 1 WLR 290.

[35] *Ibid.*, 292 per Thorpe J. When Thorpe J restated the test at 295, he dropped the 'balancing risks and needs' element. It is suggested that this has happened merely as shorthand and that Thorpe J accepted the need to balance 'risks and needs' since it is clear that he considered it very important that the risk of dying had altered from 85% to 15% following conservative treatment.

[36] *Cambridgeshire CC* v. *R* [1995] 1 FLR 50, 53.

[37] Mental Health Act Code of Practice (1999), paras. 15.10 and 15.13. The Code is currently being revised.

[38] The Law Commission, *Report on Mental Incapacity No. 231* (1995), para. 3.14: Draft Bill, clause 2(1). 'Mental disability' means 'any disability or disorder of the mind or brain, whether permanent or temporary, which results in an impairment or disturbance of mental functioning' (Draft Bill, clause 2(2)).

[39] *Ibid.*, para. 3.16: Draft Bill, clause 2(2) (a).   [40] *Ibid.*, para. 3.17.

[41] *Ibid.*, para. 3.17.

the Court of Appeal in *Re MB*,[42] and has been implemented in the Mental Capacity Act 2005, which makes competence subject to the ability to understand, retain, weigh up and use the information and communicate the decision.[43] The Code of Practice is clear that competence requires the capacity to understand the risks of the procedure and the alternatives.[44]

The assessment of capacity is decision-specific and the requisite ability depends on the decision to be made. While it might be thought that the standard should vary simply on the basis of the complexity of the decision, in *Re T*, Lord Donaldson MR argued that the capacity required for a decision depended on the importance of that decision. He stated:

> What matters is that doctors should consider whether at that time he had a capacity which was commensurate with the gravity of the decision which he purported to make. The more serious the decision, the greater the capacity required.[45]

This suggests that capacity is task-dependent and varies with the importance, or risk, of the decision. This sliding-scale risk-related standard of competence has received both academic support and criticism.[46] It has, however, received subsequent judicial approval from the Court of Appeal in *St George's Healthcare NHS Trust* v. *S*,[47] and appears to be part of English law. The Mental Capacity Act 2005 and the Code of Practice are silent on this. The Act does provide its own test of capacity but it is sufficiently vague to allow the risk-related standard to survive.

Voluntary consent   For consent to be valid it must have been freely given; consent gained by threats or fear of violence will be vitiated. Other, subtler, forms of pressure may also render consent ineffective. Whether or not the pressure is overt, it must have affected the individual to such a point that they can no longer be held responsible for their act. Thus, in *Olugboja*, Dunn LJ accepted that '"consent" . . . covers a wide range of states of mind . . . ranging from actual desire . . . to reluctant

---

[42] *Re MB (An Adult: Medical Treatment)* [1997] 2 FCR 541.

[43] Mental Capacity Act 2005, s. 3(1).

[44] Mental Capacity Act 2005 Code of Practice (2007), para. 4.30.

[45] *Re T (Adult: Refusal of Treatment)* [1992] 3 WLR 782, 796.

[46] For arguments against a risk-related standard see e.g. M. R. Wicclair, 'Patient decision-making capacity and risk' (1991) 5 *Bioethics* 91. For arguments in favour of a risk-related standard see e.g. J. Drane, 'The many faces of competency' (1985) 15 *Hastings Center Report* 17.

[47] *St George's Healthcare NHS Trust* v. *S* [1998] 3 WLR 936, 693.

acquiescence'.[48] However, the point at which the influence is strong enough to undermine the voluntary nature of the act is a matter of fact that is affected by societal beliefs, expectations and standards, which may vary over time and between communities.

Consider the nineteenth-century case of *Latter* v. *Braddell*, in which the plaintiff was a housemaid accused by her employer of being pregnant.[49] Although protesting, she submitted to an examination by the doctor summoned by her employer. Her case ultimately failed but the contrasting judgments illustrate the difficulty of determining an issue dependent on a matter of degree.

Lopes J stated:

I do not think it was correct to tell the jury that to maintain this action the plaintiff's will must have been overpowered by force or the fear of violence . . . A submission to what is done, obtained through a belief that she is bound to obey her master and mistress; or a consent obtained through fear of evil consequences to arise to herself, induced by her master's or mistress's words or conduct, is not sufficient. In neither case would the consent be voluntarily given. It would be a consent in one sense, but a consent to which the will was not a party.[50]

On the other hand, Lindley J stated:

The plaintiff was not a child; she knew perfectly well what she did and what was being done to her by the doctor . . . upon the evidence there is no reason whatever for supposing that any examination would have been made or attempted if she had told the doctor she would not allow herself to be examined. Under these circumstances I am of the opinion that there was no evidence of want of consent as distinguished from reluctant obedience or submission to her mistress's orders, and that in the absence of all evidence of coercion, as distinguished from an order which the plaintiff could comply with or not as she chose, the action cannot be maintained.[51]

When the case reached the Court of Appeal the plaintiff's case was dismissed since her submission was 'not through fear of violence'.[52] The requirement of force or violence is not the current law and in this sense *Latter* v. *Braddell* may 'safely be consigned to the archives'.[53] Lindley J's

---

[48] *R* v. *Olugboja* [1982] QB 320, 331; S. Gardner, 'Appreciating *Olugboja*' (1996) 16 *Legal Studies* 275, 279–80.

[49] *Latter* v. *Braddell* (1881) 50 LJQB 166, Common Pleas Division; (1881) 50 LJQB 448, CA.

[50] *Latter* v. *Braddell* (1881) 50 LJQB 166, 167–8.   [51] *Ibid.*, 168.

[52] *Latter* v. *Braddell* (1881) 50 LJQB 448 per Bramwell LJ.

[53] A. Grubb 'Consent to treatment: The competent person', in A. Grubb and J. Laing (eds.), *Principles of Medical Law*, 2nd edn (Oxford: Oxford University Press, 2004), pp. 131, 202, n. 422.

argument, in the Common Pleas hearing, was that the housemaid could still have refused consent and that, had she done so, she would not have been compelled to submit. It is suggested that this argument, although not explicit, is – like the Court of Appeal's judgment – relying on the lack of force present. However, as Lopes J's argument makes clear, coercion arises where the plaintiff believes that she has little option but to submit. Thus, the plaintiff only consented because she feared losing her job and her home if she acted otherwise. It is likely that Lopes J's judgment would be the preferred argument today and this is supported by the South African criminal case of *R* v. *McCoy*.[54]

The complainant had broken the rules of her employment as an air hostess by failing to use her seat belt during descent, which meant that she would either be grounded or dismissed. Since she was in debt and her work permit depended on her remaining in her current employment she was under pressure to remain on flying duty. Her boss, the appellant, suggested that this would be possible if she accepted a caning as an alternative punishment. The appellant was convicted of criminal assault and appealed. His appeal was dismissed partly because the caning was *malum in se*. However, the court also argued that her agreement was not really consent, 'but only submission under duress'.[55] For the court, the threat of losing her job was coercion and this undermined the effectiveness of the consent she gave.[56]

Whether an external influence is 'undue' is a matter of degree. Lopes J's argument and the judgment in *McCoy* suggest that this point is reached when the decision is no longer the individual's *own* decision: the decision was made only to avoid an unjust threat and the threat was irresistible. Whether influence will reach a sufficient degree of pressure to be considered undue depends both on the defendant's behaviour and on the contextual circumstances. The question of what circumstances are sufficient to vitiate consent arose in *Freeman* v. *Home Office*.[57]

The plaintiff in *Freeman*, who was serving a prison sentence, was given certain drugs to control his violent and antisocial behaviour. He brought an action for battery claiming, inter alia, that his consent under such circumstances could not be valid. His counsel submitted that the pressures and discipline of prison life meant that a prisoner would never be able to give a valid consent. Sir John Donaldson MR approved the statement made by the judge at first instance who held that the court should be alert to the risk that the context in which the consent was sought might affect the ability of the person to give a voluntary

---

[54] *R* v. *McCoy* [1953] 2 SA 4.   [55] *Ibid.*, 5.   [56] *Ibid.*, 11–12.
[57] *Freeman* v. *Home Office* [1984] 1 All ER 1036.

consent.[58] In the prison setting, the doctor may have a greater influence than in ordinary healthcare. However, this does not preclude the possibility of an effective consent; the context merely raises that possibility and is a factor to be taken into account.[59] This is not very helpful in determining when consent is vitiated by duress. All that may be taken from the case is that certain situations must alert the court to the possibility but that ultimately the question of whether influence has been undue is one of fact.

Lord Donaldson returned to the issue of undue influence in *Re T*.[60] T was pregnant and required a caesarean section following a road traffic accident. Her mother was a Jehovah's Witness, and shortly after her visit, T refused any blood transfusions that may have become necessary. After the operation she deteriorated and required ventilation on the intensive therapy unit. While there, she required a life-saving transfusion and the court was asked to consider whether her prior refusal was still operative. In the Court of Appeal, Lord Donaldson MR argued that others could advise the patient and influence in the form of persuasion was perfectly acceptable. Provided the patient's will has not been overborne the influence will not be undue and the consent will be effective. For Lord Donaldson:

> The real question in each such case is: does the patient really mean what he says or is he merely saying it for a quiet life, to someone else or because the advice and persuasion to which he has been subjected is such that he can no longer think and decide for himself? In other words, is it a decision expressed in form only, not in reality?[61]

This approach was followed by the Court of Appeal in *Mrs U* v. *The Centre for Reproductive Medicine*.[62]

Real consent   For any consent to be valid it must relate to the act performed. Thus, consent to an operation on the right ear will not be sufficient to negate liability for battery if the surgeon operates on the left ear, even where the left ear was more diseased than the right.[63] This is true even where the operation is beneficial to the patient.[64] The courts have held that a patient may consent to 'leave the nature and extent of

---

[58] *Ibid.*, 1044–5.   [59] *Freeman* v. *Home Office* [1984] 2 WLR 130, 145.
[60] *Re T (Adult: Refusal of Treatment)* [1992] 3 WLR 782.   [61] *Ibid.*, 797.
[62] *Mrs U* v. *The Centre for Reproductive Medicine* [2002] EWCA Civ 565, [22].
[63] *Mohr* v. *Williams* 104 NW 2 (1905). See also: *Cull* v. *Royal Surrey County Hospital* (1932) 1 BMJ 1195 in which a surgeon was liable for battery when he removed the plaintiff's uterus (womb) even though she had only consented to an abortion.
[64] *Devi* v. *West Midlands RHA* (1981) unreported, Transcript 491.

the operation to be performed to the discretion of the surgeon'.[65] However, consent to a particular act will be insufficient unless it is 'real'. Bristow J laid down the elements of a 'real consent' in *Chatterton* v. *Gerson*,[66] in which the plaintiff's action for battery failed because '[she] had been under no illusion as to the general nature of the operations performed by the defendant'.[67] Bristow J stated:

In my judgment once the patient is informed in broad terms of the nature of the procedure which is intended, and gives her consent, that consent is real, and the cause of the action on which to base a claim for failure to go into risks and implications is negligence, not trespass.[68]

The House of Lords, in *Sidaway* v. *Governors of Bethlem Royal Hospital*, subsequently confirmed Bristow J's approach.[69]

Bristow J's reasoning behind his decision to deny an action in battery may be criticised because he made no attempt to consider the purpose of obtaining the patient's consent. The only case used in support of his decision was the Canadian case of *Reibl* v. *Hughes*.[70] The Ontario Court of Appeal reversed the first instance decision because battery was inappropriate when a doctor acts in good faith. Instead of basing his decision on reasoned legal argument and principle Bristow J appeared to resort to policy. He claimed: 'it would be very much against the interests of justice if actions which are really based on a failure by the doctor to perform his duty adequately to inform were pleaded in trespass'.[71] No attempt was made to relate the obligation to obtain consent with the patient's right to self-determination as clearly stated by Justice Cardozo more than 60 years earlier. Bristow J ignored the issue of informed consent that had troubled the American courts.

When Bristow J gave his judgment, *Reibl* v. *Hughes* had only reached the Court of Appeal. However, the Supreme Court's decision is compatible with Bristow J's and, since the issues of risk and 'informed consent' were considered more fully, it is instructive to consider that case. In *Reibl* the plaintiff underwent carotid artery surgery, which, although competently performed, resulted in a massive stroke leaving him with a right-sided paralysis.[72] The plaintiff had formally consented but alleged that he had not been adequately informed of the risks (estimated at 10% risk of a stroke and a 4% risk of death). At first instance the trial judge

[65] *Breen* v. *Baker* (1956) The Times, 27 January.
[66] *Chatterton* v. *Gerson* [1981] 1 All ER 257.   [67] *Ibid.*, 258.   [68] *Ibid.*, 264–5.
[69] *Sidaway* v. *Governors of Bethlem Royal Hospital* [1985] 1 AC 871.
[70] *Reibl* v. *Hughes* (1978) 21 OR (2d) 14.
[71] *Chatterton* v. *Gerson* [1981] 1 All ER 257, 265.
[72] *Reibl* v. *Hughes* (1981) 114 DLR (3d) 1.

held that the risks involved were material rather than collateral and that
the defendant was liable in battery. In the Supreme Court, Laskin CJC –
giving the judgment of the court – held that the failure to disclose risks did
not give rise to liability for battery.[73]

The Supreme Court considered Morden J's test – described in *Kelly* v.
Hazlett[74] – for determining whether a failure to disclose risks would
support liability in battery or negligence.[75] Morden J distinguished
'collateral' risks from those that are central to the nature of the procedure.[76] He argued that a failure to disclose 'collateral risks' was more
properly considered in negligence. However:

> The more probable the risk the more it could be said to be an integral feature of
> the nature and character of the operation. Further, even if a risk is truly col-
> lateral, but still material, it could be said that its disclosure is so essential to an
> informed decision to undergo the operation that lack of such disclosure should
> vitiate the consent.[77]

Laskin CJC, however, rejected this distinction. He held that risk disclosure arose from the doctor's duty of care to the patient and that, in
the absence of bad faith, any breach of duty was negligence rather than
battery.[78]

The nature of a procedure also includes its purpose. Thus, in *Appleton*
v. *Garrett*, where the defendant performed unnecessary dental work on
the plaintiffs for purely financial gain, the judge held that the plaintiffs'
consents were not 'real'.[79] Furthermore, the patient must know the
identity of the treating professional. In *R* v. *Richardson* the appellant
dentist continued treating her patients even though she had been suspended from the General Dental Council's register.[80] She was charged
with assault and the judge ruled that her patients' apparent consents
were vitiated because she allowed them to think she was still registered.
She changed her plea to guilty and then appealed against the judge's
ruling.

The Court of Appeal allowed her application. Otton LJ stated:

> the Crown contended that the concept of the 'identity of the person' should be
> extended to cover the qualifications or attributes of the dentist on the basis that
> the patients consented to treatment by a qualified dentist and not a suspended
> one. We must reject that submission . . . the complainants were fully aware of

---

[73] *Ibid.*, 8–9.   [74] *Kelly* v. *Hazlett* (1976) 75 DLR (3d) 536.
[75] This test was adopted by Haines J, the trial judge in *Reibl*.
[76] *Kelly v Hazlett* (1976) 75 DLR (3d) 536, 558–9.   [77] *Ibid.*, 559.
[78] *Reibl v Hughes* (1981) 114 DLR (3d) 1, 10–11.
[79] *Appleton* v. *Garrett* [1997] 8 Med LR 75.   [80] *R* v. *Richardson* (1998) 43 BMLR 21.

the identity of the appellant. To accede to the submission would be to strain or distort the everyday meaning of the word 'identity', the dictionary definition of which is 'the condition of being the same'.[81]

Effectively the Court of Appeal rejected the argument that the consent was to 'dental treatment by a registered dentist' in favour of 'dental treatment by Ms Richardson'. Although the head-note states that 'a person's professional status or qualifications did not constitute part of their identity',[82] Otton LJ rejected the Crown's argument that 'there was no distinction between an unqualified dentist and one who is suspended'.[83] It may, therefore, have been important that she was a qualified dentist even though she was not registered at the time.

Richardson may be compared with *R* v. *Tabassum*.[84] Three women consented to be shown how to perform a breast examination by the accused, who was preparing a computer software package on breast cancer. The women all stated that they only consented to the examination because they believed the accused to be medically qualified. However, no sexual motive was alleged. The Court of Appeal held that the women had not given a true consent since, although they understood the nature of the act, they had not consented to the quality of the act. The women knew that the act was a breast examination and that it was for the purpose of preparing the software package. Thus, the Court of Appeal considered that the women's consent was to 'breast examination for the purposes of preparing a medical software package by a medically qualified person' rather than simply 'breast examination for the purposes of preparing a medical software package'. Although *Richardson* was distinguished because the decision concerned the identity of the actor rather than the nature or quality of the act, the only relevant factor in *Tabassum* was that the accused was not medically qualified,[85] which emphasises the courts' reluctance to find doctors liable for battery.

The legal regulation of consent in negligence

Legal liability in negligence requires three things: a duty of care; a breach of that duty; and a legally recognised form of damage caused by the breach. Since the duty of care is established by the professional–patient relationship it is only the latter two elements that require examination. A suitable starting point is the leading case of *Sidaway* v. *Governors of Bethlam Royal Hospital*, in which the issue of consent and the standard of

---

[81] *Ibid.*, 26.   [82] *Ibid.*   [83] *Ibid.*, 26.
[84] *R* v. *Tabassum* [2000] Lloyd's LR Med 404, CA.
[85] See also the Canadian case of *R* v. *Bolduc and Bird* [1976] 3 CCC 294, SCC.

information disclosure reached the House of Lords for the first (and only) time.[86]

Sidaway *and the standard of disclosure*

The facts and judgments The plaintiff underwent an operation to relieve recurrent neck pain. It was performed competently but the small risk (less than 1 per cent) of paraplegia associated with the operation materialised and the plaintiff was left partially paralysed. She sued in negligence alleging that the defendant had failed to inform her of this risk. At first instance Skinner J held that, while the defendant had informed the plaintiff of the risk of damaging the nerve roots (approximately 1 per cent), he had failed to inform her of the possible damage to her spinal cord (with the attendant risk of paralysis). However, Skinner J applied the *Bolam* test, which holds the defendant to a standard that a responsible body of professionals would accept as reasonable,[87] to deny the plaintiff's claim. The Court of Appeal affirmed the decision and the plaintiff appealed to the House of Lords.

It was unanimously held that the plaintiff's appeal failed because she had been unable to prove that the surgeon had breached his duty of care. Their Lordships took the opportunity to consider the standard of risk disclosure expected of the doctor. Broadly speaking, three different approaches to the standard of disclosure are detectable in their Lordships' judgments,[88] although Lord Templeman's speech might be considered sufficiently distinct to be a fourth approach.

Lord Scarman began with the premise that it is the patient's right to accept or reject the proffered treatment.[89] He argued that 'a doctor's duty of care extends not only to the health and well-being of his patient but also to a proper respect for his patient's rights [thus], the duty to warn can be seen to be a part of the doctor's duty of care'.[90] Importantly, he then went on rightly to recognise that factors other than the patient's health might be relevant to the decision.[91] These non-medical factors must be weighed against the medical advice to allow the patient to make a rational decision. Thus, the doctor's duty is both to advise a

---

[86] *Sidaway* v. *Governors of Bethlam Royal Hospital* [1985] 1 AC 871. The standard of disclosure was *obiter* to the decision in *Chester* v. *Afshar* [2004] UKHL 41, which concerned the issue of causation.

[87] *Bolam* v. *Friern HMC* [1957] 1 WLR 582.

[88] Grubb, 'Consent to treatment: The competent person', p. 184.

[89] *Sidaway* v. *Governors of Bethlam Royal Hospital* [1985] 1 AC 871, 882.

[90] *Ibid.*, 885.   [91] *Ibid.*, 886.

particular medical treatment and to provide sufficient information to allow the patient to make the decision.[92]

As to the substance of this duty, Lord Scarman rejected the *Bolam* principle and opted instead for the 'prudent patient' standard adopted in *Canterbury* v. *Spence*.[93] This requires disclosure of 'material' risks, defined as follows:

a risk is . . . material when a *reasonable person*, in what the physician knows or should know to be the patient's position, would be likely to attach significance to the risk or cluster of risks in deciding whether or not to forego the proposed therapy.[94]

This limits the role of the medical experts to determining the probability and seriousness of a risk materialising and also the 'character of the risk'.[95] The judgement of whether the risk should have been disclosed, however, is for the court to make based on the 'prudent patient' test. There was one caveat to this test: the risk need not be disclosed where the doctor reasonably believes that disclosure would harm the patient's health.[96]

Lord Diplock argued that the doctor's duty of care was indivisible and included risk disclosure.[97] His Lordship considered that the *Bolam* test was simply a modern restatement of the ancient rule of common law.[98] Thus, he stated: 'no convincing reason has in my view been advanced . . . that would justify treating the *Bolam* test as doing anything less than laying down a principle of English law that is comprehensive and applicable to every aspect of the duty of care owed by a doctor to his patient'.[99]

Lord Diplock's judgment contained two other notable points. First, he argued that a 'highly educated man of experience' such as a judge, would want to exercise his right to self-determination. In order to make a rational judgement about whether to consent or refuse consent to treatment, such a man would need to be 'fully informed of any risks'.[100] Similarly, there are enquiring patients who ask questions and should be told by the doctor what they want to know. However, these types of patient must be distinguished from unenquiring patients who must rely on the doctor's skill and judgement to define what they are told. Second, he stated that the only possible effect of risk disclosure would be to deter patients from consenting to the intervention recommended by the

---

[92] *Ibid.*, 886.   [93] *Canterbury* v. *Spence* 464 F 2d 772, 780 (1972).
[94] *Ibid.*, 787; emphasis added by Lord Scarman.
[95] *Sidaway* v. *Governors of Bethlam Royal Hospital* [1985] 1 AC 871, 889.
[96] *Ibid.*, 889–90.   [97] *Ibid.*, 893–5.   [98] *Ibid.*, 892.   [99] *Ibid.*, 893.   [100] *Ibid.*, 895.

doctor.[101] The implication of this claim, followed – as it is – by endorsement of the *Bolam* standard, is that doctors are under no obligation to inform patients of a risk if they reasonably believe that knowledge will deter them from giving consent.

Lord Bridge, with whom Lord Keith agreed, also held that the *Bolam* test was the appropriate standard. He examined the role of medical expertise in risk disclosure and noted that, in *Reibl*, Laskin CJC argued that medical experts are necessary to determine what risks are associated with a particular procedure but that the materiality of risk should not be determined by expert medical evidence alone. In a somewhat confused and self-contradictory discussion Lord Bridge stated:

I fully appreciate the force of this reasoning, but can only accept it subject to the important qualification that a decision what degree of disclosure of risks is best calculated to assist a particular patient to make a rational choice must primarily be a matter of clinical judgment.[102]

In other words, Lord Bridge accepted it was the patient's right to know but only if rubber-stamped by 'clinical judgment'. However, while the force of Laskin's reasoning had not convinced him that the professional standard was inappropriate, it was enough for Lord Bridge to hold that adopting the *Bolam* test did not entirely hand the matter over to the medical profession. There were some risks, such as the 10 per cent risk of a stroke, that were 'so obviously necessary to an informed choice' that no reasonable doctor would fail to disclose them.[103]

Although not specifically mentioning the *Bolam* test, Lord Templeman's judgment was arguably closer to Lord Bridge's than Lord Scarman's or Lord Diplock's judgment. Thus, while he acknowledged it was the patient's right to decide and the doctor's duty to provide adequate information, Lord Templeman concluded that: 'At the end of the day, the doctor, bearing in mind the best interests of the patient . . . must decide what information should be given to the patient and in what terms that information should be couched.'[104] Lord Templeman distinguished 'general' from 'specific' risks: for a general risk it is sufficient that patients are simply aware 'that a major operation may entail serious consequences'.[105] If patients want more information this must be specifically requested. Lord Templeman's argument relied on the view that too much information may be just as harmful as too little information. In addition, patients' medical conditions may make them ill-prepared to

---

[101] *Ibid.*, 895.   [102] *Ibid.*, 900.
[103] *Ibid.*, 900. The 10 per cent risk of stroke came for the case of *Reibl* v. *Hughes*.
[104] *Ibid.*, 905.   [105] *Ibid.*, 902.

cope with detailed information, which doctors should not thrust upon them. It is sufficient if patients are aware that the procedure is risky, but still in their best interests unless they specifically ask for further information or the risk is of a 'special nature'.

Unfortunately, Lord Templeman did not provide a clear explanation of the distinction between a 'general' and a 'specific' risk. At one point his argument suggests that for a general risk the patient simply needs to know that the operation carries the risk of 'serious consequences'.[106] Later, however, he stated that: 'In the case of a general danger the court must decide whether the information afforded to the patient was sufficient to alert the patient to the possibility of serious harm of the kind in fact suffered.'[107] This is inconsistent with his previous statement, since to be aware of the 'kind of harm' requires information of a different order from that needed to know that 'serious consequences' might follow. Like Lord Bridge, Lord Templeman turned to the 10 per cent risk of stroke in *Reibl* for an illustration of what would count as a special risk. However, he also made a point of including the 4 per cent risk of death as a 'specific risk'. Since death can occur as a consequence of any operation involving a general anaesthetic, Lord Templeman must have placed a great weight on the probability of a particular harm in determining whether it is specific to the operation.

Echoes of the *Bolam* test are discernable in Lord Templeman's argument that if doctors fail to disclose a risk, for which disclosure was the accepted medical practice, then the court will find them liable unless they can justify their actions. However, where medical practice:

is divided or does not include express mention, it will be for the court to determine whether the harm suffered is an example of a general danger inherent in the nature of the operation and if so whether the explanation . . . was sufficient to alert the patient to the general dangers of which the harm suffered is an example.[108]

This, less ambiguously than Lord Bridge's argument, reserved for the court the right to choose between two opposing schools of thought within the medical profession. However, Lord Templeman tempered this statement by deciding that the court should be slow to hold a conscientious doctor liable for a failure to disclose. The general tenor, therefore, of Lord Templeman's judgment is that, while the court has the final word, doctors are acting conscientiously in the patient's best interests and – unless the patient has specifically requested the

[106] *Ibid.*, 902.   [107] *Ibid.*, 903.   [108] *Ibid.*, 903.

information in question – will only be found liable where they have unjustifiably acted independently of medical practice.

Sidaway *and the standard of care*   Given the variance between the judgments it is not surprising that commentators disagreed on the interpretation and implications of the case. Kennedy and Grubb argued that Lord Diplock was in the minority and that the majority rejected the *Bolam* test.[109] Kennedy went so far as to claim that 'The message of *Sidaway* is clear. Those who advise doctors already know it. Medical paternalism has had its day.'[110] Others argued that *Sidaway* simply reaffirmed the professional standard,[111] while the majority adopted a middle ground, focusing on the speeches of Lords Bridge and Templeman and concluding that *Bolam* had been retained but modified. For some, the rejection of the prudent-patient test meant that the House of Lords had undermined the law's declared commitment to autonomy and left it in an 'unsatisfactory state'.[112] Others, however, were cautiously optimistic,[113] arguing that *Sidaway* was a step in the right direction.[114]

These disparate views were perhaps a consequence of the inherent ambiguity in the *Bolam* test. It is possible to interpret the test either to leave the standard of care entirely within the hands of the medical profession, or to retain for the court the right to determine that the relevant common practice is not reasonable. If this latter view is adopted then Lord Diplock's and Lord Bridge's judgments converge and any distinction between Lord Diplock and the 'majority' was a 'matter of semantics', merely serving to clarify rather than change or reject *Bolam*.[115] Although Lord Templeman did not discuss the standard in terms of the *Bolam* test, the general gist of his argument, despite its lack of clarity, is compatible with the latter view of that standard. If, however,

---

[109] I. Kennedy, 'The patient on the Clapham omnibus', in *Treat Me Right: Essays in medical law and ethics* (Oxford: Clarendon Press, 1988), p. 175; A. Grubb, 'Contraceptive advice and doctors – A law unto themselves' (1988) 47 *The Cambridge Law Journal* 12, 13. See also, S. Lee, 'Operating under informed consent' (1985) 101 *Law Quarterly Review* 316.

[110] Kennedy, 'The patient on the Clapham omnibus', p. 210.

[111] M. Brazier, 'Patient autonomy and consent to treatment: The role of the law?' (1987) 7 *Legal Studies* 169, 182.

[112] K. Williams, 'Pre-operative consent and medical negligence' (1985) 15 *Anglo-American Law Review* 169, 179–80.

[113] D. Giesen and J. Hayes, 'The patient's right to know – A comparative view' (1992) 21 *Anglo-American Law Review* 101, 103.

[114] Teff, 'Consent to medical procedures: Paternalism, self-determination or therapeutic alliance', 450.

[115] C. Newdick, 'The doctor's duties of care under *Sidaway*' (1985) 36 *Northern Ireland Legal Quarterly* 243, 247, 249–50.

the *Bolam* test is given Lord Scarman's interpretation, then the judgments diverge and there is no clear majority opinion.[116]

Answering questions   While the issue was *obiter*, their Lordships considered the doctor's response to questioning and his obligation to tell the truth. Although not specifically addressing the issue, Lord Scarman implied that a doctor should respond truthfully to any direct questions. He argued that the moral ideal would be to disclose what that particular patient subjectively needed to know but the law was constrained by practical considerations to an objective obligation.[117] Since it was the evidentiary difficulties alone that led him to accept the 'prudent patient' test, it follows that if a patient, through direct questioning, alerts the doctor to their own particular needs, then the doctor would be obliged to meet them.[118]

Lord Diplock commented that: 'No doubt if the patient in fact manifested this attitude [of wanting to be fully informed] by means of direct questioning, the doctor would tell him whatever it was the patient wanted to know.'[119] This was unqualified but was stated as if in the alternative to the *Bolam* test, which implies that direct questioning creates an exception to the *Bolam* test and it becomes the doctor's duty to provide whatever information is requested. The difficulty with this is that questioning can be more or less specific and the extent of the response may be similarly varied. Given his otherwise wholehearted support of *Bolam*, it is likely that Lord Diplock would also gauge the appropriateness of the doctor's response to direct questions by the *Bolam* test unless the questions were so precise as to require a particular answer.

Lord Bridge argued that specific questions must be answered 'truthfully and ... fully'.[120] Again, this seems fairly explicit in relation to precise questions but Lord Bridge's statement also leaves the vague or general question at the mercy of the *Bolam* test. Similarly, Lord Templeman allowed that a direct question creates a greater duty of disclosure requiring an accurate answer.[121]

The conclusion that may be drawn from their Lordships' judgments is that direct questioning requires a truthful and complete response. Thus, precise questions should be given precise answers. In respect of more

---

[116] J. Montgomery, *Health Care Law*, 2nd edn (Oxford: Oxford University Press, 2003), p. 245.
[117] *Sidaway* v. *Governors of Bethlam Royal Hospital* [1985] 1 AC 871, 888.
[118] Except possibly when covered by the therapeutic privilege.
[119] *Sidaway* v. *Governors of Bethlam Royal Hospital* [1985] 1 AC 871, 895.
[120] *Ibid.*, 898.   [121] *Ibid.*, 902.

general questions, their Lordships' statements are ambiguous. Take Lord Bridge's dictum that the answer must be as 'full' as the questioner requires. The problem here is that the doctor must try and determine from the question what it is that the patient wishes to know. Questions may be quite general and the doctor is left with discretion to determine the exact response. In these circumstances their Lordships have not ruled out the *Bolam* test as a guide to the standard expected.

Even where the question appears to be specific, it may be that the patient had something more general in mind. For example, the question 'What are the risks of this procedure?' has more than one possible interpretation. It might mean any one of the following:

1 What risks do you think are significant?
2 What risks do you think I need to know about?
3 What are *all* the risks?
4 What are the common risks?
5 What are the most serious risks?

The third option is the only one of these five possibilities that denies the doctor any discretion and even here the situation is not clear-cut. Are doctors obliged to disclose every adverse consequence ever recorded, or only those recorded in major textbooks, or those recorded in academic journals, or only those that they are – or ought to be – aware of? It is likely that they would only be expected to disclose those risks that they ought to be aware of and this would be judged in relation to their fellow professionals.[122] The *Bolam* test creeps back in.

Developments in the standard of care since Sidaway

Pre-Bolitho   Because these cases are now largely historical in significance I will deal with them briefly. There are two relevant Court of Appeal cases and both interpreted *Sidaway* restrictively. In *Blyth* v. *Bloomsbury*, the *Bolam* test was applied to determine the doctor's duty to disclose in response to general questions.[123] In *Gold* v. *Haringey* the Court of Appeal applied *Bolam* to disclosure of information regarding non-therapeutic interventions.[124] A widely held view amongst academics at the time was that *Bolam* provided a carte blanche for common

---

[122] See *Crawford* v. *Board of Governors of Charing Cross Hospital* (1953) The Times, 8 December. Also, see later discussion of *Blyth* v. *Bloomsbury HA* [1993] 4 Med LR 151 (decided 1987).
[123] *Blyth* v. *Bloomsbury HA* [1993] 4 Med LR 151 (decided 1987).
[124] *Gold* v. *Haringey HA* [1988] 1 QB 481.

practice and some saw *Sidaway* as removing that privilege. With that in mind, it is not surprising that these judgments received heavy criticism.[125]

One of the problems with the *Bolam* test is that the courts may apply it uncritically allowing the standard of care to be set by the medical profession. This view, which is reflected in Lord Scarman's judgment (see above), is supported by the judgments in both non-disclosure and other cases of clinical negligence.[126] However, the courts, albeit 'comparatively rare[ly]',[127] have exercised their right to reject expert medical evidence. In *McAllister* v. *Lewisham and North Southwark HA*,[128] Rougier J accepted that the *Bolam* test was the appropriate standard for determining disclosure. However, following Lord Bridge's judgment in *Sidaway*, he noted the caveat that, in the absence of 'cogent clinical reason' to justify withholding information, there were certain risks that ought to be disclosed regardless of common practice.[129] This was because, 'within certain limitations, a patient is entitled to be given sufficient information on the risks of an operation to allow him or her to exercise a balanced judgment; after all it is their life that is going to be affected'.[130]

Although the courts of first instance have been willing to challenge the opinion of expert witnesses, the Court of Appeal has arguably been more deferential.[131] Consider, for example, *Eyre* v. *Measeday*, a case in contract that concerned an unsuccessful sterilisation.[132] One of the plaintiff's allegations was that the surgeon had not warned her of the risk of failure and thus there was an implied collateral warranty that she would be rendered irreversibly sterile. In rejecting her claim for breach of

---

[125] See e.g. J. Montgomery, 'Power/Knowledge/Consent: Medical decisionmaking' (1988) 51 *Modern Law Review* 245, 248; I. Kennedy, 'Consent to treatment: The capable person', in C. Dyer (ed.), *Doctors, Patients and the Law* (Oxford: Blackwell Scientific Publications, 1992), pp. 44, 68–9; J. Healy, *Medical Negligence: Common law perspectives* (London: Sweet & Maxwell, 1999), pp. 152, 161.

[126] Lord Woolf, 'Are the courts excessively deferential to the medical profession?' (2001) 9 *Medical Law Review* 1; M. Brazier and J. Miola, 'Bye-bye Bolam: A medical revolution?' (2000) 8 *Medical Law Review* 85; A. Maclean, 'Beyond Bolam and Bolitho' (2002) 5 *Medical Law International* 205.

[127] M. A. Jones, 'Informed consent and other fairy stories' (1999) 7 *Medical Law Review* 103, 116.

[128] *McAllister* v. *Lewisham and North Southwark HA* [1994] 5 Med LR 343.

[129] *Ibid.*, 351.

[130] *Ibid.*, 351. See also *Smith* v. *Tunbridge Wells HA* [1994] 5 Med LR 334, 339; *Gascoine* v. *Sheridan* [1994] 5 Med LR 437, 441–4, in which Mitchell J was able to find a similar authority in Lord Diplock's judgment in *Sidaway*; *Doughty* v. *North Staffordshire HA* [1992] 3 Med LR 81; and *Newell and Newell* v. *Goldenberg* [1995] 6 Med LR 371, 374.

[131] See *Gold* and *Blyth* above. But, see *Loveday* v. *Renton* [1990] 1 Med LR 117.

[132] *Eyre* v. *Measeday* [1986] 1 All ER 488.

contract, Purchas LJ stated that 'in withholding this information the defendant was following a practice acceptable to current professional standards and was acting in the best interests of the plaintiff'.[133] Although the plaintiff did not pursue a claim in negligence, it is clear from this statement, that she would have been unsuccessful.[134]

The dichotomy seen in the courts' judgments is, at least in some cases, arguably caused by the court focusing on the status of the experts,[135] while in other cases it focuses on the opinion expressed by the expert witnesses.[136] Where judges focus on the body of professionals they almost invariably find in favour of the doctors. Where the spotlight is more appropriately on the opinion expressed then the judgment may go either way depending on the reasonableness of the opinion. That the Court of Appeal appears to have focused more deferentially on the body of professionals, rather than the opinion that body expresses, is illustrated by *Ratty* v. *Haringey HA*.[137] The trial judge accepted the plaintiff's experts' opinion but the Court of Appeal reversed the judgment on this point.[138] Kennedy LJ accepted that the *Bolam* test as applied in *Maynard* was the proper approach. He stated that 'it was important in the present case, once it was accepted that Mr Mann and Mr Addison represented a responsible and respectable body of colorectal opinion, to accept without qualification their formulation of the Marnham rule'.[139]

Prior to *Bolitho*, the law regarding the standard of care expected from doctors was noticeably inconsistent. This flowed from two sources. First were the disparate judgments given by their Lordships in *Sidaway*. Second, and perhaps of more fundamental importance, is the inherent

---

[133] *Ibid.*, 497.

[134] See also, *Palmer* v. *Eadie* Lexis Transcript 18 May 1987.

[135] See e.g. *Abbas* v. *Kenney* [1996] 7 Med LR 47, 57 per Gage J: 'Since Mr Shepherd is acknowledged to be a very experienced and distinguished surgeon, it seems to me quite impossible to conclude that the defendant fell below the ordinary skill of a surgeon practising in this field.'

[136] See, *Judge* v. *Huntingdon HA* [1995] 6 Med LR 223, 227; *Waters* v. *West Sussex HA* [1995] 6 Med LR 362, 366–9; *Early* v. *Newham HA* [1994] 5 Med LR 214, 216. For a rare pre-*Bolitho* example of the Court of Appeal looking beyond the expert's qualifications, see *Loveday* v. *Renton* [1990] 1 Med LR 117, 125.

[137] *Ratty* v. *Haringey HA* [1994] 5 Med LR 413. See also *De Freitas* v. *O'Brien* [1995] 6 Med LR 108, especially at 114. Although not a non-disclosure case, *De Freitas* is another example of the Court of Appeal applying the normative test to the 'body' rather than the opinion.

[138] Although liability was upheld in relation to the plaintiff's damaged bladder and ureters.

[139] *Ratty* v. *Haringey HA* [1994] 5 Med LR 413, 416. See also Evans LJ, 419 and Balcombe LJ, 420. See also the first instance cases of *Stobie* v. *Central Birmingham HA* (1994) 22 BMLR 135, 144 per Turner J; *Heath v West Berkshire HA* [1992] 3 Med LR 57, 59; *Bancroft v Harrogate HA* [1997] 8 Med LR 398, 404.

ambiguity within the *Bolam* test. This ambiguity allowed the courts, particularly the Court of Appeal, to adopt a deferential attitude to medical opinion based on the status of the expert witness. By focusing on whether the professional body was responsible rather than applying the normative question to the proffered opinion it is arguable that the courts have been too quick to accept the common practice as reasonable. In doing so, the courts have applied what should be an ethical test as if it were a sociological one.[140] Rather than focusing on what the reasonable doctor believes should be done the courts have tended to focus on what the reasonable doctor actually does. However, reasonable people do not always act reasonably and, when subject to pressure, they make take shortcuts that increase the risk. These shortcuts may become established practice and so become what the reasonable doctor does. This does not mean that these shortcuts are themselves reasonable; an action is not reasonable simply because it is done by reasonable people.

Bolitho, *beyond* Bolam?   In *Bolitho* v. *City and Hackney HA* the House of Lords again considered the *Bolam* test, albeit not in the context of disclosure.[141] Lord Browne-Wilkinson held:

> the court has to be satisfied that the exponents of the body of opinion relied upon can demonstrate that such opinion has a logical basis. In particular in cases involving, as they so often do, the weighing of risks against benefits, the judge before accepting a body of opinion as being responsible, reasonable or respectable, will need to be satisfied that, in forming their views, the experts have directed their minds to the question of comparative risks and benefits and have reached a defensible conclusion on the matter.[142]

Lord Browne-Wilkinson's argument clearly retains the court's right (and duty) to critically analyse the expert witnesses' evidence to ensure that the opinion, and not just the body, is reasonable. However, he heavily qualified his statement by suggesting that: 'In the vast majority of cases the fact that distinguished experts in the field are of a particular opinion will demonstrate the reasonableness of that opinion.'[143] This again suggests that the status of the witness will go a long way to satisfying any test of reasonableness even before the expert has proffered an opinion. Thus, Lord Browne-Wilkinson emphasised that the courts will only rarely conclude that the expert's opinion is not logically defensible.

---

[140] J. L. Montrose, 'Is negligence an ethical or a sociological concept?' (1958) 21 *Modern Law Review* 259.
[141] *Bolitho* v. *City and Hackney HA* [1998] AC 232.
[142] *Ibid.*, 241–2.   [143] *Ibid.*, 243.

Similar to the response following *Sidaway*, the academic reaction to *Bolitho* was mixed. Some commentators welcomed the judgment with open arms,[144] while others were far more cautious.[145] Still others suggested that *Bolitho* would have minimal effect.[146]

Some academics have considered *Bolitho*'s impact with the benefit of subsequent case law. Brazier and Miola argued that *Bolitho* will make a difference to malpractice litigation because it was decided 'amidst a host of other relevant developments affecting the provision of health care'.[147] These developments include: more demanding guidelines issued by a number of medical bodies, including the General Medical Council (GMC) and the Royal Colleges; the government's intention to establish national standards; the attitude of the Law Commission; and the coming into force of the Human Rights Act 1998.[148] Thus, although *Bolitho* alone would be unlikely to have a huge impact, in conjunction with these other developments the judiciary will come under increasing pressure to scrutinise professional practice. The effects of *Bolitho*, Brazier and Miola have claimed, can already be seen in the Court of Appeal decision in *Marriott* v. *West Midlands HA*.[149] Further, in the context of information disclosure they noted the combined effects of *Pearce* v. *United Bristol Healthcare NHS Trust*,[150] and *Smith* v. *Tunbridge Wells HA*,[151] which signalled 'that announcements of the stillbirth of "informed consent" in England were premature'.[152]

Lord Woolf has since commented, extra-judicially, that he was 'attracted' by the Brazier and Miola article, which supported his belief 'that the courts are going to take Lord Browne-Wilkinson's injunction to review the logical basis of the expert medical testimony seriously'.[153] Other commentators, however, were more cautious. Thus, Montgomery, Skegg and Jones all argued that it was too early to determine the impact of *Bolitho*.[154] In a survey of 64 cases carried out in 2001, four

---

[144] Grubb, 'Consent to treatment: The competent person', p. 196. See also, W. Scott, '*Bolam* and *Bolitho*: A new standard of care for doctors?' (1998) 148 *New Law Journal* 64.

[145] J. Keown, 'Reining in the *Bolam* test' (1998) 57 *The Cambridge Law Journal* 248, 249; H. Teff, 'The standard of care in medical negligence – Moving on from Bolam?' (1998) 18 *Oxford Journal of Legal Studies* 473.

[146] Healy, *Medical Negligence*, p. 66.   [147] Brazier and Miola, 'Bye-bye Bolam', 112.

[148] *Ibid.*, 110–13, 114.   [149] *Marriott* v. *West Midlands HA* [1999] Lloyd's LR Med 23.

[150] *Pearce* v. *United Bristol Healthcare NHS Trust* (1998) 48 BMLR 118.

[151] *Smith* v. *Tunbridge Wells HA* [1994] 5 Med LR 334.

[152] Brazier and Miola, 'Bye-bye Bolam', 113.

[153] The quote is from Lord Woolf, 'Are the courts excessively deferential to the medical profession?' (2001) 9 *Medical Law Review* 1, 10.

[154] J. Montgomery, 'Time for a paradigm shift?', 375; P. D. G. Skegg, 'English medical law and "informed consent": An antipodean assessment and alternative' (1999) 7

years after *Bolitho*, I found that *Bolam* and *Bolitho* were inconsistently applied and that there was little evidence to support Brazier and Miola's position.[155] Even cases that they strongly relied on, such as *Marriott*, are open to more critical analysis that reveals much less support for their opinion than they claimed.[156] That survey, however, was not specific to disclosure cases and it is to those cases that I now turn.

In *Pearce* v. *United Bristol Healthcare NHS Trust*, the Court of Appeal was asked to consider the standard of risk disclosure required to enable the claimant to decide whether to accept the defendant's advice to follow a conservative non-interventional approach.[157] The claimant, who was pregnant, had gone past the expected date of delivery and was extremely concerned for the safety of her fetus. She saw the consultant obstetrician, who counselled her that the safest course was to allow labour to begin naturally. He did not disclose that there was a small (0.1–0.2 per cent) risk of stillbirth, which unfortunately materialised. The woman brought a claim for failure to disclose the risk, which was rejected both at first instance and by the Court of Appeal.

Despite the fact that the claimant lost her case, Lord Woolf MR's judgment does appear, at first glance, to advance the cause of patient autonomy. He argued that:

if there is a significant risk which would affect the judgment of a reasonable patient, then in the normal course it is the responsibility of a doctor to inform the patient of that significant risk, if the information is needed so that the patient can determine for him or herself as to what course he or she should adopt.[158]

However, the appellant's case was dismissed, which weakens the strength of any support the judge's words may imply. Speaking the right words is far easier than putting those words into practice and it is only when that happens that the words are likely to achieve their maximum practical impact.

Another weakness of the case is the implication that the duty to disclose a risk 'which would affect the judgment of a reasonable patient' only applies where that risk is obviously and objectively significant. Although reluctant to discuss the meaning of 'significant' in terms of 'precise percentages', Lord Woolf MR appeared to focus on 10 per cent, which had been presented by one of the experts as the level of risk that would incur a duty of disclosure. He then argued that the 0.1–0.2

Medical Law Review 135, 145–46; Jones, 'Informed consent and other fairy stories', 117–118.
[155] Maclean, 'Beyond Bolam and Bolitho'.   [156] *Ibid.*, 212–13.
[157] *Pearce* v. *United Bristol Healthcare NHS Trust* (1998) 48 BMLR 118.   [158] *Ibid.*, 124.

per cent risk in this case was not significant. Lord Woolf MR was correct to suggest that 'precise percentages' have little to do with the significance of a risk. However, his judgment was somewhat confused in that he then did exactly that against which he had counselled.

The main difficulties with his approach are that it ignored the nature of the risk and related the relevance of the risk to an objectively reasonable patient without requiring that the subjective position of the patient be taken into account. These difficulties are compounded by Lord Woolf MR's apparent reliance on the expert medical witnesses to determine that the risk was not significant. Since the judgment of significance preceded the assessment of whether disclosure would have affected the reasonable patient's decision, it acts as a filtering device which, being placed in the medical profession's hands, undermines the apparent weight given to patient autonomy. Before the reasonable-patient test is engaged the medical expert acts as gatekeeper determining the significance of the risk, and 'insignificant' risks are excluded from further consideration.[159]

The nature of the risk is crucial to its significance. In *Pearce* the risk was of a stillbirth. If it was suggested to someone that they should consent to a course of action that would result in death in 1:500–1:1,000 occasions it seems reasonable to suggest that they would consider the risk to be significant if not common. The supposed lack of significance of the risk of stillbirth seems ridiculous when contrasted to the lesser (0.05 per cent) risk of vasectomy failure and yet it is accepted that it is negligent to fail to disclose that risk.[160] A frequency of 1:10 is such a high cut-off that, in the world of modern medicine, it excludes most of the risks of serious permanent harm. A 1:100 risk of permanent paralysis, for example, may be seen as a very significant risk but, on the basis of Lord Woolf MR's judgment, disclosure would be left to the doctor's discretion.

This apparently exclusive reliance on percentages also excludes the very relevant factors of the risks associated with alternative courses of action. In *Pearce*, the risks associated with a caesarean should have been compared with the risks associated with non-intervention in order to determine whether the risk of stillbirth from non-intervention was significant. Furthermore, the significance of a risk also depends on how it will impact on the patient's life should it materialise. While it may be appropriate to objectify this assessment, Lord Woolf MR's argument

---

[159] Maclean, 'Beyond Bolam and Bolitho', 213–14; A. R. Maclean, 'The doctrine of informed consent: Does it exist and has it crossed the Atlantic?' (2004) 24 *Legal Studies* 386, 408–9.

[160] See the information leaflets provided on the Family Planning Association website at www.fpa.org.uk.

does not explicitly include any scope for the patient's circumstances to be considered. As I have argued elsewhere, if the prudent-patient standard is relevant then 'The question should not be whether the doctor thinks the risk is significant but whether the reasonable person, pregnant, post term and concerned to deliver a healthy baby, would find the risk significant.'[161]

Brazier and Miola suggested that:

Even the cynic must concede that, whatever the outcome on the facts, the 'reasonable doctor' test received a body blow in *Pearce*. It survives only if the 'reasonable doctor' understands that he must offer the patient what the 'reasonable patient' would be likely to need to exercise his right to make informed decisions about his care.[162]

While it is true that this argument does reduce the test to that of the 'reasonable patient' it is subject to the crucial caveat of who decides what counts as a significant risk. Following Lord Woolf MR's approach, the courts would still rely on the experts to determine the significance of a particular risk.[163] As I have noted elsewhere:

This approach turns the Brazier and Miola argument back on its head. The standard becomes: the doctor must disclose those risks that the reasonable doctor believes the reasonable patient ought to find significant to a decision. This view may be cynical, but the judgment in *Pearce*, and the court's apparent reliance on percentages and expert assessment of significance, does nothing to dispel that cynicism.[164]

The practical impact of *Pearce* remains to be seen. In theory it has inched towards a standard marginally more respectful of patient autonomy than *Bolam simpliciter*. However, as I have argued, Lord Woolf MR's judgment is not wholly consistent or coherent and leaves the standard open to divergent interpretations. It would be speculative to try and second-guess the direction the courts will take, although if the previous trend is continued the law will, in fits and starts, stumble towards the doctrine of informed consent as espoused in *Canterbury* v. *Spence*. This continued trend towards the prudent-patient standard is confirmed by *Wyatt* v. *Curtis*, which concerned the duty to disclose the risks of chickenpox to a pregnant woman.[165] Sedley LJ generously interpreted Lord Woolf's test

---

[161] Maclean, 'The doctrine of informed consent', 409.
[162] Brazier and Miola, 'Bye-bye Bolam', 110. See also, A. Grubb, 'Medical negligence: Duty to disclose after Bolitho' (1999) 7 *Medical Law Review* 61, 63.
[163] The expert opinion would still be subject to the *Bolitho* caveat.
[164] Maclean, 'Beyond Bolam and Bolitho', 214.
[165] *Wyatt* v. *Curtis* [2003] EWCA Civ 1779.

to recognise the patient's subjective appreciation of the risks, which was conspicuously absent from Lord Woolf's judgment. Sedley LJ stated:

> Lord Woolf's formulation refines Lord Bridge's test by recognising that what is substantial and what is grave are questions on which the doctor's and the patient's perception may differ, and in relation to which the doctor must therefore have regard to what may be the patient's perception.[166]

Thus, what may not be significant to the doctor may well be relevant to the patient's decision and ought to be disclosed.

This goes further than what Lord Woolf actually said – or did – in *Pearce* (see above), and appears to reflect the Brazier and Miola interpretation of the judgment. However, although a Court of Appeal judgment, it was *obiter* to the decision as the appeal concerned one doctor trying to join a second doctor in liability. Since the first doctor had been found liable for the failure to disclose, and the appeal concerned the liability of the second doctor, it was not a case of doctor against patient but doctor against doctor. These particular circumstances may allow the court the luxury of a more generous interpretation of the duty to disclose and means that their words do not have to be backed by action. Lord Woolf's test is capable of Sedley LJ's interpretation, but the meaning of a test lies in both the words and its application. Since the Court of Appeal in *Wyatt* did not need to apply the test, it remains uncertain how sensitive to the patient's subjective appreciation it will be in practice.

Information disclosure and understanding   It would be too onerous to insist on ensuring actual understanding.[167] However, the courts have held that the professional's duty does not end with simple disclosure.[168] In *Smith* v. *Tunbridge Wells HA*,[169] Moorland J argued that the doctor's duty to inform included the use of appropriately simple language, which makes it possible for the patient to make an informed decision. Thus, the doctor's duty is to 'take reasonable care to ensure that his explanation of the risks is intelligible to his particular patient'.[170] This duty requires the doctor to have some regard to the patient's condition and, where a patient is less receptive, for example because of illness or the after-effects of medication or treatment, the onus lies with

---

[166] *Ibid.*, [16].
[167] See, M. A. Somerville, 'Structuring the issues in informed consent' (1981) 26 *McGill Law Journal* 740, 778.
[168] *Lybert* v. *Warrington HA* (1995) 25 BMLR 91.
[169] *Smith* v. *Tunbridge Wells HA* [1994] 5 Med LR 334.   [170] *Ibid.*, 339.

the doctor to adapt his practice of disclosure accordingly which may require repetition of the information on a subsequent occasion.[171]

Deriche v. *Ealing Hospital NHS Trust*[172] concerned a doctor who was aware that the patient had already been counselled regarding the risks of chickenpox infection to the patient's fetus. The question for the court was how far the defendant could rely on the earlier counselling. Buckley J decided in favour of the claimant because the defendant had failed 'to ensure that she [the claimant] fully understood the nature of the risks under discussion'.[173] This decision, while only first instance, appears to require that the doctor does indeed ensure understanding. As suggested earlier, this is an onerous duty and one that the courts have generally shied away from. In *Deriche*, Buckley J relied on the expert witness' evidence which he took to say that the defendant should have ensured his patient 'fully understood the nature of the risks and should not simply have taken Dr Adedze's notes as read'.[174] The gist of this is that the defendant should not have simply relied on the notes but should have checked with the patient that she had been made aware of the risks and that they were potentially serious for the fetus. This is a lesser duty than ensuring 'understanding', which would require the doctor to enquire into the patient's appreciation of the risk, rather than simply whether she could recite the risks back to the doctor. However, since it was not fully explained, the extent of the duty is uncertain and will only be clarified by subsequent case law.

There may also be a duty to ensure that a misunderstanding does not occur. This duty is limited to reasonable misunderstandings where patients have already indicated their concern to their physician.[175] In *Cooper* v. *Royal United Hospital Bath NHS Trust*,[176] the poor communication and lack of coordination between the doctors caring for the claimant meant that she was understandably confused about her options. It also meant the hospital 'team' made erroneous assumptions about her wishes, which resulted in the claimant being presented with a management plan that led to the failure to detect a recurrence of her breast cancer. Butterfield J held that the defendants were liable in negligence for misleading the claimant and depriving her of 'her right to choose the treatment she would prefer and address the risks that she . . . not Dr Goddard was facing'.[177]

---

[171] *Smith* v. *Salford HA* (1994) 23 BMLR 137, 149. See also, *Lybert* v. *Warrington HA* (1995) 25 BMLR 91.
[172] *Deriche* v. *Ealing Hospital NHS Trust* [2003] EWHC 3104.   [173] *Ibid.*, [44].
[174] *Ibid.*, [42].   [175] *Crouchman* v. *Burke* (1997) 40 BMLR 163, 176.
[176] *Cooper* v. *Royal United Hospital Bath NHS Trust* [2005] EWHC 3381.
[177] *Ibid.*, [58].

In *Cooper*, the misunderstanding clearly arose from the doctors' failure to communicate effectively, both with each other and with the patient. The approach in that case may be contrasted with *Al Hamwi* v. *Johnston*, in which the origin of the misunderstanding was unclear and the doctor had provided the patient with factually correct information. In finding for the defendant, Simon J concluded that there was no duty to ensure understanding and misunderstandings were inevitable in clinical practice.[178] Thus, 'clinicians should take reasonable and appropriate steps to satisfy themselves that the patient has understood the information which has been provided',[179] but this was satisfied by the provision of accurate information and required nothing more than a superficial enquiry as to whether the patient understood the information. The restricted nature of the duty is indicated by Simon J's acceptance that the defendant's approach was appropriate when she stated:

> I understand it is alleged that in response to the fact that (the Claimant) changed her mind in the course of the consultation I should have asked her why she had changed her mind. I would never ask a patient to explain or justify the decision they have made. I would not do so because I would be concerned that by doing so the patient may interpret this as criticism of their choice.[180]

This limited approach to ensuring that patients understand the information and are truly exercising their autonomy may be affected by the context of the counselling. *Al Hamwi* concerned the advice given to the claimant about having amniocentesis to detect fetal chromosomal abnormality. It is perfectly correct, as the judge noted, that clinicians should not allow their religious beliefs to colour their advice.[181] However, a distinction can be made between directive advice based on personal religious or moral views and directive advice based on clinical and social factors. Simon J emphasised the fact that the patient was provided with written information and that the defendant had satisfied her duty by disclosing factually correct information. It was immaterial that the claimant had, in fact, misunderstood the level of risk associated with amniocentesis. The doctor's duty was restricted to disclosing information and the communicative process itself was essentially irrelevant.[182]

Simon J's judgment, which allowed the clinician to simply accept the patient's decision without question, implies that any duty to ensure understanding is limited to the way in which information is presented

---

[178] *Al Hamwi* v. *Johnston, The North West London Hospitals NHS Trust* [2005] EWHC 206, [69].
[179] *Ibid.*, [69].   [180] *Ibid.*, [73].   [181] *Ibid.*, [64].
[182] J. Miola, 'Autonomy rued OK?' (2006) 14 *Medical Law Review* 108, 111–12.

and does not include a requirement to challenge a decision. It may, of course, be relevant that the decision was not wholly irrational. The problem with deciding whether or not to undergo an amniocentesis is that, depending on one's views, it may be just as rational to refuse the intervention as it is to consent to it. This means that the clinician gets no clue from the decision itself without engaging with the patient's values, beliefs and reasoning. In other words, without asking patients to explain their decision it may not be possible to know whether the decision is irrational. However, that kind of engagement with the patient is not part of the healthcare professional's legal duty. It remains open whether the clinician has a duty to enquire into the patient's understanding where the decision appears to be objectively irrational.

The professional's duty to persuade   Apart from the limited duty to facilitate understanding, Simon J's judgment in *Al Hamwi* indicates that clinicians are not under a duty to persuade, or attempt to persuade patients to change their minds if their decisions seem unwise. This follows from Simon J's acceptance that 'Counselling should be non-directive, avoiding influencing or dictating the parents' decision and allowing them a sense of control over the pregnancy.'[183] It also follows from his approval of the defendant's approach to accepting the patient's decision without question (see above). That there is currently no legal duty to (attempt to) persuade is confirmed more explicitly by the judgment in *Attwell* v. *McPartlin*,[184] in which the judge argued:

It is for the patient, not the doctor, to decide whether the risks of any particular treatment or procedure are acceptable. It would, in my opinion, be a novel and serious departure for established practice throughout a wide range of professional relationships . . . to hold that a doctor is under a legal duty, not just to advise and warn fairly and appropriately but to persuade or . . . to express his wishes in such a way as to secure compliance. Some doctors may wish to make an effort to persuade a reluctant patient to act in what the doctor sees as the patient's best interests; some doctors may even feel the need to adopt an overbearing or bullying attitude in order to secure compliance. But, in the end, in the ordinary case it is for the professional to advise and for the patient . . . to decide. There is no scope for a duty to 'push'.[185]

Although there is no duty to attempt to persuade the patient, the High Court has held that there is a duty not to present the information in such

---

[183] *Al Hamwi* v. *Johnston, The North West London Hospitals NHS Trust* [2005] EWHC 206, [44]. The quote is from an obstetrics textbook. See also *Enright* v. *Kwun* [2003] EWHC 1000.
[184] *Attwell* v. *McPartlin* [2004] EWHC 829.   [185] *Ibid.*, [60].

a way that the patient's right to make his or her own decision is usurped. In *Thompson* v. *Bradford*, the parents of a young boy with an unusual perianal abscess that required surgery were told that they could proceed with immunising their child.[186] This resulted in him contracting polio. Wilkie J held that, while the defendant had not acted negligently in advising the parents to proceed with immunisation, he was negligent 'for the way in which he gave advice'.[187] The defendant had been 'unnecessarily dismissive' of the parents' concerns and had 'failed to inform them that the recurrent perianal abscess was unique in his experience and extremely unusual',[188] which caused the parents to passively accept 'his confident advice'.[189] However, the decision was reversed on appeal on the grounds that contracting polio following immunisation was an unforeseeable consequence that undermined any possible duty to advise postponing immunisation.[190]

The Court of Appeal rejected the argument that the unusual presentation of the abscess should have put the doctor on alert that the risks of vaccination may be affected and held the reasonable general practitioner was entitled to rely on the information in the 'Green Book', which advised that '[m]inor infections without fever or systemic upset are not reasons to postpone immunisation'.[191] This essentially factual reason for allowing the appeal allowed the Court of Appeal to avoid dealing with Wilkie J's criticism of the defendant for his dismissively paternal approach to advising the claimants.

These cases appear to indicate that the courts have accepted that counselling should be non-directive although it is acceptable for doctors to indicate what they recommend.[192] Information should be presented as factual numerical risks and the patients left to make their own decision.[193] There is no duty to attempt to persuade the patient. In *Attwell*, the judge appears to have accepted that doctors may attempt to persuade patients and may even do so in an 'overbearing or bullying' way. In *Thompson*, the High Court appears to have rejected that approach as undermining patient autonomy. However, when *Thompson* reached the Court of Appeal, the relevance of the doctor's manner was sidestepped. Arguably, this leaves the legal rules in a confused state, making it difficult for healthcare professionals to know what is allowed and what is expected of them. This is particularly so as the judge in *Attwell* appears

---

[186] *Thompson* v. *Bradford* [2004] EWHC 2424.   [187] *Ibid.*, [27].   [188] *Ibid.*, [27].
[189] *Ibid.*, [32].   [190] *Thompson* v. *Bradford* [2005] EWCA Civ 1439.
[191] *Ibid.*, [11]. For information on the 'Green Book' see www.dh.gov.uk/PolicyAndGuidance/HealthAndSocialCareTopics/GreenBook/fs/en.
[192] *R (Burke) v GMC* [2005] EWCA 1003, [51] per Lord Phillips MR.
[193] *Enright* v. *Kwun* [2003] EWHC 1000, [56].

to have failed to appreciate the distinction between rational persuasion and other methods of getting the patient to make the desired decision. While rational persuasion respects, and is arguably required to respect, autonomy, 'bullying' is unacceptable and is an example of undue influence.

Non-treatment decisions   While there is an obligation to disclose information about the alternative treatments available,[194] there is no obligation to provide particular treatments. Consent is the expression of the negative right to self-determination and it affords no positive claims to a right to treatment. This was made clear by the Court of Appeal in *R (Burke)* v. *GMC*.[195] Lord Phillips MR stated:

> The doctor will describe the treatment that he recommends or, if there are a number of alternative treatments that he would be prepared to administer in the interests of the patient, the choices available, their implications and his recommended option. In such circumstances the right to refuse a proposed treatment gives the patient what appears to be a positive option to choose an alternative. In truth the right to choose is no more than a reflection of the fact that it is the doctor's duty to provide a treatment that he considers to be in the interests of the patient and that the patient is prepared to accept.[196]

Although there is no right to particular treatments,[197] it is at least arguable that Article 8 of the European Convention on Human Rights – incorporated into domestic law by the Human Rights Act 1988 – allows patients the right to be involved in, or at least to be informed of, decisions not to offer treatment.[198] In *Glass* v. *UK*,[199] the European Court of Human Rights (ECtHR) held that the claimant's rights under Article 8 had been breached by doctors who failed to seek the court's authorisation when their management plan differed from what Mrs Glass believed to be in her son's best interests. In *W* v. *UK*, which involved decisions regarding children who had been taken into care, the ECtHR stated:

> In the Court's view, what therefore has to be determined is whether, having regard to the particular circumstances of the case, and notably the serious nature of the decisions to be taken, the parents have been involved in the decision-making process . . . to a degree sufficient to provide them with the requisite protection of their interests.[200]

---

[194] *Smith* v. *Salford HA* (1994) 23 BMLR 137, 148.
[195] *R (Burke)* v *GMC* [2005] EWCA 1003.   [196] *Ibid.*, [51].
[197] *North West Lancashire HA* v. *A, D & G* [1999] Lloyd's LR Med 399.
[198] See e.g. *Tysiac* v. *Poland* (2007) 45 EHRR 42, [115], ECtHR.
[199] *Glass* v. *UK* [2004] 1 FLR 1019.   [200] *W* v. *UK* (1988) 10 EHRR 29, 50.

If parents have an Article 8 right to be involved in the decision-making process regarding their children then, given that Article 8 protects individual autonomy,[201] individuals should also be involved in the decision-making process about their medical treatment. While such a right is not traditionally available through either battery or negligence, and thus is not protected by the legal regulation of consent to medical treatment, it is a right that the courts should protect.

The therapeutic privilege   Although the doctrine is generally associated with informed consent and the prudent-patient standard of information disclosure, a similar doctrine operates in English law as a component of the professional standard of disclosure.[202] As Grubb suggested: 'The need for a "therapeutic privilege" . . . is at the heart of the majority view in *Sidaway* that at least *prima facie*, *Bolam* should apply.'[203] Thus, if a reasonable body of physicians would withhold the information because it might 'harm' the patient then the requisite standard of care would be satisfied. That the principle is part of English law is shown by Lord Templeman's judgment in *Sidaway*. He stated that 'the doctor impliedly contracts to provide information which is adequate to enable the patient to reach a balanced judgment, subject always to the doctor's own obligation to say or do nothing which the doctor is satisfied will be harmful to the patient'.[204]

In principle the privilege should only apply to situations where disclosure would harm the patient or make them so distressed that a rational decision is no longer possible. However, it has been applied more loosely. In the US case of *Nishi* v. *Hartwell*, for example, the majority held that the doctor's duty to disclose was subject to what was in the patient's best interest.[205] In *McAllister* v. *Lewisham*, Rougier J took a similar approach arguing that the therapeutic privilege applies where it is in the patient's best interest for the doctor to be 'somewhat economical with the truth'.[206] This, he held, was wholly in keeping with the principle of the *Bolam* test.

Disclosure and causation

In order to succeed in negligence, the claimant must prove that the damage suffered was caused by the defendant's negligence. In

---

[201] *Pretty* v. *UK* (2002) 35 EHRR 1, 17.
[202] Jones, 'Informed consent and other fairy stories', 113.
[203] Grubb, 'Contraceptive advice and doctors', 13.
[204] *Sidaway* v. *Governors of Bethlam Royal Hospital* [1985] 1 AC 871, 904.
[205] *Nishi* v. *Hartwell* 473 P 2d 116, 119 (1970).
[206] *McAllister* v. *Lewisham and North Southwark HA* [1994] 5 Med LR 343, 352.

non-disclosure cases the risk itself is not caused by the defendant's negligence. Instead, the defendant's negligence must have caused the claimant to be exposed to this non-negligent risk. This means that, to complete the causal association between the defendant's negligence and the damage, claimants must show that, but for the negligent failure to disclose the risk, they would have adopted a different course of action and so avoided harm.[207]

This raises two issues: first, should the test be subjectively based on what this patient would have done or should it be objectively based on the 'reasonable patient'; second, what counts as a different course of action? Both of these raise questions about the protection of patient autonomy. If the test is subjective and the second question interpreted broadly then patient autonomy is protected far more than it is by an objective test and an insistence that the patient must have completely rejected the proffered intervention.

The nature of the test   In *Bolam*, McNair J treated causation as subjective.[208] On this limited evidence the issue is treated as a straightforward causation problem with claimants having to prove on the balance of probabilities that they would have refused the treatment had they been in possession of all the facts. In *Chatterton* v. *Gerson*, Bristow J affirmed the subjective test,[209] but also appeared to introduce an objective element. He stated: 'I should add that . . . I would not have been satisfied that if properly informed Miss Chatterton would have chosen not to have [the operation]. The whole picture on the evidence is of a lady desperate for pain relief, who has just been advised by Mr Crymble to let Dr Gerson try again.'[210] The consequence of this is a mixed test: plaintiffs must show what they would actually have done had they been properly informed, but this subjective claim is then subjected to an objective test of credibility. This mixed approach to causation has subsequently been applied (*obiter*) by the Court of Appeal in *Pearce* v. *United Bristol Healthcare NHS Trust*.[211]

---

[207] For example, see *Bolam* v. *Friern HMC* [1957] 1 WLR 582, 590.
[208] *Bolam* v. *Friern HMC* [1957] 1 WLR 582, 591.
[209] *Chatterton* v. *Gerson* [1981] 1 All ER 257, 265.
[210] *Ibid.*, 267. For other evidence of a mixed approach see *Hills* v. *Potter* [1984] 1 WLR 641; *Smith* v. *Barking, Havering and Brentwood HA* [1994] 5 Med LR 285, 289 (Decided 1988).
[211] *Pearce* v. *United Bristol Healthcare NHS Trust* (1998) 48 BMLR 118. The objective approach is underscored by Lord Woolf MR's argument (at 125) that 'if *Mrs Pearce had been able to understand* what she had been told about the increased risk, her decision would still have been to follow, reluctantly, the advice of the doctor' (emphasis added).

Sometimes the objective element of the test can work for the claimant but this will generally be where the procedure is an elective lifestyle choice or where it is particularly risky and medical opinion is divided as to its appropriateness. In *McAllister* v. *Lewisham and Southwark HA*, the plaintiff succeeded in establishing liability for a failure to warn her of the risks associated with surgery to correct a cerebral arterio-venous malformation. In allowing her claim, Rougier J applied a complex test involving both subjective and objective elements.

The main subjective elements were the plaintiff's 'own personality' and the fact that she thought she would have sought a second opinion. The objective elements included the expert evidence that the decision to operate was by no means straightforward and there would have been divided medical opinion. Thus, Rougier J argued that:

[a] second opinion would have been much more keenly aware of the dangers of operating and would, in whatever way it was expressed, have not been in favour of operation. That I feel would have tipped the balance in Mrs McAllister's mind. After all, few would want to undergo surgery of this magnitude and risk unless they felt that the arguments in favour were, if not compelling, at least very much more powerful than those against.[212]

This clearly objective standard was arguably also relevant in Rougier J's acceptance that the plaintiff's employment situation was such that at least she would have delayed the surgery.[213] Finally, the objective component is most clearly seen in Rougier J's argument that, given sufficient evidence, the judge could make a decision regarding the plaintiff's hypothetical decision even where the plaintiff herself was 'reluctant to hypothesise'.[214]

The case law suggests that the English courts, while purporting to adopt a subjective standard, subject the plaintiff's evidence to objective scrutiny so that it will only be accepted if it accords with what the judge believes is objectively reasonable. The rationale behind this is the risk of hindsight and self-serving testimony, which accords with the reasoning in the United States and Canada that led to their courts more openly adopting an objective standard.[215] Robinson CJ explained that a

---

[212] *McAllister* v. *Lewisham and North Southwark HA* [1994] 5 Med LR 343, 353–4.

[213] See also *Smith* v. *Tunbridge Wells HA* [1994] 5 Med LR 334, in which Morland J clearly sympathised with the plaintiff, a sexually active young man who had not been warned of the risk of impotence following an operation for a rectal prolapse (at 341).

[214] *McAllister* v. *Lewisham and North Southwark HA* [1994] 5 Med LR 343, 353. See also *Gowton* v. *Wolverhampton HA* [1994] 5 Med LR 432, 435–6.

[215] *Canterbury* v. *Spence* 464 F 2d 772 (1972), 791 per Robinson CJ (delivering the judgment of the court); *Reibl* v. *Hughes* (1981) 114 DLR (3d) 1, 14–17.

subjective test would be 'purely hypothetical . . . hardly . . . more than a guess, perhaps tinged by the circumstances that the uncommunicated hazard has in fact materialized'.[216] Where patients have been injured by the materialisation of an undisclosed risk it is only natural to say that they would not have agreed to undergo the procedure had they known of the risk.

Although the English courts have retained the subjective standard of causation, the application of that standard in practice has been strongly constrained by the use of objective criteria to determine the credibility of the plaintiff's assertions. The use of these objective criteria means that it is improbably difficult for patients to succeed unless they are claiming a course of action that the judge accepts as 'reasonable'. This is more likely where the treatment is controversial, with medical opinion divided, or where it is particularly risky. However, in most cases plaintiffs must be able to show that there is something distinct about their situation that allows the judge to understand why they might have rejected the doctor's advice. As a consequence causation becomes a significant hurdle for the injured claimant that compounds the professional standard of disclosure.[217]

Although the subjective test is the most respecting of the patient's self-determination, it may be difficult to apply it in practice without allowing the concept of reasonableness to creep in. However, Giesen and Hayes suggested that a wholly subjective test is possible and that German law has found a way of dealing with the problem of hindsight. They argued that the Federal Supreme Court of Germany, in a 1984 ruling, took the 'correct' approach in requiring the plaintiff to give a 'plausible reason' in the face of a 'real conflict' to explain why he would have refused consent.[218] While this may be preferable to a purely objective test, it would be difficult to accept arguments as plausible unless the reason provided by the claimant is at least credible, and the most credible reasons are those that are objectively 'reasonable' based on the knowledge that the judge possesses of the patient's circumstances. This does not mean that the reasoning must be rationally logical but that the process of reasoning is one that would make sense to a 'reasonable man' as perceived by the judge. As such, the 'plausible reason' test is unlikely to be any less objective than the mixed test applied in England.

Even if the courts were able to adopt a purely subjective standard this would still fall short of the right to give or refuse consent that the patient

---

[216] *Canterbury* v. *Spence* 464 F 2d 772 (1972), 790 per Robinson CJ.
[217] Skegg, 'English medical law and "informed consent"', 149.
[218] Giesen and Hayes, 'The patient's right to know', 121–2.

possesses since the patient may give or refuse consent for no reason whatsoever.[219] The postcedent requirement for reasons, whether subjective, credible or wholly objective, undermines the antecedent right to decide irrespective of having a reason for the decision. The very requirement to prove the causal link, while a necessary element of negligence liability, undermines the patient's right to irrational self-determination. I will return to this in the following chapter.

The content of the test   The test in *Chatterton* appears to imply that, in order to prove causation, claimants must show that they would have undertaken a different course of action. Although this test describes the basic position, subsequent developments have made it easier to recover damages. As mentioned earlier, in *McAllister* Rougier J allowed causation because he accepted that, at the very least, the patient would have delayed surgery. More recently, this very issue came before the Court of Appeal in *Chester* v. *Afshar*.[220] The claimant was a 51-year-old journalist who suffered severe back pain. Although she was reluctant to undergo surgery, Mr Afshar reassured her sufficiently for the claimant to give consent. Unfortunately, following the surgery she was left with severe neurological deficit. At trial, the court accepted that Mr Afshar had failed to disclose the risk of nerve damage or paralysis and that, had he done so, she would at least have sought second and third opinions before deciding whether to undergo the operation. The trial judge awarded damages for the failure to disclose and Mr Afshar appealed against the decision.

Following the majority decision in the Australian case of *Chappel* v. *Hart*,[221] and basing the judgment on the individual's right to self-determination, the Court of Appeal held that:

The object is to enable the patient to decide whether or not to run the risks of having that operation at that time. If the doctor's failure to take that care results in her consenting to an operation to which she would not otherwise have given her consent, the purpose of that rule would be thwarted if he were not to be held responsible when the very risk about which he failed to warn her materialises and causes her an injury which she would not have suffered then and there . . . It would in our judgment be unjust to hold that the effective cause of the claimant's injury was the random occurrence of the 1 to 2% risk referred to above rather than the defendant's failure to bring such risk to her attention.[222]

[219] *Re MB (An Adult: Medical Treatment)* [1997] 2 FCR 541, 553.
[220] *Chester* v. *Afshar* [2002] EWCA Civ 724.   [221] *Chappel* v. *Hart* [1998] HCA 55.
[222] *Chester* v. *Afshar* [2002] EWCA Civ 724, [47].

The House of Lords subsequently upheld the Court of Appeal decision. Their Lordships in the majority justified what they saw as 'a narrow and modest departure from traditional causation principles'[223] by arguing that, because of the patient's right to autonomy,[224] to do otherwise would strip the duty to disclose 'of all practical force' and render it 'devoid of all content'.[225] Following *Chester*, the current test for causation appears to be that claimants will succeed if they can show that disclosure of the risk would simply have altered their decision. Claimants no longer need to show that they would have refused consent to the proffered treatment.

As a final point, damages may sometimes be awarded even though the claimant has been unable to prove causation in relation to the materialised risk. These cases are where the materialised risk had additional consequences that might have been avoided had the claimant been forewarned. In *Newell and Newell* v. *Goldenberg*, for example, the omission to mention the risk that the man's sterilisation might fail put strain on the marriage when his wife became pregnant.[226] The judge sympathised with the claimant in the worry that his wife may have been unfaithful and he awarded damages to compensate for the distress caused.[227]

Legally recognised damage

The final aspect of legal liability is the type of harm that the courts are prepared to recognise. Traditionally the courts have accepted that damages may be awarded to compensate for physical harm, or – in more limited circumstances – psychiatric harm or economic loss. Where the damage arises as a result of an undisclosed risk materialising, the situation is relatively unproblematic since the harm is obvious. However, where the claim is simply that consent was invalid and the procedure was a battery, the situation is less straightforward. Where the procedure is medically indicated, then the patient has probably benefited from its performance.[228] This is particularly problematic where the treatment was life-preserving since the courts generally consider life to be a benefit.[229]

---

[223] *Chester* v. *Afshar* [2004] UKHL 41, [24] per Lord Steyn.
[224] *Ibid.*, [18–24] per Lord Steyn; [77] per Lord Hope; [92–3] per Lord Walker.
[225] *Ibid.*, [86–7] per Lord Hope. See also Lord Walker [101].
[226] *Newell and Newell* v. *Goldenberg* [1995] 6 Med LR 371.
[227] See also the Scottish case *Goorkani* v. *Tayside HB* 1991 SLT 94.
[228] C. Gavaghan, 'Anticipatory refusals and the action of "wrongful living"' (2000) 5 *Medical Law International* 67, 72–5.
[229] *McKay* v. *Essex AHA* [1982] 1 QB 1166, CA; *McFarlane* v. *Tayside Health Board* [2000] 2 AC 59, 72–5.

Although in *Malette* v. *Shulman*, a Jehovah's Witness was awarded $20,000 following a blood transfusion contrary to an advance directive, the English approach may be different.[230] Thus, commenting on *Malette* in *Re T*, Butler-Sloss LJ stated: 'I do not believe an English court would give damages in those particular circumstances.'[231]

A similar problem arose in negligence with the wrongful pregnancy cases, in which an unwanted pregnancy results from the defendant's negligence leaving the claimants with the cost of raising an unplanned child. In *MacFarlane* v. *Tayside HB*,[232] the House of Lords held that the birth of a healthy child was an unquantifiable blessing that could not be offset against the economic loss arising from the maintenance costs associated with raising the child. Subsequently, in *Rees* v. *Darlington*,[233] the House of Lords acknowledged that the mother's autonomy had been infringed. With a majority of 4:3, their Lordships awarded the conventional sum of £15,000 in recognition of the harm done.

It would be possible for the courts to award a similar amount in other cases where the harm was primarily to the claimant's autonomy. Mason and Brodie in fact criticised the decision in *Chester* because, they argued, the harm was to the patient's autonomy rather than the physical consequences of the risk materialising.[234] Thus, they suggested that an award of a conventional sum, as in *Rees*, would have been more appropriate. Given that Article 8 of the European Convention on Human Rights protects the right to personal autonomy,[235] an infringement of this right should be acknowledged by an appropriate award of damages. In *Cornelius* v. *De Taranto*, for example, the court made an award of £3,000 for the mental distress caused by a breach of confidence in order to recognise the seriousness of breaching a protected human right.[236] However, in the wrongful pregnancy cases the award may reflect judicial sympathy for the harshness of a law that precludes any recovery at all for the maintenance costs associated with the unplanned child. The award of damages in these cases may simply be a way of mitigating that harshness and thus the courts may be less inclined to make a similar award in other cases.

---

[230] *Malette* v. *Shulman* [1991] 2 Med LR 162; 67 DLR (4th) 3.
[231] *Re T (Adult: Refusal of Treatment)* [1992] 3 WLR 782, 800. See also, Staughton LJ's similar comment, 805.
[232] *McFarlane* v. *Tayside Health Board* [2000] 2 AC 59.
[233] *Rees* v. *Darlington Memorial Hospital NHS Trust* [2003] UKHL 52, HL.
[234] K. Mason and D. Brodie, 'Bolam, Bolam – wherefore art thou Bolam?' (2005) 9 *Edinburgh Law Review* 298, 305.
[235] *Pretty* v. *UK* (2002) 35 EHRR 1, 17.
[236] *Cornelius* v. *De Taranto* [2001] EMLR 12, [65–9]. The case went to appeal, but the Court of Appeal did not overrule this aspect: (2002) 68 BMLR 62.

Conclusion

In this chapter I have described the current legal regulation of consent. I noted that battery law regulates direct invasions of bodily integrity but all other interventions fall within the penumbra of the law of negligence. It is battery law that allows the patient the right to refuse treatment, regardless of the reason, and it is this branch of law that requires the patient to be competent and for consent to be given without undue influence. While battery law has the advantage of focusing on the right to bodily integrity, which allows patients to exercise their autonomy by giving or withholding consent, it is readily satisfied by minimal disclosure of the nature and purpose of the procedure in broad terms. Further disclosure is required to satisfy the healthcare professional's duty under negligence law.

The duty to disclose in negligence law most importantly covers risks and alternative treatments. Currently the duty is determined by the professional standard but phrased in such a way as to approach the prudent-patient standard. Incorporated within this standard is the therapeutic privilege, which retains for the healthcare professional a degree of paternalistic control over the information disclosed. The law requires disclosure of information in a way that at least recognises the need for understanding. However, there is little in the way of positive obligations to foster comprehension and no requirement to ensure understanding. Furthermore, there is no duty to make more than a cursory enquiry of whether the patient has understood and there is certainly no duty to challenge an irrational decision or try to persuade patients to change their minds. Like the duty to disclose, the rules regarding causation have become more sensitive to individual autonomy. The law now allows that causation is satisfied if claimants can show that they would simply have made a different decision had the risk been disclosed. While this is more sensitive to autonomy than a rule requiring claimants to prove that they would have refused consent, it still demands that the change of decision is credible. This means that it must be objectively reasonable, which is arguably inconsistent with the antecedent right to refuse treatment (which can be for irrational reasons or no reason at all).

In this chapter I compare the current legal regulation of consent against the model developed in Part I and I argue that the current regulation of consent falls short. However, this is not to suggest that the shortfall must be met by direct legal regulation. There are a number of alternative responses, which include allowing further development of the common law, legislation with or without a code of practice and a regulatory body, an enhanced role for professional regulation or some combination of these. Ultimately the decision is a political one that will be guided by the cost, the support of the various lobbies and the vision of the type of healthcare system that the government wants to develop; a market approach to healthcare supports a very different regulatory model of consent than more social, welfare or communitarian visions.

The model I have developed is a socio-liberal one in which respect for individual autonomy is seen as the guiding principle but that autonomy is situated in the professional–patient relationship and the wider network of relationships that constitutes the community. This allowed me to argue for a model of relational consent that incorporates both consent as a permission and consent as agreement. It also justifies a clear distinction between harm caused by an infringement of the right to consent and the harm caused by the materialisation of a risk. Furthermore, the relational aspect of both autonomy and consent requires that the obligations arising from the professional–patient relationship fall on both parties and not just the professional. With that in mind, I turn now to critique the law.

The split between battery and negligence

The first thing to note is that the legal regulation of consent is split between the two distinct torts of battery and negligence. In principle my model of consent could support this approach with battery governing consent as permission while negligence regulates consent as agreement. Since battery makes unjustified contact unlawful, the individual is granted a legally protected right to bodily integrity. In allowing the individual to waive this right, by granting consent, the tort focuses attention on the wrong done to the victim rather than on the actor's behaviour. This makes battery conceptually attractive because it is consistent with the central theory of consent as permission. Negligence, on the other hand, focuses on the professional's duty while allowing the patient's behaviour to be taken into account through the defence of contributory negligence. Since there is no need for bodily contact, negligence encompasses both treatment decisions – including those not involving direct contact – and non-treatment decisions. Thus, negligence is better situated than battery to regulate consent as agreement.

The major problem with this view is that the current legal regulation arose not for conceptual reasons but because the judiciary were disinclined to hold doctors liable for battery, with the judiciary 'deploring' the use of that tort.[1] This reluctance arose for two main reasons: first, to avoid the association of battery with the criminal law and, second, because negligence provides judges with greater control of liability than is possible in battery law.[2] The judicial antipathy to claims of battery was given practical effect when risk disclosure was divorced from the requirements of a 'real' consent and made a duty in negligence.

The regulatory split between negligence and battery has a number of consequences. First, because it reflects a judicial reluctance to use the tort of battery, the usefulness of that tort is undermined and it only becomes relevant where there has been a gross failure to obtain consent or where the healthcare professional has acted in bad faith. Thus, where a dentist secured his patient's consent to expensive dental restorative work by convincing them it was clinically necessary he was liable in battery.[3] However, where an anaesthetist, acting in good faith and beneficently, performed a caudal (local) anaesthetic even though the patient had only consented to a general anaesthetic he was not liable.[4] On the one hand this limits its usefulness as a general means of regulating consent to medical treatment. On the other hand it does allow the courts to condemn a particularly serious failure to respect the patient's autonomy by finding the defendant liable for battery.

---

[1] See *Davis* v. *Barking, Havering and Brentwood Health Authority* [1993] 4 Med LR 85, 90 per McCullough J. Also see, *Sidaway* v. *Governors of Bethlam Royal Hospital* [1985] 1 AC 871, 885 per Lord Scarman.

[2] Brazier, 'Patient autonomy and consent to treatment', 180; Robertson, 'Informed consent to medical treatment', 123–4. See also Grubb, 'Consent to treatment: The competent person', pp. 172–3.

[3] *Appleton* v. *Garrett* [1997] 8 Med LR 75.

[4] *Davis* v. *Barking, Havering and Brentwood Health Authority* [1993] 4 Med LR 85.

A second consequence of the split is that risk disclosure is regulated in negligence rather than battery. This again undermines the use of battery as means of regulating consent to medical treatment. As noted above, the split was made for largely pragmatic, rather than conceptual, reasons, which creates uncertainty regarding the purpose of risk disclosure: if it is not necessary for consent then what is its purpose and why does causation require that the claimant would have made a different consent decision had the information been disclosed? However, if risk disclosure is necessary for consent then it ought to be required for the patient's consent to be real.

In the Canadian case of *Reibl* v. *Hughes*, although acknowledging that an 'informed choice' requires knowledge of the risks, Laskin CJC held that the duty to disclose risks derives from a general 'anterior' duty of care arising by virtue of the doctor's role.[5] However, if patients require knowledge of the risks to make an 'informed choice' then they require that knowledge in order to maximise their autonomy. If the law of battery is to protect individual autonomy, at least in the liberal sense of rational self-determination, then it should require disclosure of those risks that are essential to an informed choice. To make risk disclosure part of the doctor's general duty of care is to shift the emphasis away from a patient-centred right to autonomy. Thus, the patient's right to be informed of risks is currently a derivative right dependent on the doctor's duty of care rather than the individual's right to self-determination.

The split also affects the question of competency, although this point has not been acknowledged in practice. In principle one need only be competent to understand the information necessary to make the consent decision.[6] Since risk information is unnecessary for a real consent then there is no need for the patient to understand it. However, the current *Re C* test includes the ability to weigh up the risks as part of the decision-making process.[7] Although Hale J avoided explicit reference to risks in *Cambridgeshire CC* v. *R*, the Mental Health Act Code of Practice quotes the tripartite *Re C* test as the appropriate test for competence and states that the knowledge required for consent includes: 'the purpose, nature, likely effects and risks of th[e] treatment including the likelihood of its success and any alternatives to it'.[8] Neither the Mental Capacity Act 2005 nor the Code of Practice specifically refer to risks (the Code

---

[5] *Reibl* v. *Hughes* (1981) 114 DLR (3d) 1, 10–11.
[6] Gunn, 'The meaning of incapacity'.
[7] *Re C (Adult: Refusal of treatment)* [1994] 1 WLR 290, 292 per Thorpe J.
[8] Mental Health Act Code of Practice (1999), paras. 15.10, 15.13. The Code is currently under review.

talks of 'likely consequences')[9] but the test of capacity in the Act is similar to, and informed by, the *Re C* test.[10] This means that the ability to understand the risks of the procedure is likely to continue to be part of the test of competency, particularly as healthcare professionals will be making the competency assessments and currently risk disclosure is widely seen as a necessary part of consent in medical ethics and practice.[11]

Because risk disclosure is regulated by the duty of care in negligence, an inability to understand the risks does not affect the patient's capacity to give a 'real' consent. Thus, rather than making the patient incompetent to consent, it simply negates the duty to disclose. This follows because it would be nonsensical to require a duty to do something that is futile.[12] It is evident from the court's approach to causation, where claimants are required to show that the information would have affected whether or not they would have given consent, that the duty to disclose risks relates to the treatment decision.[13] However, if patients are unable to use the risk information effectively because they cannot understand it then the purpose of the duty evaporates. There may, of course, be other reasons that justify a duty to disclose the risks. For example, risk disclosure may be required to forewarn patients so that they may be more prepared should the risk materialise, but even here the purpose of disclosure is frustrated where the patient is unable to understand the risk. This means that, in principle, patients incapable of understanding risk information may still give a valid consent, but they lose the right to complain about a failure to disclose the risk.

While this conceptual inconsistency may be ignored in practice it reflects a failure of the law to be truly sensitive to the patient's autonomy as the principle underlying the right to give or withhold consent. It may also threaten the coherent development of the law. Where the rules are based on unclear or inconsistent reasons this increases the possibility of divergent interpretations of those rules, which may cause the development of an increasingly incoherent law. Furthermore, any development of the legal rules should relate to the reasons justifying the existence of the duty given substance through those rules; if the duty to disclose is

---

[9] Mental Capacity Act Code of Practice (2007), para. 4.48.

[10] The Lord Chancellor, *Making Decisions*, Cm (1999) 4465, para. 1.6; The Law Commission, *Report on Mental Incapacity No. 231* (1995), para. 3.15; Mental Capacity Act 2005, s. 3(1).

[11] M. Mayberry and J. Mayberry, *Consent in Clinical Practice* (Abingdon: Radcliffe Medical Press Ltd, 2003) pp. 82–91.

[12] *Airedale NHS Trust v. Bland* [1993] 1 All ER 821; *LCB v. UK* (1998) 27 EHRR 212, 222.

[13] See the discussion on causation in the previous chapter.

related to consent then any change in the duty ought to be consistent with the justifications for requiring consent. However, if the duty is predicated on some other ground then its development should be sensitive to that basis. It is, therefore, problematic that the justification for risk disclosure in negligence is uncertain.

There are four ways in which to conceptualise the negligence-based duty to disclose. First, the duty may be seen as wholly independent of consent. Second, consent in battery can be valid but nonetheless negligently obtained if the professional has failed to disclose a material risk. Third, there are two 'consents': one a legal consent required by the law of battery, the other an ethical consent predicated on the patient's right to autonomy, which must be obtained if the professional is to avoid liability in negligence. The fourth possibility is the same as the third except that the ethical consent is driven by the healthcare professional's duty of beneficence rather than the patient's autonomy. For present purposes it is unnecessary to explore which model is most plausible and I have argued elsewhere that the third and fourth models are the most coherent being equated to the prudent patient and the reasonable doctor standards respectively.[14] The important point is that each of these four models is a possible interpretation and this lack of conceptual clarity carries the potential for an inconsistent or incoherent development of the law.

Currently, therefore, the legal regulation of consent is conceptually confused. While this does not preclude a rational development of the law, it increases the risk that the law will develop inconsistently with the ethical justification underlying the legal rights and concomitant duties. Given the primary reason for the way in which the law has developed – the judicial reluctance to use the law of battery – it seems unlikely that the conceptual confusion will be clarified by the common law. Furthermore, even if the split between negligence and battery could be reversed and risk disclosure included as part of a 'real' consent, reliance on the law of battery may still not be the answer since the requirement for directness restricts the extent of the tort to healthcare interventions that involve a degree of contact between the healthcare professional and the patient.[15] This means that negligence would still be required for 'consent' to the non-contact interventions and for decisions not to provide a particular intervention. While reserving battery law for serious infringements of patient autonomy may be defensible, and – as I mentioned earlier – would fit with my model, it can only deal with those

---

[14] Maclean, 'The doctrine of informed consent', 399–401.
[15] See *Morgan* v. *MacPhail* 704 A 2d 617, 620 (1997).

cases where the infringement involves direct bodily contact. It is therefore better to acknowledge the need for a specific law that can be more sensitive to the context of healthcare.

Consent and negligence

Although negligence may be an appropriate vehicle for regulating consent as agreement, it falls short of the ideal with respect to consent as permission. The first weakness is the conceptual basis for negligence. While battery focuses on the wrong done to the patient, negligence concentrates on the behaviour of the healthcare professional. Since autonomy is the primary justification for consent, patient-centred regulation is more appropriate than professional-centred law. The role of consent is to give the actor permission to do something that would otherwise be illegitimate. For patients to be able to give that permission they must control those things that will be affected by the act. If it is the patient's permission that is important then it makes sense to focus the regulation on whether patients are given an adequate opportunity to exercise that control. Ideally, then, regulation of consent should start by focusing on the conditions under which patients are required to make consent decisions and not whether the professional has acted reasonably in creating those circumstances.

Since it may be necessary to refer to what may be reasonably expected of the healthcare professional (and provider) in order to determine the extent of necessary circumstances, this point may be dismissed as simply a matter of emphasis. But, this emphasis may affect the ease with which compromises to patient autonomy are accepted. If consent is seen primarily as a role-specific obligation the rules may be more readily tempered by the role-specific principle of beneficence, which perhaps explains the law's readiness to accept the paternalistic therapeutic privilege (see below) and the apparent distinction between the level of risk disclosure required for non-therapeutic interventions (e.g. sterilisation) as opposed to therapeutic procedures (e.g. management of pregnancy and delivery). Despite this, if the conceptual criticism were the sole problem then it may be reasonable to accept the status quo. However, the law of negligence has other shortfalls that raise questions regarding its suitability as a vehicle for regulating consent.

A second weakness of negligence is that traditionally it requires the claimant to demonstrate actual damage. This is easiest to show where the damage is physical although, under certain conditions, the claimant may also be able to recover where the only damage is economic loss. In cases where there is uncertainty how a third party might have behaved, the claimant may also recover for loss of chance.[16] The loss of chance claim may be characterised as the loss of an opportunity to control, as far as possible, one's life. It is, therefore, an autonomy-based claim. However, in cases involving the possibility of avoiding the materialisation of medical risks, the English courts have so far refused to recognise the relevance of such a claim. While the possibility of such a claim succeeding has not been completely ruled out,[17] the House of Lords decision in *Gregg* v. *Scott* makes it of diminishing likelihood.[18] In *Rees* v. *Darlington*, however, the House of Lords has recognised a breach of autonomy as a form of damage allowing recovery of a conventional sum.[19] The damage in that case also included the claimant's pregnancy, which was characterised as physical harm. It is, therefore, uncertain whether the courts will recognise an infringement of autonomy when it occurs in the absence of recoverable physical damage.

The likelihood of the courts allowing claims where harm to autonomy is the only damage may be increased by virtue of the Human Rights Act 1998. It is arguable under Article 8 (the right to a private and family life) that this type of damage should be recognised by the courts independently of any physical harm. However, this is speculative and the current requirement that the breach of duty caused physical harm, exemplified by the House Lords decision in *Chester* v. *Afshar*, remains a weakness if autonomy and consent are seen as important rights. It might be countered that the courts have, on occasion, provided compensation for the consequences of an infringement of autonomy even though the primary claim fell at the causation hurdle.

In *Newell and Newell* v. *Goldenberg*, Mantell J held that the plaintiffs' decisions would not have been altered by disclosure of the risk that the vasectomy might fail.[20] However, he was prepared to award damages for the distress and anxiety caused by the discovery that Mrs Newell was pregnant. Although this provided a small amount of compensation to the plaintiffs it still required some tangible damage. This fails to recognise that individuals are harmed just because a choice that was theirs to make has been unjustly taken away from them. It remains, therefore,

---

[16] *Spring* v. *Guardian Assurance* [1995] 2 AC 296; *Allied Maples Group Ltd* v. *Simmons & Simmons* [1995] 1 WLR 1602.

[17] The House of Lords in *Hotson* v. *East Berkshire HA* [1987] AC 750 refused to allow population statistics to be used to circumvent the balance-of-probabilities test for causation through the use of a loss-of-chance argument.

[18] *Gregg* v. *Scott* [2005] UKHL 2. The House of Lords decision in *Barker* v. *Corus (UK) plc* [2006] UKHL 20 does, however, keep the flame burning.

[19] *Rees* v. *Darlington Memorial Hospital NHS Trust* [2003] UKHL 52.

[20] *Newell and Newell* v. *Goldenberg* [1995] 6 Med LR 371.

that while the law espouses the importance of patient autonomy, the current rules of causation and damage belie the judicial rhetoric.

Related to this problem is the inconsistency between what the law claims to be the patient's right and what it is prepared to compensate. The law proclaims that the patient can make any decision regardless of reason.[21] However, it is then only prepared to compensate those cases of a failure to disclose where claimants provide credible evidence that they would have made a different decision. To be credible, claimants must provide accessible reasons. This is inconsistent; there is a right to refuse treatment for irrational reasons (or even no reason) but in trying to show causation in a failure-to-disclose case a claimant's purported refusal of treatment must be rational. This arises because of the need to show that the breach of duty caused actual damage. If outcome responsibility were severed from the issue of consent and dealt with separately, the inconsistency would be removed since liability for failure to consent would no longer be dependent on showing that a different decision would have been made and the harm from the risk materialising avoided. Separating consent and outcome responsibility would allow these distinct harms to be dealt with in a less blunt way, which would facilitate a more just response. However, because liability for negligence requires a bad outcome, it cannot entirely separate consent and outcome responsibility.

I have already mentioned the problem of emphasis that undermines reliance on negligence. This emphasis is the root cause of a third weakness: the standard of care required. Because negligence focuses on the actor it is understandable that the standard of care is expressed in terms of what the reasonable person would have done in the same circumstances. For professional practice the *Bolam* test is the standard and, traditionally, this has been interpreted to allow significant deference to the professional with the test being determined by expert evidence of common practice.[22] There have always been instances when the court has rejected such evidence but it is only since the recent House of Lords judgment in *Bolitho* that commentators have suggested that this deference is disappearing.[23] However, in a review of post-*Bolitho* negligence cases, I found little evidence for that optimism.[24]

The consequence of the *Bolam* test is that the degree of disclosure is determined by professional practice. At its best the standard requires what can be reasonably expected of the professional. While this standard

---

[21] *Re T (Adult: Refusal of Treatment)* [1992] 3 WLR 782, 786.
[22] See, for example, Lord Scarman's statement in *Sidaway* v. *Governors of Bethlam Royal Hospital* [1985] 1 AC 871, 880.
[23] See the discussion in Chapter 4.   [24] Maclean, 'Beyond Bolam and Bolitho'.

may initially seem fair, such a judgement is parasitic on the determination of reasonableness. At its worst, the standard becomes a sociological comparison between what the defendant did and what other doctors are doing. As Lord Scarman suggested in *Sidaway*, this places the standard wholly in the hands of the profession and is insensitive to the patient's needs, interests and rights.

In *Pearce*, Lord Woolf MR delivered a judgment hailed by some as being sufficiently sensitive to the patient's needs. Certainly, the test he developed appeared to move Lord Bridge's approach towards the prudent-patient standard. However, as I argued in the previous chapter, Lord Woolf applied his test in a way that marginalised the relevance of the reasonable patient because it was the medical experts who determined the crucial question of whether the risk was significant. Thus, following *Pearce*, the standard remains largely insensitive of the patient's needs.

Sedley LJ's *obiter dictum* in *Wyatt* v. *Curtis* provides a generous interpretation of *Pearce* that appears to be more responsive to the patient's subjective appreciation of risk and effectively equates the standard with the prudent-patient test.[25] However, since the interpretation was *obiter* and Sedley LJ did not need to apply the test, it remains uncertain how it will be applied in practice. If subsequent courts follow Lord Woolf's lead and refer the question of significance back to the medical expert then any sensitivity to the patient is on shaky ground unless the expert evidence is predicated on more than just that expert's subjective opinion or anecdotal experience. If the reasonable patient is truly to have a voice in court, then it ought to be based on empirical evidence.[26] While judges continue to rely on their own, or the medical experts', intuition, their judgments risk being insensitive to the needs of the reasonable patient let alone the actual patient. This weakens the protection for the patient's autonomy and retains a degree of self-protection for the medical profession since it allows the medical experts a powerful voice in determining the reasonableness of their colleagues' behaviour.

Despite perhaps retaining too much reliance on the medical expert witness, *Pearce* and *Wyatt* have arguably introduced a standard of disclosure that is equivalent to that required by the doctrine of informed consent.[27] This doctrine does appear to focus more on the patient, as the

---

[25] *Wyatt* v. *Curtis* [2003] EWCA Civ 1779 at [16].

[26] A. R. Maclean, 'Giving the reasonable patient a voice: Information disclosure and empirical evidence' (2005) 7 *Medical Law International* 1.

[27] While it remains predicated on the *Bolam* test and the expert witnesses are still relied on it remains distinct from the doctrine. See Maclean, 'The doctrine of informed consent'.

standard requires doctors to disclose material risks, the significance of which is defined by reference to the reasonable patient. In the seminal case, Robinson CJ articulated the appropriate test by quoting with approval from an academic commentary that stated:

> [a] risk is thus material when a reasonable person, in what the physician knows or should know to be the patient's position, would be likely to attach significance to the risk or cluster of risks in deciding whether or not to forgo the proposed therapy.[28]

Even this standard of disclosure is open to criticism as, by determining the duty by reference to the hypothetical objective reasonable patient, it fails to protect individual autonomy.

A further problem with the doctrine of informed consent, at least from the claimant's perspective, is that it may make little difference to the likelihood of success. The objective test of causation adopted in the US and Canada limits the advantages of the prudent-patient test.[29] Given that we already have a subjective test of causation, it is likely that we will retain that standard and this is reinforced by Lord Woolf's approach in *Pearce*.[30] In theory this should give the claimant a better chance of success but, as I argued earlier, it is difficult for the courts to assess credibility without importing objective elements into the test and so weakening the claimant's case.

If the law of negligence settled on the prudent-patient standard with a subjective test of causation then, given that the law sets out only minimally acceptable behaviour, it would arguably have a standard that provides a reasonable degree of protection for patient autonomy (balancing patient autonomy against the facilitation of healthcare and the protection of healthcare professionals from unjust claims). However, one of the problems with the law, even with this more acceptable standard, is that it focuses on the actual risks disclosed rather than on the process of disclosure. If the law concentrated on regulating the dialogical process involved in consent as agreement, it might solve some of the difficulties of trying to determine whether a risk is significant or material to a decision. Focusing on the process itself, rather than the outcome of the process, would also allow the law more readily to acknowledge that the consent engages two parties in an imperfect

---

[28] *Canterbury* v. *Spence* 464 F 2d 772, 787 (1972), quoting from: J. R. Waltz and T. W. Scheuneman 'Informed consent to therapy' (1970) 64 NWUL Rev. 628, 640.

[29] G. Robertson, 'Informed consent ten years later: The impact of Reibl v Hughes' (1991) 70 *The Canadian Bar Review* 423, 435.

[30] *Pearce* v. *United Bristol Healthcare NHS Trust* (1998) 48 BMLR 118, 124.

process of communication that generates and requires mutual obligations of trustworthy behaviour.

This is not to suggest that the law should not be concerned with which risks were actually disclosed. Rather, by focusing on the process and the way in which the two parties communicated, the law can achieve a more holistic understanding of whether the healthcare professional respected the patient's autonomy. Looking at the way in which the two parties approached and engaged with the dialogue may provide an insight into whether a failure to disclose a particular risk was culpable. For example, if it became clear from the discussion between the healthcare professional and the patient that the patient had particular concerns then this should affect the duty to disclose.[31] Lord Woolf MR genuflected towards this idea in *Pearce* when he acknowledged that precise percentages were unhelpful in determining whether a risk should be disclosed. However, by ignoring the evidence concerning the dialogue (the woman's concern for her unborn child was clearly apparent in the case report) and by asking the medical experts for their opinion on the significance of the risk, Lord Woolf ultimately ignored the process of communication between the claimant and defendant.

An additional issue related to the standard of disclosure is how far the law recognises a right to waive information. This is not a question that the courts have been asked to adjudicate on but, while the courts may accept the patient's right to waive the healthcare professional's duty to disclose, the prudent-patient standard could be rigidly applied which would mean that all the risks that would be required by the 'reasonable' patient would need to be disclosed irrespective of the wishes of the particular patient. Whether patients are currently allowed to waive information perhaps depends on whether the law focuses on the patient's rights or the healthcare professional's duties. Since the law of negligence is duty-based, the argument that the patient has no right to waive the information is stronger than it would be under a rights-based approach. It could still be seen as negligent to fail to disclose a risk even if the patient does not want to know the risk.

In the US case of *Putensen* v. *Clay Adams Inc.* the California Court of Appeals appeared to accept that the doctor's duty to disclose was relieved by a specific request 'not to be told the intricacies' of the procedure.[32] The courts in England may well adopt a similar approach as it

---

[31] This can work both ways in that it may be clear from the dialogue that the patient did not wish to be informed of the risks.

[32] *Putensen* v. *Clay Adams Inc.* 12 Cal App 3d 1062, 1083 (1970). See also *Cobbs* v. *Grant* 502 P 2d 1, 12 (1972).

seems unjust to blame professionals for failing to disclose if they have been asked not to. It should be noted, though, that in *Putensen* two further factors were relevant. First, the plaintiff had independently looked into the procedure and 'stated she was aware of what was involved'.[33] Second, the court's justification for accepting that the doctor was relieved of the duty to disclose relied heavily on the therapeutic privilege. Although it is arguable that the courts would acknowledge the right to waive information, until they do, and until the rules for doing so are laid down,[34] some healthcare professionals may be reluctant to accept a waiver in practice. Heywood, for example, argued that the current law is confusing and may lead to doctors acting defensively and 'taking upon themselves [to] disclose excessive information about risks, which the patient may not need or actually want'.[35] Quasi-legal guidance would help, but the easiest way to resolve the issue would be through legislation.

The fourth problem with negligence is crucially related to the question of how far the courts protect patient autonomy. It is the question of which conception of autonomy are the courts relying on when determining these cases, and are they consistent in their application? If tort law is fundamentally a system of corrective justice, which associates responsibility with the desert-based principle of fault, then it reflects a liberal conception of autonomy. The liberal approach sees autonomy as essential for responsibility and as integral to the construction of identity (see Chapter 1). On this view, freedom to choose is necessary for responsibility and where that freedom has been unjustly infringed responsibility for any loss transfers to the wrongdoer. This approach is perhaps evident in the majority judgments in the House of Lords hearing of *Chester* v. *Afshar* (see Chapter 5). However, the minority judgments are, if still predicated on autonomy, explicable only by taking a more socially embedded view of autonomy.[36]

Similarly, in the wrongful birth case of *McFarlane* v. *Tayside*, the House of Lords limited the consequences of corrective justice by relying on distributive-justice arguments that may be justified either by lessening the importance of autonomy or by adopting a less individualistic conception that weakens, or even severs, the association between autonomy and responsibility for outcome. Given the primacy that the law gives autonomy in other medico-legal cases, such as those involving the right to

---

[33] *Putensen* v. *Clay Adams Inc.* 12 Cal App 3d 1062, 1083 (1970).
[34] J. W. Berg, 'Understanding waiver' (2003) 40 *Houston Law Review* 281, 334.
[35] R. Heywood, 'Excessive risk disclosure: The effects of the law on medical practice' (2005) 7 *Medical Law International* 93, 95, 96.
[36] A. Maclean, 'Risk, consent and responsibility for outcome' (2005) 14 *Nottingham Law Journal* 57, 61, 64.

refuse treatment, the better view is to explain the court's approach as based on a more socially embedded view of autonomy. This, however, is inconsistent with the majority's approach in *Chester*. If the law is to be consistent, coherent and predictable then it should be clear which conception of autonomy is relevant, and that conception should be applied universally rather than utilised in a pick-and-mix fashion to suit judicial intuition or bias.

A fifth problem with negligence is that, if disclosure is predicated on the professional's duty, it risks being restricted by his or her duty of care to provide reasonable treatment.[37] What this means is that, if the treatment is not something that the professional would recommend, and it is reasonable under the *Bolam* test to take this stance, then there may be no duty to disclose the treatment even if another doctor would have recommended it. Although the duty to disclose probably encompasses the disclosure of alternative treatments there are no UK cases directly on this point. The cases have been universally concerned with the disclosure of risks, again emphasising the link between consent and outcome responsibility. Because of the lack of English authority on this point, it is necessary to look to other jurisdictions. In *Hicks* v. *Ghaphery*,[38] the Supreme Court of West Virginia held that the informed consent duty to disclose was limited by ordinary negligence principles. Giving the majority opinion, Maynard J quoted from the Californian Court of Appeal case of *Vandi* v. *Permanente Medical Group*:

[I]t would be anomalous to create a legally imposed duty which would require a physician to disclose and offer to a patient a medical procedure which, in the exercise of his or her medical judgment, the physician does not believe to be medically indicated . . . if the procedure is one which should have been recommended it would be negligence under ordinary medical negligence principles and there is no need to consider an additional duty of disclosure.[39]

What this means is that where a responsible school of thought would not recommend a treatment then there would be no duty to disclose it as an alternative treatment.

In *Matthies* v. *Mastromonaco*,[40] the Supreme Court of New Jersey held that, while '[c]hoosing among reasonable treatment alternatives is a shared responsibility of physicians and patients', doctors only had a duty

---

[37] See E. Jackson, ' "Informed consent" to medical treatment and the impotence of tort', in S. A. M. McLean (ed.), *First Do No Harm* (Aldershot: Ashgate, 2006), pp. 271, 277.
[38] *Hicks* v. *Ghaphery* 571 SE 2d 317, 335 (2002).
[39] *Vandi* v. *Permanente Medical Group* 9 Cal Rptr 2d 463, 467 (1992).
[40] *Matthies* v. *Mastromonaco* 733 A 2d 456 (1999).

to disclose those 'courses of treatment that are medically reasonable'.[41] Although this means that 'physicians do not adequately discharge their responsibility by disclosing only treatment alternatives that they recommend',[42] the need to disclose alternatives is governed by the professional standard rather than the prudent-patient standard (or, at least, the prudent-patient standard is necessarily derived from the professional standard) and this limits patient autonomy. If a similar limit were placed on disclosure in England then doctors would only need to find an expert witness to support their view that a particular treatment need not be recommended and, unless their position was illogical, it would not help the patient to find a countervailing opinion.

The duty may protect patients from doctors recommending a somewhat controversial treatment, as in *Matthies*, but it may limit disclosure the other way: if a more controversial, or perhaps outdated, treatment would be more attractive to the patient – for whatever reason – the doctor would not be obliged to disclose it to the patient. It also restricts the patient's ability to act in accordance with his or her character. The patient may be risk averse and feel that it is better to be safe than sorry. The doctor's decision, on the other hand may be influenced by a cost-benefit analysis in deciding that an investigation is not medically indicated. Deciding that the likelihood of detecting an abnormality or preventing a risk materialising is not worth the cost of the procedure may be reasonable from the physician's perspective but the physician is not the one who will have to live with the consequences. In *Hicks*, for example, the doctor decided against inserting a vena-cava filter in a patient at risk of a deep-vein thrombosis. The Supreme Court held that, although the filter would have prevented the patient's death it was a medically reasonable decision not to insert the filter and therefore the doctor was not negligent for failing to disclose the intervention to the patient.[43]

There are three other problems associated with the standard of care required by the duty to disclose. The first problem is the failure of the courts to develop a duty to challenge an apparently irrational decision and attempt to persuade the patient to change his or her mind. If anything, as I noted in Chapter 5, the law has followed the lead of the medical profession and has accepted that, at least in some circumstances, the professional's duty is to be non-directive and any disclosure must be neutral. While this stance may be appropriate in relation to the professional's personal moral values, it reflects a barren view of autonomy as isolated independence if it is applied to decisions that risk the

---

[41] *Ibid.*, 460.   [42] *Ibid.*, 462.   [43] *Hicks v Ghaphery* 571 SE 2d 317 (2002).

patient's health or well-being. As I argued in Chapter 3, part of the professional's role is to advise and to recommend treatment, which, by definition, cannot be a neutral endeavour. It is debatable whether any act of information disclosure by a human can be neutral since even the order of disclosure may affect the way the listener interprets the information. Furthermore, insistence on neutrality sterilises the dialogue and, while it formally respects consent as permission, it undermines consent as agreement. As a final comment on persuasion, I noted earlier that the courts' approach to persuasion is confused and inconsistent. As such it currently fails to provide adequate guidance for healthcare professionals.

The second problem is the therapeutic privilege. Kennedy argued that the doctrine 'allows the doctor proper discretion in the exercise of his duty to disclose'.[44] Provided that the court determines the 'general circumstances in which the privilege may be invoked' then the law will be 'sensitive to the interests of both patient and doctor'.[45] Professional judgement could then determine whether the patient fell within one of these categories. Although cautioning that the risk of paternalism lies just beneath the surface of the privilege, which means it should be an exception rather than the rule, Kennedy suggested that 'the principle behind the doctrine is the same as that justifying informed consent: namely respect for the patient'.[46] If this is the case, then the patient should still be allowed the right to decide whether or not to be given the relevant information regardless of any 'harm' that may be caused by that information. Providing the patient is aware that the doctor believes the information might be detrimental, the choice should remain with the patient. The only exception which might be justified is where the information will significantly impair that patient's autonomous capacity to use the information and even this exception depends on whether the emphasis of respect is placed on the patient's future autonomy rather than his or her present autonomy.

If respect for the person is equated with the individual's present autonomy then the therapeutic privilege cannot be justified. For Kennedy, however, respecting the patient – at least as far as the therapeutic privilege is concerned – also engages beneficence. The acceptance that respect for the patient involves beneficence allows the doctor to make 'inroads into the principle of autonomy' and withhold information that may not be in the patient's best interests. Kennedy, however, argued that the patient is sufficiently protected because the onus of proof lies with the doctor.[47]

[44] Kennedy, 'The patient on the Clapham omnibus', p. 187.   [45] Ibid., p. 187.
[46] Ibid., p. 187.   [47] Ibid., p. 205.

While a respect for the person encompasses both a respect for autonomy and a respect for welfare, the caveat is that the person's welfare should be defined subjectively by reference to the person's own view of his or her interests. In most circumstances the only way to determine the person's welfare interests is to engage that person in dialogue and this requires an openness precluded by the therapeutic privilege. Furthermore, if, the right to give or withhold consent is based solely on the right to self-determination or on the right to autonomy the doctrine of 'therapeutic privilege' is an unjustified exception. It is hypocritical for the law to state that individuals can make whatever decision they like, even if it is harmful, and then deny the individual the very information necessary to make the decision.

Brazier suggested that the prudent-patient test combined with the therapeutic-privilege defence may be seen simply as reversing the burden of proof. Thus, 'Doctors may still rely on custom and practice to withhold information but *they* must prove the custom and practice.'[48] However, she went on to argue that this first impression of the doctrine is blinkered since:

the medical judgment relied on to invoke therapeutic privilege must be specific to that patient. It at least requires that the doctor explore his relationship with that individual and probe to discover the potential effect on him of disclosure. It is not dependent on a *general* assumption that disclosure equals harm to the patient.[49]

This is an insightful and important point. Since the professional standard reflects general practice it is not patient specific. The prudent patient combined with the doctrine of therapeutic privilege focuses attention on the individual patient. However, this advantage arises from the different linguistic emphasis of the two tests. If both tests are interpreted in a spirit of respect for the autonomy of the particular patient then the two tests begin to approach each other and the difference in burden of proof again becomes the distinguishing feature.

The advantage of the prudent-patient test is not that it requires the doctor to focus on the individual in front of him. This should also be required under the professional standard. Rather, the advantage is that the prudent-patient test makes it harder for the doctor to hide behind professional practice. Under both standards the particular patient should be the focus of what information ought to be disclosed. Thus, the professional standard should be: would a responsible body of doctors consider as reasonable the information disclosed to the particular patient

[48] Brazier, 'Patient autonomy and consent to treatment', 188.   [49] *Ibid.*, 188.

in relation to the procedure? It should not be: would a responsible body of doctors consider as reasonable the information disclosed in relation to the procedure? The problem with the professional standard is that there is no linguistic pressure to consider the individual patient and it is therefore too easy to decide the issue generically. The true advantage of the prudent-patient standard, then, is that it linguistically pressures one into considering the particular patient.

Robertson suggested that there are four reasons why information likely to cause psychological distress should be withheld from the patient:

1. The information may be counterproductive in that the resulting psychological distress might prevent rational decision-making.
2. Where the patient is being treated for emotional or psychological problems the added distress may compromise that treatment.
3. 'If disclosure would be likely to cause serious distress or psychological harm, it would be in the best interests of the patient that the information should not be disclosed.'
4. If told the risks, the patient might refuse to give consent to treatment that the doctor believes to be in the patient's best interests.[50]

As Robertson noted: 'It is the fourth possible reason for withholding information on the basis of the "best interests of the patient" principle that gives cause for concern . . . This is a clear example of . . . paternalism.'[51] The danger of this paternalism is particularly great '[g]iven that the duty to disclose is regarded as part of the overall duty of care'.[52] The third reason is also unduly paternalistic. If self-determination forms the basis for consent then the patient should be given the option of waiver where the doctor believes a particular piece of information may be distressing. Furthermore, the patient has the right to be distressed if that is appropriate and the distress – providing it is not incapacitating – may focus the patient's mind more closely on the decision at hand. This might even result in a more appropriate decision. The first reason is also interesting in that it again raises the issue of present and future autonomy as well as the question of whether autonomy requires rationality.[53] Even on the second point (assuming competency) the choice of whether to exercise or waive their right to the information should be put to the patients. Thus, the doctrine should only apply where the information is likely to cause such distress that the patient is rendered incompetent to

---

[50] G. Robertson, 'Informed consent to medical treatment' (1981) 97 *Law Quarterly Review* 102, 121.
[51] *Ibid.*, 121.   [52] *Ibid.*, 122.   [53] See Chapter 1.

make the decision. In this situation it is in patients' best interests not to be informed since they are then encouraged to exercise the maximum amount of autonomy as is possible in the circumstances. If they were to be given the information their competence would be compromised and their autonomy neutered.

Berg *et al.* argued that, because of the overlap between the privilege and the two exceptions to consent of waiver and incompetence, the doctrine could be abolished.[54] The argument is persuasive: if the patient is informed of the potentially distressing nature of the information then a waiver would allow the patient the right to decide 'that they prefer to risk being harmed by being informed than be harmed by having to make choices in the dark of nondisclosure'.[55] The doctrine of therapeutic privilege means that it is the doctor that makes this decision and the patient is presented with a fait accompli. In fact, the position in favour of waiver is even stronger since choosing to receive the information only *risks* harm whereas not being given the choice actually *does* harm by infringing the patient's autonomy. This approach, of allowing the patient to decide whether to risk the potential harm of the disclosure, must be done in a way that is sensitive to the vulnerability of the patient. However, it does serve the purpose of supporting and facilitating the patient's autonomy and allows him or her to retain as much control as is possible in the circumstances.

Despite the fact that the doctrine appears to be encompassed by the *Bolam* test (see Chapter 5), it should rarely, if ever, be allowed as a justification for withholding information. The doctrine suffers from ambiguity,[56] lack of any justified basis – either empirical or philosophical[57] – and there are sufficient exceptions to disclosure that achieve a more coherent and justifiable balance between respecting patient autonomy and improving health.

The third problem is that the standard of care required in urgent and emergency situations remains to be determined. There have been no English cases looking at whether the duty to disclose information and obtain the patient's consent is affected by the urgency of the situation.[58]

---

[54] Berg *et al.*, *Informed Consent*, p. 83.

[55] *Ibid.*, p. 83.

[56] Faden and Beauchamp, *The History and Theory of Informed Consent*, p. 37.

[57] Berg *et al.*, *Informed Consent*, p. 834; S. Bok, *Lying: Moral choice in public and private life* (New York: Vintage Books, 1978), pp. 232–55.

[58] In *Re F (Mental Patient: Sterilisation)* [1990] 2 AC 1, 74, Lord Goff indicated, in an *obiter dictum*, that non-consensual treatment would be justified by an emergency where there was no 'opportunity to communicate' with the patient. However, there are few emergencies where the patient is competent and no communication at all is possible. In *Re R (A Minor) (Wardship: Consent to Treatment)* [1992] Fam 11, 22, Lord Donaldson

Logically, one would expect that the duty would be less demanding simply because the time constraints may make it impossible to counsel the patient adequately. In the US it has been held that the doctor's duty to obtain the patient's informed consent is relieved by the emergency.[59] Clearly, the greater the urgency the less emphasis should be placed on disclosure – there is little point in respecting the patient's autonomy if the patient dies before having the opportunity to exercise that right. But while this may lessen the duty to disclose, it should not relieve the professional of the duty to ask for the patient's permission to treat. This can be done relatively quickly and it is only where the patient is rendered incompetent by the emergency that the duty should be wholly relieved.[60] Because of the unpredictable and highly variable nature of emergencies it would be impossible to set precise standards of disclosure and any duty must, therefore, be subject to the reasonableness standard.

As a final point, since negligence applies both to a failure to disclose and to careless treatment or diagnosis, a finding of negligence may be seen as implying a general carelessness not warranted by what some may see as less blameworthy than the careless performance of an operation. When a doctor, or other healthcare professional, is sued in negligence this may have both personal and professional consequences. Some doctors suffer something akin to a grief reaction; a finding of negligence may be unfairly equated with incompetence and a finding of negligence may have career consequences. It is equally important to treat the healthcare professional fairly as it is the patient and this may be more readily achieved by establishing a distinct liability for 'breach of consent to medical treatment'. While better education of doctors and other healthcare professionals may lead to a better understanding of the meaning of negligence liability it may still be appropriate to more clearly distinguish errors of communication from errors of medical treatment or diagnosis.

The problem of treatment refusal

I previously noted that, at least in principle, the law protects the right to refuse treatment regardless of the consequences for the patient (unless the person is mentally ill). The problem I want to highlight here is the gap between principle and practice. There have been a number of cases

MR equated the emergency exception with circumstances where 'the patient is unconscious or otherwise incapable of giving or refusing consent'.
[59] *Shine* v. *Vega* 709 NE 2d 58, 63–4 (1999).
[60] *Canterbury* v. *Spence* 464 F 2d 772, 788–9 (1972).

where an apparently autonomous person has been denied the right to refuse treatment. In most cases this is achieved by finding the person incompetent. For example, in *Rochdale Healthcare (NHS) Trust* v. *C*, a pregnant woman was held to be incompetent when she refused a Caesarean section because her reasoning seemed irrational to the judge. This was despite the consultant obstetrician believing she was competent to decide and despite the fact that the judge had not actually met or spoken to the woman.[61] Interestingly, in none of the seven Caesarean-section cases was the woman's decision respected while there were lives at risk.[62] Two of the women were clearly competent,[63] and a third was arguably so.[64] Thorpe LJ commented extra-judicially:

> Whatever emphasis legal principle may place upon adult autonomy with the consequent right to choose between treatments, at some level the judicial outcome will be influenced by the expert evidence as to which treatment affords the best chance of the happy announcement that both mother and baby are doing well.[65]

A sceptical analysis of the treatment refusal cases suggests that a refusal is unlikely to be respected where there is a 'socially valuable' life at risk.[66] Consider *Re E*, in which a 15-year-old Jehovah's Witness was deemed incompetent to refuse a blood transfusion despite the judge stating: 'I find that A is a boy of sufficient intelligence to be able to take decisions about his own well-being.'[67] Similarly, in *Re T*, a young woman's refusal of blood transfusions was held to be invalid because it was inapplicable in the circumstances, misinformed and made as a result of undue influence.[68] Other advance refusals have also been rejected even where made with the knowledge of the person's doctor and with the assistance of a solicitor.[69]

---

[61] *Rochdale Healthcare (NHS) Trust* v. *C* [1997] 1 FCR 274.

[62] *Re S* [1992] 4 All ER 671; *Tameside and Glossop Acute Services Trust* v. *CH* [1996] 1 FLR 762; *Norfolk and Norwich Healthcare (NHS) Trust* v. *W* [1996] 2 FLR 613; *Rochdale Healthcare (NHS) Trust* v. *C* [1997] 1 FCR 274; *Re L (An Adult: Non-consensual Treatment)* [1997] 1 FCR 609; *St George's Healthcare NHS Trust v S* [1998] 3 WLR 936; *Bolton Hospitals NHS Trust* v. *O* [2002] EWHC 2871. In *St Georges Healthcare NHS Trust*, the Court of Appeal held that here refusal of treatment should have been respected but this case was heard after the caesarean had been performed.

[63] *Re S* [1992] 4 All ER 671; *St George's Healthcare NHS Trust* v. *S* [1998] 3 WLR 936.

[64] *Rochdale Healthcare (NHS) Trust* v. *C* [1997] 1 FCR 274.

[65] Thorpe LJ, 'The caesarean section debate' (1997) 27 *Family Law* 663, 663–4.

[66] It is not suggested that this is the only explanation for the outcome of the cases; merely that it is a possible one. See A. R. Maclean 'Advance directives and the rocky waters of anticipatory decision making' (2008) 16 *Medical Law Review*, 1.

[67] *Re E (A Minor) (Wardship: Medical Treatment)* [1993] 1 FLR 386, 391.

[68] *Re T (Adult: Refusal of Treatment)* [1992] 3 WLR 782.

[69] *The NHS Trust* v. *Ms T* [2004] EWHC 1279.

In some instances the courts have upheld the individual's right to refuse, but these are where there is no life at risk, or the life at risk is arguably of limited 'social value', or where the individual's decision is seen as rational by the judge because continued life would be painful or pointless. For example, in *Re AK*, a patient with advanced motor neurone disease was held to have made a valid advance directive refusing further treatment after his ability to communicate was lost despite the fact that his competency could not be properly assessed.[70] Without the ability to communicate or use his body in any way his life could be seen as lacking any further point. In the case of *Re B*, the claimant's refusal was upheld as competent because the judge arguably accepted that the life of a paraplegic was of little value if not valued by the individual herself.[71] If Ms B had seen the point in continuing her life and undergoing rehabilitation she would have been a role model of courage in the face of adversity. As Dame Butler-Sloss stated: 'I hope she will forgive me for saying, diffidently, that if she did reconsider her decision, she would have a lot to offer the community at large.'[72] However, there is no dignity in being forced to continue life as a paraplegic against one's wishes.

In *Re C*, a 68-year-old chronic paranoid schizophrenic, confined to Broadmoor after he had stabbed his girlfriend, was held to be competent to refuse surgical amputation of a gangrenous leg despite having the delusion that he was a world-famous physician who had never lost a patient.[73] Arguably, it was of little social concern whether or not his decision resulted in his death, which would have been of little, if any, loss to the community. As a final case to help make the point, consider Ian Brady's attempt to go on hunger strike as a protest against his treatment. Hunger strikes have been allowed where the prisoners were political. However, the court held that Brady was incompetent to refuse and that the refusal was a consequence of his personality disorder, which meant that he could be force-fed under the Mental Health Act 1983.[74] It might be argued that this is an example of a person's refusal being disallowed despite the apparent lack of social value in keeping him alive. However, the social value of Ian Brady's life arises from the need to ensure that the heinous 'moors murderer' was being seen to suffer his punishment for the evil he committed in torturing and murdering children.

[70] *Re AK (Medical Treatment: Consent)* [2001] 1 FLR 129, 133.
[71] *Re B (Consent to Treatment: Capacity)* [2002] EWHC 49.
[72] *Ibid.*, [95].   [73] *Re C (Adult: Refusal of treatment)* [1994] 1 WLR 290.
[74] *R v. Collins, ex parte Brady* (2000) 58 BMLR 173.

The point of this discussion is to note the fragility of patient autonomy in the common law. Combined with a strict code of practice, legislation might bolster the protection of patient autonomy. Emphasising the right to refuse treatment and providing guidelines through a code of practice may limit the cases that are brought to court.[75] However, the vagueness of the competency criteria allows the court huge leeway and would still permit the judges to manipulate the outcomes of cases to continue to preserve 'socially valuable' lives. Legislation could introduce a more robust system of competency assessment but that is beyond the scope of this book and would be unlikely given the recent passage of the Mental Capacity Act 2005. A further possibility that might have a small, but possibly significant, effect would be to emphasise the need for healthcare professionals to challenge apparently irrational decisions. This may either allow patients to acknowledge their errors and change their decisions or it may allow healthcare professionals to understand the patient's reasoning and accept the rationality of the decision.

The problem of non-treatment decisions

I have already noted that consent is not required for non-treatment decisions since they do not invade the patient's bodily integrity. However non-treatment decisions do raise standard of care issues in negligence. It is an interesting and under-explored aspect of *Pearce* that the claimant's case was based on the doctor's failure to disclose a risk of non-treatment.[76] To briefly recap, the case concerned the doctor's obligation to disclose the risk of stillbirth associated with the conservative management of pregnancy. The possible interventions were to induce labour or to deliver the claimant's baby by caesarean section. However, the doctor's advice was to do nothing and allow 'nature to take its course'.

Technically this is a non-treatment decision and thus the patient's consent is not required. However, without any exploration of the possible problems that may be associated with the claim, the Court of Appeal appeared to deal with this as if the conservative management in this situation was simply a type of medical treatment. This is unfortunate because it meant that the Court of Appeal failed to acknowledge

---

[75] Given that only one Caesarean-section case has been brought since the Court of Appeal in *St George's Healthcare NHS Trust* v. *S* [1998] 3 WLR 936 set down guidelines there is some support for this position. While the same result appears possible through the common law the effect of the guidelines appears to have been limited to the refusal of a Caesarean section.

[76] *Pearce* v. *United Bristol Healthcare NHS Trust* (1998) 48 BMLR 118.

the difficulty of winning a claim for failure to disclose in relation to a non-treatment decision. The main problem arises in relation to proving causation. If the healthcare professional is not obliged to provide the treatment (in *Pearce* this was a caesarean section), and the courts have always held that doctors cannot be required to provide a particular treatment,[77] then it is unclear how a failure to disclose a risk can lead to liability.

Consider the situation in *Pearce* if hypothetically the Court of Appeal held that the doctor had breached his duty of disclosure. In order to prove causation in failure to disclose cases claimants must show that they would have changed their decision and not undergone the procedure on that occasion. This is necessary to link the failure to disclose to the damage consequent on the undisclosed risk materialising. However, in cases such as *Pearce*, while the claimant may be able to satisfy the court that she would have refused to agree to conservative management or non-treatment, she cannot show that the failure to disclose caused the damage. This follows because the patient cannot require the doctor to intervene and the doctor may insist on non-treatment even in the face of the patient's disagreement. Since the failure to disclose the risk did not affect the management of the patient it cannot be said to have caused the damage when the risk materialised.

It might be suggested that the disclosure may prompt the patient to seek a second opinion and this might lead to a change in management. There are two points to note here. First, while the second opinion is being sought the management will remain conservative and so, depending on how long it takes to organise the consultation the stillbirth may still happen. Second, the second opinion may support the original doctor's advice, particularly if it is the standard clinical approach to post-term pregnancy. The difficulty here is that the duty to treat is driven by the healthcare professional's duty of care rather than by the patient's autonomy. Thus, unless the management plan is itself negligent, the claimant would find it very difficult to succeed in a case for failure to disclose where the plan is one of non-intervention.

The situation could change if the law were to accept that doctors could be obliged to provide treatment. However, this is extremely unlikely. Alternatively, the law would have to recognise infringement of autonomy as an independent harm, disassociated from the damage caused by the materialised risk. This is possible, but again seems unlikely at present.

[77] See e.g. *R (Burke)* v. *GMC* [2005] EWCA 1003.

The problems of the common law

The first difficulty to note here is that the common law is reactive rather than proactive. This means that it can only develop in response to an actual case. If an issue is not brought before the courts then the judges cannot address that issue and determine the law's stance. While it may be argued that this means that the law only deals with the most important questions, this is not necessarily the case. The driving force is more likely to be money rather than an important point of principle. On top of this, cases that do reach court must be decided within the common-law institutional constraints of precedent and legal policy. Furthermore, any development is likely to be piecemeal and decisions may be inconsistent with each other.

All of this leads to a law that may be out of synch with ethical mores, uncertainty and a lack of predictability, which makes life more difficult for practitioners trying to decide what the law requires of them.[78] As Jones suggested: 'Although the case law can gradually fill in some areas of doubt it can never be a comprehensive framework.'[79] This applies as much to the regulation of consent as any other aspect of the common law and may be exacerbated by the incoherent split between battery and negligence. Consider, for example, the uncertainty that lies in the amount of information that need be disclosed and whether patients can waive their right to information.

Related to this, the law of tort is limited in the flexibility of its remedies. The National Audit Office found that disgruntled patients often want an explanation, an apology or an indication that steps will be taken to prevent the problem recurring.[80] For the most part the patient only has the option of damages and the remedies of an explanation or an apology are not available. Similarly, the courts have no power to ensure that adequate measures are taken to remedy the situation, whether through changes in the system or through retraining, education or referral to the relevant professional regulatory body.

It is arguable that these issues are not the law's concern and that the profession is capable of managing them through bodies such as the GMC without the court's involvement. There is certainly strength in the argument that it should not be necessary to go to court to get an apology or an explanation. However, the complaints system does not always

---

[78] See e.g. R. Worthington, 'Ethical dichotomies and methods of seeking consent' (2004) 59 *Anaesthesia* 525, 526.

[79] Jones, 'Informed consent and other fairy stories', 106.

[80] NAO, *Handling Clinical Negligence Claims in England*, paras. 3.22–3.24.

work, and the threat of litigation, in what may be seen as a counter-productive manner, may cause the doctor to maintain silence rather than risk an apology being misconstrued as an admission of liability. It is precisely because the court and the common law are unable to deal with this that legislation ought to be considered; providing an alternative to the courts with a wider and more flexible range of remedies is an option that is closed to the common law. Although the NHS Redress scheme goes some way to resolving this, by including an explanation and an apology in the package of remedies available under the scheme, it is only applicable to small claims.[81] Furthermore, it does not apply to claims in battery, which may further marginalise that tort in this context.

A further problem with the common-law approach to consent is that regulation is, as I suggested earlier, focused more on the outcome of the process that culminates in consent rather than on the process itself. This results in the law devaluing the relational aspect of the professional–patient relationship and establishes a number of dichotomies that treat autonomy as an all-or-nothing concept (consent or no consent; voluntary or involuntary; competent or incompetent) rather than as a variable characteristic capable of degrees of existence. This is partly to do with liability, at least in negligence, depending on the materialisation of a risk. If outcome responsibility and consent are distinguished, the law could develop a more sensitive approach to regulating the iterative dialogical process between the healthcare professional and the patient. However consent is regulated, the law would be unable to escape the use of thresholds to establish liability. But, either through legislation or the development of professional regulation, the law could engage with the variable nature of autonomy and establish a number of thresholds that would allow for different remedies or differing amounts of compensation.

The penultimate problem with common-law regulation is that, while it is presently developing in a way that seeks to provide an increased protection for individual autonomy, it could equally well shift in the opposite direction. The law of negligence has previously seen such oscillations, for example, in the development of the rules used to determine whether a novel claim should be recognised,[82] and in cases of indeterminate causation.[83] The law also tends to follow the dominant

---

[81] NHS Redress Act 2006; Department of Health, *NHS Redress: Statement of policy* (Leeds Department of Health, 2005) at para. 34.

[82] See *Anns* v. *Merton London Borough* [1978] AC 728; *Junior Books* v. *Veitchi* [1983] 1 AC 520; and *Caparo Industries plc* v. *Dickman* [1990] 2 AC 605.

[83] Rules of causation relaxed in *Fairchild* v. *Glenhaven* [2002] 1 AC 32, but tightened up in *Barker* v. *Corus (UK) Ltd* [2006] UKHL 20.

ethical arguments, although with an extensive lag period which means that just as the law reacts to the ethical and social mores so those mores change. The present developments are leading to increased protection for a liberal conception of the autonomous person. There is now, however, a noticeable movement to constrain that approach by highlighting the relational nature of autonomy, the obligations of patients and the relevance of other communitarian concerns. In addition, there is currently concern regarding the 'compensation culture' to the point that the Compensation Act 2006 has been introduced to reverse, or at least slow down the rise in negligence claims.[84]

The effects of these developments may be that the law will pull on the reins of informed consent and reverse the expansion of liability seen in cases such as *Chester* v. *Afshar*. While this is not necessarily inappropriate the problem is that the piecemeal development of the common law will mean that any such reversal of judicial policy will inevitably cause confusion and a lack of certainty regarding the current rules of disclosure and consent.

A final point is the inability of tort law to engage with or develop a coherent philosophy for the community's system of healthcare. This is something that is properly the purview of the government, which has both the authority and the tools to develop such a philosophy. Although the courts may be influenced by government policy, and may be able to fine-tune liability, they are constrained by precedent and the institution of law. The courts are often reluctant to rely on policy arguments and when they do attend to the wider implications of a judgment it creates the types of problems exemplified by the somewhat arbitrary appeal to distributive justice in the recent series of wrongful pregnancy cases.[85] However, the extent of the requirements for a valid and effective consent are – or ought to be – inextricably linked to the whole philosophy of healthcare in the context of its delivery within the particular community. Given the constraints of the common law, it may be better to legislate for consent in a way that would be compatible with the values and pragmatic concerns of healthcare as well as being sensitive to the needs of the patients served by the institution of healthcare itself.

---

[84] See the prime minister's speech on the compensation culture delivered to the Institute of Public Policy Research on 26 May 2005, available at www.number10.gov.uk/output/Page7562.asp.

[85] *McFarlane* v. *Tayside Health Board* [2000] 2 AC 59; *Parkinson* v. *St James and Seacroft University Hospital* [2001] EWCA Civ 530; *Rees* v. *Darlington Memorial Hospital NHS Trust* [2002] EWCA Civ 88; *Rees* v. *Darlington Memorial Hospital NHS Trust* [2003] UKHL 52.

Addressing the gap between practice and principle

There are broadly three alternative approaches. First, the common law could be allowed to continue to develop, guided by criticism and debate. However, this is a haphazard and uncertain process that could drag the protection of patient autonomy into the depths of libertarian isolation or revert to a more protectionist paradigm of limited paternalism through the reliance on medical experts and the development of the therapeutic privilege. Currently, it seems unwilling or unable to develop the law creatively in a way that is sensitive to a more nuanced and mature view of patient autonomy in the context of the professional–patient relationship. Furthermore, after some thirty years of developing the law in this area, we are still left with a situation in which the realities of informed consent may be described as a 'fairy story', with medical practice falling short of both legal and ethical expectations. It is, therefore, arguable that any amount of 'tinkering' with the common law will inevitably be inadequate and that a more radical solution is required.[86]

A second approach would be to start from first principle and legislate on the issue. This would have the advantage of allowing the development of a conceptually coherent law, with well-defined guidance that reflects the political approach to healthcare and provides secure protection for patient autonomy balanced by the recognition that the right to autonomy is not free-floating but is grounded in relationships and the obligations inherent to those relationships. Although Heywood's suggestion that 'The law can never be viewed as a proactive mechanism protecting patients' rights'[87] is a fair criticism of the common law, it is less accurate in relation to new legislation. This is especially so if the legislative process is accompanied by a consultation process, which serves to enhance the consciousness-raising effect of new legislation. Furthermore, if a code of practice and an independent regulator are part of the new legislation, the law can be both proactive and flexible. Added to which, passing new legislation has an important symbolic effect, which would serve to emphasise the relative value the community places in autonomy, self-determination and health. Thus, legislation could be a positive influence on medical practice both on the individual practitioner and on the profession as a whole.

The final option is to develop professional regulation so as to allow a more proactive role for the professional regulatory bodies. It is likely that

[86] See, Jackson, ' "Informed consent" to medical treatment and the impotence of tort', p. 272.
[87] Heywood, 'Excessive risk disclosure', 105.

some form of professional regulation will always play an important role in encouraging the virtue of professionalism; regulating the healthcare professional's character dispositions requires an active supervision that falls outside the courts' role. However, there is still the question of whether professional regulation could be developed sufficiently to negate the need for a direct legislative response.

In recent years the GMC, for example, has been active in producing guidelines, which should improve practice and are likely to indirectly influence legal standards. In addition to this they could also be given the power to provide limited remedies, such as a small amount of compensation for the harm done to the patient's autonomy, an explanation, a formal apology and assurance that something will be done to prevent the same thing happening to others. The main problem with that approach is the possible perception that the professional regulatory bodies are insufficiently independent of the practitioners and are biased in their favour. The GMC, for example, has over recent years been subject to much criticism[88] and, while it has engaged more openly with the public in recent consultation exercises,[89] there may be insufficient public confidence in these bodies at present to support an expanded role. However, given the time and support to develop and become more proactive and independent, professional regulation may gain a new lease of life.

Any reliance on professional regulation would, of course, need to address the problem of coordinating the different regulatory bodies, such as the GMC and the Nursing and Midwifery Council (NMC), to ensure consistent and coherent regulation of healthcare practice. If that can be addressed, professional regulation may be able to paper over the deficiencies in the common law.

Conclusion

To conclude this chapter, I will briefly summarise my argument. In analysing the regulation of consent and information disclosure in the torts of battery and negligence, I have shown that both of these torts have their deficiencies. These include both conceptual and practical flaws. Battery, for example, has connotations of criminality and fails to deal with non-interventional management or non-contact treatment.

---

[88] See e.g. J. Smith, *The 5th Shipman Report, Safeguarding Patients: Lessons from the past – proposals for the future*, Cm 6394 (2004), Chapter 15; D. Irvine, *The Doctors' Tale: Professionalism and public trust* (Oxford: Radcliffe Medical Press, 2003).
[89] In 2005 the GMC held five public seminars entitled 'What is Good Medical Practice?'.

Negligence, on the other hand, is constrained by the need to show that the failure to disclose caused legally recognised damage, and carries the baggage of reliance on medical experts and deference to the profession. The standard of care expected is inadequately defined at present and the reluctance of the courts to require a duty to persuade underlines the barren nature of the legal conception of autonomy. Furthermore, while lacking the criminal associations of battery, it does perhaps imply that the doctor is generally negligent rather than that the error was confined to a failure of communication.

Just as there are problems with either tort, so there are difficulties with the combined regulation, which is the current approach taken by the law. Conceptually it makes little sense to distinguish risk information from the 'nature' of the procedure and this association of risk disclosure and negligence creates a particular link between consent and responsibility for outcome. While this may be appropriate, I argued earlier that it was not necessary and legislating for consent would provide an opportunity to rethink that association. Furthermore, the common law's focus on the end product of the duty to disclose, rather than on the process of dialogue that precedes consent as permission, restricts its sensitivity to individual autonomy. Finally, I also briefly raised some of the problems of regulating consent to medical treatment within the common-law system, which includes its reactive rather than proactive approach, its costs and the inflexibility of remedies available.

While none of these problems is fatal on its own, together they add up to a powerful argument in favour of at least considering the value of legislating or developing more extensive professional regulation. This approach is given additional support by three further weaknesses of current English law.[90] First, the legal requirements remain vague, contested and perhaps not well known by healthcare professionals, although this may have been ameliorated to some extent by the publication of the Department of Health's guidance.[91] Second, the law has been developed in relation to doctors and it is unclear whether the same obligations apply to other healthcare professionals. Third, and finally, litigation is expensive and some injured parties may be put off legal recourse by the cost, which may unjustly preclude patients receiving at least recognition that they have been wrongly treated. These criticisms are unlikely to be adequately addressed by tinkering with the common law.

---

[90] Skegg, 'English medical law and "informed consent"', 148–59.
[91] Department of Health, *Reference Guide to Consent*.

7 Constructing consent: Future regulation and the practice of healthcare

Over the course of the book I have explored the moral justification for the legal protection afforded to the individual's right to give or withhold consent. I have argued that any model of consent must be sensitive to the context and that consent should be situated at the heart of the relationship between the healthcare professional and the patient. Following this approach I constructed a relational model of consent. This model acknowledges the limits of individual autonomy and accommodates the bilateral obligations that exist by virtue of the professional–patient relationship.

Having explored the concept of consent, its moral basis and its contextual setting, I turned to examine the law, comparing the legal model of regulation to the theoretical model of relational consent. While the law works to a passable level it was found wanting, both conceptually and normatively. Part of the problem with the law is that it has developed within the confines of the existing common law torts of battery and negligence. This has led to a blunt system of regulation, with an unimaginative approach to consent and a thin view of autonomy. Furthermore, the institutional constraints of the common law, and the necessary association of consent and responsibility for outcome, shackle the future development of the legal regulation of consent.

In this final substantive chapter I will examine how the common law might develop in the future and I will compare that vision to the alternative regulatory approach should a relational model be implemented. I will set the scene for this comparison by briefly recapping the development of the law to date.

The developing law

Prior to the House of Lords hearing of *Sidaway*, the legal regulation of consent was deferential to doctors and supportive of the endemic paternalism that existed in the medical profession. It was an essentially illiberal approach that subjugated the personal autonomy of the patients to a community perspective of what constituted the good life. This community perspective was mediated by the medical profession and prioritised clinical interests over all other values. In this context *Sidaway* was a landmark judgment that, despite the subsequent cases of *Blyth* and *Gold*, marked a turning point in judicial attitude.

The four judgments delivered in *Sidaway* represent three distinct political approaches to consent. Lord Scarman's speech was the most liberal, emphasising the patient's right to self-determination and arguing that the prudent-patient standard should be preferred to the reasonable-doctor test. Lord Diplock's judgment was the most traditional preserving the paternalistic communitarian view that the patient's medical best interests, as determined by the doctor, should be prioritised over his or her autonomy. Lords Bridge and Templeman delivered judgments that sat between these two approaches, although they were perhaps closer to Lord Diplock's position than to Lord Scarman's.

Following *Sidaway*, *Blyth* and *Gold* in the late 1980s temporarily entrenched Lord Diplock's paternalism. However, in the 1990s the deference to the medical profession was unravelling as the courts developed a more liberal approach that reflected the approach of Lords Bridge and Templeman. In the late 1990s the Court of Appeal in *Pearce* advanced this approach. Although Lord Woolf MR ostensibly relied on Lord Bridge's judgment in *Sidaway*, his formulation of the *Bolam* test inched the standard ever closer to the prudent-patient standard espoused by Lord Scarman. Lord Woolf's formulation of the test, and its application in the case itself, is open to criticism (see earlier); however, there is no doubt that the law has now shifted to a liberal position that prioritises the patient's right to self-determination. This is confirmed by the dicta in *Wyatt* v. *Curtis* and the majority judgments in the House of Lords hearing of *Chester* v. *Afshar*. While it may not apply in all contexts, the law has perhaps reached its libertarian nadir in *Al Hamwi* v. *Johnston*, a case involving genetic counselling in which the judge accepted that the doctor's duty was satisfied simply by disclosing accurate information, leaving the patient with the mandatory responsibility of deciding what to do. In this extreme vision, autonomy is seen as independent and obligatory self-determination.

The cycle of criticism and the scope for further development

Many concepts are capable of spawning a variety of conceptions that depend on one's political view of the world, which allows the current conception to be criticised and makes it possible for change without the need to abandon the core concept itself. There is always motivation to apply pressure for change, which is a necessary part of any meaningful democracy. Over time, if the pressure for change is consistent enough the concept will metamorphose into a new conception. Once that new conception becomes the norm it too will be subject to critical pressure and will subsequently develop into a new conception. Of course that change can go backwards as well as forwards and prior conceptions may be revisited as part of this continuous cycle of criticism and change.

As with all concepts, consent has a basic core that cannot be changed by criticism without the concept being effectively abandoned. In this context the core concept is that consent is a derivative right allowing the rights-holder to control the primary right to bodily integrity by granting another person permission to act in a way that would otherwise breach the primary right. However consent can be varied by moving along the continuum between the two extremes of consent as a state of mind and consent as an act of communication. The scope for change and criticism that this variable allows is increased by the recognition that the preferred conceptions of autonomy and rationality, both of which are crucially connected to consent, are determined by political perspective.

The core concept of autonomy is subject to two variables. One axis is a continuum that extends from complete independence through relational dependence to complete dependence. Relational dependence still acknowledges the individual as an agent but one who is reliant on others to support his or her autonomy. Going beyond this point to a position of complete dependence undermines the concept of autonomy, which must then be abandoned. The two ends of this axis roughly correspond to libertarian and communitarian perspectives.

Interacting with this continuum is the discontinuous axis of rationality. At one extreme is the conception of instrumental rationality. At the other end of the axis is recognitional rationality, which sees the rational choice as determined by an objective determination of the good. In between these two extremes are the two constructivist approaches. Lying more closely to instrumental rationality is the neo-Humean conception of reflective rationality. Further along the axis towards the recognitional end is Kant's approach to rationality, which equates rationality and morality. O'Neill's accessible-ends model of rationality lies even further along the axis. These insights may be applied to the way in which the law has developed.

Traditionally judges treated consent as a state of mind, although only in respect of battery law.[1] This liberal approach to consent was,

---

[1] *Sidaway* v. *Governors of Bethlem Royal Hospital* [1985] 1 AC 871, 894 per Lord Diplock.

therefore, confined to situations where there was a gross failure to obtain the patient's consent or the healthcare professional acted with bad faith. Even then the liberal approach was tempered by the recognition of the role communication plays in providing the healthcare professional with permission. Thus, patients would be estopped from denying either that they had the relevant information or that they had consented if they acted in such a way as to cause the healthcare professional reasonably to believe that an effective permission had been given.[2] However, the duty to disclose the additional information beyond that required for a real consent essentially focused on consent as communication.

The healthcare professionals' duty was based on the need for rational decision-making where rationality was recognitional and determined by clinical goals. Thus, the healthcare professionals determined the amount, the manner and the timing of any information disclosed. The basis for disclosure balanced the patient's self-determination against his or her medical best interests, but it was best interests that took priority where conflict arose. While this tension is apparent in *Sidaway*, it is perhaps most explicit in the Scottish case of *Moyes* v. *Lothian HB*.[3] Following *Sidaway*, Lord Caplan acknowledged the patient's right to self-determination and to be 'fully informed'. The doctor's duty, however, remained governed by 'medical criteria'.[4] The doctor's primary concern was the patient's health and the patient's right to self-determination was 'essentially an aspect of the [doctor's] duty to take reasonable care for his safety'.[5]

As the law developed through the 1990s and up to the present day the emphasis on the patient's right to self-determination was given increasing prominence and the healthcare professional's duty of beneficence became a secondary concern. The reliance on recognitional rationality diminished and the legal approach to rationality shifted towards the liberal constructivist and libertarian instrumental models of rationality. Along with this change in the conception of rationality, the courts treated autonomy as independent self-determination and developed an approach, culminating in *Al Hamwi*, that takes a minimalist view to the role of communication so that the duty to disclose becomes simply about providing accurate information presented in lay terms. Thus, over the last quarter of a century the law has gone from a paternalistic, communitarian approach to a liberal view of consent that, at its worst, abandons patients to their own devices.

While the courts have increasingly emphasised the patient's right to independent self-determination they have also managed to retain a

---

[2] *Ibid.*   [3] *Moyes* v. *Lothian HB* [1990] 1 Med LR 463.   [4] *Ibid.*, 469.   [5] *Ibid.*

curiously dichotomous attitude that permits healthcare professionals to act paternalistically provided they satisfy their duty to disclose, which is measured purely by the outcome of the process. Thus, the judges have shown themselves to be distinctly uninterested in the manner of communication[6] and it is acceptable for healthcare professionals to be wholly unsupportive and disengage themselves from the patient.[7] However, it is equally acceptable for healthcare professionals to manipulate or even bully their patients into making the decision they see as right.[8]

From this brief synopsis it can be seen that the law's approach to consent and self-determination has gone from one extreme to the other in the cycle of criticism: from doctor decides to the abandonment of patients. The deference to the medical profession, in particular to the ethics of the medical profession,[9] has remained and this perhaps goes a long way to explaining the law's approach to paternalism. Although paternalism has been rejected in regard to the prima facie duty to disclose, it remains protected in the therapeutic privilege and the absolute discretion given to doctors in how the information is communicated.

Just as the traditional approach was subject to pressure to change so the current position remains open to criticism and is likely to alter over time, particularly given the reactive nature of the common law. While the common law provides scope for development it is constrained by the forms of action, the doctrine of precedent, the often-indirect nature of the influence on the judges, their training, background and experience. These institutional influences are exacerbated by the reaction of the healthcare profession and its associated machinery. As the threat of litigation has increased so too has the risk-management industry, which takes a functional and defensive approach to satisfying the legal duty. This has encouraged a tendency to satisfy the duty to disclose largely by reference to the amount of information disclosed; if there is any uncertainty whether a risk should be disclosed the safest approach – in avoiding litigation – is to disclose it. Thus, *full* disclosure – if such a thing is possible – satisfies the duty to make *adequate* disclosure and removes the problems of any grey areas that have yet to be defined by the courts.

Since the law has only just reached the abyss of consent predicated on libertarian self-determination, most of the academic effort has been directed at criticising the failure of the courts to protect the patient's autonomy. This has recently changed and there is growing criticism of

---

[6] *Thompson* v. *Bradford* [2005] EWCA Civ 1439.
[7] *Al Hamwi* v. *Johnston* [2005] Lloyd's LR Med 309.
[8] *Attwell* v. *McPartlin* [2004] EWHC 829, [60].
[9] See J. Miola, *Medical Ethics and Medical Law: A symbiotic relationship* (Oxford: Hart Publishing, 2007).

the current situation that prioritises patient choice as justification for consent. One of the leading critics has been Onora O'Neill and this culminated in her recent book, written with Neil Manson, *Rethinking Informed Consent in Bioethics*. I have already addressed aspects of their approach in earlier chapters and I turn now to compare their model of consent to my own. I will explain the place that their model might – or perhaps should – take in the cycle of criticism. It is, I will argue, a necessary step in the development of consent, but it provides inadequate support for the patient and thus, if it is adopted at all, it should only be a transitional measure. However, before I address Manson and O'Neill's approach I will briefly explain the philosophy of healthcare provision that underlies my own approach to consent.

The nature of healthcare delivery

I have argued that consent must be situated within the context of the professional–patient relationship and I have explained how the obligations that arise from the relationship influence the conception of consent. Just as consent sits at the heart of the relationship so the relationship can be defined by how consent is regulated. However, this iterative interaction does not exist in a vacuum but occurs in the context of the provision of healthcare. The philosophy behind the provision of healthcare inevitably affects the nature of the relationship between the professional delivering the care and the patient receiving it. To fully appreciate the relationship and its obligations, one must understand the view of healthcare that motivates its provision.

The point I am getting at here is that the nature of the professional–patient relationship, and thus how consent should be regulated, is dependent on the desired type of healthcare system. If health is treated as a commodity that can be managed using a market approach to the delivery of healthcare then a more libertarian approach to consent, which prioritises patient choice rather than patient-centred care, is appropriate. However, if health, and hence healthcare, is valued for more than just its objectively rational economic worth then a more communitarian or social approach is justified.

While health is of instrumental rather than intrinsic value, it is so fundamentally important to our sense of well-being and to our ability to achieve our goals that any attempt to value it economically would be arbitrary and would ultimately fail to do justice to the role that health plays in each of our lives. A community that fails to care for the health and well-being of its members is an unjust community because those people whose health is affected to the point at which their goals are threatened are placed at a disadvantage to those who are not so affected. This disadvantage is exacerbated if a market approach is taken to the delivery of healthcare; not only do sick people have to cope with the effects of the illness – they also have to meet the costs of the care, or risk not having the care because it is economically inefficient to provide it. This prejudices the sick and prioritises the interests of those who are lucky enough to have good health.

While this short discussion perhaps oversimplifies the argument, the basic point holds that health is too important a value to trust to the harshness of liberal market economics. How we respond to the sick and disadvantaged reflects our humanity. To treat health and well-being as if their only value is economic dehumanises us. It undermines the care that we should feel towards other creatures capable of suffering. For these reasons the provision of healthcare should be based on a social or communitarian approach. I am not, however, suggesting that one can ignore the cost; merely that value of health exceeds its economic worth.

While the health of each member of the community concerns the whole community the interests of the community should not be allowed to smother the interests of the individual. Health is important, but it remains of instrumental value and thus may be superseded by other goals or values that are intrinsic to the integrity of the individual. In other words, the community's interest in the individual's health does not justify prioritising health over the individual's other interests. This means that there must be a balance between the community's interest in the individual's health and the individual's wider interests. This is best achieved by taking a relational approach to the individual agent that recognises the importance of individual agency but also acknowledges the relevance of its social context.

Manson and O'Neill's model of genuine consent

Manson and O'Neill launch a two-pronged attack on the current approach to consent,[10] a theme also pursued by O'Neill elsewhere.[11] First, they criticise the reliance on a libertarian conception of autonomy as justifying the ethical importance of informed consent. Second, they attack the liberal approach to consent that emphasises the importance of the agent's state of mind to the detriment of the relevance of communication. Both of these are valid arguments that have also formed part of my criticism of the current legal model of regulation and I have already

---

[10] Manson and O'Neill, *Rethinking Informed Consent.*
[11] O'Neill, 'Some limits of informed consent'; O'Neill, *Autonomy and Trust.*

examined both of these points in earlier chapters. It is, however, worth recapping their arguments because it will help in understanding the limits of the model they subsequently propose.

In criticising the current approach to consent, Manson and O'Neill argue that autonomy as self-determination allows choices that have no moral value and thus do not deserve the protection afforded by the rules of consent. For them, Kant's version of autonomy of the will is the only conception of autonomy that could provide the requisite moral worth but it cannot be translated into the precise rules required to regulate consent. I have already criticised their discussion for completely ignoring the conception of relational autonomy and their claim that Kant's conception of autonomy cannot be 'operationalised by informed consent procedures'.[12] I will not repeat that criticism here. However, it should be noted that it is Kant's conception of autonomy, in the form of the categorical imperative that all self-legislated rules should be universalisable, that forms the basis for the healthcare professional's obligation in their model.

The consequence of Manson and O'Neill's approach is that, rather than the rules of consent being based on the patient's right to autonomy, they are derived from the universalisable obligations that fall on all agents capable of exercising their autonomous wills to self-legislate. This shifts the focus from the patient's right to autonomy to the healthcare professional's duties under the categorical imperative. Their argument emphasises the importance of communication in the process of obtaining consent and this crucially interacts with the Kantian duty-based approach to consent because effective communication is only possible where the parties behave in a trustworthy way that allows the person to rely on the information imparted. Thus, consent is genuine where the healthcare professional has neither coerced nor deceived the patient.

Their approach to communication relies on an agency model of information, which requires the person imparting the information to take into account, as far as possible, the context of the person receiving the information. Because the person receiving the information is likely to rely on it, the information must be accurate, relevant and intelligible. Furthermore, because it is ultimately the agent's right to give or withhold consent, he or she must remain in control of how much information is imparted. Finally, their approach to consent and communication recognises that both parties must engage with the process.

To summarise, Manson and O'Neill's model has a number of characteristics. First, it recognises that the right to consent is derived from an

[12] Manson and O'Neill, *Rethinking Informed Consent*, p. 18.

underlying right. Second, it denies that the patient's autonomy provides consent decisions with their moral worth. Third, it focuses on the healthcare professional's obligations rather than on the patient's rights. Fourth, it emphasises the importance of consent as an act of communication rather than simply as a state of mind. Fifth, it utilises an agency-based approach to information, rather than the container model that underlies the current approach. Finally, consent is context-dependent and thus different rules may be required in different circumstances.

The first problem with their model relates to their approach to communication and information. For Manson and O'Neill a genuine consent has essentially three features: the person granting consent has not been coerced or deceived and has retained control of the amount of information that is disclosed. While their approach prioritises consent as communication it does so by focusing primarily on the healthcare professional's obligations required for effective communication. The consequence of this focus is that the normative rules of communication they espouse essentially relate to disclosure and thus maintain the two parties at a distance that allows the healthcare professional to avoid engaging with the patient in a way that promotes good decision-making. The emphasis is on truthful disclosure rather than on a cooperative – or communal – interaction.

The norms of communication that are given particular emphasis are those of intelligibility, relevance and adequate accuracy. In addition to these norms of communication, Manson and O'Neill recognise that the consent transaction involves the parties making conditional commitments that require the consent to be freely given, which means that it must be given in circumstances free of 'force, duress, constraint . . . coercion . . . fraud and deceit'.[13] While all of these conditions of an effective consent are reasonable, they impose only minimal positive obligations on the professional and the duty remains primarily one of disclosure. This focus is exacerbated by the second problem with their model, which is their assertion that autonomy is not the ethical justification for consent. This means that they are not concerned with whether the person makes a good decision. Manson and O'Neill's approach to consent is essentially restricted to communication as effective disclosure. Their insights into the container model of information, and their arguments in favour of the agency model, are apposite and important. However, their approach still permits a superficial engagement with the patient that avoids the deeper commitments to the patient's good, which constitutes the duty of beneficence.

[13] Manson and O'Neill, *Rethinking Informed Consent*, pp. 86–94, 92.

A third problem with Manson and O'Neill's model is that they have made no attempt to consider how the model would work in practice. There are two aspects to this. First, they reasonably note that consent is context-dependent. However, while they later go on to look at information in the contexts of data protection and genetics, they make little, if any, attempt to explain how other contexts affect the relevant duties. Second, they do not examine the possible interaction between their theoretical model, the institutional constraints imposed by law, the reaction of the healthcare professionals and the impact of the machinery of risk management. In other words, they have not engaged with the problems of implementation that may act to distort their model. This is unfortunate since it is just these influences that have caused the liberal model of consent to mutate into a consumerist caricature.

Although somewhat speculative, it is worth considering how Manson and O'Neill's model might be affected were it to be implemented. First, the law already has rules that prohibit coercion, duress and fraud and, given the continuing respect afforded to the medical profession and its ethics, the judges are likely to see little need to alter their approach with regard to the law of battery. This means that any changes that occur are likely to be restricted to the law of negligence. This law is parasitic on professional practice and already expects the professional to disclose intelligible, accurate and relevant information. These requirements mirror the important norms of communication that Manson and O'Neill focus on.

The law currently determines the extent of the duty by reference to the reasonable patient's informational needs as determined by the reasonable professional. In principle this means that the duty to disclose is determined by the circumstances or context of the disclosure and reserves the prima facie duty as a matter for clinical judgement, albeit one that is subject to the court's scrutiny. Beyond the prima facie duty, patients control additional disclosure but only if they ask the appropriate questions. Manson and O'Neill's model suggests that the patient is put in control of the information received by being given access to extendable information. This would perhaps be best achieved by requiring a dialogue between the professional and the patient, backed by a duty on the professional to support and facilitate the patient's access to, and their understanding of, the requisite information. However, the model of genuine consent does not require this. Like the law it demands a limited amount of relevant, accurate and intelligible information with the patient given control of additional disclosure.[14]

---

[14] O'Neill, 'Some limits of informed consent', 6.

One of Manson and O'Neill's concerns is that the patient is not simply overburdened with information in a futile attempt to achieve full disclosure. This has also been the law's concern and, in *Sidaway*, Lord Templeman explicitly cautioned against this. In fact, when implanted into the current common law, Manson and O'Neill's model of consent and information seems very similar to the approach taken by Lord Templeman in particular, but also Lord Bridge. The difference between the two comes down to the emphasis in *Sidaway* on clinical judgement. In Manson and O'Neill's model it is the patient who ostensibly has control of the flow of information. While this is a crucial difference in principle, it is difficult to see how it will have much effect in practice given Manson and O'Neill's rejection of autonomy as the ethical foundation for consent. In effect, the limited information disclosed initially must be a matter for clinical judgement and access to further information can only be controlled by the patient requesting it or asking questions. As I discussed in Chapter 5, questions are rarely so specific that they leave no discretion to the person answering them and thus clinical judgement remains an important factor. The information put in leaflets made available to patients can only be based on what the reasonable patient would want to know. What goes into the leaflets will ultimately be determined by those writing them and not by the patient, who must rely on questions for more personalised information.

One of the problems with the law is that it allows professionals to satisfy their duty by the bare disclosure of accurate, relevant and intelligible information. There is no further duty to facilitate effective communication, assist understanding or support decision-making. There is nothing in Manson and O'Neill's approach to suggest that implementing their model of genuine consent would affect this somewhat laissez-faire attitude to the patient as decision-maker. This is exacerbated by the law's focus on the outcome of disclosure as a measure of the duty to disclose. Again, there is no reason why this would change and the pressure of risk management and defensive practices are likely to reinforce this.

The easiest way to avoid litigation where the measure of the duty is based on the outcome of disclosure is to focus attention on what needs to be disclosed rather than on the process of disclosure itself. Adequate disclosure becomes determined by whether a particular risk, or packet of information, is disclosed and all of the dangers of focusing on the conduit model of information resurface. Although Manson and O'Neill rightly caution against reliance on the conduit model, it is likely that their approach to consent, when subject to the constraints of the common law, and the forces of risk management and defensive practice, would do little to avoid that reliance.

Their argument has an important symbolic power and if taken on board by virtuous professionals it may be applied to the benefit of the patient. Importantly, it may also rein in the worst excesses of information disclosure that reflect the libertarian monster of mandatory autonomy. In this regard it may be an important and necessary step in the further development of the regulation of consent. However, their approach may simply be used to justify a restricted standard of disclosure that strongly resembles the standard defined in the judgments of Lords Templeman and Bridge. Furthermore, it may do little to counteract the law's acceptance of paternalism that coexists somewhat inconsistently with its current emphasis on the patient's right to autonomy. Finally, Manson and O'Neill's model fails to require the supportive engagement necessary to foster good decision-making.

The relational model of consent

The main strengths of Manson and O'Neill's model are its focus on an agency approach to information and its emphasis on the importance of context. As a consequence of this they expose the unhelpful approach to consent and information that demands full disclosure. At best, full disclosure is a meaningless requirement, but it may also be positively disadvantageous because it places unrealistic demands on healthcare professionals and risks overloading patients with unhelpful and possibly confusing information. However, while Manson and O'Neill recognise the importance of context they provide little in the way of explaining how their approach should be implemented in these different circumstances. In particular their context-specific focus is limited to an examination of informational privacy and genetic information.

In the previous section of this chapter I suggested that if their model was to be implemented in clinical practice it would have the important consequence of reining in the current approach to disclosure. However, I suggested that the concept of a genuine consent should only be seen as an intermediary step in the development of a model that both respects and supports the patient's agency. The model developed in the first part of this book is designed to meet both of those requirements while also recognising the limits of consent as a derivative right that is effective only in relation to an underlying primary right.

This recognition that consent is a derivative right is an increasingly acknowledged constraint on the role that consent plays. It is a feature that is common to both my concept of relational consent and Manson and O'Neill's model of a genuine consent. My model also shares a similar approach to information and the importance of the process of communication. However, although they emphasise the importance of communication, Manson and O'Neill's model appears to treat it as an arm's-length process. This represents a major point of divergence from my model, which highlights the importance of the relationship between the patient and the professional. It is this relationship that provides the primary context for consent and generates specific obligations that inform the rules implemented to ensure an adequate consent.

While the interaction between the two parties is crucial, my model also recognises that both the doctor and the patient are autonomous agents. This reflects another distinction between the concept of relational consent and Manson and O'Neill's model of a genuine consent. Unlike Manson and O'Neill, who severed the connection between autonomy and consent, I argued that autonomy remains the primary justification for affording the individual the right to give or withhold consent and hence to control the relevant underlying right. However, autonomy should not be equated with simple self-determination or liberty.

My model engages all three types of autonomy. As simple self-determination, autonomy is important because it reflects the liberty of the individual and means that the competent adult must ultimately be allowed to decide whether to accept or reject the healthcare professional's advice. As rational self-determination, autonomy is relevant to the determination of competence. Finally, as moral, rational self-determination, a relational conception of autonomy is important to generating the obligation on the healthcare professional to support and facilitate the patient's autonomy. It is relational autonomy that requires the two parties to engage with each other in the process of negotiation and mutual persuasion, which reflects consent as an agreement and precedes consent as permission.

The final point of divergence is that Manson and O'Neill's model implicitly maintains the connection between consent and responsibility for outcome. In fact, they do not engage with the issue at all, which is perhaps a consequence of their failure to engage with the legal regulation of consent in any meaningful way. Legal claims are inevitably triggered by a bad outcome of treatment, but, as I argued in Chapter 4, there is nothing in the concept of consent that automatically requires responsibility for outcome to flow from it. Outcome responsibility is a matter of justice and consent is only one factor to be taken into account. As such, my approach to consent severs the usual connection between consent and responsibility for outcome.

Implementing relational consent

At the end of the preceding chapter I argued that there were essentially three routes available to implement relational consent: the common law could be allowed to develop; the common law could be supplemented by specifically developing professional regulation; or legislation could be used to change the law. I argued that, given the reactive nature of the common law and the other institutional constraints, it would be better to choose a more interventional approach. Given past experience, it would take about twenty years for the law to make the kind of changes necessary and the process is entirely dependent on the judges hearing the cases. Furthermore, it is unlikely the model would be implanted without significant distortion. I also argued that it would be unsatisfactory to simply try and paper over the cracks by developing professional regulation. This is not to suggest that professional regulation has no role to play. Rather it is that the legal and professional regulation should work synergistically and this is best achieved by specifically constructing the law and the professional regulation with that view in mind.

There are three tiers of regulation that must interact to provide a coherent and cohesive system. The bottom tier is legal regulation, which provides the minimum standards of acceptable behaviour. The second tier incorporates regulation primarily by the professional bodies but also by the employing institution. The final tier is the self-regulation by the virtuous professional who aspires to standards that reflect not just the letter of the regulatory rules of the lower tiers but also the spirit that underlies those rules. This hierarchy of regulation provides the framework for implementing the relational model of consent.

In the past, the regulation of consent has developed haphazardly with the law trying to adapt the blunt tools of tort law to the specific context of clinical care. Professional regulation has tended to reiterate the law. Where it does provide distinct guidance, such as the GMC guidance on consent, it is unclear whether the professional body is trying to set out rules of expected behaviour or simply indicating aspirational standards. With the risk of being sued and the growth of risk management, the professionals themselves often react in a defensive way and treat the duty to seek the patient's consent as a functional duty following only the letter of the rule and ignoring, or misunderstanding, the spirit behind it. Thus, all levels of regulation are currently deficient and this is best resolved by constructing a system of regulation *de novo*.

The proposed principles

In recent legislation there has been a tendency to set out the underlying principles that pervade the statute, indicate the spirit behind the rules and aid interpretation of the particular rules. This is helpful because it facilitates a synergistic coordination between the different tiers of regulation. By setting out the basic principles, a hierarchical tier of rules and guidance may be designed to implement the model in a way that acknowledges the need for trust and trustworthiness but which recognises that a system of accountability to others cannot provide a complete answer to the risk of trusting others.

The first principle is that the professional–patient relationship is central to the regulatory framework for consent. The relationship provides an important part of the context for consent. It is also partly responsible for the obligations on both the patient and the professional to engage with the other party, to permit the other party to fulfil his or her obligations and to respect and care about both the other party and the relationship itself.

The second principle is that consent to clinical interventions engages both consent as permission and consent as agreement. As discussed in Part I of the book, consent as permission is central to the theory of consent and respects the patient's agency while consent as agreement is an attribute that reflects the relational nature of autonomy and the interaction between two autonomous agents.

The third principle is that consent as permission is derived from the underlying right to bodily integrity, which is broadly conceived to include both direct and indirect interferences.

The fourth principle is that, while consent as permission is not relevant to non-treatment decisions, consent as agreement requires the patient to be involved in any such decisions. This does not mean that the patient must agree to non-treatment, although this would be desirable. However, it does require the healthcare professional to engage the patient in a dialogue to explain why the treatment will not be offered. It also requires the healthcare professional to remain open to persuasion that the patient should be given the treatment.

The fifth principle is that an effective consent involves both consent as a state of mind and consent as an act of communication. This means that any regulation must balance those two aspects of consent. It must recognise the need for communication and the norms that govern such an interaction between the parties to the relationship.[15] However,

---

[15] Manson and O'Neill, *Rethinking Informed Consent.*

it must also recognise the agency and integrity of the person giving consent.

The sixth principle is that the value of autonomous agency provides the justification for requiring consent. There are two caveats to this principle. First, neither autonomy nor consent is an absolute, limitless right. Second, different aspects of autonomy justify different aspects of consent. In this regard autonomy is relational, with both rational and moral requirements. Relational autonomy has three main features: the basic liberty of self-determination, which allows the moral agent the right to be wrong and grounds consent as permission; the requirement for the capacity for rationality, which is relevant to the determination of competence; and the requirement for moral concern, which is relevant to consent as agreement and provides part of the basis for the obligation on both the patient and the healthcare professional to engage in the dialogical process of mutual persuasion.

The seventh principle is that consent may not be necessary or sufficient to provide the requisite justification for the intervention. This principle, which defines the limits of consent, is based on two features of consent. First, the underlying justification for consent, which lies in the liberty and autonomy of agency, does not require that consent be seen as an absolute right. Just as an individual's autonomy may be justifiably constrained where it risks harm to others, so too may consent. Where providing treatment protects others from direct harm that is greater than the harm caused by the infringement of autonomy and bodily integrity resulting from non-consensual treatment, the person's consent is not necessary to justify the intervention.

Second, since consent is a derivative right there must be an underlying right that requires protection before the need for consent arises. It is only where autonomy is seen as the supreme and exclusive interest that consent provides the sole justification for infringement of an underlying right. For persons capable of exercising their autonomy, the right to respect for autonomy means that each person determines his or her own interests and the weighting that should be given to them. However, where the person lacks capacity the autonomy-based justification for affording the individual a right to consent is no longer effective and some other justification must be found that allows the underlying right to be infringed. Such an alternative justification must be possible where, in the absence of a right to consent, the individual is threatened by the primary right.

The eighth principle is that, as a right, autonomy should not be seen as a mandatory obligation except insofar as it is necessary to exercise autonomy in waiving the right to make the substantive decision. This means that the patient is entitled to cede the decision to the healthcare professional provided the healthcare professional is prepared to act as sole decision-maker. This transfer of decision-making responsibility should have no effect on the allocation of responsibility for outcome. This is because the healthcare professional is acting as the patient's agent and not as an agent in his or her own right.

The ninth principle is that patients should have control over the information that they receive. This is subject to three caveats. First, the patient must be given sufficient information to know that there is a decision to make and to know what he or she is being asked to decide. This does not require the patient to have sufficient information to actually make the requisite decision. However, it must be enough to allow the patient to decide whether to cede the decision or whether to retain decisional authority and possibly seek further information. Provided the patient is aware that more information is available and that any decision made with this basic information would be made in conditions of unnecessary uncertainty, the patient is entitled to waive the right to further information.

The second caveat is that the response to any request for further information, or to any questions asked by the patient, must be interpreted by the healthcare professional. This necessarily engages the healthcare professional's clinical judgement and so requires some leeway for clinical autonomy in making the appropriate response. The healthcare professional's clinical autonomy is also relevant to the third caveat. While the healthcare professional has an obligation to disclose the necessary information, there should be some discretion over how that information is communicated and the timing of the disclosure.

The tenth principle is that there is no necessary relationship between consent and outcome responsibility. Responsibility for outcome should be determined by principles of distributive justice. While agency and consent may be factors to be considered in the allocation of risk, they are not the only factors. However, where there is an opportunity to seek the person's consent, as in the context of non-emergency healthcare, then that consent may be necessary to specifically include the person in the allocation exercise. The effect of this principle is that the harm caused by any infringement of the person's agency may be distinguished from the harm caused by the materialisation of any risk associated with the procedure itself.

While these principles provide guidance as to the spirit of the law, and so will aid interpretation, they are insufficiently precise to adequately guide behaviour. More specific rules must be drafted and, as I suggested in the previous chapter, a code of practice should be used to support these rules. It is inappropriate to include here either draft legislation or a draft code of practice. However, I will develop these principles in more depth and illustrate how they might be implemented in practice.

Fleshing out the principles

One of the criticisms I raised against the current legal approach is that the law places too much emphasis on the outcome of disclosure at the expense of the communicative process itself. This importance of the communicative process is highlighted in Manson and O'Neill's analysis. However, as I argued earlier, they subsequently focus most closely on the healthcare professional's negative duties to avoid coercion, deceit and manipulation. My criticism of this focus was not directed at the inclusion of these duties but at the failure to require a greater obligation to positively support the patient's ability to make an autonomous decision. The negative duties provide the necessary foundation for consent as permission and a failure to satisfy those fundamental duties wholly undermines the normative effect of the patient's consent.

The law currently treats the use of coercion, fraud or dishonesty as a complete failure of consent. Any person relying on a consent given under such circumstances would be liable for battery. There would also be the possibility of criminal charges. However, the judiciary have shown a reluctance to use the law of battery to regulate consent, in part because of the criminal connotation inherent to a finding of battery. Where the healthcare professional's motive is beneficent this reluctance may be justified. It may also be reasonable even where the healthcare professional's motive is mixed. For example, consider the dentist in *R* v. *Richardson*.[16] She was charged with battery after continuing to practise having been suspended from the Dental Register. Although her motive was not explored in the case one might speculate that she continued to practise both for her own benefit (the fees paid by her patients) and for her patients' benefit. Compare this with the dentist in *Appleton* v. *Garrett* who deceived his patients into believing that they needed expensive dental restoration.[17] His motive was entirely selfish, with no concern for benefiting the patients.

The different circumstances may justify a more nuanced approach to the regulation of these fundamental negative duties. The law should recognise that the healthcare professional acting with a wholly selfish motive and no intention to benefit the patient should be subject to a greater sanction than the healthcare professional whose intention and

---

[16] *R* v. *Richardson* (1998) 43 BMLR 21.   [17] *Appleton* v. *Garrett* [1997] 8 Med LR 75.

motive are consistent with his or her basic obligation of beneficence even if they act in a way that is unjustifiably paternalistic. To reflect this, the legal rules should provide that the criminal law and the civil battery claim are only available where the healthcare professional acts in bad faith and coerces, deceives or manipulates the patient to gain his or her consent where there is no intention to provide him or her with a benefit from the intervention, or the way in which the intervention is performed.[18] To deal with other failures of consent, whether partial or complete, there should be a new category of civil claim that provides for a range of remedies dependent on the precise nature of the breach. This new category of claim may be termed a breach of consent and would replace civil liability for both battery and negligence.

To illustrate the basic distinction between a bad-faith breach and other failures of consent, consider the Australian case of *R* v. *Mobilio*.[19] The accused was a radiographer who performed trans-vaginal ultrasound when he could have carried out the examination trans-abdominally. He was initially convicted for rape but the conviction was overturned on appeal. The Supreme Court of Victoria held that the radiographer's sexual motive was irrelevant as the women had consented to the examination and understood that it involved the use of a vaginal ultrasound probe.[20]

Under the approach proposed here, the women's consent would be deemed ineffective to legitimate the act because the decision to perform the examination trans-vaginally rather than trans-abdominally was intended to benefit the radiographer by providing sexual gratification. Although the women knew what was to be done, and the examination did benefit them, the same benefit could have been achieved by the trans-abdominal procedure. This would have involved a less invasive and less sensitive infringement of the women's bodily integrity and they should have been given the choice. This holds even where the more invasive procedure is clinically better than the less invasive one because clinical benefit is only one factor in determining overall benefit and satisfying patients' preferences should also be included in the balance. Furthermore, the infringement of the patient's autonomy is a harm, which may act to counter the benefit of a more clinically efficacious procedure.

---

[18] For example, where a breast exam is clinically indicated but carried out in an inappropriate way for sexual gratification: see *Kumar* v. *The Queen* [2006] EWCA Crim 1946 (CA).

[19] *R* v. *Mobilio* [1991] 1 VR 339 (Supreme Court of Victoria).

[20] *R* v. *Mobilio* [1991] 1 VR 339, 351–2.

This approach to rendering consent ineffective is not wholly inconsistent with the existing law. In *R* v. *Tabassum*, the Court of Appeal characterised the nature of the act as a non-medical one because the accused was not a medical professional. Thus, the accused was found guilty despite the women involved understanding that he would be touching their breasts in order to demonstrate breast self-examination. The Court of Appeal's approach to characterising the act as medical or non-medical could be further developed to include the need for the act to benefit the patient.

This discussion highlights the need to define both the extent of the regulation as well as the extent of an effective consent. My analysis of consent has been confined to consent to medical treatment interventions, which includes both diagnostic and therapeutic procedures. The term medical is not used to restrict the regulation to doctors but includes all healthcare professionals, including those providing alternative therapies. Thus, the accused in *R* v. *Tabassum* would not be excluded from these regulatory proposals simply because he had no formal training or qualification. However, the act of demonstrating breast self-examination for the purpose of developing a software package would take the case outside the remit of the proposals: developing a software package is neither therapeutic nor diagnostic.

Research interventions, particularly those that are non-therapeutic, fall outside the scope of the regulation. There may be a case for including therapeutic research interventions but this would require further consideration, which will have to wait for another occasion. However, educational or training interventions may be included where they are integrated into the therapeutic or diagnostic process. The main reason for inclusion is that it will serve to familiarise the trainees or students with the regulatory requirements that set out the legal duties imposed on them once qualified. It will also provide a seamless transition from student to qualified practitioner. Furthermore, although the intervention could have been performed, or may need to be repeated, by a qualified or more experienced practitioner, this does not prevent them from also being therapeutic or diagnostic. Inserting a drip, taking a blood sample or performing a lumbar puncture, for example, remain therapeutic or diagnostic even if they are also educational. Rather than try to draw a line between those educational interventions that are also therapeutic or diagnostic and those that are purely educational, it is better to incorporate all of them into the regulatory framework.

Cosmetic interventions should also be included within the regulatory framework where there is some therapeutic intention behind the intervention. This would include those done to repair any damage caused, for example, by burns, other injury or disease. It should also include interventions justified by the psychological impact of the feature to be modified, which would include 'bat' ears and sex-change operations.

Because it is difficult to draw a line between those that have a psychological impact and those that do not, it may be better to include all cosmetic interventions performed in a healthcare context. This is a bright line. However, it is justified so as to ensure that none of the cosmetic interventions with a therapeutic dimension evade the regulatory framework. Furthermore, by drawing the line at the healthcare context it includes all the interactions where a healthcare professional–patient relationship is present. It would not include those relationships that are essentially commercial, such as those between the beauty therapist, tattooist or piercer and their customers.

Returning to the extent of an effective consent, it would prima facie include all of those interventions that fall under the scope of the regulations. However, following the earlier discussion, it would exclude those therapeutic and diagnostic interventions where the professional has gained the patient's consent by bad faith. This exclusion applies where the healthcare professional's intention is essentially self-serving rather than for the patient's benefit. It does not apply simply because there is a coincidental benefit to the healthcare professional. Thus, the exclusion applies only where, for selfish reasons, the healthcare professional deceives, manipulates or coerces the patient into granting consent.

Consider again the case of *R* v. *Mobilio*. Because the accused could have offered the women the option of trans-abdominal ultrasound but chose not to in order to gratify his sexual desire, he has manipulated the women into granting consent. The sexual motive of the accused, rather than the patient's benefit, was the operative factor. However, had the trans-vaginal route been the only way of performing the ultrasound then the accused would not have manipulated the patient's consent and the sexual gratification he received from the intervention would have been coincidental.

The aim of this distinction is to weed out the most reprehensible behaviour where there is a breach of trust that wholly undermines the therapeutic nature of the healthcare professional–patient relationship. The professional that falls foul of this provision would be liable for civil-law battery and may also be guilty of a criminal offence.[21] This failure of consent should only occur in rare cases. Other cases, where the failure has arisen through oversight, carelessness, misunderstanding of the legal

---

[21] Which criminal offence is engaged is beyond the scope of the present discussion.

requirements or misguided paternalism, will be regulated by the rules establishing liability for breach of consent.

Apart from the requirement that the healthcare professional was acting in good faith, the other prerequisite is that the patient is competent to consent. The issue of competency assessment is beyond the scope of this book and has recently been addressed by the legislature through the Mental Capacity Act 2005. I will not address it any further here.

The basic regulatory framework addresses both consent as agreement and consent as permission. This requires attention to both the process leading up to the patient's consent$_P$ as well as the outcome of that process. Although it is easier to regulate practice by looking at outcomes, which are more readily assessed than processes, this encourages a defensive formalism that, in the hands of risk management, is likely to result in precisely the same problem that has affected the current approach to consent. This may be avoided, but only if the process of disclosure and negotiation are appropriately scrutinised.

Regulating the process   There are certain ground rules that must be set. The least contentious of these are that the disclosure and dialogue must be relevant to the decision and be in terms that the patient is able to understand.[22] In other words, the professional should use lay language and explain any technical terms that may be used. It is also not contentious to require the healthcare professional to pay attention to the patient's condition and his or her ability to appreciate the information and the decision to be made.[23] Where the patient's condition makes it likely that he or she will have difficulty comprehending and retaining the information then more time must be spent in the dialogue leading up to the consent decision. Alternatively, if feasible the discussion should be delayed or repeated on another occasion when the patient is better able to engage with it. Where the consent decision cannot be delayed then the healthcare professional must make a judgement on whether the patient is competent to make a decision.

A third ground rule is that the discussion should take place in an environment that is conducive to an unhurried and supportive dialogue. Given the imbalance in power in the professional–patient relationship and the healthcare professional's role and relationship obligations, it is his or her responsibility to facilitate any dialogue. This includes making an adequate amount of time available for the process of communication.

---

[22] See *Smith* v. *Tunbridge Wells HA* [1994] 5 Med LR 334, discussed in Chapter 5.
[23] See *Smith* v. *Salford HA* (1994) 23 BMLR 137, 149.

Time is a precious commodity in the pressured environment of modern healthcare. There is a balance between how much time is spent treating patients as persons and treating the patients' pathologies. At one extreme is the factory model of healthcare, but at the other extreme there is a danger that waiting lists will grow and patients' treatment will be unduly delayed. Precisely where the balance is made will depend on priorities. However, in addition to the infringement of the patient's autonomy it may be counterproductive to set the balance too far towards the factory model approach since there is evidence to suggest that keeping patients well informed and engaged with their care results in a better clinical outcome.[24]

It is not possible to prescribe how long should be spent with each patient as this will depend on a number of factors. These include: the patient's condition; the nature of the patient's illness and the complexity of the treatment; the urgency of the treatment; how involved the patient wants to be; and how effective the healthcare professional and patient are at communicating with each other. The law should take all of these into account when determining whether the healthcare professional has acted reasonably in creating an environment that will facilitate dialogue.

A second concern is to ensure that the discussion occurs in a suitably private location. Many medical matters are intensely personal and the patient may be inhibited if discussion is initiated in a situation where others might overhear. These include other patients, non-essential medical staff and healthcare workers or ancillary staff not involved directly in the patient's care. Teaching ward rounds, for example, have traditionally involved an entourage of students and are inappropriate for making major management decisions without giving the patient the opportunity to discuss the issues with the treating professional in more private circumstances.

Again, the law should only demand that healthcare professionals do what is reasonable. However, this may require healthcare professionals to use a ward consulting or treatment room where the dialogue involves sensitive and personal matters and the patient's condition permits it. Less sensitive or important matters may be discussed at the bedside with the curtains drawn provided the healthcare professional is sensitive to the possibility that the conversation may be audible to neighbouring patients. What will be reasonable will ultimately depend on the circumstances. However, it is important for the professional to have regard to the conditions of communication and the law should require

---

[24] See e.g. Valimaki *et al.*, 'Self-determination in surgical patients in five European countries', 309.

professionals to provide evidence that they considered the matter and acted reasonably in the circumstances.

The responsibility for creating a suitable environment lies with both the Trust or hospital and with the treating healthcare professional. The healthcare institution must make suitable facilities available and ensure sufficient staffing levels to enable the healthcare professional to create the requisite conditions for effective communication. The healthcare professional then has the responsibility to use the appropriate facilities and allow sufficient time for the process. While the responsibility lies with the healthcare professional treating the patient this does not preclude the delegation of part or all of the process. One option would be to train people specifically for the role of facilitating communication with patients and these facilitators could be used to free-up clinicians' time allowing them to treat more patients.

Apart from establishing a suitable environment the healthcare professional should have certain obligations to facilitate the process of communication that precedes the patient's consent. This applies both to those situations where the patient's consent is required and to those non-treatment decisions where the patient's involvement in the process is required even though consent is strictly unnecessary. These obligations must be based on what may reasonably be expected of the healthcare professional given the circumstances of the case. For example, the obligations should be less exacting in an emergency. Similarly, where there are other patients with an equal call on the healthcare professional's attention this may affect what is reasonable. However, the Trust, or hospital, has a responsibility to ensure that there are sufficient personnel and resources available. The onus would be on the Trust and the healthcare professional to show that they acted reasonably.

The starting point, which accords with Manson and O'Neill's approach, is that beyond the minimum disclosure required for patients to know that they have a decision to make, patients should be allowed to control how much information they receive. This is the standard position, which should be followed subject to certain exceptions discussed below. It requires that information is communicated in stages and that the amount and type of information reflects the needs of the patient. This may be facilitated by the use of leaflets and other decision aids and the patient should be provided with at least one form of permanent reminder of the key information. However, recorded information and decision aids, while valuable supportive tools, are no substitute for the personal engagement of professional and patient since the communicative process of dialogue, negotiation and mutual persuasion requires the involvement of at least two rational agents. Furthermore, the communicative process is an opportunity to support the trust that is integral to a good relationship.

A number of rules flow from the principle that both the professional and the patient should have regard to the communicative norms. Again this is consistent with the agency model of communication explicated by Manson and O'Neill in their proposals for rethinking informed consent.[25] If these norms are to have a real impact they should be emphasised and explained in the accompanying code of practice. Furthermore, the law should require both parties to meet reasonable obligations required by the norms.

In addition to the ground rules discussed above, effective communication is dependent on mutual trust and requires that both parties are trustworthy. This means that any communicative interaction must be truthful, which allows the other party to rely on the information. Any information disclosed by the healthcare professional should be sufficient to allow patients to make the requisite decision, whether that be to request further information, to waive their right to further information or to cede the decision to the healthcare professional. The information should be 'adequately accurate' and the healthcare professional should explain the limitations and relevance of the information.[26] For example, if the risk of a particular operation is disclosed, the healthcare professional should make clear whether this is based on data from his or her own practice or not. Where possible, the patient should be provided with data from both personal and national practice and the healthcare professional should honestly explain any difference in the figures. However, such data does not always exist.

Ensuring that the patient has sufficient information requires both parties to engage with the communicative process. The law should make it clear that patients have the responsibility of engaging with the healthcare professional. This requires patients to be open and honest about their informational needs, their desire to make or be involved in the decisional process, their goals and values and their understanding of the information and the decision. This will allow the healthcare professional to respond appropriately to questions and to assess how well the patient has understood the information and the decision to be made. However, despite the patients' obligations, the onus remains on healthcare professionals to facilitate their patients' involvement and their ability to meet those obligations. The process involves an interaction between both the patient and the healthcare professional and neither party's

---

[25] Manson and O'Neill, *Rethinking Informed Consent*, p. 64.   [26] *Ibid.*

actions may be fully assessed without considering the role played by the other.

In scrutinising the process the law might divide it into a number of stages. Once the healthcare professional has established that there is a decision to be made the next stage would be to discover what level of involvement the patient would like. It is the healthcare professional's responsibility to enquire whether the patient requires additional information. Patients may explicitly waive their right to information and, for evidentiary reasons this waiver should be in writing. If the patient chooses to waive information then the healthcare professional should explain the implications of the waiver, which are that any decision made by the patient will be made under conditions of unnecessary uncertainty and that the waiver has implications for outcome responsibility (see later). The healthcare professional should also check whether the waiver of information is actually meant to be an attempt to cede the decision.

If the patient wishes to cede the decision to the healthcare professional this should be permitted, although it should be made in writing. Before making a final decision, the healthcare professional should make a reasonable enquiry into the patient's goals and values that might have a bearing on the decision to be made. It is the patient's responsibility to respond openly and honestly to any such enquiry. However, in the absence of any evidence to the contrary it would be reasonable to assume that the decision to cede decisional responsibility to the healthcare professional implies that the patient's health is the most important value to be taken into account.

Should the patient not waive the right to information the healthcare professional has the responsibility to determine how much information to provide. This is necessarily an iterative process that requires a dialogue with the patient. However, if the patient wants to retain decisional responsibility then it would be reasonable to take as the starting point the information that would be required by a reasonable person in the patient's position. This is now a familiar standard for the law.

Following the initial disclosure the healthcare professional should then enquire whether the patient requires any additional information, or if any of the information requires clarification. The healthcare professional should also explore any particular concerns that the patient might have. The aim of the dialogue is to allow the professional and the patient to expose the particular patient's informational needs so that those needs may be met. At this juncture the healthcare professional should encourage the patient to ask questions. Any questions should be answered honestly and reasonably. It is difficult to be precise since questions may not be phrased so exactly as to leave no discretion for the professional. The important point is that the professional approaches the process with the aim of facilitating good decision-making. The need for this trustworthy and supportive attitude should be emphasised in the code of practice and any evidence that the professional has acted inconsistently may be taken into account in determining whether there has been a breach of consent.

This process of enquiring whether the patient has any further questions should be repeated until the patient is happy with the information and his or her understanding of the information. It is the patient's responsibility to be open and honest with the healthcare professional as to whether the information is sufficient and whether anything is unclear. However, given the power imbalance the healthcare professional should be supportive and facilitate the dialogue encouraging the patient to say if anything is unclear.

For both treatment and non-treatment decisions the patient should be offered the opportunity to be involved in the clinical decision-making process. While patients cannot dictate what treatment, if any, should be given, they should have the decision-making process explained and the healthcare professional should explain the reasons behind any decision. The patient should then be given an opportunity to negotiate the decision as an aspect of the process of mutual persuasion, which I will discuss below.

>*The obligation to facilitate understanding and good decision-making*   It would be unhelpful to impose an obligation on the healthcare professional to ensure that patients understand the information disclosed and the decision to be made. It is impossible to guarantee understanding without some formal assessment, which would be unreasonably demanding, both for healthcare professionals and patients. However, this does not mean that the law should not impose an obligation on healthcare professionals to facilitate understanding. As I noted in Chapter 5, the law already does this, but only on the superficial level of creating the conditions necessary to enable understanding: the use of lay terms and disclosure of information at a time when the patient is in a suitable condition. Beyond that the current legal obligation would be satisfied by disclosure of accurate and relevant information.

Although Manson and O'Neill's model derives from an approach that emphasises the importance of communication it seems unlikely that, if implemented, it would require anything beyond what the law already requires. As discussed earlier, their model essentially requires negative duties of non-interference – allowing the patient to remain in control of the information, and not deceiving, manipulating or coercing the patient. The law already requires the few positive duties included in their model and the obligation to disclose may be more limited than the existing duty. The main reason for this unsupportive approach is their claim that autonomy does not provide consent with its moral value. I have argued that this is unhelpful. While it may reflect the way consent is currently approached that does not mean that it reflects the way that consent ought to be approached.

The model I am proposing relies on a relational approach to autonomy. One consequence of making this connection is that autonomy is given moral content and this, along with their role and relationship obligations of beneficence and respect for the other person's autonomy and agency, requires healthcare professionals to support and facilitate their patients' decision-making. The ultimate aim is to achieve a decision that is acceptable to both parties and is autonomous. While it must involve the patient as decision-maker, the decision does not have to be made independent of other people. However, any interaction with the patient's decision-making must be supportive and facilitatory rather than overbearing. Furthermore, whether the decision is seen as a 'good' one should be assessed from the patient's perspective and must be based on the patient's goals and values as well as his or her obligations to relational others such as a spouse or child.

In order to be in a position to assess whether a decision is reasonably autonomous the healthcare professional must engage in a dialogue with the patient to gain some understanding of the patient's perspective. This understanding may be limited but it is an important aspect of respecting others as moral agents to try and understand their point of view. It should allow a more balanced assessment of the rationality of the patient's decision although any such judgement is likely to remain heavily influenced by the healthcare professional's clinical expertise. This should not be seen as problematic because the professional's clinical expertise is the reason why the patient has sought help and advice. However, it does mean that healthcare professionals must be open to persuasion that their assessment is wrong.

This process of mutual persuasion is crucial to an approach that aims to achieve as good a decision as is possible and it respects both the patient's agency and autonomy. It requires the healthcare professional to engage with the patient's decision-making process and to sensitively challenge the resultant decision. This should not be seen as an adversarial challenge. Rather it should be a gentle probe to allow the healthcare professional the opportunity to assess the patient's reasons for his or her decision. By looking at the reasons for a decision the healthcare professional should be able to assess whether the patient has understood both the information and the decision to be made.

If healthcare professionals have a duty to seek their patients' reasons then the patients have an obligation, arising from the healthcare professional–patient relationship, to engage in the dialogue, to reflect on and to explain their decisions, as far as is possible. This should assist the healthcare professionals to fulfil their own obligations. The duty on the patient should not be directly enforceable because the aim is to facilitate and support good decision-making not to compel it, which would undermine the patient's agency and his or her responsibility for the decision. However, if a patient fails to engage sufficiently this may be taken into account when determining whether the healthcare professional has satisfied the legal duty and in allocating responsibility for the outcome of the decision.

The obligation to seek the patient's reasons for a decision is to enable the healthcare professional to assess the patient's understanding and to facilitate good decision-making. It will, of course, require an investment of time and for many decisions, such as the consent to chest auscultation, abdominal palpation or taking the patient's temperature or blood pressure, it would be unduly time-consuming to require this in all cases. For these kinds of interactions it would be reasonable for the obligation to be triggered by an objectively irrational decision. This would be a decision that the reasonable healthcare professional would see as irrational. Where a patient agrees to the chest or abdominal examination there would be little value to be gained from requiring the professional to enquire why the patient had agreed. However, where the patient refuses then this denies the healthcare professional important information required to provide the best treatment. In such circumstances, it would be reasonable to ensure that the patient understands the implications of the decision and to enquire into the reasons behind the decision.

For interventions of a more invasive nature, or where the implications of the decision would have a significant impact on the patient's health or life then the healthcare professional should have an obligation to enquire into the patient's reasons for the decision regardless of whether the decision appears to be irrational. There are two main reasons for this. First, if the healthcare professional only challenged objectively irrational decisions it might be interpreted as an unjustified criticism of the patient's choice. By challenging all decisions, and not just the irrational ones, the healthcare professional's intervention can be more readily explained as a concern to facilitate good decision-making from the patient's perspective. If the patient's reasons are sought for all such decisions it becomes the expected norm and will look less like a criticism of the actual choice and should be seen as part of the normal process of making such a decision. The second reason is that for some decisions all of the outcomes may be rational from an objective clinical perspective.

Consider the circumstances that arose in *Al Hamwi* v. *Johnston*,[27] which involved a woman whose decision was whether or not to undergo an amniocentesis. On one side of the equation is her desire to avoid the birth of a child with Down's syndrome. On the other side is her desire to avoid the miscarriage of a healthy child. The rational outcome of her choice will depend on the strengths of those two desires taking into account the likelihood of the risk materialising in either case. From an objective perspective either choice might be rational. It would be perfectly reasonable for the woman to have a stronger desire to avoid the miscarriage of a healthy child than to avoid giving birth to a child with Down's syndrome. Even though the risks of amniocentesis were lower than the risk of her having a Down's syndrome child, this is outweighed by her greater desire to avoid a miscarriage. Thus, it is rational to reject the amniocentesis. On the other hand, if her stronger desire were to avoid the birth of a child with Down's syndrome then it would be irrational to refuse the amniocentesis.

In this case it would be impossible for the healthcare professional to know whether the woman has made an irrational decision without engaging with the reasoning behind the decision. It is only by entering into a dialogue with her that one can determine the rationality of her choice. In the actual case the court held that it was reasonable for the doctor to simply provide accurate information and then accept whatever decision the woman made. In the event she made what turned out to be an irrational decision because she had misunderstood the level of risk associated with amniocentesis. This was not apparent to the doctor because she had excluded any dialogue. Had she discussed the decision the misunderstanding may have been revealed and the bad decision avoided.

While the duty to enquire into the patient's reasons for a decision may reveal a misunderstanding and an irrational decision it may not cause patients to change their decisions. To support and facilitate good decision-making the healthcare professional would need to go further than this and the law should require the professional to attempt to persuade the patient to change his or her mind. If this duty to persuade is to respect the patient's autonomy and agency then it must be restricted to the use of rational argument and should avoid any manipulative tactics such as deception, bullying or undue exploitation of the patient's guilt. Thus, any such engagement must be done in a way that shows sensitivity

---

[27] *Al Hamwi* v. *Johnston, The North West London Hospitals NHS Trust* [2005] EWHC 206.

to the patient's situation. Furthermore, the healthcare professional has a concomitant duty to be open to persuasion.

One of the difficulties with the evaluation of a decision is that the healthcare professional may judge a subjectively rational decision as objectively irrational. Since the aim is to enable a decision that is good for the patient, the aim is to achieve subjective rationality. However, even following a period of dialogue the healthcare professional may still not fully appreciate the patient's perspective. The professional's bias is to assess rationality from a clinical perspective. This is appropriate since it is the healthcare professional's clinical expertise that justifies his or her role and provides the authority to advise and treat the patient. The patient has specifically sought advice and treatment precisely because of that clinical expertise. Thus, the healthcare professional has a duty to try and persuade the patient to make a decision that is rational from an objective clinical perspective. However, because the decision might be subjectively rational while appearing objectively irrational, the healthcare professional should remain open to persuasion that the decision is, in fact, a rational one.

Although the healthcare professional has an obligation to engage in a process of mutual persuasion, this does not provide a power to override the patient's decision. If the patient persists with his or her decision then, following a reasonable process of mutually persuasive dialogue, the healthcare professional should accept that, as an autonomous moral agent, the patient ultimately has the right to make the decision even if it is an unwise choice. The healthcare professional's obligation is to make a reasonable attempt to support and facilitate, but not compel, good decision-making. The caveat to this duty is that the patient should also have a duty to engage in mutual persuasion and be open to the healthcare professional's advice.

Information disclosure – measuring the outcome The relational model of consent is more concerned with the process of disclosure than what is actually disclosed. By engaging in dialogue with the aim of supporting and facilitating good decision-making it is more likely that the informational and decisional needs of the patient are met. This focus on the process requires the healthcare professional to approach the dialogue with the right kind of attitude and this is more difficult to regulate than standards of disclosure that determine the duty by reference to particular pieces of information that must be disclosed. To assess the process the law must address more intangible issues such as whether the healthcare professional was supportive or dismissive of the patient's concerns.

As well as assessing the healthcare professional's attitude the law might judge the process by considering whether certain key dialogical features were present. As I have already suggested, these include a suitably supportive environment, adequate time and the use of decisional supports to assist patient decision-making. The law may also assess whether the patient has been empowered to ask questions and whether the healthcare professional has made a reasonable attempt to facilitate good decision-making through the use of rational persuasion. However, because it is more difficult to assess the process, rather than the outcome of the process, the law should require a default position of disclosure.

The default position would require a duty to disclose a certain basic level of information. A failure to disclose this core information would result in liability unless the healthcare professional is able to show that the patient waived his or her right to it. As discussed previously, there is an absolute minimum of information that cannot be waived. Before patients are in a position to waive any information they must at least know that there is a decision to be made, that they have a right to be informed, that they may waive the right or indeed cede the decision and the legal implications of doing so. As an example of what should be required consider the patient with appendicitis. That patient must be told, in lay terms, that they will need an abdominal operation to excise the infected appendix. For example, it would be sufficient to say 'we need to do an operation to make you better'. The patient is not free to waive this very basic information, which is required to make the patient aware of the intervention and the need for a decision. This minimal duty, however, would not satisfy the duty to disclose core information.

The duty to disclose core information would only be satisfied either by the patient's waiver or by the disclosure of the requisite information. This core information includes the nature and purpose of the procedure, the person performing the procedure,[28] the material risks and the alternative options. Although this looks like the familiar prudent-patient standard there are some important distinctions and it might be better to refer to it as the generic-patient standard. Terms like 'reasonable' or 'prudent' imply that anyone requiring a different level of disclosure is being unreasonable or imprudent. Furthermore, the prudent patient is a construct and what is reasonable for one person may not be for another. On top of this, the measure of what is reasonable is determined largely by intuition, which may be subject to particular biases.

---

[28] This could, but need not, be a named individual. It would also be acceptable to identify the operator as a member of a team.

The development of consent in the UK, with the gradual shift towards the prudent-patient standard, has resulted in an approach that is crucially different from the US,[29] Canadian and Australian approach. As I discussed previously, in *Pearce* Lord Woolf applied the standard by reference to what the reasonable doctor would think the reasonable patient would want to know. Again this may introduce a bias that results in a test that fails to reflect what ordinary patients actually would want to know. The purpose behind the standard is to provide a degree of certainty for the healthcare professionals. However, there is no reason why this needs to be based on a flawed intuitive conception of the prudent patient. Rather, it could be determined by reference to an evidence-based standard.

Empirical studies may be performed to provide insights into what the average patient would want to know.[30] While it may not be possible to carry out studies for every possible intervention, the studies may be used to provide evidence about the type and degree of risk that particularly concerns patients and these standards may be abstracted across a range of interventions. The studies will also provide insights into the other types of information that may be relevant. Furthermore, such research would provide a range of views that might be useful in encouraging dialogue with the patient. For example, the healthcare professional might prompt the patient by saying that 'some patients want to know about . . .'. This would give the patient permission to request such information while also allowing the patient to turn down the offer.

Another distinction between the proposed and the current standard is that the proposed standard will be applied differently. Crucially, it is a default test not the final measure of the healthcare professional's duty. Where it is shown that the healthcare professional has breached the dialogical duties then liability will be found irrespective of whether the healthcare professional satisfied the duty to disclose the core information of the generic-patient standard.

The standard is relevant in three ways. First, where there is insufficient evidence regarding the process then the generic-patient standard may be used to determine liability. In this way it acts as a 'safety-net' obligation where evidence regarding the dialogical process is insufficient to determine the issue. Second, where the patient is unwilling to engage in the process of negotiation but does not formally waive his or her right to information then the generic-patient standard will determine the healthcare professional's default obligation. Third, the standard

---

[29] I refer here to the minority of states that apply the prudent patient standard.
[30] Maclean, 'Giving the reasonable patient a voice'.

provides the healthcare professional with a useful opening gambit in the dialogue. It would, for example, be reasonable to offer the patient the information that patients generally want.

This third use of the standard is subject to the caveat that if the professional offers the patient this starting package of information then it must be made clear that it is perfectly reasonable to want more or less information. The offer should only be used as a way in to discussing what the patient does actually want to know. It is not a substitute for dialogue.

Exceptions   The only exception to the duty is where the patient would suffer serious harm as a consequence of any delay in treatment.[31] In other words, where there is an emergency and time precludes a full engagement in the dialogical process. This is a context-dependent exception that must ultimately depend on what is reasonable to expect under the circumstances. However, a brief discussion may help to explicate the extent of the exception.

A distinction should be drawn between the process leading up to consent as permission and the actual decision to grant permission. In urgent situations, where a delay in treatment may cause permanent harm then there may not be time to negotiate consent as agreement or engage in persuasion, or even satisfy the reasonable-patient standard of disclosure. However, there may still be time to disclose the minimum information that a particular intervention is required to treat the patient. Similarly, there may be time to ask for the patient's permission. While time may preclude an autonomous decision in the fullest sense of the word, there may still be time to respect the patient as an agent and to seek the patient's authority to intervene.

In the most extreme emergencies the patient is likely to lack the capacity to make an autonomous decision and give an effective consent. However, this does not mean that the patient should not be engaged with what is being done as far as time and other circumstances allow. Where the patient retains capacity but time precludes anything but the most notional of disclosures then the emergency exception should apply and the healthcare professional should be relieved of any duty to obtain the patient's consent. In part, this is justified by the difficulties of formally assessing capacity in such circumstances. It is better to err on the side of preserving health and aim to restore the person's autonomy than to mistakenly allow a patient to suffer severe harm that may significantly

---

[31] I considered and rejected the therapeutic privilege in Chapter 6.

restrict that person's future autonomy. The other justification is that if there is only time to disclose the minimum information then the patient's decision may not be autonomous and again it may be better to err on the side of preserving health.

I am not suggesting that emergency treatment should simply be forced on the unwilling patient. Healthcare professionals should try to gain their patients' cooperation and permission to intervene even if the permission would not satisfy the requirements for a legally effective consent. In these circumstances, the justification for intervention derives from a respect for the person's welfare given that the time constraints prevent the healthcare professional from being able to respect the person's autonomy. While the patient's agency should be respected as far as possible, it is important to facilitate the provision of such emergency care and it may be counterproductive to impose a legal obligation on the healthcare professional to engage in even a limited dialogical process beyond that necessary to assist the provision of treatment.

To summarise, where treatment is required urgently to prevent the patient suffering serious harm then the duty to engage in dialogue must be modified depending on the precise circumstances. The duty to obtain the patient's permission remains, however, unless the situation is such an emergency that imposing a duty on the healthcare professional would be counterproductive and inhibit the provision of care. In determining the extent of any duty the seriousness of the harm risked by delaying treatment must be balanced against the invasiveness of the intervention. Other relevant circumstances include the patient's condition and the nature of the emergency. Even though the patient might retain competence it is likely that the stress of the emergency and any injuries will affect his or her ability to make an autonomous decision. Furthermore, if the patient is being treated in the field, rather than in hospital, the difficulties of providing care in such an environment may also be taken into account in determining what may reasonably be expected. Similarly, where the emergency is a major incident then the duty must be modified to reflect the healthcare professional's obligation to treat multiple patients in difficult circumstances that make it impossible to engage in meaningful dialogue.

While healthcare professionals may be able to rely on an urgent case to modify the obligation, or an emergency case to relieve them of the duty, it will be for the healthcare professional to justify the exception. Where the healthcare professional relies on the urgent treatment exception the courts should judge the modified duty against what would be reasonable to expect in the circumstances. Where the emergency exception is pleaded then the test should be an 'honest belief' that situation was an emergency.

This lesser standard reflects the more pressured circumstances of an emergency and the public interest in facilitating emergency care.

The form of consent   As the law currently recognises, the form in which consent is granted should not matter. Whether given verbally, by behaviour or in writing, provided it is clear that permission has been granted then the consent should be morally and legally effective. The purpose behind requiring consent to be in writing is to ensure that there is a record of the process. However, the record serves only as evidence and not as proof of consent. Nevertheless, where subsequent disagreement may arise it is sensible to make a record. This is particularly so for more invasive procedures and those where the patient will be anaesthetised. However, the recording of consent should be seen as a matter of good practice rather than legal necessity. Thus, the law may leave such matters to the healthcare professional's employers or regulatory body.

Where permission is explicit, as with verbal or written consent, it may readily be accepted as legally effective. However, where consent is implied by the patient's behaviour the law should be more circumspect. It is acceptable to allow implied consent for minor interventions or procedures where the patient is conscious and able to withdraw consent. For more significant or sensitive interventions, and for those where the patient is anaesthetised or sedated then explicit consent should be required. For example, implied consent to blood sampling for routine tests or superficial examination of a non-sensitive part of the body should be legally valid. For genital, anal or female breasts examination consent should be explicit. Similarly, consent should be explicit for non-standard blood tests, particularly those such as testing for HIV that carry social and possibly psychological implications.

This distinction balances the facilitation of healthcare with the protection of both the patient and the healthcare professional. However, although healthcare professionals should be allowed to rely on implied consent they should be encouraged, through the code of practice, to seek explicit consent. This is because an explicit consent is less likely to be misunderstood. To reduce the risk of misunderstanding associated with implied consent, the healthcare professional should be shielded from liability only where the inference of consent was both honest and reasonable.

The effect of consent   Consent as permission has the effect of transforming the moral and legal status of the relevant intervention. It does so by allowing the otherwise forbidden act to be performed. A failure to gain consent means that the intervention remains forbidden and its performance is a moral and legal wrong. The wrong is essentially an infringement of the patient's right to autonomous agency. Given the importance of autonomous agency this wrong should be recognised by the law.

The law does currently protect the individual's autonomy by providing remedies for a failure to obtain an effective consent or a failure to disclose the material risks of the intervention. In doing so the law essentially connects consent and responsibility for outcome. As I discussed in Chapter 4, there is no reason – other than convention – why the two must be tied in this way. This means that the healthcare professional can be required to compensate the infringement of the patient's autonomous agency while not necessarily being held responsible for the materialisation of a remote risk.

Whether the healthcare professional should be held responsible for the consequences of a risk materialising depends on a number of factors. The default position is that responsibility for outcome responsibility should fall on the patients because the interventions are performed for their benefit. This would not apply where the intervention is part of a research project or where the intervention is done for the benefit of the community where the community should bear the cost of any harm that results. In this regard it would be fair to treat immunisation differently to other interventions that are done solely for the individual's benefit.

Although patients have the default responsibility, this can be transferred to the healthcare professional where there has been a complete failure to obtain consent or where the healthcare professional has acted in bad faith. For example, where the healthcare professional has misled the patient into consenting for personal gain then the healthcare professional should be responsible for any bad outcome. This might occur in private practice where the healthcare professional stands to gain financially. It might also occur in the NHS where, for example, the healthcare professional is keen to gain the experience of performing a particular procedure and persuades the patient to consent despite the availability of other more appropriate options.

More commonly, the question of responsibility may arise where there has been a failure to disclose a risk but the procedure is recommended for the patient's benefit. Where the healthcare professional has paternalistically withheld information in order to gain consent then the intentional deception fails to respect the patient as an autonomous agent. As such, the patient's default responsibility is undermined and the healthcare professional should bear the cost of a bad outcome.

Where the failure to disclose a risk that should have been disclosed is a matter of carelessness then the issue should be determined by two factors. First, how remote was the risk? The remoteness of the risk should be determined by considering both the nature of the harm and the likelihood that the harm would materialise. There is no easy formula for deciding the centrality of the risk, but the more central the risk the more reasonable it is to transfer responsibility for outcome. The second factor is how far the failure is simple human error as opposed to a generally careless approach to communication reflecting a lack of respect for the patient's autonomous agency. This should be determined by an assessment of the process leading up to the patient's consent. If the healthcare professional has genuinely engaged with the dialogical process but has simply forgotten to disclose the risk this should be taken into account in determining whether responsibility for outcome remains with the patient or is transferred to the healthcare professional. Both of these factors have a role in determining whether outcome responsibility should stay with the patient or be transferred to the healthcare professional.

This approach to outcome responsibility is predicated on two contingent factors. First, healthcare professionals will either be indemnified by the NHS or will have insurance that will cover liability.[32] This means that the loss is spread amongst either the community of healthcare professionals or the wider community via NHS indemnification (funded by taxation). Second, the state provides a reasonable level of social support that also acts to spread the cost of any consequential harm. Further, there is nothing in this model that precludes the introduction of a no-fault system of compensation and this would arguably be the best approach to dealing with the harmful consequences of a materialised risk given that the provision of healthcare benefits both the individual and the community.

Refusal of consent Although I have argued that both the healthcare professional and the patient have an obligation to engage in the dialogical process of mutual persuasion this does not affect the patient's right to refuse treatment by withholding consent. The obligation of mutual persuasion is aimed at supporting good decision-making. The obligation does not include any power to compel a particular decision and it remains the patient's right to make what others see as a poor decision. As is the current law, the patient may refuse consent for irrational reasons or no reason at all. However, where the patient refuses to engage in a dialogue to explore his or her decision, and the reasons behind that decision (whether or not those reasons are explicit), then the

---

[32] This might not be available where the professional has acted in bad faith.

healthcare professional will satisfy his or her dialogical obligations by making a reasonable attempt to engage the patient.

Non-treatment decisions   While consent is not currently relevant to non-treatment decisions I argued earlier that including consent$_A$ as an attribute of consent to medical treatment would allow non-treatment decisions to be included in the regulation. This would be consistent with what is arguably required under Article 8 of the ECHR. It was also implicitly accepted in *Pearce*, in which the decision not to treat was referred to as conservative treatment and the legal duty was dealt with as if 'allowing nature to take its course' was a healthcare intervention.[33] As such there was no discussion of whether the healthcare professional's obligations differed from where the professional was recommending an intervention that would infringe the patient's bodily integrity.

Since the patient's permission is not required for non-treatment decisions, the patient is in a weaker position and this arguably imposes a greater obligation on the professional to engage the patient in a dialogue that supports and facilitates the patient's autonomy. In other words, the healthcare professional should enter the discussion prepared to listen to, and be persuaded by, the patient's opinion. It is inappropriate to simply present the patient with a decision that has already been made. Although the healthcare professional should advise the patient and recommend a management course, the final decision should wait until the patient has had the opportunity to discuss the options with the professional. It is also important that the patient's agreement is sought. This agreement is not required to legitimise a non-treatment decision since the patient cannot oblige the professional to provide a treatment. However, the law should require the patient's opinion to be taken into account in making the decision and, as part of the process, should also require the healthcare professional to seek the patient's agreement. To assess whether this obligation has been met the courts will have to focus on the dialogical process and examine the attitude adopted by the professional.

Liabilities and remedies   The model of relational consent allows for a range of liabilities and remedies. Where the healthcare professional has acted in bad faith the law could simply rely on the existing tort of battery. In this situation the court should not be reluctant to use that tort and the compensation payable can reflect both the dignitary

---

[33] *Pearce v. United Bristol Healthcare NHS Trust* (1998) 48 BMLR 118.

harm to the patient's agency and the injury caused by the non-consensual intervention.

Where the healthcare professional has acted beneficently there should be civil liability for a 'breach of consent'. All such breaches should provide for an apology and explanation of the steps that will be taken to avoid a recurrence of the breach.[34] Affected patients should also be eligible for compensation recognising the harm caused by an infringement of their autonomous agency. This compensation should be more than nominal damages. Finally, in cases where responsibility for outcome is transferred to the healthcare professional (see above) then damages should be available for the consequential loss caused by a materialised risk.

While the claimant will have to prove that the damage was caused by a materialisation of the risk rather than by a progression of an underlying pathology, there will be no need to show that he or she would have made a different decision had the risk been disclosed. This is because both the patient and the healthcare professional have exercised their agency in causing the intervention and thus both are causally linked to the materialised risk. For the healthcare professional, the causal relationship to the harm is fully determined by the causal link to the infringement of the patient's agency. By causing an infringement of the patient's agency, healthcare professionals allow themselves to be included in the determination of how the responsibility for outcome should be fairly distributed. This distribution, which is a desert-based system based on the degree of infringement of the patient's agency and the healthcare professional's culpability, has been discussed in a previous section of this chapter.

---

[34] This would be in line with the approach taken in the NHS redress scheme proposed by the Chief Medical Officer and given statutory force through the NHS Redress Act 2006. See CMO, *Making Amends* (2003). See also National Audit Office, *Handling Clinical Negligence Claims in England*, paras. 3.22–3.24; NHS Redress Act 2006; Department of Health, *NHS Redress: Statement of policy* (2005).

Summary and conclusion

My aims in writing this book were to expose the flaws of the current legal regulation of consent and to suggest how the deficiencies might be addressed. In achieving these aims I have not attempted to provide a complete or final solution, if such a thing is possible. Indeed, my position is that consent is inherently political, which means that the current approach will always be open to criticism. However, I do not see this as a weakness but as the strength of a democratic polity. Such criticism does not necessarily require change but it does prevent the arrogance of complacency and it means that our beliefs and assumptions are constantly being challenged. My arguments fit into this cycle of criticism as a challenge to the way consent has developed since bioethics emerged in the 1960s.

The growth of bioethics, along with the developments of groups such as the Patients Association, growing media scrutiny and the rise of a consumerist society have all contributed to an increasingly liberal approach to autonomy and consent. This has resulted in an approach to autonomy that risks abandoning patients and emphasises a respect for individual boundaries at the expense of a care for the person's welfare. However, the problems with consent do not end there. Apart from critiquing current ethical approaches to consent, a main objective has been to examine how the legal regulation has developed against the backdrop of this concern for individual autonomy. The difficulty for the law is that, unless the matter is legislated, any developments are necessarily shaped by the institutional constraints of the common law. Combined with the judicial reluctance to use the tort of battery and the reactive nature of the common law, these institutional constraints have resulted in legal rules that lack coherence and focus on the outcome of disclosure. This in turn encourages a defensive risk-management response that prioritises risk disclosure over other aspects of consent and the communicative process that precedes it. My objectives were to expose these priorities as misguided and to argue for an alternative approach based on a relational approach to consent.

I began my critique by exploring the moral basis for consent which – despite recent attacks – remains the individual's autonomous agency. I then went on to consider the other moral influences that shape the boundaries arising out of the primary justification. These abstract moral arguments were subsequently situated within the context of the professional–patient relationship. Using this textured moral landscape I then developed a model of consent that became the comparator enabling a critique of the current law.

In Chapter 1 I considered the meaning, value and implications of personal autonomy, which is the primary rationale for protecting the individual's right to consent. Because the capacity and liberty to be autonomous are essential to moral agency, personal responsibility and the integrity of the individual, autonomy is intrinsically valuable and, in any democracy, it deserves legal protection. Without agency, and hence autonomy, reactive attitudes are meaningless – except as training tools – and humanity is lost to automatism. Since the main reasons for valuing autonomy all require a conception of autonomy that at least includes rationality as an integral part, I argued that it is meaningful to distinguish the autonomous person from the autonomous act. This then raised the question of how society should respond to irrational decisions that risk serious, and possibly catastrophic, harm to the decision-maker.

Despite the fact that a bad decision could significantly harm the patient's future autonomy, I argued that a society in which all such important decisions were scrutinised and overridden if made badly would be too high a price to pay since, if that approach were adopted consistently the whole concept of autonomy would be eroded to the point that its very essence was destroyed. However, while autonomy may be integral to humanity, it is necessarily relational, not isolationist, and respect for that autonomy does not mean that individuals should be abandoned to their fates. As Mill argued in his defence of liberty, the principle at least requires that an apparently irrational decision be challenged.[1]

In the final section of Chapter 1 I examined two recent challenges that have been raised against the connection between autonomy and consent. These challenges, while raising some important questions about autonomy ultimately failed to sever the connection with consent. Autonomy, however, is not the sole value to guide our interactions and in Chapter 2 I explored other values, principles and moral approaches that define the contours of autonomy. I argued that beneficence is best understood as being shaped by the individual's autonomy. The duty of beneficence

[1] Mill, 'On Liberty', p. 84.

requires that the beneficiary's autonomy is supported and enhanced. Although irrational decisions may not be overridden, they do not reflect the individual's autonomy and beneficence requires the healthcare professional's intervention to persuade the patient to reconsider his or her decision.

In Chapter 2 I also considered the relevance of justice and virtue to the principle of respect for autonomy. Justice is relevant in three ways. First, it requires that if respect for autonomy is required then that respect should be given equally to all moral agents unless there is some morally relevant reason why any particular agent or group of agents should be treated differently. Second, because respect for autonomy requires the use of scarce resources, justice is relevant to ensuring that those resources are fairly distributed. Third, the distribution of outcome responsibility should also be justly determined. Attention to virtue is important because the indeterminacy of rules generated from the even more abstract principles necessitates interpretation. A virtuous individual is more likely to interpret the rules within the spirit of the principle giving due accord to the values protected by the rule.

In Chapter 3 I examined the professional–patient relationship as the context for the application for these moral approaches. Rather than draw analogies with other relationship models, as other authors have done, I discussed the interaction between healthcare professional and patient as a unique relationship characterised by specific needs and obligations. While both parties are autonomous persons, that autonomy is constrained by the other's autonomy and also by the obligations that arise from the relationship. The healthcare professional's autonomy is also constrained by the professional obligations that justify the social mandate to practise the profession.

The professional–patient relationship should be one of mutual trust and respect, which requires that both parties are trustworthy. Because the power within the relationship lies mostly, although by no means exclusively, with the professional, and because of the professional's role-specific obligations, healthcare professionals should foster and support the patient's autonomy. Thus, the relationship context of the various healthcare interactions, exemplified by consent, requires the healthcare professional to sensitively inform patients of any relevant information, assist them in understanding the information, advise them and if necessary persuade them to reconsider any apparently irrational decisions.

In Chapter 4, taking the prior discussions into account, I analysed the concept of consent. I argued that consent should not be restricted to being just an actively permissive state of mind. Communication to the healthcare professional is crucial to justify any interaction. Although consent as permission justifies an action, it is necessary but insufficient to determine outcome responsibility for any action performed as a consequence of that consent. Rather, as I discussed in Chapter 2, outcome responsibility is a matter of distributive justice with agency simply being one factor to be taken into account.

Relying on a theory-based approach to concepts, I argued that the basic theory is satisfied by consent as permission. However, a context-sensitive conception of consent, situated in the professional–patient relationship as discussed in Chapter 3, also engages with consent as agreement. Consent as agreement requires a process of negotiation and shared decision-making that precedes and culminates in the final consent decision. Consent as agreement also forms the basis of the professional's obligation to discuss reasonable alternatives with the patient and to engage the patient in any non-treatment decisions. However, neither consent as permission nor consent as agreement actually requires the healthcare professional to offer or provide any particular treatment. Any such obligation arises from the professional's duty of care rather than from the duty to respect the patient's autonomy.

As an addendum to Chapter 4 I described a model of consent that I subsequently used as a basis for critiquing the current legal regulation of consent to medical treatment. In that model, consent as permission was a secondary right derived from the underlying right to bodily integrity. Once consent has been given an intervention becomes a justified breach of bodily integrity. Thus, consent is the act of communicating to the healthcare professional the patient's permissive propositional attitude towards the proposed procedure. It lasts until it is either withdrawn or circumstances change to mean that the permission no longer applies. Consent as agreement is a process of negotiation and persuasion, which requires mutual trust and the virtuous engagement of both parties. It allows the professional to advise and persuade the patient to consent to a particular course of action. However, it also crucially requires the professional to be open to persuasion.

This approach relies on the assumption that both parties come to the relationship with a common goal. This is to determine the best course of action for the patient within the constraints of available resources. Thus, it allows the professional to challenge apparently irrational decisions. The healthcare professional's duty of beneficence and respect for autonomy makes the power to persuade (and be open to persuasion) an obligation, but one that must be exercised with sensitivity to the patient's condition. However, because patients should retain their right to be wrong, which is an essential aspect of autonomy, any attempts to persuade should be limited to rational argument. Bullying and coercion are unacceptable and are not permitted in this model.

Because consent is predicated on autonomy, the patient must be competent, the decision must be made voluntarily and the patient should have sufficient knowledge to enable a rational decision. This requires that the professional both makes adequate disclosure and takes reasonable steps to help the patient to understand the information enough to use it to make a reasonable decision. Ordinarily this will involve disclosing information that relates to the implications of the proposed course of action, which includes the implications of rejecting any alternatives. However, patients may waive their right to this information, either in full or in part. In this regard, it is one of the patient's obligations to assist the healthcare professional in determining what information should be disclosed. Where all treatment-related information is refused, this does not end the healthcare professional's obligation since the healthcare professional must ensure that the patient understands the legal implications of that waiver.

Just as patients may waive their right to information, so they may waive their right to consent. As with the informational waiver, they should be informed of the legal consequences of the waiver. Because patients must actively waive their right, they must exercise their autonomy. In this minimal sense, autonomy is mandatory, but consent to medical treatment is not an inalienable right.

The model recognises that the competent patient should have a prima facie right to consent or refuse consent to any proffered treatment. The right is not absolute because other justifications, such as where non-treatment poses a risk of serious harm to others, may permit non-consensual treatment. There may also be occasions, where an act harms the community, when consent is ineffective to justify intervention. Barring these exceptions, a refusal of consent should ultimately be accepted. However, as I noted above, where the refusal is irrational, temporary infringement of the right to refuse is justified, and indeed required, while the healthcare professional attempts to persuade the patient to reconsider the decision. This allows healthcare professionals to fulfil their obligations to the patient (see earlier). The patient, in entering into a relationship with the professional, should accept the obligation to allow the professional to fulfil those duties. Thus, patients should be willing to explain their decision and be reasonably open to persuasion.

Finally, the model recognises a distinction between responsibility for the treatment decision and responsibility for the outcome of treatment. Because consent is based on autonomy and is seen as a right, the patient is harmed by any unjustified failure to obtain an effective consent. The model allows this harm to be recognised independently of the outcome of treatment. Whether or not a risk materialises is irrelevant to the wrong. How far the damage caused by a materialised risk should be compensated for may be dependent on the interaction between the healthcare professional and the patient in making the treatment decision; but responsibility for outcome should be a distinct judgement that takes into account, but is not determined by, the adequacy of any consent.

In Chapter 5 I explored the legal regulation of consent to medical treatment. I noted that the courts had distinguished certain elements of the duty to disclose, most notably information about risks and alternative options. The primary reason for this was to avoid the associations of criminality inherent to battery liability. It also allows the judges much greater control over liability than would have been possible in battery law. However, in creating this battery/negligence divide the law has largely emasculated the tort of battery except for the most extreme cases of failure to gain consent. Although battery protects the patient's right to bodily integrity, and so is conceptually attractive, it is limited in its practical use for regulating consent because of the relative ease with which its requirements may be satisfied. Furthermore, it is only concerned with those interventions that involve the direct application of force to the patient. This leaves large areas of medical practice outside the penumbra of the protection provided by battery law.

The traditional difficulties that claimants face in bringing negligence claims include a doctor-friendly standard of care, the problems of proving causation and the need to show actual damage. In my analysis I showed how the standard of care has shifted slightly from the reasonable doctor towards the prudent-patient standard. At present, it is uncertain how much protection is provided for individual autonomy since in *Pearce*,[2] Woolf LJ still relied on expert medical evidence to act as a gatekeeper restricting the claimant's access to the autonomy sensitive part of the test. Also, the therapeutic privilege remains an important 'get out of jail free' card. However, other developments have also resulted in a shift in favour of greater protection for the patient's autonomy. In particular, the rules of causation no longer require claimants to show that they would never have undergone the procedure had the risk been disclosed. This move towards a greater protection for individual autonomy is limited by the persisting need to show actual damage, usually as a result of the undisclosed risk materialising.

[2] *Pearce* v. *United Bristol Healthcare NHS Trust* (1998) 48 BMLR 118.

In Chapter 6 I compared the legal regulation of consent against the relational model developed in the first part of the book. I argued that both torts have their problems, whether considered individually or together. While battery law may be a more conceptually appropriate vehicle, it has undesirable associations with criminality. The law of negligence, however, which is centred on the defendant's duty rather than the claimant's right and requires actual damage, is conceptually less attractive. Furthermore, the battery/negligence divide is conceptually unclear and the association between risk disclosure and consent has been inappropriately severed leaving the current requirement for competence an incoherent test.

The law of battery is limited by the need for the direct application of force, which significantly limits its relevance to significant areas of healthcare practice. The necessary association of consent and responsibility for outcome hampers both torts. Furthermore, the law's protection of autonomy appears to be relying on the thin view of autonomy as self-determination that I argued in Part I was an inadequate conception of autonomy. Thus, the courts have inadvisably rejected the need for any duty on the healthcare professional to attempt to persuade their patients to make rational decisions. The courts' focus on the outcome of the interaction between the healthcare professional and the patient is at the expense of the process and, given the importance of the process of decision-making to whether a decision is autonomous, this limits the current protection provided for a more textured conception of autonomy. What protection there is risks being undermined by the vague and paternalistic therapeutic privilege. Finally, the legal remedies available are limited to tort law's corrective justice role of compensating a wrongful loss.

The common law is restricted in the way it can develop. It is reactive and depends on the relevant cases being brought before the court. Even then, it is constrained by precedent and has a limited range of remedies available. Furthermore, just as the law may evolve to provide a greater and more sensitive protection for autonomy, so too may it rein in or even reverse that process. It is also hampered by the court's limited role in policy matters. The rules of consent, central as consent is to the professional–patient relationship, should be developed as part of a coherent philosophy of healthcare provision. This is something that is more properly the role of parliament than the courts. For these reasons I suggested that simply allowing the common law to continue to develop the rules piecemeal is the least attractive of the three possible options.

I am not suggesting that the current approach is not workable; it provides passably fair protection for both patient and professional. It is bolstered by the regulation such as that provided by bodies such as the GMC or the NMC and developing that professional regulation could cover some of the gaps and deficiencies of the common law. Unfortunately, public trust in these bodies has been shaken recently by a number of scandals and is perhaps at a nadir. If they can rebuild public trust it is feasible that they could, in conjunction with the common law, provide an appropriate regulatory regime.[3] Given the recent report by the CMO,[4] commissioned by the Secretary of State for Health following publication of the fifth report by the Shipman Inquiry, this may be an ideal opportunity to harness the regulation of consent to any reforms recommended following the public consultation. However, the conceptual difficulties would remain, as would the legal focus on outcome rather than process with the current lack of remedy for a bare infringement of autonomy.

An additional problem faced by a regulatory system based on a reactive common law that is, to a significant extent, dependent on professional standards is that any change in professional guidelines and practice are likely to influence the courts' approach to the standard of care. The current approach to consent has recently been challenged by the influential philosopher Baroness Professor O'Neill. Along with her co-author Neil Manson she has argued that the healthcare professions should focus on a 'genuine' rather than informed consent. I addressed their approach in Chapter 7. While their model has a lot to recommend it, particularly the focus on the agency model of information, there is a strong risk that, if implemented in practice, the theoretical model will be misshapen by the risk-management machinery and the constraints of the common law.

While they emphasise the importance of communication, this is undermined by their insistence that consent has nothing to do with autonomy. As such, the model they propose is largely focused on the negative duties of non-interference, avoiding coercion and deception and allowing the patient to control the amount of information disclosed. Because of this, the emphasis remains on the healthcare professional's duty to disclose, albeit a duty to do so in a trustworthy way. Once this model is exposed to the practical concerns of legal liability the duty is likely to be measured by the outcome of the disclosure process. As such it resembles the approaches of Lords Bridge and Templeman in

---

[3] It has even been suggested that the current Council should be disbanded and the 'its successor reformed with members . . . who can give it a convincing fresh start': D. Irvine, 'Good doctors: safer patients – the Chief Medical Officer's prescription for regulating doctors' (2006) 99 *Journal of the Royal Society of Medicine* 1, 2.
[4] Chief Medical Officer, *Good Doctors, Safer Patients*.

Sidaway. It may be that Manson and O'Neill's model is a necessary stage in the cyclical development of consent; however, since it fails to provide adequate support for good decision-making it should be at most a temporary stopping-off point.

The final option for reform is legislation, which could resolve the problems I have highlighted and 'send a strong signal about society's values'.[5] One of the problems, however, is that legislation may be poorly drafted.[6] This is not uncommon and it may, contrary to intention, result in more complex and less coherent regulation.[7] This is obviously a risk. However, the existing regulation provided for by the common law at least ensures formal justice, which means that, even if the substantive justice provided could be improved, it provides a sufficient degree of fair protection and legislation does not need to be rushed. With appropriate care it should be possible to avoid the pitfalls of drafting that may accompany more hurried legislation. The risk of poor drafting could be further minimised by producing a more civilian style of legislation, favouring general and less particular regulation,[8] accompanied by a 'statement of intent'[9] and a code of practice to flesh out the principles and rules set out in the statute. Such an approach could 'leave sufficient room for judicial flexibility, while giving better guidance than is presently available'.[10]

Other disadvantages of legislation include:[11]

- the problems associated with the legislative process, including the differential access of interested parties to the legislators and the political process that may require amendments to be accepted
- the expense and resource implications of legislation
- the difficulty and time involved in amending legislation
- the inflexibility and unresponsiveness of statute law.

---

[5] Working Group on Hate Crime, *Consultation Paper* (Edinburgh: Scottish Executive, 2004), para. 3.4. Available at http://www.scotland.gov.uk/Resource/Doc/1099/0001954. pdf.

[6] The Law Reform Commission, *Foreign State Immunity*, *Report No. 24* (Canberra: Australian Government Publishing Service, 1984), p. 31; L. Campbell, 'Drafting styles: Fuzzy or fussy?' (1996) 3 *E Law – Murdoch University Electronic Journal of Law*, para. 7.

[7] D. Renton, *The Preparation of Legislation: Report of a committee appointed by the Lord President of the Council*, Cmnd 6053 (1975), pp. 27–8.

[8] Campbell, 'Drafting styles: Fuzzy or fussy?', para. 1.

[9] Renton, *The Preparation of Legislation*, p. 30.

[10] The Law Reform Commission, *Foreign State Immunity*, p. 31.

[11] Robyn Kennedy & Co. Pty Ltd, *National Community Housing Forum: A regulatory framework for community housing in Australia, vol. 2: Regulatory options, final report* (2001), p. 46. Available at: www.nchf.org.au/downloads/regulationvol2.pdf.

Some of these problems could be avoided or minimised by legislating at the level of general principles and rules, allowing the detail to be filled in by the code of practice and the courts. This would improve the flexibility and responsiveness of the law as well as improve its clarity and accessibility while providing sufficiently detailed and comprehensive guidance. Delegated legislation may limit the difficulties of amending legislation. This means that the remaining objections to legislation are the initial cost and the democratic deficiencies of the legislative process.

Whether legislation is the preferred option – and it may be that a combination of developing professional regulation and concurrent legal reform would be best – depends on how central consent is seen to be to healthcare. It has been my position that consent should be seen as central to the professional–patient relationship. This relationship, as I noted in Chapter 3, is valued both by patients and professionals and arguably is crucial to a mature conception of patient-centred care. The nature of that relationship may be defined by the approach to consent and the process of communication that envelops it. As such, I have argued that the principles and rules of consent to medical treatment should be given a statutory basis and I addressed how the relational model of consent might be translated into principles and general rules in the second half of Chapter 7.

Ultimately, the response to the current deficiencies in the regulation of consent must balance ethical values against cost and economic efficiency. However, if patient-centred care is a genuine aim then it is important to extend the present commitment beyond the consumerist focus on choice and service provision. It is necessary to engage with consent, which lies at the heart of the professional–patient relationship and, if conceived of expansively, forms the basis of healthcare interactions. Investing in the development of the regulation of a more textured consent would be money well spent if it emphasises the importance of, and provides and protects a sensitive and mature respect for, both the patient's and the professional's autonomy.

Bibliography

Adler, H. M. 'The sociophysiology of caring in the doctor–patient relationship' (2002) 17 *Journal of General Internal Medicine* 883.

Agell, A. 'The conceptual relationship between medical malpractice and the lack of informed consent', in L. Westerhall and C. Phillips (eds.), *Patients' Rights – Informed consent, access and equality* (Stockholm: Nerenius & Santerus Publishers, 1994), p. 85.

Ainsworth-Vaughan, N. *Claiming Power in Doctor-Patient Talk* (New York: Oxford University Press, 1998).

Alderson, P. and Goodey, C. 'Theories of consent' (1998) 317 *British Medical Journal* 1313.

Alexander, L. 'Introduction to issues 2 and 3: Symposium on consent in sexual relations' (1996) 2 *Legal Theory* 87.

'The moral magic of consent (II)' (1996) 2 *Legal Theory* 165.

Appleby, J., Harrison, A. and Devlin, N. *What is the Real Cost of More Patient Choice?* (London: King's Fund, 2003).

Aristotle (tr. J. A. K. Thomson) *The Ethics of Aristotle: The Nichomachean Ethics* (London: Penguin Books, 1976).

(tr. E. Barker) *Politics III* (Oxford: Oxford University Press, 1998).

Arneson, R. J. 'Mill versus paternalism' (1980) 90 *Ethics* 470.

Association of Anaesthetists *Consent for Anaesthesia* (2006).

Austoker, J. 'Gaining informed consent for screening' (1999) 319 *British Medical Journal* 722.

Aveyard, H. 'The requirement for informed consent prior to nursing care procedures' (2002) 37 *Journal of Advanced Nursing* 243.

Baker, J. H. *An Introduction to English Legal History*, 3rd edn (London: Butterworths, 1990).

Baker, J. H. and Milsom, S. F. C. *Sources of English Legal History: Private Law to 1750* (London: Butterworths, 1986).

Barclay, L. 'Autonomy and the social self', in C. Mackenzie and N. Stoljar (eds.), *Relational Autonomy: Feminist perspectives on autonomy, agency and the social self* (New York: Oxford University Press, 2000), p. 52.

Barilan, Y. M. and Weintraub, M. 'Persuasion as respect for autonomy: An alternative view of autonomy and the limits of discourse' (2001) 26 *Journal of Medicine and Philosophy* 13.

Barneschi, M. G., Novelli, G. P., Miccinesi, G. and Paci, E. 'Informed consent to anaesthesia' (1998) 15 *European Journal of Anaesthesiology* 517.

Baud, R. H., Lovis, C., Rassinoux, A-M. and Scherrer, J.-R. 'Alternative ways for knowledge collection, indexing and robust language retrieval' (1998) 37 *Methods of Information in Medicine* 315.

Beauchamp, T. L. and Childress, J. F. *Principles of Biomedical Ethics*, 5th edn (New York: Oxford University Press, 2001).

Beck, J. C. 'When the patient threatens violence: An empirical study of clinical practice after Tarasoff' (1982) 10 *Bulletin of the AAPL* 189.

Benson, J. 'Who is the autonomous man?' (1983) 58 *Philosophy* 5.

Benson, P. 'Feeling crazy: Self-worth and the social character of responsibility', in C. Mackenzie and N. Stoljar (eds.), *Relational Autonomy: Feminist perspectives on autonomy, agency and the social self* (New York: Oxford University Press, 2000), p. 72.

Berg, J. W. 'Understanding waiver' (2003) 40 *Houston Law Review* 281.

Berg, J. W., Appelbaum, P. S., Lidz, C. W. and Parker, L. S. *Informed Consent: Legal Theory and Clinical Practice*, 2nd edn (New York: Oxford University Press, 2001).

Bergsma, J. 'Cancer and autonomy' (2002) 47 *Patient Education and Counseling* 205.

Bergsma, J. and Thomasma, T. *Autonomy and Clinical Medicine: Renewing the health professional relation with the patient* (Dordrecht: Kluwer Academic Publishers, 2000).

Berlin, I. *Four Essays on Liberty* (Oxford: Oxford University Press, 1969).

Berofsky, B. 'Identification, the self and autonomy' (2003) 20 *Social Philosophy and Policy* 199.

Beste, J. 'Instilling hope and respecting patient autonomy: Reconciling apparently conflicting duties' (2005) 19 *Bioethics* 215.

Biegler, P. 'Should patient consent be required to write a do not resuscitate order?' (2003) 29 *Journal of Medical Ethics* 359.

Bigwood, R. 'Undue influence: "Impaired consent" or "Wicked exploitation"?' (1996) 16 *Oxford Journal of Legal Studies* 503.

Bishop, M. 'The possibility of conceptual clarity in philosophy' (1992) 29 *American Philosophical Quarterly* 267.

Bix, B. 'Conceptual questions and jurisprudence' (1995) 1 *Legal Theory* 465.

Black, C. 'Still striving for Utopia' (2006) 332 *British Medical Journal* 47.

Black, C. and Craft, A. 'The competent doctor: A paper for discussion' (2004) 4 *Clinical Medicine* 527.

Bogart, J. H. 'Commodification and phenomenology: Evading consent in theory regarding rape' (1996) 2 *Legal Theory* 253.

Bok, S. *Lying: Moral choice in public and private life* (New York: Vintage Books, 1978).

Bordieu, P. 'The force of law: Toward a sociology of the juridical field' (1986–1987) 38 *Hastings Law Journal* 814.

Brahams, D. 'The law and foreseeability' (2006) 74 *Medico-Legal Journal* 41.

Brazier, M. 'Patient autonomy and consent to treatment: The role of the law?' (1987) 7 *Legal Studies* 169.

'Competence, consent and proxy consents', in M. Lobjoit (eds.), *Protecting the Vulnerable: Autonomy and consent in health care* (London: Routledge, 1991), p. 34.

Brazier, M. and Miola, J. 'Bye-bye Bolam: A medical litigation revolution?' (2000) 8 *Medical Law Review* 85.

Brennan, M. 'A concept analysis of consent' (1997) 25 *Journal of Advanced Nursing* 477.

Bridson, J., Hammond, C., Leach, A. and Hester, M. R. 'Making consent patient centred' (2003) 27 *British Medical Journal* 1159.

Brink, D. O. 'Kantian rationalism: Inescapability, authority and supremacy', in G. Cullity and B. Gaut (eds.), *Ethics and Practical Reason* (Oxford: Clarendon Press, 1997), p. 255.

The British Medical Association *Medical Ethics Today: Its practice and philosophy* (London: BMJ Publishing Group, 1993, reprinted 1998).

Brock, D. W. 'Decisionmaking, competence and risk' (1991) 5 *Bioethics* 105.
  Life and Death: Philosophical essays in biomedical ethics (New York: Cambridge University Press, 1993).

Brody, D. S. 'The patient's role in clinical decision making' (1980) 93 *Annals of Internal Medicine* 718.

Brody, H. *The Healer's Power* (New Haven: Yale University Press, 1992).

Brown, H. I. *Rationality* (London: Routledge, 1988).

Brownsword, R. 'The cult of consent: Fixation and fallacy' (2004) 15 *King's College Law Journal* 223.

Buchanan, A. 'Medical paternalism' (1978) 7 *Philosophy and Public Affairs* 370.

Burkitt Wright, E., Holcombe, C. and Salmon, P. 'Doctors' communication of trust, care, and respect in breast cancer: qualitative study' (2004) 328 *British Medical Journal* 864.

Burrows, B. J. 'The patient's view of anaesthesia in an Australian teaching hospital' (1982) 10 *Anaesthesia and Intensive Care* 20.

Byrne P. 'Divergence on consent: A philosophical assay', in G. R. Dunstan and M. J. Seller (eds.), *Consent in Medicine: Convergence and divergence in tradition* (London: King Edward's Hospital Fund, 1983), p. 45.
  'What may a patient properly expect of his doctor?', in G. R. Dunstan and M. J. Seller (eds.), *Consent in Medicine: Convergence and divergence in tradition* (London: King Edward's Hospital Fund, 1983), p. 26.

Campbell, L. 'Drafting styles: Fuzzy or fussy?' (1996) 3 *E Law – Murdoch University Electronic Journal of Law*.

Campbell, T. D. 'Humanity before justice' (1974) 4 *British Journal of Political Science* 1.

Cane, P. *Responsibility in Law and Morality* (Oxford: Hart Publishing, 2002).

Caplan, A. L. 'Informed consent and provider-patient relationships in rehabilitation medicine' (1988) 69 *Arch. Phys. Med. Rehabil.* 312.

Capron, A. M. 'Informed consent in catastrophic disease research and treatment' (1974) 123 *University of Pennsylvania Law Review* 340.

Cassell, E. 'The function of medicine, (1977) 7 *Hasting Center Report* 16.

Cassell, E. J. *The Healer's Art* (Cambridge, Mass.: MIT Press, 1985).
  The Nature of Suffering and the Goals of Medicine (New York: Oxford University Press, 1991).

Chapman, I. H. 'Informed consent – Survey of Auckland, NZ anaesthetists' practice and attitudes' (1997) 25 *Anaesthesia and Intensive Care* 671.

Charles, C., Gafni, A. and Whelan, T. 'Shared decision-making in the medical encounter: What does it mean? (Or it takes at least two to tango)' (1997) 44 *Social Science and Medicine* 681.

Charlesworth, M. *Bioethics in a Liberal Society* (Cambridge: Cambridge University Press, 1993).

Chavkin, W., Allen, M. H. and Oberman, M. 'Drug abuse and pregnancy: Some questions on public policy, clinical management, and maternal and fetal rights' (1991) 18 *Birth* 107.

Chee Saw, K., Wood, A. M., Murphy, K., Parry, J. R. W. and Hartfall, W. G. 'Informed consent: An evaluation of patients' understanding and opinion (with respect to the operation of transurethral resection of the prostate)' (1994) 87 *Journal of the Royal Society of Medicine* 143.

Chell, B. 'Competency: What it is, what it isn't, and why it matters', in J. F. Monagle and D. C. Thomasma (eds.), *Health Care Ethics: Critical issues for the 21st century* (Gaithersburg, Md.: Aspen Publishers Inc., 1998), p. 117.

Cherniak, C. *Minimal Rationality* (Cambridge, Mass.: MIT Press, 1986).

Chief Medical Officer. *An Organisation with a Memory* (London: Department of Health, 2000).

Good Doctors, Safer Patients (London: Department of Health, 2006).

Childs, B. 'Pause for thought: Contributory negligence and intentional trespass to the person' (1993) 44 *Northern Ireland Legal Quarterly* 334.

Clark, C. C. 'Trust in medicine' (2002) 27 *Journal of Medicine and Philosophy* 11.

Clement, G. *Care, Autonomy, and Justice: Feminism and the ethic of care* (Boulder, Colo.: Westview Press, 1998).

Cohen, J. 'Patient autonomy and social fairness' (2000) 9 *Cambridge Quarterly of Healthcare Ethics* 391.

Coulter, A., *The Autonomous Patient: Ending paternalism in medical care* (London: The Stationery Office, 2002).

Coulter, A., Entwistle, V. and Gilbert, D. 'Sharing decisions with patients: Is the information good enough?' (1999) 318 *British Medical Journal* 318.

'Whatever happened to shared decision-making?' (2002) 5 *Health Expectations* 185.

Cruess, S. R., Johnston, S. and Cruess, R. L. 'Professionalism for medicine: Opportunities and obligations' (2002) 177 *Medical Journal of Australia* 208.

Cullity, G. and Gaut, B. 'Introduction', in G. Cullity and B. Gaut (eds.), *Ethics and Practical Reason* (Oxford: Clarendon Press, 1997), p.1.

Culver, C. M. and Gert, B. *Philosophy in Medicine* (New York: Oxford University Press, 1982).

Cunliffe, J. and Reeve, A. 'Dialogic authority' (1999) 19 *Oxford Journal of Legal Studies* 453.

Dawes, P. J. D. and Davison, P. 'Informed consent: What do patients want to know?' (1994) 87 *Journal of the Royal Society of Medicine* 149.

Department of Health. *Patient and Public Involvement in the New NHS* (Health Service Circular: HSC (99) 210) (London: Department of Health, 1999).

Good Practice in Consent Implementation Guide: Consent to examination or treatment (London: Department of Health, 2001).

Reference Guide to Consent for Examination or Treatment (London: Department of Health, 2001).

Learning from Bristol: The Department of Health's response to the report of the public inquiry into children's heart surgery at the Bristol Royal Infirmary 1984–1995, Cm 5363 (London: The Stationery Office, 2002).

NHS Improvement Plan 2004: Putting people at the heart of public services, Cm 6268 (London: Department of Health, 2004).

Creating a Patient-led NHS: Delivering the NHS Improvement Plan (London: Department of Health, 2005).

Dickenson, D. *Moral Luck in Medical Ethics and Practical Politics* (Aldershot: Avebury, 1991).

Risk and Luck in Medical Ethics (Cambridge: Polity Press, 2003).

Dodd, F. J., Donegan, H. A., Kernohan, W. G., Geary, R. V. and Mollan, R. A. B. 'Consensus in medical communication' (1993) 37 *Social Science and Medicine* 565.

Dodds, S. 'Choice and control in feminist bioethics', in C. Mackenzie and N. Stoljar (eds.), *Relational Autonomy: Feminist perspectives on autonomy, agency and the social self* (New York: Oxford University Press, 2000), p. 213.

Doukas, D. J. 'Where is the virtue in professionalism?' (2003) 12 *Cambridge Quarterly of Healthcare Ethics* 147.

Doyal, L. 'The moral foundation of the clinical duties of care: Needs, duties and human rights' (2001) 15 *Bioethics* 520.

'Good clinical practice and informed consent are inseparable' (2002) 87 *Heart*, 103.

Drane, J. 'The many faces of competency' (1985) 15 *Hastings Center Report* 17.

Draper, H. and Sorrell, T. 'Patients' responsibilities in medical ethics' (2002) 16 *Bioethics* 335.

Draper, K. 'The personal and impersonal dimensions of benevolence' (2001) 36 *Nous* 201.

Dupus, H. M. 'Professional autonomy: A stumbling block for good medical practice: An analysis and interpretation' (2000) 21 *Theoretical Medicine* 493.

Dworkin, G. *The Theory and Practice of Autonomy* (Cambridge: Cambridge University Press, 1988)

'Moral paternalism' (2005) *24 Law and Philosophy* 305–19.

Dworkin, R. *Law's Empire* (London: Fontana Press, 1986).

Life's Dominion (London: HarperCollins, 1993).

Dworkin, R. B. 'Getting what we should from doctors: Rethinking patient autonomy and the doctor–patient relationship' (2003) 13 *Health Matrix* 235.

Dyer, A. R. and Bloch, S. 'Informed consent and the psychiatric patient' (1987) 13 *Journal of Medical Ethics* 12.

Earle, M. 'The future of informed consent in British common law' (1999) 6 *European Journal of Health Law* 235.

Eekelaar, J. and Maclean, M. 'Marriage and the moral bases of personal relationships' (2004) 31 *Journal of Law and Society* 510.

Elliott, C. *Bioethics, Culture and Identity: A philosophical disease* (New York: Routledge, 1999).

Emanuel, E. J. and Emanuel, L. L. 'Four models of the physician-patient relationship' (1992) 267 *Journal of the American Medical Association* 2221.

Endacott, R. 'Clarifying the concept of need: A comparison of two approaches to concept analysis' (1997) 25 *Journal of Advanced Nursing* 471.

Ende, J., Kazis, L. and Moskowitz, M. A. 'Preference for autonomy when patients are physicians' (1990) 5 *Journal of General Internal Medicine* 23.

Engelhardt Jr, H. T. 'The many faces of autonomy' (2001) 9 *Health Care Analysis* 283.

English, D. A. 'Moral obligations of patients: A clinical view' (2005) 30 *The Journal of Medicine and Philosophy* 139.

Entwistle, V., Watt, I. S., Gilhooly, K., Bugge, C., Haites, N. and Walker, A. E. 'Assessing patients' participation and quality of decision-making: Insights from a study of routine practice in diverse settings' (2004) 55 *Patient Education and Counseling* 105.

Epstein, M. 'Why effective consent presupposes autonomous authorisation: A counterorthodox argument' (2006) 32 *Journal of Medical Ethics* 342.

Erh-Soon Tay, A. 'The sense of justice in the common law', in E. Kamenka and A. Erh-Soon Tay (eds.), *Justice* (London: Edward Arnold, 1979), p. 79.

Evans, G. *The Varieties of Reference* (Oxford: Clarendon Press, 1982).

Faden, F. R. and Beauchamp, T. L. *The History and Theory of Informed Consent* (New York: Oxford University Press, 1986).

Faulder, C. *Whose Body Is It? The troubling issue of informed consent* (London: Virago, 1985).

Feinberg, J. *Harm to Others* (New York: Oxford University Press, 1984).
Harm to Self (New York: Oxford University Press, 1986).
'Autonomy', in J. Christman (ed.), *The Inner Citadel* (New York: Oxford University Press, 1989), p. 27.

Fennell, P. 'Inscribing paternalism in the law: Consent to treatment and mental disorder' (1990) 17 *Journal of Law and Society* 29.

Fifoot, C. H. S. *History and Sources of the Common Law* (London: Stevens & Sons Ltd, 1949).

Foot, P. *Virtues and Vices* (Oxford: Clarendon Press, 2002).

Foucault, M. *The Birth of the Clinic* (New York: Vintage Books, 1973).
'Body/Power', in C. Gordon (ed.), *Power/Knowledge* (Brighton: The Harvester Press, 1980), p. 55.
'Two lectures', in C. Gordon (ed.), *Power/Knowledge* (Brighton: The Harvester Press, 1980), p. 78.
The Archaeology of Knowledge (London: Routledge, 1995).

Frankfurt, H. 'What we are morally responsible for', in J. M. Fischer and M. Ravizza (eds.), *Perspectives on Moral Responsibility* (Ithaca, NY: Cornell University Press, 1993), p. 286.
'Freedom of the will and the concept of a person', reprinted in R. Kane (ed.), *Free Will* (Malden, Mass.: Blackwell Publishers, 2002), p. 127.

Fuller, L. L. *The Morality of Law*, 2nd edn (New Haven: Yale University Press, 1969).

Gadamer, H.-G. *Truth and Method*, 2nd edn (London: Sheed & Ward, 1975).

Gardiner, P. 'A virtue ethics approach to moral dilemmas in medicine' (2003) 29 *Journal of Medical Ethics* 297.

Gardner, S. 'Appreciating *Olugboja*' (1996) 16 *Legal Studies* 275.

Gaut, B. 'The structure of practical reason', in G. Cullity and B. Gaut (eds.), *Ethics and Practical Reason* (Oxford: Clarendon Press, 1997), p. 161.

Gauthier, C. C. 'Moral responsibility and respect for autonomy: Meeting the communitarian challenge' (2000) 10 *Kennedy Institute of Ethics Journal* 337.
'The virtue of moral responsibility in healthcare decisionmaking' (2002) 11 *Cambridge Quarterly of Healthcare Ethics* 273.

Gavaghan, C. 'Anticipatory refusals and the action of "wrongful living"' (2000) 5 *Medical Law International* 67.

General Medical Council *Seeking Patients' Consent: The ethical considerations* (London: GMC, 1999).

Giesen, D. 'From paternalism to self-determination to shared decision making in the field of medical law and ethics', in L. Westerhall and C. Phillips (eds.), *Patient's Rights – Informed consent, access and equality* (Stockholm: Nerenius & Santerus Publishers, 1994), p. 19.

Giesen, D. and Hayes, J. 'The patient's right to know – A comparative view' (1992) 21 *Anglo-American Law Review* 101.

Gilbert, M. 'Agreements, coercion, and obligation' (1993) 103 *Ethics* 679.

Gilberthorpe, J. *Consent to Treatment* (London: The Medical Defence Union, 1999).

Gillon R. *Philosophical Medical Ethics* (Chichester: John Wiley & Sons, 1985, 1992 Reprint).
'Ethics needs principles – four can encompass the rest – and respect for autonomy should be "first among equals"' (2003) 29 *Journal of Medical Ethics* 307.

Glazebrook, P. R. 'Assaults and their consequences' (1986) *The Cambridge Law Journal* 379.

Goodyear-Smith, F. and Buetow, S. 'Power issues in the doctor-patient relationship' (2001) 9 *Health Care Analysis* 449.

Gordon, E. J. and Daugherty, C. K. '"Hitting you over the head": Oncologists' disclosure of prognosis to advanced cancer patients' (2003) 17 *Bioethics* 142.

Gordon, R. and Barlow, C. 'Competence and the right to die' (1993) *The New Law Journal* 1719.

Gostin, L. 'Consent to treatment: The incapable person', in C. Dyer (ed.), *Doctors, Patients and the Law* (Oxford: Blackwell Scientific Publications, 1992), p. 72.

Greenawalt, K. 'The perplexing borders of justification and excuse' (1984) 84 *Columbia Law Review* 1897.
'Legal enforcement of morality', in D. Patterson (ed.), *A Companion to Philosophy of Law and Legal Theory* (Oxford: Blackwell, 1996), p. 475.

Gregg Bloche, M. and Quinn, K. P. 'Professionalism and personhood', in D. C. Thomasma, D. N. Weisstub and C. Herve (eds.), *Personhood and Health Care* (Dordrecht: Kluwer Academic Publishers, 2001), p. 347.

Grice, H. P. 'Logic and conversation', in R. M. Hamish (ed.), *Basic Topics in the Philosophy of Language* (New York: Harvester Wheatsheaf, 1994), p. 57.

Griffin, J. 'Virtue ethics and environs', in E. F. Paul, F. D. Miller and J. Paul (eds.), *Virtue and Vice* (Cambridge: Cambridge University Press, 1998), p. 56.

Grisso, T. and Applebaum, P. S. *Assessing Competence to Consent to Treatment* (Oxford: Oxford University Press, 1998).

Grubb, A. 'Contraceptive advice and doctors – A law unto themselves' (1988) 47 *The Cambridge Law Journal* 12.

'Medical negligence: Duty to disclose after Bolitho' (1999) 7 *Medical Law Review* 61.

'Consent to treatment: The competent person', in A. Grubb and J. Laing (eds.), *Principles of Medical Law*, 2nd edn (Oxford: Oxford University Press, 2004), p. 131.

Gunn, M. 'The meaning of incapacity' (1994) 2 *Medical Law Review* 8.

Gunn, M. J., Wong, J. G., Clare, I. C. H. and Holland, A. J. 'Decision-making capacity' (1999) 7 *Medical Law Review* 269.

Gupta, G. 'Ethics, treatment and consent' (1999) 12 *Current Opinion in Psychiatry* 605.

Gutheil, T. G., Bursztajn, H. and Brodsky, A. 'Malpractice prevention through the sharing of uncertainty: Informed consent and the therapeutic alliance' (1984) 311 *New England Journal of Medicine* 49.

Gylling, H. A. 'Autonomy revisited' (2004) 13 *Cambridge Quarterly of Healthcare Ethics* 41.

Habiba, M. W. 'Examining consent within the patient–doctor relationship' (2000) 26 *Journal of Medical Ethics* 183.

Hall, M. A. 'Law, medicine and trust' (2002) 55 *Stanford Law Review* 463.

Hallenbeck, J. L. 'What's the story – How patients make medical decisions' (2002) 113 *The American Journal of Medicine* 73.

Halpin, A. 'Concepts, terms, and fields of enquiry' (1998) 4 *Legal Theory* 187.

Harrington, J. A. 'Privileging the medical norm: Liberalism, self-determination and refusal of treatment' (1996) 16 *Legal Studies* 348.

Harris, J. 'Consent and end of life decisions' (2003) 29 *Journal of Medical Ethics* 10.

Harris, J. and Keywood, K. 'Ignorance, information and autonomy' (2001) 22 *Theoretical Medicine* 415.

Harrison, K. and Bell, B. 'Assaulting our common sense – The impact of DPP v K' (1990) 53 *Modern Law Review* 518.

Haug, M. R. and Lavin, B. 'Practitioner or patient – Who's in charge?' (1981) 22 *Journal of Health and Social Behavior* 212.

Haworth, L. *Autonomy: An essay in philosophical psychology and ethics* (New Haven: Yale University Press, 1986).

Hayry, H. *The Limits of Medical Paternalism* (London: Routledge, 1991).

Hayry, M. 'Prescribing cannabis: Freedom, autonomy and values' (2004) 30 *Journal of Medical Ethics* 333.

Healy, J. *Medical Negligence: Common law perspectives* (London: Sweet & Maxwell, 1999).

Hembroff, L. A., Holmes-Rovner, M. and Wills, C. E. 'Treatment decision-making and the form of risk communication: Results of a factorial survey' (2004) 4 *BMC Medical Informatics and Decision Making* 20.

Henry, M. S. 'Uncertainty, responsibility, and the evolution of the physician/patient relationship' (2006) 32 *Journal of Medical Ethics* 321.

Hermeren, G. 'Informed consent from an ethical point of view', in L. Westerhall and C. Phillips (eds.), *Patient's Rights – Informed consent, access and equality* (Stockholm: Nerenius & Santerus Publishers, 1994), p. 39.

Heywood, R. 'Excessive risk disclosure: The effects of the law on medical practice' (2005) 7 *Medical Law International* 9.

'Re-thinking the decision in Pearce' (2005) *Contemporary Issues in Law* 264.

Hill, T. 'A lost chance for compensation in the tort of negligence by the House of Lords' (1991) 54 *Modern Law Review* 511.

Hirst, M. 'Assault, battery and indirect violence' (1999) *Criminal Law Review* 557.

Honoré, T. 'Responsibility and luck' (1988) 104 *Law Quarterly Review* 530.

'The dependence of morality on law' (1993) 13 *Oxford Journal of Legal Studies* 1.

'The morality of tort law', in D. G. Owen (ed.), *Philosophical Foundations of Tort Law* (Oxford: Clarendon Press, 1995), p. 73; reprinted in: *Responsibility and Fault* (Oxford: Hart Publishing, 2002), p. 67.

Hoogland, J. and Jochemsen, H. 'Professional autonomy and the normative structure of medical practice' (2000) 21 *Theoretical Medicine* 457.

Horner, J. S. 'Autonomy in the medical profession in the United Kingdom – An historical perspective' (2000) 21 *Theoretical Medicine* 409.

Horton, R. 'The context of consent' (1994) 344 *Lancet* 211.

Hughes, G. 'Two views on consent in the criminal law' (1963) 26 *The Modern Law Review* 233.

Huntington, P. 'Toward a dialectical concept of autonomy' (1995) 21 *Philosophy and Social Criticism* 37.

Hurd, H. M. 'The moral magic of consent' (1996) 2 *Legal Theory* 121.

Hurka, T. 'Why value autonomy?' (1987) 13 *Social Theory and Practice* 361.

Hurley, S. L. *Justice, Luck, Knowledge* (Cambridge, Mass.: Harvard University Press, 2003).

Husak, D. N. 'Paternalism and autonomy' (1981) 10 *Philosophy and Public Affairs* 27.

Ingelfinger, F. J. 'Informed (but uneducated) consent' (1972) 287 *New England Journal of Medicine* 465.

Irvine, D. *The Doctors' Tale: Professionalism and public trust* (Oxford: Radcliffe Medical Press, 2003).

'Good doctors: safer patients – the Chief Medical Officer's prescription for regulating doctors' (2006) 99 *Journal of the Royal Society of Medicine* 1.

Jackson, E. '"Informed consent" to medical treatment and the impotence of tort', in S. A. M. McLean (ed.), *First Do No Harm* (Aldershot: Ashgate, 2006), p. 271.

Jackson, J. *Truth, Trust and Medicine* (London: Routledge, 2001).

Jacob, J. 'Biomedical law: Lost horizons regained' (1983) 46 *The Modern Law Review* 21.

Jones, M. A. 'Informed consent and other fairy stories' (1999) 7 *Medical Law Review* 103.

Kamenka, E. 'What is justice?', in E. Kamenka and A. Erh-Soon Tay (eds.), *Justice* (London: Edward Arnold, 1979), p. 1.

Kant, I. (ed. V. Politis) *Critique of Pure Reason* (London: Everyman's Library, 1993).

(tr. M. Gregor) *Groundwork of the Metaphysics of Morals* (Cambridge: Cambridge University Press, 1998).

(tr. M. Gregor) *The Doctrine of Virtue: Part two of the metaphysics of morals* (New York: Harper & Row, 1964).

Katz, J. *The Silent World of Doctor and Patient* (Baltimore: Johns Hopkins University Press, 1984, 2002).

Kaufert, J. M. and O'Neil, J. D. 'Biomedical rituals and informed consent: Native Canadians and the negotiation of clinical trust', in G. Weisz (ed.), *Social Science Perspectives on Medical Ethics* (Dordrecht: Kluwer Academic Publishers, 1990), p. 41.

Kay, R. and Siriwardena, A. K. 'The process of informed consent for urgent abdominal surgery' (2001) 27 *Journal of Medical Ethics* 157.

Kell, D. 'Social disutility and the law of consent' (1994) 14 *Oxford Journal of Legal Studies* 121.

Kelleher, D., Gabe, J. and Williams, G. 'Understanding medical dominance in the modern world', in D. Kelleher, J. Gabe and G. Williams (eds.), *Challenging medicine* (London: Routledge, 1994), p. xi.

Kelley, M. 'Limits on patient responsibility' (2005) 30 *The Journal of Medicine and Philosophy* 189.

Kennedy, I. *Treat Me Right: Essays in medical law and ethics* (Oxford: Clarendon Press, 1988).

'Consent to treatment: The capable person', in C. Dyer (ed.), *Doctors, Patients and the Law* (Oxford: Blackwell Scientific Publications, 1992), p. 44.

Learning from Bristol: The report of the public inquiry into children's heart surgery at the Bristol Royal Infirmary 1984–1995, Cm 5207 (2001).

Kennett, J. *Agency and Responsibility: A common-sense moral psychology* (Oxford: Clarendon Press, 2001).

Keown, J. 'The ashes of AIDS and the phoenix of informed consent' (1989) 52 *The Modern Law Review* 790.

'Reining in the *Bolam* test' (1998) 57 *The Cambridge Law Journal* 248.

Kernohan, A. 'Social power and human agency' (1989) 86 *The Journal of Philosophy* 712.

Kessel, A. S. 'On failing to understand informed consent' (1994) 52 *British Journal of Hospital Medicine* 235.

Ketler, S. K. 'The rebirth of informed consent: A cultural analysis of the informed consent doctrine after Schreiber v Physicians Insurance Co. of Wisconsin' (2001) 95 *Northwestern University Law Review* 1029.

Kligman, M. and Culver, C. M. 'An analysis of interpersonal manipulation' (1992) 17 *The Journal of Medicine and Philosophy* 173.

Korsgaard, C. M. 'Personal identity and the unity of agency: A Kantian response to Parfit' (1989) 18 *Philosophy and Public Affairs* 101.

'The normativity of instrumental reason', in G. Cullity and B. Gaut (eds.), *Ethics and Practical Reason* (Oxford: Clarendon Press, 1997), p. 215.

'Self-constitution in the ethics of Plato and Kant' (1998) 3 *The Journal of Ethics* 1.

Kraetschmer, N., Sharpe, N., Urowitz, S. and Deber, R. B. 'How does trust affect patient preferences for participation in decision-making?' (2004) 7 *Health Expectations* 317.

Krupat, E., Fancey, M. and Cleary, P. D. 'Information and its impact on satisfaction among surgical patients' (2000) 51 *Social Science & Medicine* 1817.

Kultgen, J. *Autonomy and Intervention: Parentalism in the caring life* (New York: Oxford University Press, 1995).

Ladenson, R. F. 'A theory of personal autonomy' (1975) 86 *Ethics* 30.

The Law Commission Consultation Paper No. 134 *Consent and Offences Against the Person* (London: HMSO, 1994).

Law Commission Consultation Paper No. 135 *Consent in the Criminal Law* (London: HMSO, 1995).

The Law Commission *Report on Mental Incapacity No. 231* (London: HMSO, 1995).

The Law Reform Commission *Foreign State Immunity, Report No. 24* (Canberra: Australian Government Publishing Service, 1984).

Lee, S. 'Operating under informed consent' (1985) 101 *Law Quarterly Review* 316.

'A reversible decision on consent to sterilisation' (1987) 103 *Law Quarterly Review* 513.

'Towards a jurisprudence of consent', in J. Eekelaar and J. Bell (eds.), *Oxford Essays in Jurisprudence* (Oxford: Oxford University Press, 1997), p. 199.

Lehrer, K. 'Freedom, preference and autonomy' (1997) 1 *The Journal of Ethics* 3.

'Reason and autonomy' (2003) 20 *Social Philosophy and Policy* 177.

Leino-Kilpi, H., Valimaki, M., Arndt, M., Dassen, T., Gassull, M., Lemonidou, C., Scott, P. A., Bansemir, G., Cabrera, E., Papaevangelou, H. and McParland, J. *Patient's Autonomy, Privacy and Informed Consent* (Amsterdam: IOS Press, 2000).

Lelie, A. and Verweij, M. 'Futility without a dichotomy: Towards an ideal physician–patient relationship' (2003) 17 *Bioethics* 21.

Levi, B. H. *Respecting Patient Autonomy* (Chicago: University of Illinois Press, 1999).

Loewy, E. H. *Moral Strangers, Moral Acquaintance, and Moral Friends: Connectedness and its conditions* (Albany, NY: State University of New York Press, 1997).

The Lord Chancellor *Making Decisions: The government's proposals for making decisions on behalf of mentally incapacitated adults*, Cm 4465 (1999).

Lunney, M. 'What price a chance?' (1995) 15 *Legal Studies* 1.

Lysaught, M. T. 'Respect: Or, how respect for persons became respect for autonomy' (2004) 29 *Journal of Medicine and Philosophy* 665.

MacDonald, C. 'Clinical standards and the structure of professional obligation' (1999) 8 *Professional Ethics* 7.

'Relational professional autonomy' (2002) 11 *Cambridge Quarterly of Healthcare Ethics* 282.

MacIntyre, A. 'Patients as agents', in S. Spicker and H. T. Engelhardt (eds.), *Philosophical Medical Ethics: Its nature and significance* (Boston: D. Reidel Publishing Co., 1975), p. 197.

After Virtue, 2nd edn (London: Duckworth, 1985).

Maclean, A. 'Consent and the legal protection of autonomy' (2000) 17 *Journal of Applied Philosophy* 277.

'Beyond Bolam and Bolitho' (2002) 5 *Medical Law International* 205.

'Risk, consent and responsibility for outcome' (2005) 14 *Nottingham Law Journal* 57.

'Magic, myths and fairytales: Consent and the relationship between law and ethics', in M. Freeman (ed.), *Law and Bioethics*, Current Legal Issues vol. 11 (Oxford: Oxford University Press, 2008),

Maclean, A.R. 'Distributing the burden of a blessing' (2004) 1 *Journal of Obligation and Remedies* 23.

'The doctrine of informed consent: Does it exist and has it crossed the Atlantic?' (2004) 24 *Legal Studies* 386.

'Consent and sensibility' (2005) 4 *International Journal of Ethics* 31.

'Giving the reasonable patient a voice: Information disclosure and empirical evidence' (2005) 7 *Medical Law International* 1.

'Advance directives and the rocky waters of anticipatory decision making' (2008) 16 *Medical Law Review* 1.

Makoul, G. 'Essential elements of communication in medical encounters: The Kalamazoo consensus statement' (2001) 76 *Academic Medicine* 390.

Malm, H.H. 'The ontological status of consent and its implications for the law on rape' (1996) 2 *Legal Theory* 147.

Manchester, A.H. *Modern Legal History of England and Wales 1750–1950* (London: Butterworths, 1980).

Manson, N.C. and O'Neill, O. *Rethinking Informed Consent in Bioethics* (Cambridge: Cambridge University Press, 2007)

Mappes, T.A. and Zembaty, J.S. 'Biomedical ethics', in T.A. Mappes and J.S. Zembaty (eds.), *Biomedical Ethics*, 3rd edn (New York: McGraw-Hill Inc., 1991), p. 1.

Marta, J. 'Whose consent is it anyway? A poststructuralist framing of the person in medical decision-making' (1998) 19 *Theoretical Medicine* 353.

Mason, K. and Brodie, D. 'Bolam, Bolam – wherefore art thou Bolam?' (2005) 9 *Edinburgh Law Review* 298.

May, T. 'Assessing competency without judging merit' (1998) 9 *The Journal of Clinical Ethics* 247.

'Rights of conscience in health care' (2001) 27 *Social Theory and Practice* 111.

Mayberry, M. and Mayberry, J. *Consent in Clinical Practice* (Abingdon: Radcliffe Medical Press Ltd, 2003).

Mazur, D.J. 'Information disclosure: How do patients understand and use the information they report they want?' (2000) 20 *Medical Decision Making* 132.

McConnell, T. *Inalienable Rights: The limits of consent in medicine and the law* (New York: Oxford University Press, 2000).

McCullough, L.B. 'Trust, moral responsibility, the self, and well-ordered societies: The importance of basic philosophical concepts for clinical ethics' (2002) 27 *Journal of Medicine and Philosophy* 3.

McGrath, P. 'Autonomy, discourse, and power: A postmodern reflection on principalism and bioethics' (1998) 23(5) *Journal of Medicine and Philosophy* 516.

McGregor, J. 'Force, consent, and the reasonable woman', in J.L. Coleman and A. Buchanan (eds.), *In Harm's Way: Essays in honor of Joel Feinberg* (New York: Cambridge University Press, 1994), p. 231.

'Why when she says no she doesn't mean maybe and doesn't mean yes: A critical reconstruction of consent, sex, and the law' (1996) 2 *Legal Theory* 175.

McIlwain, J. C. 'Clinincal risk management: Principles of consent and patient information' (1998) 24 *Clinical Otolaryngology & Allied Sciences* 255.

McKay, A. C. 'Supererogation and the profession of medicine' (2002) 28 *Journal of Medical Ethics* 70.

McKinstry, B. 'Do patients wish to be involved in decision making in the consultation? A cross sectional survey with video vignettes' (2000) 321 *British Medical Journal* 867.

McLean S. and Maher G. *Medicine, Morals and the Law* (Aldershot: Gower Publishing Co. Ltd, 1983).

McLean, S. A. M. *A Patient's Right to Know: Information disclosure, the doctor and the law* (Aldershot: Dartmouth, 1989).

'Talking to patients: Information disclosure as "good" medical practice', in L. Westerhall and C. Phillips (eds.), *Patients' Rights: Informed consent, access and equality* (Stockholm: Nerenius & Santerus Publishers, 1994), p. 171.

Mechanic, D. 'In my chosen doctor I trust' (2004) 329 *British Medical Journal* 1418.

Meisel, A. and Kuczewski, M. 'Legal and ethical myths about informed consent' (1996) 156 *Archives of Internal Medicine* 2521.

Messer, N. G. 'Professional–patient relationships and informed consent' (2004) 80 *Postgraduate Medical Journal* 277.

Meyer, M. J. 'Patients' duties' (1992) 17 *The Journal of Medicine and Philosophy* 541.

Meyers, C. 'Cruel choices: Autonomy and critical care decision-making' (2004) 18 *Bioethics* 104.

Micah Hester, D. 'Narrative as bioethics: The "fact" of social selves and the function of consensus' (2002) 11 *Cambridge Quarterly of Healthcare Ethics* 17.

'What must we mean by "community"? A processive account' (2004) 25 *Theoretical Medicine* 423.

Mill J. S. 'On Liberty' (1859), in J. Gray (ed.), *On Liberty and Other Essays* (Oxford: Oxford University Press, 1998).

Milsom, S. F. C. 'Trespasses from Henry III to Edward III. Part I: General writs' (1958) 74 *Law Quarterly Review* 195.

'Trespasses from Henry III to Edward III. Part III: More special writs and conclusions' (1958) 74 *Law Quarterly Review* 561.

Historical Foundations of the Common Law, 2nd edn (London: Butterworths, 1981).

Miola, J. 'Autonomy rued OK?' (2006) 14 *Medical Law Review* 108.

Medical Ethics and Medical Law: A symbiotic relationship (Oxford: Hart Publishing, 2007).

Mitchell J. 'ABC of breast diseases: A fundamental problem of consent' (1995) 310 *British Medical Journal* 43.

Mold, M. S. A. (ed.) *Select Cases of Trespass from the King's Courts 1307–1399*, vol. 1 (London: Seldon Society, 1985).

Montgomery, J. 'Power/Knowledge/Consent: Medical decisionmaking' (1988) 51 *The Modern Law Review* 245.

'Victims or threats?: The framing of HIV' (1990) 12 *The Liverpool Law Review* 25.

'The role of law in raising standards of consent', in P. Alderson (ed.), *Consent to Health Treatment and Research: Differing perspectives* (London: The Social Science Research Unit, 1994), p. 35.

'Time for a paradigm shift? Medical law in transition' (2000) 53 *Current Legal Problems* 363.

Health Care Law, 2nd edn (Oxford: Oxford University Press 2003).

Montrose, J. L. 'Is negligence an ethical or a sociological concept?' (1958) *Modern Law Review* 259.

Morgan, D. *Issues in Medical Law and Ethics* (London: Cavendish Publishing, 2001).

Mulcahy, L. 'Threatening behaviour? The challenge posed by medical negligence claims', in M. Freeman and A. Lewis (eds.), *Law and Medicine, Current Legal Issues*, vol. 3 (Oxford: Oxford University Press, 2000), p. 81.

Murphy, G. L. and Medin, D. L. 'The role of theories in conceptual coherence' (1985) 92 *Psychological Review* 289.

Murphy, L. B. 'Institutions and the demands of justice' (1998) 27 *Philosophy and Public Affairs* 251.

Murphy, P. 'Are patients' decisions to refuse treatment binding on health care professionals?' (2005) 19 *Bioethics* 189.

Myles, P. S., Williams, D. L., Hendrata, M., Anderson, H. and Weeks, A. M. 'Patient satisfaction after anaesthesia and surgery: Results of a prospective survey of 10,811 patients' (2000) 84 *British Journal of Anaesthesia* 6.

Nagel, T. *Mortal Questions* (New York: Cambridge University Press, 1979).

The Last Word (New York: Oxford University Press, 1997).

Nathan, N. M. L. *The Concept of Justice* (London: Macmillan Press, 1971).

National Audit Office *Handling Clinical Negligence Claims in England* (2001) HC 403 Session 2000–2001.

Neale, G. 'Informed consent' (2000) 46 *Gut* 5.

Nedelsky, J. 'Reconceiving autonomy: Sources, thoughts and possibilities' (1989) 1 *Yale Journal of Law and Feminism* 7.

Nessa, J. 'Autonomy and dialogue: About the patient–doctor relationship', in D. C. Thomasma, D. N. Weisstub and C. Herve (eds.), *Personhood and Health Care* (Dordrecht: Kluwer Academic Publishers, 2001), p. 355.

Newdick, C. 'The doctor's duties of care under *Sidaway*' (1985) 36 *Northern Ireland Legal Quarterly* 243.

Noggle, R. 'The public conception of autonomy and critical self-reflection' (1997) 35 *The Southern Journal of Philosophy* 495.

Oakley, J. 'A virtue ethics approach', in H. Kuhse and P. Singer (eds.), *A Companion to Bioethics* (Oxford: Blackwell Publishing, 1998), p. 86.

Omerod D. 'Consent and offences against the person: Law Commission consultation paper no. 134' (1994) 57 *Modern Law Review* 929.

O'Neill, O. *Towards Justice and Virtues* (Cambridge: Cambridge University Press, 1996).

Bounds of Justice (Cambridge: Cambridge University Press, 2000).

Autonomy and Trust in Bioethics (Cambridge: Cambridge University Press, 2002).

Ong, L. M. L., De Haes, C. J. M., Hoos, A. M. and Lammes, F. B. 'Doctor–patient communication: A review of the literature' (1995) 49 *Social Science and Medicine* 903.

Oshana, M. 'How much should we value autonomy' (2003) 20 *Social Philosophy and Policy* 99.

Osuch, J. R. 'The power of the doctor, the vulnerability of the patient, and informed consent' (2004) 61 *Surgical Neurology* 494.

The Oxford English Dictionary (Oxford: Oxford University Press, 1971).

Parfit, D. *Reasons and Persons* (Oxford: Clarendon Press, 1984).

Patel, V. L. and Kushniruk, A. W. 'Understanding, navigating and communicating knowledge: Issues and challenges' (1998) 37 *Methods of Information in Medicine* 560.

Paul, E. F., Miller, F. D. and Paul, J. 'Introduction', in E. F. Paul, F. D. Miller and J. Paul (eds.), *Virtue and Vice* (Cambridge: Cambridge University Press, 1998), p. vii.

Pellegrino, E. D. 'Patient and physician autonomy: Conflicting rights and obligations in the physician–patient relationship' (1994) 10 *Journal of Contemporary Health Law and Policy* 47.

Pellegrino, E. D. and Thomasma, D. C. *The Virtues in Medical Practice* (New York: Oxford University Press, 1993).

Peters, E. and Challis, M. 'Most doctors see consent from functionalist perspective' (1999) 318 *British Medical Journal* 735.

Philipp, E. E. and Johnson, E. S. 'Considerations governing a doctor's advice to his patient', in G. R. Dunstan and M. J. Seller (eds.), *Consent in Medicine: Convergence and divergence in tradition* (London: King Edward's Hospital Fund, 1983), p. 89.

Pollock, A. M. *NHS plc: The privatisation of our health care* (London: Verso, 2004).

Pollock, F. and Maitland, F. W. *The History of English Law*, vol. 2, 2nd edn (Cambridge: Cambridge University Press, 1898).

Potter, H. *An Historical Introduction to English Law and its Institutions*, 3rd edn (London: Sweet & Maxwell Ltd, 1948).

Potter, S. J. and McKinlay, J. B. 'From a relationship to encounter: An examination of longitudinal and lateral dimensions in the doctor-patient relationship' (2005) 61 *Social Science and Medicine* 465.

The President's Commission for the Study of Ethical Problems in Medicine and Biomedical and Behavioral Research *Making Health Care Decisions: The ethical and legal implications of informed consent in the patient–practitioner relationship, vol. one: Report* (Washington D.C., 1982).

Prichard, M. J. 'Trespass, case and the rule in Williams v Holland' (1964) *Cambridge Law Journal* 234.

Provis, C. and Stack, S. 'Caring work, personal obligation and collective responsibility' (2004) 11 *Nursing Ethics* 5.

Putman, D. 'Virtue and the practice of modern medicine' (1988) 13 *Journal of Medicine and Philosophy* 433.

Quante, M. 'Precedent autonomy and personal identity' (1999) 9 *Kennedy Institute of Ethics Journal* 365.

Quill, T. E. and Brody, H. 'Physician recommendations and patient autonomy: Finding a balance between physician power and patient choice' (1996) 125 *Annals of Internal Medicine* 763.

Quist, N. 'The paradox of questions and answers: Possibilities for a doctor–patient relationship' (2003) 14 *The Journal of Clinical Ethics* 79.

Renton, D. *The Preparation of Legislation: Report of a committee appointed by the Lord President of the Council*, Cmnd 6053 (London: HMSO, 1975).

Reynolds, M. 'No news is bad news: Patients' views about communication in hospital' (1978) 1 *British Medical Journal* 1673.

Rhoden, N. K. 'The judge in the delivery room: The emergence of court-ordered cesareans' (1986) 74 *California Law Review* 1951.

Rhodes, R. 'Understanding the trusted doctor and constructing a theory of bioethics' (2001) 22 *Theoretical Medicine* 493.

Rich, B. A. 'Personhood, patienthood, and clinical practice: Reassessing advance directives' (1998) 4 *Psychology, Public Policy, and Law* 610.

Richards, D. A. J. 'Rights and autonomy' (1981) 92 *Ethics* 3.

Richman, K. A. *Ethics and the Metaphysics of Medicine: Reflections on health and beneficence* (Cambridge, Mass.: The MIT Press, 2004).

Roberts, E. '*Re C* and the boundaries of autonomy' (1994) 10 *Professional Negligence* 98.

Roberts, P. 'Consent to injury: How far can you go?' (1997) 113 *The Law Quarterly Review* 27.

Robertson, G. 'Informed consent to medical treatment' (1981) 97 *Law Quarterly Review* 102.

'Informed consent ten years later: The impact of Reibl v Hughes' (1991) 70 *The Canadian Bar Review* 423.

Robyn Kennedy & Co. Pty Ltd *National Community Housing Forum: A regulatory framework for community housing in Australia, vol. 2: Regulatory options. Final report* (2001).

Rodgers, B. L. 'Concepts, analysis and the development of nursing knowledge: The evolutionary cycle' (1989) 14 *Journal of Advanced Nursing* 330.

Rogers, W. A. 'Is there a moral duty for doctors to trust patients?' (2002) 28 *Journal of Medical Ethics* 77.

Rössler, B. 'Problems with autonomy' (2002) 17 *Hypatia* 143.

Roter. D. 'The medical visit context of treatment decision-making and the therapeutic relationship' (2000) 3 *Health Expectations* 17.

Roth, L. H., Meisel, A. and Lidz, C. W. 'Tests of competency to consent to treatment' (1977) 134 *American Journal of Psychiatry* 279.

Rothman, D. J. 'The origins and consequences of patient autonomy: A 25-year retrospective' (2001) 9 *Health Care Analysis* 255–64.

Rudinow, J. 'Manipulation' (1978) 88 *Ethics* 338.

Ryan, A. 'Introduction', in A. Ryan (ed.), *Justice* (Oxford: Oxford University Press, 1993), p. 1.

Salmon, P. and Hall, G. M. 'Patient empowerment or the emperor's new clothes' (2004) 97 *Journal of the Royal Society of Medicine* 53.

Sandel, M. J. *Liberalism and the Limits of Justice*, 2nd edn (Cambridge: Cambridge University Press, 1998).

Sandin, R. H., Enlund, G., Samuelsson, P. and Lennmarken, C. 'Awareness during anaesthesia: A prospective case study' (2000) 355 *Lancet* 707.

Sang, B. 'Choice, participation and accountability: Assessing the potential impact of legislation promoting patient and public involvement in health in the UK' (2004) 7 *Health Expectations* 187.

Savulescu, J. 'Rational non-interventional paternalism: Why doctors ought to make judgments of what is best for their patients' (1995) 21 *Journal of Medical Ethics* 327.

Scheffler, S. 'Relationships and responsibilities' (1997) 26 *Philosophy and Public Affairs* 189.

Schneider, C. and Farrell, M. 'The limits of informed consent', in M. Freeman and A. Lewis (eds.), *Law and Medicine, Current Legal Issues*, vol. 3 (Oxford: Oxford University Press, 2000), p. 107.

Schneider, C. E. *The Practice of Autonomy: Patients, doctors, and medical decisions* (New York: Oxford University Press, 1998).

Schuck, P. H. 'Informed consent in the US: Perspectives from tort law', in L. Westerhall and C. Phillips (eds.), *Patient's Rights: Informed consent, access and equality* (Stockholm: Nerenius & Santerus Publishers, 1994), p. 383.

Scoccia, D. 'Paternalism and autonomy' (1990) 100 *Ethics* 318.

Scott, R. *Rights, Duties and the Body: Law and ethics of the maternal-fetal conflict* (Oxford: Hart Publishing, 2002).

Scott, W. '*Bolam* and *Bolitho*: A new standard of care for doctors?' (1998) 148 *New Law Journal* 64.

Seabourne, G. 'The role of the tort of battery on medical law' (1995) 24 *Anglo-American Law Review* 265.

Secker, B. 'The appearance of Kant's deontology in contemporary Kantianism: Concepts of patient autonomy in bioethics' (1999) 24 *Journal of Medicine and Philosophy* 43.

Seeman, M. and Seeman, T. E. 'Health behavior and personal autonomy: A longitudinal study of the sense of control in illness' (1983) 24 *Journal of Health and Social Behavior* 144.

Sher, G. 'Ethics, character and action', in E. F. Paul, F. D. Miller and J. Paul (eds.), *Virtue and Vice* (Cambridge: Cambridge University Press, 1998), p. 1.

Sherwin, E. 'Infelicitous sex' (1996) 2 *Legal Theory* 209.

Sillender, M. 'Can patients be sure they are fully informed when representatives of surgical equipment manufacturers attend their operations?' (2006) 32 *Journal of Medical Ethics* 395.

Simester, A. P. and Sullivan, G. R. *Criminal Law: Theory and doctrine* (Oxford: Hart Publishing, 2000).

Skegg, P. D. G. 'English medical law and "informed consent": An antipodean assessment and alternative' (1999) 7 *Medical Law Review* 135.

Slote, M. 'The justice of caring', in E. F. Paul, F. D. Miller and J. Paul (eds.), *Virtue and Vice* (Cambridge: Cambridge University Press, 1998), p. 171.

Slote, M. A. 'Desert, consent, and justice' (1973) 4 *Philosophy and Public Affairs* 323.

Smith, D. G. and Newton, L. H. 'Physician and patient' (1984) 5 *Theoretical Medicine* 43.

Smith, D. H. and Pettegrew, L. S. 'Mutual persuasion as a model for doctor–patient communication' (1986) 7 *Theoretical Medicine* 127.

Smith, J. *The 5th Shipman Report, Safeguarding Patients: Lessons from the past – proposals for the future*, Cm 6394 (2004).

Smith, J. C. *Justification and Excuse in the Criminal Law* (London: Stevens & Sons, 1989).

Smith, R. 'GMC under the cosh' (1998) 316 *British Medical Journal* 945.

'GMC: Expediency before principle' (2005) 330 *British Medical Journal* 1.

Somerville, M. A. 'Structuring the issues in informed consent' (1981) 26 *McGill Law Journal* 740.

Speeding, E. J. and Rose, D. N. 'Building an effective doctor–patient relationship: From patient satisfaction to patient participation' (1985) 21 *Social Science and Medicine* 115.

Stauch, M. 'Causation, risk, and loss of chance in medical negligence' (1997) 17 *Oxford Journal of Legal Studies* 205.

Stirrat, G. M. and Gill, R. 'Autonomy in medical ethics after O'Neill' (2005) 31 *Journal of Medical Ethics* 127.

Stone, J. 'Justice not equality', in E. Kamenka and A. Erh-Soon Tay (eds.), *Justice* (London: Edward Arnold, 1979), p. 97.

Strong, P. M. 'Sociological imperialism and the profession of medicine: A critical examination of the thesis of medical imperialism' (1979) 13A *Social Science and Medicine* 199.

Szasz, T. *The Theology of Medicine* (New York: Syracuse University Press, 1988).

Takala, T. 'Concepts of "person" and "liberty", and their implications to our fading notions of autonomy' (2007) 33 *Journal of Medical Ethics* 225.

Tauber, A. I. 'Historical and philosophical reflections on patient autonomy' (2001) 9 *Health Care Analysis* 299.

'Sick autonomy' (2003) 46 *Perspectives in Biology and Medicine* 484.

Patient Autonomy and the Ethics of Responsibility (Cambridge, Mass.: MIT Press, 2005).

Taylor, J. S. 'Autonomy and informed consent: A much misunderstood relationship' (2004) 38 *The Journal of Value Inquiry* 383.

Teff, H. 'Consent to medical procedures: Paternalism, self-determination or therapeutic alliance' (1985) 101 *The Law Quarterly Review* 432.

Reasonable Care (Oxford: Clarendon Press, 1994).

'The standard of care in medical negligence: Moving on from Bolam?' (1998) 18 *Oxford Journal of Legal Studies* 473.

Thompson, P. 'Home birth: Consumer choice and restriction of physician autonomy' (1987) 6 *Journal of Business Ethics* 481.

Thorpe, Lord Justice, 'The caesarean section debate' (1997) *Family Law* 663.

Tomlinson, T. 'The physician's influence on patients' choices' (1986) 7 *Theoretical Medicine* 105.

Trinidade, F. A. 'Intentional torts: Some thoughts on assault and battery' (1982) 2 *Oxford Journal of Legal Studies* 211.

Tsanoff, R. A. 'Social morality and the principle of justice' (1956) 67 *Ethics* 12.

Ulrich, L. P. *The Patient Self-Determination Act: Meeting the challenges in patient care* (Washington D.C.: Georgetown University Press, 1999).

Usher, K. J. and Arthur, D. 'Process consent: A model for enhancing informed consent in mental health nursing' (1998) 27 *Journal of Advanced Nursing* 692.

Valimaki, M., Leino-Kilpi, H., Gronroos, M., Dassen, T., Gasull, M., Lemonidou, C., Scott, P. A. and Sr. Benedicta, M. 'Self-determination in surgical patients in five European countries' (2004) 34 *Journal of Nursing Scholarship* 305.

Varelius, J. 'Autonomy, subject-relativity, and subjective and objective theories of well-being in bioethics' (2003) 24 *Theoretical Medicine* 363.

Veatch, R. M. 'Models for ethical medicine in a revolutionary age' (June 1972) 2 *Hastings Center Report* 5.

'Doctor does not know best: Why in the new century physicians must stop trying to benefit patients' (2000) 25 *Journal of Medicine and Philosophy* 701.

Waldron, J. 'Vagueness in law and language: Some philosophical issues' (1994) 82 *California Law Review* 509.

Waller, B. M. 'The psychological structure of patient autonomy' (2002) 11 *Cambridge Quarterly of Healthcare Ethics* 257.

Walton, D. N. 'What is reasoning? What is an argument?' (1990) 87 *The Journal of Philosophy* 399.

Waltz, J. R. and Scheuneman, T. W. 'Informed consent to therapy' (1970) 64 NWUL Rev. 628.

Warren, M. A. 'On the moral and legal status of abortion', in L. Gruen and G. E. Panichas (eds.), *Sex, Morality and the Law* (London: Routledge, 1997), p. 302.

Wear, S. 'Patient autonomy, paternalism, and the conscientious physician' (1983) 4 *Theoretical Medicine* 253.

Informed Consent: Patient autonomy and clinician beneficence within health care, 2nd edn (Washington D.C.: Georgetown University Press, 1998).

Werner, A. and Malterud, K. 'It is hard work behaving as a credible patient: Encounters between women with chronic pain and their doctors' (2003) 57 *Social Science and Medicine* 1409.

Wertheimer, A. 'Consent and sexual relations' (1996) 2 *Legal Theory*, 89.

Wertheimer, A. 'What is consent? And is it important?' (2000) 3 *Buffalo Criminal Law Review* 557.

West, R. 'A comment on consent, sex, and rape' (1996) 2 *Legal Theory* 233.

White, S. M. 'Consent for anaesthesia' (2003) 30 *Journal of Medical Ethics* 286.

Whitney, S. 'A new model of medical decisions: Exploring the limits of shared decision making' (2003) 23 *Medical Decision Making* 275.

Wicclair, M. R. 'Patient decision-making capacity and risk' (1991) 5 *Bioethics* 91.

'The continuing debate over risk-related standards of competence' (1999) 13 *Bioethics* 149.

Wilks, I. 'Asymmetrical competence' (1999) 13 *Bioethics* 154.

Williams, B. *Moral Luck* (New York: Cambridge University Press, 1981).

Williams, G. 'Consent and public policy' (1962) *Criminal Law Review* 74.

'The logic of exceptions' (1988) 47 *Cambridge Law Journal* 261.

Williams, G. and Hepple, B. A. *Foundations of the Law of Tort*, 2nd edn (London: Butterworths, 1984).

Williams, G. C., Rodin, G. C., Ryan, R. M., Grolnick, W. S. and Deci, E. L. 'Autonomous regulation and long-term medication adherence in adult outpatients' (1998) 17 *Health Psychology* 269.

Williams, G. L. 'The foundations of tortious liability' (1939) 7 *Cambridge Law Journal* 111.

Williams, K. 'Pre-operative consent and medical negligence' (1985) 15 *Anglo-American Law Review* 169.

'Comprehending disclosure: Must patients understand the risks they run?' (2000) 4 *Medical Law International* 97.

Wilson, J. 'Is respect for autonomy defensible?' (2007) 33 *Journal of Medical Ethics* 353.

Winick, B. J. 'Competency to consent to treatment: The distinction between assent and objection', in D. B. Wexler and B. J. Winick (eds.), *Essays in Therapeutic Jurisprudence* (Durham, NC: Carolina Academic Press, 1991), p. 41.

Wolf, S. 'Sanity and the metaphysics of responsibility', in F. Schoeman (ed.), *Responsibility, Character and the Emotions* (Cambridge: Cambridge University Press, 1987), p. 46.

'The importance of free will', in J. M. Fischer and M. Ravizza (eds.), *Perspectives on Moral Responsibility* (Ithaca, NY: Cornell University Press, 1993), p. 101.

Lord Woolf 'Are the courts excessively deferential to the medical profession?' (2001) 9 *Medical Law Review* 1.

Working Group on Hate Crime, *Consultation Paper* (Edinburgh: Scottish Executive, 2004).

Worthington, R. 'Clinical issues on consent: Some philosophical concerns' (2002) 28 *Journal of Medical Ethics* 377.

'Ethical dichotomies and methods of seeking consent' (2004) 59 *Anaesthesia* 525.

Wright, M. 'Medical treatment: The right to refuse' (1993) *Journal of Social Welfare and Family Law* 204.

Young, P. W. *The Law of Consent* (North Ryde, NSW: The Law Book Company Ltd, 1986).

Young, R. 'Autonomy and the "inner self"', in J. Christman (ed.), *The Inner Citadel* (New York: Oxford University Press, 1989), p. 77.

Index

abilities
  justice and 61
abortion 95, 116
action
  autonomous acts 12, 19, 45, 91
  freedom of 12
  offensive actions 35
actual bodily harm 153
agency 44, 136, 137, 244, 261
  autonomy and 23–4, 235
  future selves and 39, 41
  model of information 227
  moral 75, 76
agreements
  consent as 112, 126, 142, 263
arbitrary claims 13
Arneson, R. J. 54
Association of Anaesthetists 106
autonomy 9, 45, 48, 53, 111, 139, 215,
  222, 227, 261
  action for harm to 197, 202
  autonomous acts 12, 19, 45, 91
  autonomous persons 12, 19, 45
  children 75
  consent and 41–5, 46, 144, 261, 264
    relational model 232
  etymology 10
  failure to lead autonomous life 26
  justice and 58, 59–63
  limits of 29–30, 46
    future selves 38–41
    harm principle 30–3, 36
    other limiting principles 33–5
    protection of future autonomy 36–8
  locus of control and 91
  mandatory 97–101
  as moral basis for consent 41–5
  nature of 9–11
  paternalism and 55
  professional–patient relationships and
    76, 80, 84, 86, 90, 94–5
  protection of future autonomy 36–8

relational model 235, 247, 266
as self-determination 11–13
  as moral rational self-determination
    17–22, 45
  as rational self-determination 13–17,
    45, 59
  value of 23–9, 46

Barilan, Y. M. 85
battery 150–2, 190, 191–6, 218, 238, 260,
  265, 266
  consent and 153–4, 195, 222, 237
Beauchamp, T. L. 56, 57, 129
behaviour
  justice and 62
  professional–patient relationships and
    94
beneficence principle 48, 49–51, 56, 70,
  223, 237, 261, 263
  paternalism and 51
  professional–patient relationships and
    88, 89, 90, 92
Berg, J. W. 208
best interests of patients 207
Biegler, P. 127–8
bioethics 260
Bolam test 164–5, 166, 167, 168, 169, 170,
  172, 198, 203, 208
  Bolitho case and 172–7
Brazier, M. 173, 176, 177, 206
breach of consent 238, 259
Bristol Royal Infirmary Inquiry 69
British Medical Association (BMA) 49
Brock, D. W. 51
burden of proof
  battery 153
Burkitt Wright, E. 93

capacity *see* competence and capacity
care 74, 203
  delivery of care 106, 225–6
  holistic approach to care 107

professional–patient relationships and
    89, 90, 103, 125, 162
  standard of 167–8, 169–83, 198, 204,
    265
  team approach to care 107
carelessness 209
categorical imperative 20, 21, 227
causation 200, 213, 259
  disclosure of information and 183–4,
    190
    content of test 187–8
    nature of test 184–7, 200
caveat emptor 108
challenging decisions 83, 89, 204
chance
  loss of 197
children
  autonomy 75
  parental involvement in decisions about
    128
  refusal of consent 132
  refusal of treatment 210
  relationships with 75
Childress, J. F. 56, 57, 129
choice
  consent as 124–7
codes of practice 217–18, 246
coercion 158, 229, 237
collateral risks 161–2
common law
  problems of 214–16, 219, 224, 266
communication 81, 244
  consent and 119, 120, 121, 143, 145,
    223, 228, 232, 234, 267
  professional–patient relationships 244
  trust and 244
communitarianism 10, 11, 108, 222
  health service delivery and 225, 226
compassion 74, 103
competence and capacity
  for autonomy 37, 38, 60, 140
  to benefit 62
  consent and 140–1, 154–6, 193, 241
  emergency treatment 253
  for rationality 19
  refusal of treatment and 210, 212
complaints system 214
compulsory testing and treatment 82
conduit model of information 230
confidence
  loss of 91
conscience
  rights of 95
consent 9, 62, 67, 69, 72, 79, 110, 142–3,
    222, 262

absent 146
addressing gap between practice and
    principle 217–18
  as agreement 112, 126, 142, 263
  answering questions and 168–9, 236,
    245, 246
  autonomy and 41–5, 46, 144, 261, 264
    relational model 232
  battery 153–4, 195, 222, 237
  breach of consent 238, 259
  as choice 124–7
  competence and 140–1, 154–6, 193, 241
  definition 110–13, 121
  development of law 220–1
    cycle of criticism and scope for further
      development 221–5
  disclosure of information and 163–9,
    190
  duration 124
  effect of 255–7
  emergency treatment and 208, 253–5
  form of 255
  ineffective 146
  information, knowledge and risk 134–9
  informed 41–2, 125, 151, 160, 193, 199,
    216, 217, 226
  legal regulation *see* legal regulation of
    consent
  limits to 122, 235
  Manson and O'Neill's model of genuine
    consent 226–31, 232, 267
  as mental state 113, 114, 119, 121, 124,
    142, 234
  model 143, 191
  nature and function of consent to
    medical treatment 113–22, 141–2
  negligence and 162–3, 196–209
    Sidaway case and standard of
      disclosure 163–9
    standard of care 167–8, 169–83, 198
  non-treatment and 127–9, 182–3,
    212–13, 234, 258
  obligation to facilitate understanding and
    good decision-making 246–50
  outcome responsibility and 118, 119,
    232, 236, 256–7, 264
  as permission 113, 115, 126, 142, 234,
    255–7, 263
  power and control and 133–4
  presumed 145
  problems of common law 214–16, 219,
    224, 266
  process of 122–4, 241–6
  professional–patient relationships and 76
  real 159–62, 194

consent (*cont.*)
    refusal 130–2, 143, 146, 257–8, 264
    relational model 231–3, 247, 266
        implementation 233
    shared decision-making and 129–30
    therapeutic privilege 183, 202, 205,
        206, 208
    voluntariness and 139–40, 156–9
    waiver of right to 100, 123, 264
consequences 48
consequentialism 54
constructivist model of decision-making
    14
consultation process 217
context dependence 229
control 90
    consent and 133–4
    locus of 91
    over information 236, 243
controversial treatments 204
cooperation
    professional–patient relationships and 92
corporal punishment 158
corrective justice 63, 64, 202
cosmetic treatments 239
counselling 179, 180, 181
critical self-reflection 18

damage 188–9, 196
damages 128, 188
day surgery 106
deception 85, 87, 90
decision-making
    rationality and 14
defensive approach to consent 106
deferring decisions 82
delays 242
delivery of care 106, 225–6
deontology 68
Department of Health 106
dependency 100, 222
determinism 10, 18, 25, 26
development of law 220–1
    cycle of criticism and scope for further
        development 221–5
Dickenson, D. 65
disclosure of information 134, 174, 190,
    193, 201, 203, 204, 213, 218, 224
    causation and 183–4, 190
    content of test 187–8
        nature of test 184–7, 200
    emergency treatment and 208, 253–5
    exceptions 253–5
    genuine consent model 229–31
    measuring outcome 250–3

obligation to facilitate understanding and
    good decision-making 246–50
relevance 241
Sidaway case and standard of disclosure
    163–9
timing of 56
understanding and 177–80, 193
dishonesty 237
distress
    information likely to cause 207, 208
distributive justice 63, 125, 202
doctor–patient relationships *see*
    professional–patient relationships
duration of consent 124
duress 229
Dworkin, Gerald 10, 39

education 105
Eekelaar, J. 77
effect of consent 255–7
emergency treatment 243
    consent and 208, 253–5
empathy 74, 78, 79
equality
    justice and 57, 61
ethics 214, 224
    bioethics 260
    virtue ethics 67–70, 71
experts 43
    expert evidence 170, 199
explanation of decisions 96, 146

factory model of care 108
false consciousness argument for
    mandatory autonomy 99
Feinberg, J. 32
fiduciary relationships 74
Ford, Henry 38
form of consent 255
fraud 229, 237
future
    development of law 220–1
        cycle of criticism and scope for further
            development 221–5
    future selves 38–41
    legal regulation 220
    proposed principles 234–6, 237–41
    protection of future autonomy 36–8

garrison model 32
Gaut, B. 14
Gauthier, C. C. 17
General Medical Council (GMC) 214, 218
general risk 166
genetic counselling 83

genuine consent model 226–31, 232, 267
Giesen, D. 186
Gill, R. 125
Gillon, R. 111
goals 53
good life 14, 34
goods 27
government and the state 28, 216, 257
  healthcare systems and 108
  justice and 58
Grubb, A. 183
guilt 86

harm principle 30–3, 36, 60
Harris, J. 132
Hayes, J. 186
Hayry, M. 34
Helsinki Declaration 119
Heywood, R. 217
Hippocratic Oath 49
holistic approach to care 107
Honoré, T. 64
Hume, David 15, 20
humility 104
Hurd, H. M. 114, 115, 116

identity
  autonomy and 26, 99
  future selves 38–41
  real consent and 161–2
indemnity 257
indeterminacy 67
information 80, 82
  agency model 227
  conduit model 230
  consent and 134–9
  control over 236, 243
  disclosure see disclosure of information
  likely to cause distress 207, 208
  misinterpretation 87
  misunderstanding 86
  overburdening with 230
  questions 168–9, 236, 245, 246
  understanding see understanding
  waiver of right to 100, 201–2, 207, 245,
    251, 264
informed consent 41–2, 125, 151, 160,
  193, 199, 216, 217, 226
institutions 73
  professional–patient relationships and
    106–7
instrumental approach to rationality 15,
  222
instrumental value of autonomy 27
insurance 257

integrity 104
intention
  consent as 114
Internet 80
interpretation 67, 68
irrationality 52, 53, 55, 82, 96, 198

Jones, M. A. 173, 214
justice 57–9, 70, 71, 104, 262
  autonomy and 58, 59–63
  corrective justice 63, 64, 202
  distributive justice 63, 125, 202
  resources and 58, 61–3
  responsibility and 58, 63–7

Kant, Immanuel 15, 16, 17, 20, 21, 22,
  44, 222, 227
Kennedy, I. 205
knowledge
  consent and 134–9
Korsgaard, C. M. 16, 39, 40
Kuczewski, M. 122

language 67
Law Commission
  competence/capacity and 154
legal regulation of consent 149–50, 190,
  191, 195, 218, 233, 260, 265, 266
  future 220
    obligation to facilitate understanding
      and good decision-making
      246–50
    proposed principles 234–6, 237–41
    regulation of process 241–6
  negligence and 162–3
legislation 217, 268–9
Levi, B. H. 28, 37
liabilities 258–9
liberalism
  autonomy and 10, 11, 15, 18, 44, 202,
    216, 260
  consent and 223, 226, 260
libertarianism 80
  autonomy and 10, 11, 18, 44, 222,
    226
limits
  autonomy 29–30, 46
    future selves 38–41
    harm principle 30–3, 36
    other limiting principles 33–5
    protection of future autonomy 36–8
  consent 122, 235
locus of control 91
logical argument for mandatory autonomy
  100

loss of chance claim 197
luck 118
lying 22, 87

Maclean, M. 77
mandatory autonomy 97–101
manipulation 85, 86, 87, 90
Manson, Neil C. 15, 21, 44, 45, 46, 136,
    137, 138, 139, 225, 237, 243, 244,
    246, 266
  model of genuine consent 226–31, 232,
    267
market systems 107, 225, 226
marriage 77
May, T. 95
McKinstry, B. 81
medical treatment 35
  beneficence principle 48, 49–51, 56, 70,
    223, 237, 261, 263
    paternalism and 51
    professional–patient relationships and
    88, 89, 90, 92
  consent to see consent
  controversial treatments 204
  doctor–patient relationships see
    professional–patient relationships
  experts 43
    expert evidence 170, 199
  medically indicated 95
  moral luck and 65
  paternalism and 52–4, 56, 57
  recommending treatment 205
  risk of see risk
Meisel, A. 122
mental illness
  consent and 153
  information likely to cause distress 207
  refusal of treatment and 211
mental state
  consent as 113, 114, 119, 121, 124, 142,
    234
Mill, J. S. 27, 30, 34, 35, 38, 83
Miola, J. 173, 176, 177
misinterpretation 86, 87
mistakes
  learning and 34
  paternalism and 52
misunderstanding 86, 178
Montgomery, J. 73, 173
moral luck 65
moral responsibility 78
moral status
  children 75
morality
  autonomy and 23, 25, 34

autonomy as moral basis for consent
    41–5
moral argument for mandatory
    autonomy 99–100
moral rational self-determination 17–22,
    45
murder
  consent and 116
Murphy, L. B. 59

National Audit Office 214
National Institute for Health and Clinical
    Excellence (NICE) 88
necessity defence 154
Nedelsky, J. 18
negligence 127–8, 191–6, 215, 218, 229,
    265, 266
  causation and 183–4, 190
    content of test 187–8
    nature of test 184–7, 200
  consent and 162–3, 196–209
    Sidaway case and standard of
    disclosure 163–9
    standard of care 167–8, 169–83, 198
  legally recognised damage 188–9
neo-Humeans 15, 20, 222
NHS Redress scheme 215
no-fault compensation system 119
non-interference 246
non-maleficence principle 48
  professional–patient relationships and 88
non-reciprocal relationships 93
non-treatment 127–9, 182–3, 212–13, 234,
    258
novel claims 215
Nursing and Midwifery Council (NMC)
    218

offensive actions 35
O'Neill, Onora 15, 17, 21, 23, 44, 45, 46,
    136, 137, 138, 139, 222, 225, 237,
    243, 244, 246, 266
  model of genuine consent 226–31, 232,
    267
outcome responsibility
  consent and 118, 119, 232, 236, 256–7,
    264
  justice and 58, 63–7
overriding decisions 54, 250

Parfit, D. 36, 38, 39, 40
paternalism 51–7, 60, 69, 70, 111, 167,
    207, 220, 221, 224
Patients Association 260
Pellegrino, E. D. 69

permission
  consent and 113, 115, 126, 142, 234,
    255–7, 263
persuasion 84, 87, 96, 156, 247, 266
  professional's duty to persuade 180–2
politics
  consent and 107
power
  consent and 133–4
  professional–patient relationships and
    81, 87, 90, 94, 95, 145, 241
pressure for change 222
presumed consent 145
prisoners
  consent and 158
privacy 242
private treatment 127
privilege
  therapeutic 183, 202, 205, 206, 208
procedural dependency 100
professionalism 102–5
professional–patient relationships 72–9,
    108–9, 111, 112, 120, 215, 232, 234,
    262, 269
  communication and 244
  consent and 225
  duty of care 89, 90, 103, 125, 162
  external factors 105–8
  obligation to facilitate understanding and
    good decision-making 246–50
  patient's obligations 93–7, 143
    mandatory autonomy and 97–101
  power and 81, 87, 90, 94, 95, 145, 241
  professional's obligations 79–93
  virtue of professionalism and
    professional virtues 102–5
  virtuous patient 101–2
prophylaxis argument for mandatory
    autonomy 98
prudence 104
  prudent-patient standard 164, 167, 168,
    200, 206, 221, 251
public-health concerns 153
public interests 32

questions
  answering 168–9, 236, 245, 246

rape
  consent and 115, 121
rationality 33, 222, 223
  autonomy as rational self-determination
    13–17, 45, 59
  definition 13
  rational self-reflection 26

reaction 24
real consent 159–62, 194
reasons for decisions 248–50
recognitional model of decision-making 14
recognitional rationality 222, 223
recommending treatment 205
reductionism 36
refusal of treatment 83, 95, 126, 150,
    209–12
  non-treatment 127–9, 182–3, 212–13,
    234, 258
  refusal of consent 130–2, 143, 146,
    257–8, 264
  religious grounds 159, 210
  withholding treatment 127–9
regulation 233, 265
  consent 149–50, 190, 191, 195, 218,
    233, 260, 265, 266
    future 220
    negligence and 162–3
    obligation to facilitate understanding
      and good decision-making
      246–50
    proposed principles 234–6, 237–41
    regulation of process 241–6
relational dependence 222
relational model of consent 231–3, 247,
    266
  implementation 233
relationships see professional–patient
    relationships
religion
  refusal of treatment and 159
remedies 258–9
  damages 128, 188
research
  consent and 118, 151, 239
resources 127
  justice and 58, 61–3
respect
  professional–patient relationships and
    78, 94
responsibility
  consent and 118, 119, 232, 236, 256–7,
    264
  justice and 58, 63–7
  moral 78
Richards, D. A. J. 25
rights 133
  bodily integrity 234
  consent and 117, 122, 124, 227, 231,
    235
  see also self-determination
risk 54, 69, 95, 260
  collateral risks 161–2

risk (*cont.*)
  consent and 134–9
  disclosure of information and 163–9,
    174, 190, 193
  failure to disclose 256
  general 166
  material 164
  specific 166
Robertson, G. 207
Rössler, B. 26

Schneider, C. 97, 98, 99, 100
second opinions 213
self-determination 10, 28, 37, 45, 99, 207,
    221, 223, 227
  autonomy as 11–13
  as moral rational self-determination
    17–22, 45
  as rational self-determination 13–17,
    45, 59
  legal right 149
  paternalism and 52
self-fulfilment 28
self-help groups 94
self-knowledge 27
self-reflection
  critical 18
  rational 26
self-regulation 233
shared decision-making
  consent and 129–30
Skegg, P. D. G. 173
social conditioning 105
specific risk 166
Stirrat, G. M. 125
Stone, J. 57
submission
  consent and 113
substantive dependency 100
Szasz, T. 48

Taylor, J. S. 41, 42, 43, 44, 46
team approach to care 107
temperance 104
test results 57
therapeutic argument for mandatory
    autonomy 98–9

therapeutic privilege 183, 202, 205, 206,
    208
Thomasma, D. C. 69
threats 156
time constraints 242
timing of disclosure of information 56
tolerance 104
tort law 216
trust
  communication and 244
  professional–patient relationships and
    77, 90, 92, 93, 97, 105

unaffordable treatment 127
understanding
  disclosure of information and 177–80,
    193
  misunderstanding 86, 178
  obligation to facilitate understanding and
    good decision-making 246–50
undue influence 158
universalisability constraint 17
US President's Commission 130
utility 88

values 53
virtues 262
  virtue ethics 67–70, 71
  virtue of professionalism and
    professional virtues 102–5
  virtuous patient 101–2
voluntariness
  consent and 139–40, 156–9
vulnerability 94

waiver
  of right to consent 100, 123, 264
  of right to information 100, 201–2, 207,
    245, 251, 264
Weintraub, M. 85
welfare need 62
withholding treatment 127–9
witnesses
  expert evidence 170, 199
Wolf, S. 24
wrong acts
  consent and 116, 117